MERGERS AND ECONOMIC PERFORMANCE

MERGERS AND ECONOMIC PERFORMANCE

Keith Cowling, Paul Stoneman, John Cubbin
John Cable, Graham Hall, Simon Domberger and
Patricia Dutton
UNIVERSITY OF WARWICK

CAMBRIDGE UNIVERSITY PRESS
CAMBRIDGE
LONDON · NEW YORK · MELBOURNE

Published by the Syndics of the Cambridge University Press
The Pitt Building, Trumpington Street, Cambridge CB2 1RP
Bentley House, 200 Euston Road, London NW1 2DB
32 East 57th Street, New York, NY 10022, USA
296 Beaconsfield Parade, Middle Park, Melbourne 3206, Australia

First published 1980

Photoset and printed in Malta by
Interprint Limited

Library of Congress Cataloguing in Publication Data

Main entry under title:

Mergers and economic performance.

'Findings of a project . . . organised under the auspices of the Centre for Industrial Economic and Business Research at the University of Warwick.'
1. Consolidation and merger of corporations – Great Britain. 2. Consolidation and merger of corporations. I. Cowling, Keith. II. University of Warwick. Centre for Industrial Economic and Business Research.
HD2845.M47 338.8'3'0941 78-16279
ISBN 0 521 22394 6

CONTENTS

PREFACE

This book represents the findings of a project commissioned in late 1973 by the then Department of Trade and Industry but later taken over by the Office of Fair Trading. We are most grateful to them for their financial assistance. The project was organised under the auspices of the Centre for Industrial Economic and Business Research at the University of Warwick and has been supervised by Keith Cowling of the Department of Economics. Paul Stoneman, John Cubbin and John Cable, also of the Department of Economics, were involved in all aspects of the project from the beginning and Graham Hall was appointed to work on the project full-time from 1974. Simon Domberger and Pat Dutton were awarded studentships to pursue research in connection with the project. In addition to the above authors who were all connected with the University of Warwick, Mike Kelly (Lanchester Polytechnic) produced the section of Chapter 12 dealing with Diversification and Performance.

The report in general reflects the work of the group as a whole but individual members have been largely responsible for specific chapters. Cowling and Stoneman shared most of the work of editing and were responsible with Cable for the Introduction (Chapter 1) and also for putting together the views of the group in the concluding chapter (Chapter 14). Cable and Cowling put together the Welfare Framework (Chapter 2) and Cowling adapted the earlier work of Cowling and Mueller to provide an estimate of the welfare loss incident to monopoly in the UK (Chapter 3). Chapter 4 on the measurement of efficiency was the work of Cubbin and the postscript on data sources was provided by Domberger. The series of studies of specific mergers in Chapter 5 were mainly provided by Cubbin and Hall, and Stoneman was responsible for co-ordination and integration. Cubbin and Dutton provided the comparative study of GEC and British Leyland (Chapter 6), Hall the study of the Brewing industry (Chapter 7), Dutton the study of mergers and the labour market (Chapter 8), Stoneman the study of mergers and technological change (Chapter 9) and Cowling the study of vertical integration (Chapter 10). These various case studies are followed by

Cable on aspects of diversification (Chapter 11), a review and extension of results on structure–performance relationships by Cowling, Stoneman and Kelly (Chapter 12), and an assessment of the effect of mergers/market structure on the rate of price adjustment by Domberger (Chapter 13).

The report would not have been possible without the excellent secretarial and data-processing assistance we received. Clive Hicks and Valerie Jephcott gave invaluable clerical and computing assistance throughout, and Mark Partridge, Bob Webley and Warren Ho supplied specific assistance during summer projects. First class secretarial help was provided by Shirely Patterson, Joy Gardner and Yvonne Slater in the Department of Economics and Maureen Garcia and Jane Wright in the CIEBR. We are also most grateful to Mr A. K. Pepper of the Department of Industry for unstinting help in the provision and assembling of price data. Our gratitude also extends to Malcolm Sawyer and Mike Waterson who allowed us access to their own data. We would like also thank Ian Slicer for preparing the Index, and Chapman and Hall for their permission to use material in Chapters 7 and 9 previously published in *Applied Economics.*

The views expressed in this book are those of the authors and do not necessarily represent the views of the Office of Fair Trading.

1
Introduction

This study is aimed at an assessment of the impact of merger activity within the UK. The investigation differs from previous investigations in identifying the impact of merger in social welfare terms. Previous studies have concentrated on measures of performance which have relevance to stockholders or managers but the relevance of which in social welfare terms may need severe qualification. The central issue to which this report is addressed is the possibility of a welfare trade-off between economic power and technical efficiency. In terms of horizontal mergers, and, as we will argue later, vertical mergers, the narrowest interpretation of this trade-off is in terms of product market power and efficiency related to size, and indeed this question occupies much of the body of this report, but we will also be concerned with broader issues of the power of large corporations in the economy and in society. We will therefore also focus on the labour and capital market implications of the evolution of the large firm via merger and, to some extent, on the interrelationships between large corporations and the state.

Our approach to the investigation is primarily a case-study one. We have attempted to look in depth both at specific cases of merger and at specific industries which have been transformed by a series of mergers. We feel that this approach is necessary if we are really to unearth the elements of the welfare trade-off. However we will also examine cross sectional evidence on the links between merger, market-structure and performance and provide estimates of the welfare implications of the existence of monopoly power more generally within the economy.

To justify an investigation such as this we need to be clear that merger activity has been quantitatively important and that it has significantly contributed to the increasing concentration of industry in the UK. It is to these questions that we now turn.

A merger for our purposes can be defined as the coming together of two or more enterprises to form a new enterprise. We are not concerned, in this context, with joint directorships or minority shareholdings or other interconnections between firms, simply the forming of one enterprise from more than one enterprise.

Table 1.1 *Merger activity 1954–75*

Year	Total net assets acquired (£m.)	No. of quoted acquisitions	Expenditure on new subsidiaries (£m.)
1954	76.99	35	72
1955	61.79	37	60
1956	60.49	33	76
1957	102.55	58	86
1958	113.63	52	83
1959	147.60	72	201
1960	256.75	77	202
1961	322.75	67	243
1962	182.45	53	344
1963	152.16	59	251
1964	179.57	52	341
1965	257.09	48	328
1966	998.0	63	228
1967	2,273.0	96	482
1968	8,499.0	133	1,295
1969	3,714.0	126	628
1970	2,598.0	80	—
1971	1,687.0	110	—
1972	3,588.0	114	—
1973	4,870.0	134	—
1974	7,621.0	141	—
1975	5,786.0	160	—

Sources: Columns 1 and 2: 1954–65, Utton (1969), covering quoted companies in manufacturing; 1966–75, statistics supplied by the Office of Fair Trading. Column 3; Meeks (1977) p. 4.

In Table 1.1 we detail the pattern of merger activity 1954–75. As a yardstick, in the boom year of 1968, the total expenditure on acquisitions exceeded total gross domestic fixed capital formation. Although comparisons over the years should be avoided because of differing data bases (see below), the figures give some idea of the extent of merger activity.[1] For our study we have concentrated mainly on mergers that have taken place post-1965.

1 It should be noted that the data referred to relates only to larger mergers. The total number of mergers in the economy would be far in excess of this, e.g. press reports indicated a total of 884 mergers in 1971 in contrast to the 110 reported in Table 1.1. Utton's (1969) data refers only to mergers between quoted companies in manufacturing industry. Private companies have been excluded. For further detail on data in column (2), see Gribben (1974) but they essentially cover most consummated mergers involving assets acquired in excess of £5m.

Our first task is to break down the sum total of merger activity into the traditional horizontal, vertical, diversified categories. In Table 1.2 we detail the pattern of merger activity 1958–68 according to its inter-industry breakdown. The first point to note here is the differences in merger activity in different sectors, thus, for example, the Drink sector has experienced heavy merger activity, whereas Leather has not experienced any merger within the limits of the data requirements imposed by the source. The second observation on this table is the dominance of the main diagonal, i.e. the overriding importance in this ten year period of horizontal merger activity. One should note however that with a finer industrial classification this dominance could well be less marked.

More detailed statistics on the incidence of types of merger over the past twenty years or so are available from two sources. The first derives from an analysis of mergers between quoted companies in manufacturing by Utton (1969). The second (see Gribben (1974)) results from the work of the Mergers Panel for whom merger proposals are screened for reference to the Monopolies Commission under the terms of the 1965 Monopolies and Mergers Act. Annual statistics on the incidence of mergers of all types from these two sources are set out in Tables 1.3 and 1.4 respectively.

The two tables are not strictly comparable for a number of reasons. Utton's series are confined to quoted companies in manufacturing, whereas the Panel statistics relate to industrial, commercial and financial mergers involving both quoted and unquoted firms. Moreover the Panel series records merger proposals, not all of which are consummated. For all these reasons one would expect to find a higher merger incidence recorded in Table 1.4 than in Table 1.3. However, the Panel statistics *exclude* mergers outside the scope of the 1965 Act, that is those which escape both the 25% market share and the £5 million gross assets tests. Moreover, the basis for classifying a merger as diversified rather than horizontal or vertical is not necessarily the same in the two sources, and assets are shown gross in the Panel statistics and net in Utton's series. The net effect of these various differences is hard to assess. In the one year common to both series, 1965, the total number of mergers of all types recorded is the same (48) but the classification by merger type is different, and there is a further complication in that the Panel statistics only relate to part of 1965.

These problems of non-comparability concern us in the context of determining the level and possible trend in the intensity of different merger types. Utton's statistics show an unmistakable decline in importance of diversified mergers between the late 1950s and early 1960s, when there was a small drop in absolute numbers and a much more striking fall in diversifying mergers as a proportion of all mergers, both by number and by value (Table 1.5). However, there is reason to suppose that this decline was a short-term cyclical effect rather than part of a long-term trend, reflecting a peak of activity in 1959–60 – 'when a new wave of (conglomerate) companies came into the picture' (Econtel Research (1969) p. 4).

Table 1.2 *Distribution by industry class of net assets transferred as a result of mergers 1958–68 (£m)*

Net assets acquired by acquiring companies / Net assets of companies acquired	1	2	3	4	5	6	7	8	9	10	11	12
1 Food	**86**	5	15	7								
2 Drink		**590**		5								
3 Tobacco			**5**									
4 Chemical and allied industries	3	1		**76**						2	26	
5 Metal manufacture				14	**71**	3	2				1	
6 Non-electrical engineering				21	14	**116**	34		25	36	5	
7 Electrical engineering					11	1	**649**		22	1		
8 Ship and marine engineering								**23**	3			
9 Vehicles					20	5			**328**	1	7	
10 Metals n.e.s.				2	10	17	7			**26**	1	
11 Textiles				46	3					6	**276**	
12 Leather, etc.												**0**
13 Clothing and footwear					1						19	
14 Bricks, pottery, glass, cement				1	2		2			1		
15 Timber, furniture, etc.												
16 Paper, printing, publishing					1							
17 Other manufacturing			2		1						9	
18 Construction												
19 Transport	33											
20 Wholesale distribution	6	22			8	3	1	1		1	34	
21 Retail distribution	6		2	22			45				7	
22 Miscellaneous services												
23 Sub-total	134	618	24	194	139	148	740	24	378	74	385	0

Notes: The data covers companies (a) with assets exceeding £0.5m in 1961; (b) mainly engaged in the UK;
Source: Department of Trade and Industry (1970) p. 30.

Accurate comparison of the early and late 1960s is precluded by the non-consistency of the two data sources, but the post-1965 Merger Panel statistics do serve to show a dramatic increase in the absolute and relative importance of diversifying mergers between 1965–69 and 1970–74. Between these sub-periods the number of diversifying mergers more than doubled and also rose from around 13% to not much less than a quarter of all merger cases. Moreover it is clear that not only did diversifying mergers become absolutely and relatively more numerous in the second sub-period, but they also become much larger on average. Thus in the period 1965–69 the 13% of mergers in the diversified category had a less than proportionate share in the total value of mergers (approximately 7%),

13	14	15	16	17	18	19	20	21	22	Sub-total	Not in population	Total	
								41	2	156	15	171	1
				3				10		608	0	608	2
										5	0	5	3
			7			1				116	55	171	4
			9		2		1			103	9	112	5
	1	1	9	10	3		6		6	287	35	322	6
			2			2			9	697	62	759	7
										25	2	28	8
		2	3				1		2	369	6	375	9
6						2	3	1		75	19	94	10
4	2	1		1			2	1		342	17	359	11
										0	1	1	12
18	1							9	1	49	1	50	13
	69				30					105	8	113	14
		3				12	4			19	2	21	15
			212	1		2			1	218	22	240	16
			1	**16**	7		1			37	1	38	17
	10				**4**					14	11	25	18
		4				**12**				49	0	49	19
1	9	11					**25**	6	3	131	44	175	20
80							3	**74**	2	241	18	259	21
						80	1	21	**38**	140	18	158	22
109	92	18	247	31	46	111	47	164	64	3,787	346	4,133	23

(c) quoted in 1961.

as in earlier periods. In 1970–74, however, the 23.5% of mergers which were diversifying accounted for nearly 32% of all mergers by value, and in 1972 the 27% of mergers which were of this type accounted for 50% of the total gross assets involved (Table 1.4).

Explanation of this increase in the importance of conglomerate mergers is beyond the scope of the present analysis. It can, however, be pointed out from Table 1.4 that the growth of conglomerate merger does not appear to be wholly due to horizontal and vertical merger opportunities becoming exhausted. Thus the number of horizontal mergers also rose, from 382 in 1964–69 to 415 in 1970–74, while the (very low) number of vertical mergers remained roughly the

Table 1.3 *Incidence of merger types in manufacturing 1954–65*

Year	Horizontal		Vertical		Diversified		Diversified mergers as percentage of total	
	Total net assets acquired (£m.)	Number of quoted acquisitions	Total net assets acquired (£m.)	Number of quoted acquisitions	Total net assets acquired (£m.)	Number of quoted acquisitions	Total net assets acquired (%)	Number of quoted acquisitions (%)
1954	41.96	23	24.71	5	10.32	7		
1955	53.73	28	0.72	4	7.34	5		
1956	48.40	23	3.42	3	8.67	7		
1957	73.59	39	9.30	10	19.66	9		
1958	91.49	30	10.31	9	11.83	13		
1959	124.53	50	13.00	12	10.07	10		
1954–59	433.70	193	61.46	43	67.89	51	13.7	17.9
1960	240.83	62	6.12	5	9.80	10		
1961	259.37	49	17.73	10	45.65	8		
1962	163.80	39	12.86	8	5.79	6		
1963	105.87	35	39.41	15	6.88	9		
1964	139.10	39	20.88	6	19.49	7		
1965	207.69	31	26.26	6	23.14	11		
1960–65	1,115.66	255	123.26	50	110.75	51	8.9	14.4
Total	1,549.36	448	184.72	93	178.64	102	9.3	15.9

Source: Utton (1969).

same (24 in the first period and 26 in the second). However, some evidence of a depletion of horizontal merger opportunities *at large sizes* is conceivably discernible from the fact that the total value of horizontal mergers fell from £15,015 million in 1965–69 to £13,235 in 1970–74, a fall which would have been much greater after allowance for inflation.

Assuming that the Merger Panel statistics may be taken at face value, and that apparent trends are not due simply to variations in classification procedure, it seems fair to conclude that diversifying mergers have become relatively more important over the past 10 years or so. Whether or not the level of conglomerate activity in recent years has been at a peak and whether this high level is above or below previous peaks is impossible to say in the absence of longer time series on a consistent basis.

There remains, however, a question as to whether the statistics give an accurate indication of the relative importance of the diversifying and horizontal merger cases for public policy. The question arises out of the criteria applied in classifying mergers to the two categories, and how narrow or broad a definition of diversification is embodied in them – the breadth of the definition varying inversely with that of the industry groups used for classification purposes.

Examination of individual cases suggests that the Merger Panel statistics are based on rather narrow industry definitions, e.g. gas *vs* electrical and 'traditional' *vs* 'newer' domestic appliances; diamond abrasive wheels *vs* cutting tools; animal feeds *vs* other agricultural products; different types of goods supplied to builders merchants; subsectors of the ethical pharmaceutical industry; and so on. As is widely recognised in the literature, there is bound to be some arbitrariness in decisions over what is diversification in practice and what is not. But it would seem open to argument that the merger of firms engaged in narrowly defined industries such as the above could lead to market power effects of a horizontal nature. In terms of the US nomenclature, the OFT diversified category would seem to include mergers of the product and market extension type as well as pure conglomerates.

The Merger Panel's diversified category would certainly seem to be broader than that which would result from a Minimum List Heading, or 3-digit industry classification. To confirm this, the OFT list of mergers which were classified as diversified, and which subsequently took place in the period 1965–70, were checked against the Kuehn[2] data tape, which lists all the industrial activities of firms as indicated by the *Stock Exchange Yearbook* and similar sources. Of a total of 50 cases 13 involved firms outside the manufacturing sector (mainly mining companies or investment trusts, banks, etc.) or foreign firms. These were excluded from further consideration on grounds of data availability and/or maintaining comparability in subsequent analysis. Comparison of the industrial activities

2 We wish to thank Doug Kuehn for making these data available to us.

Table 1.4 *Industrial, commercial and financial mergers classified by type of integration 1965–75*

Criteria	1965 (part) no. or value	%	1966 no. or value	%	1967 no. or value	%	1968 no. or value	%	1969 no. or value	%	1970 no. or value	%
Horizontal												
number	39	81	49	78	83	86	109	82	102	81	67	84
value (£m)	946	84	850	85	2,095	92	7,741	91	3,383	91	2,047	78
Vertical												
number	5	10	7	11	5	5	5	4	2	2	1	1
value (£m)	96	9	79	8	80	4	145	2	11	0	5	0
Diversified												
number	4	9	7	11	8	9	19	14	22	17	12	15
value (£m)	83	7	69	7	98	4	613	7	320	9	556	22

Source: Supplied by the Office of Fair Trading (see also Gribben (1974)).

Table 1.5 *Incidence of diversifying merger by sub-period 1955–74*

Period	Number	Total assets[a]	No. as % total	Assets as % total
1955–59	44	57.57	17.5	11.9
1960–64	40	87.61	12.2	8.0
1965–69	60	1,183.00	12.9	7.1
1970–74	136	6,494.00	23.5	31.9

Sources: Derived from Tables 1.3 and 1.4.
[a]Net assets acquired 1955–64, gross assets 1965–74.

of the partners in the remaining 37 cases revealed 15 instances where the acquired and acquiring firms had no industry in common and 22 with one or more industry. In the majority of this second group of cases, only one or two industries of several were common to both firms. But the exceptional cases included one in which there were two firms each with five industries of which four were common to both; three cases in which the acquiring firm operated in a single industry and the acquired in that industry and one other; one in which the acquiring firm operated in two industries and the acquired *only* in one of these; and one case in which both firms were listed as active in only one industry.

The OFT and the 3-digit industrial classification principles clearly produce very different results, and the question arises as to whether the broad OFT classification overstates the relative importance of diversified merger by classifying mergers as conglomerate which by their determining causes and their

1971		1972		1973		1974		1975		1965–75	
no. or value	%	no. or value	%	no. or value	%	no. or value	%	no. or value	%	no. or value	%
83	76	75	66	94	70	96	68	113	71	910	76
1,111	66	1,444	40	3,703	76	4,940	65	4,468	77	32,718	76
7	6	8	7	5	4	7	5	8	5	60	5
66	4	340	10	79	2	163	2	210	4	1,274	3
20	18	31	27	35	26	38	27	39	24	235	19
510	30	1,804	50	1,096	22	2,518	33	1,108	19	8,775	21

effects belong in the horizontal category. This question is important not merely from the point of view of the accuracy of the statistical record but also for the application of merger policy, since classification as diversified rather than horizontal may have an important bearing on whether or not a particular case is referred for investigation to the Monopolies and Merger Commission. However, it is clear that the great majority of mergers have been horizontal even if the share of diversified mergers has increased over time.

Part of the case that we wish to analyse is whether the gains in market power that mergers can yield are adequately offset by efficiency gains resulting from the merger. These market power effects can only occur if the pattern of industrial concentration is significantly affected by merger activity. It becomes necessary for us therefore to trace out this link between mergers and industrial concentration. The analysis of the effect of mergers on the level of concentration has had a chequered history – it is generally agreed however that this is one area where US and UK experience do not match, primarily because horizontal merger is of much more importance in the UK. Thus the UK literature stands on its own. This point is successfully argued by among others Utton (1971) and Hannah (1974). The UK literature is not extensive, but is reasonably conclusive. As our main concern is with the 1960s we will concentrate on results for that period.

In general it must be accepted that merger will at least in the short run lead to an increase in the level of concentration.[3] The literature attempts to provide estimates of the proportion of the changes in the concentration level that are

3 Although Utton (1971) illustrates where, given his measure of concentration, a decrease can be indicated (p. 49 n. 3).

Table 1.6 *Classification of product groups according to the number of the 100 largest manufacturing firms included among their leading three sellers*

No. of firms from top 100 in leading three	No. of product groups in sample	Average sales 1963 (£'000)	Weighted average concentration ratio (%)
0	15	33,119	40.1
1	8	46,262	60.4
2	4	105,995	67.8
3	3		

due to merger activity, or, equivalently, how different the time path of concentration is from that which would have existed if the merger activity had not occurred. This question posed in the latter way indicates:

(a) factors other than merger can lead to increased levels of concentration, e.g. differential internal growth rates of firms;

(b) pressures may lead to increased concentration, e.g. changes in minimum efficient scales, for which merger is purely a means to achieve at an earlier date a result that market forces might have brought about later;

(c) the specification of the counter factual is critical for the results achieved.

The discussion proceeds on two levels, the first looking at aggregate concentration, the second at concentration in individual industries. A good place to start is to see how these two interact i.e. how large companies dominate individual markets. The data in Table 1.6 are from Utton (1974). He concludes that:

> the picture that emerges is of a manufacturing sector where a relatively small group of very large concerns not only dominates overall but probably plays an influential part in about half the product groups in manufacturing. A recent estimate for the share of the 100 largest enterprises in manufacturing output in 1970 was 46%. The large volume of merger activity in the middle and late 1960s undoubtedly played an important part in this increase.

How important a part is assessed by Aaronovitch and Sawyer (1975a, 1975b). They look at a population of firms (covering 70% of the UK quoted sector) with assets exceeding £5m at the end of 1957 operating mainly in the manufacturing and distribution industries. The financial, agricultural and mining sectors are excluded. Analysing the change in concentration ratios (CR25, 50, 100)[4] at the aggregate level for the period 1958–67, they identify four factors influencing the level of concentration:

4 CRN is defined as the proportion of total sales, assets or employment (depending on source) attributable to the top N firms.

Table 1.7 *Effects of mergers on aggregate concentration*

	Aaronovitch & Sawyer			Hannah & Kay		
	1958	1967	% change due to merger	1957	1969	% change due to merger
CR25	31.37	35.28	110	—	—	—
CR50	40.92	49.23	62.3	48.4	60.6	116.4
CR100	51.65	62.03	54.3	60.1	74.9	102.7
CR500				88.9	97.0	116.0

Source: Aaronovitch and Sawyer (1975a), Hannah & Kay (1977).

(a) the relative growth of firms who survive;
(b) the effect of disappearances through acquisition;
(c) changes in the population relative to the whole quoted sector;
(d) the impact of firms not in their basic population.

Acquisition effects arise directly from (b), indirectly from (a) and perhaps (c) and (d), plus any interaction. In Table 1.7 we detail their estimates of the effect of influence (b). Using essentially the same data, Hannah and Kay (1977) also calculate the effects of mergers at the level of aggregation and their results are also presented in Table 1.7. The differences in the results are quite marked as are the estimates of concentration for similar years, but for our purposes the rough magnitude of the estimates is the main point. At least 50% of the increase in concentration is due to merger.[5]

To produce such estimates of the effect of mergers on concentration the basic method is as follows. Between the base date and the end date a number of mergers have occurred. To compare with base year concentration (C_1) one constructs a figure for what base year concentration would have been had all the subsequent mergers occurred in the base year (C_2) by the simple expedient of combining merging firms base year assets before calculating the concentration ratio. If end year concentration is C_3, then the % change in concentration due to merger is calculated as $C_2 - C_1/C_3 - C_1 \times 100$.

The figure of 50% calculated for the aggregate level above is supported by the work of Hart, Utton and Walshe (1973) at the disaggregated level. Walshe (1974) in his study of 32 monopoly products in the UK states:

> Eleven of the thirty two products considered became monopolies or near monopolies as a result of merger activity. In the majority of

5 In Table 1.7 the figures, especially those of Hannah & Kay can show that the percentage change due to merger may exceed 100%. This essentially implies that without merger concentration would have fallen.

> cases, high concentration is explained by internal growth of a few firms which has eliminated the competition of many others, or by the fact that few firms have entered production of the commodity in question. Nevertheless in ten of the thirty two cases mergers were an important tool used to prevent the erosion of market shares once market power had been obtained by internal growth.

Thus one may argue that mergers rank equal to internal growth in generating increases in concentration, and they also have a role to play in preventing the reduction in concentration levels.

For quantitative estimates of the effect of mergers on concentration at the industry level we have two further sources, Utton (1971) and Hannah & Kay (1977). Using basically the same methods as above, but with different concentration measures, they have generated the results in Table 1.8. The two estimates by Utton differ in that the first is calculated using the method whereby all mergers are allowed to take place in the base year. The second is constructed allowing all mergers to occur in the end year. To calculate the end year figures the assets of a firm on the eve of merger are grossed up by the growth rate of the main industry to predict what the assets would have been in the end year if it had not merged. One then calculates the hypothetical end year concentration figures as if no mergers had occurred and this is then compared with the actual.

The figures presented confirm the conclusions derived from the analysis of aggregate data, i.e. at least 50% of the increase in concentration is due to merger. In fact this is probably an unduly conservative estimate.

One other contribution in this area deserves some discussion before drawing our conclusions. Prais (1976) is generally credited with the opinion that merger does not have any significant effect on the level of concentration. If however we use Prais' estimate that in the 1967–72 period takeovers led to an increase in CR100 of 0.3 percentage points per annum, and that between 1968 and 1970 CR100 increased at the most by 1 percentage point (a result established from Prais' Table 1.1 p. 4), then one can attribute 60% of the increase to mergers. This is a result in line with our earlier results. However Prais argues that 'a merger is a method of growing: it does not explain the motive for that growth', and moreover that the operation of Gibrat's Law is sufficient to generate a series on concentration matching quite closely observed increases in concentration. The point is essentially that Prais' counter factual is one with increasing concentration as opposed to that used in the above studies where the counter factual is based on an assumption that without merger the concentration increases resulting from it would not occur. An argument about the appropriate counter factual can never be satisfactorily resolved, but for the present purposes we can sidestep the issue. Prais' result can be interpreted as that merger leads to increased concentration, but to *explain* increases in concentration we need to know why firms merge. In the present context our task is to identify the effect on performance of merger

Table 1.8 *Industry level estimates of the effects of mergers on concentration*

Measure . . .	Variance of log of firm size				CR10		
	Utton				Hannah & Kay		% change due to merger
	Level of concentration		% due to merger		Level of concentration		
	1954	1965	Utton 1	Utton 2	1957	1969	
Industry							
Food	3.43	5.44	77	66	62.1	80.5	70.1
Drink	2.76	5.37	58	71	40.8	87.2	76.3
Tobacco	—	—	—	—	100	100	—
Chemicals	3.72	5.51	49	52	80.6	86.4	31.2
Metal manufacture	3.97	5.64	69	72	58.7	74.3	107.1
Electrical engineering	3.82	5.41	39	52	60.4	81.2	105.8
Non-electrical engineering					39.0	32.1	—
	2.29	3.18	38	21			
Shipbuilding					80.3	93.3	80.8
Vehicles	3.40	5.12	46	57	57.2	85.8	70.6
Metal goods n.e.s.	2.08	2.63	—	—	67.2	77.1	129.2
Textiles	2.36	2.70	—	—	55.9	74.2	127.8
Building materials	2.12	3.88	45	22	71.2	65.0	—
Paper and publishing	3.18	4.37	60	41	63.6	78.1	111.1
Other manufactures	1.98	2.16	—	—	—	—	—
Clothing and footwear	1.76	2.02	—	—	—	—	—
Miscellaneous	—	—	—	—	58.3	65.6	95.9

Source: Cols. 1–4, Utton (1971); cols. 5–7, Hannah & Kay (1977).

activity, and part of the analysis must refer to the effect on performance of the resultant increase in concentration. It is not necessary for this purpose to *explain* why concentration increases, only to know that it increases significantly after merger activity.

As surveyed above, therefore, the literature definitely supports an assumption of *at least* 50% and on some estimates a much greater % of the change in concentration can be attributed to merger,[6] whether we look at the aggregate or disaggregated data: the differing measures and data used making this a result that is remarkably robust.

We are thus in a position to establish that:

(a) merger activity has been substantial since 1950;

(b) that the majority of this activity has been horizontal, but probably a declining share; and

(c) the net consequence has been a much increased degree of concentration in the economy.

This latter is a matter of prime concern to us, and we approach it and its consequences in a number of ways. Thus we review the evidence on the link between concentration and economic performance (Chapter 12) and also specifically investigate the rather neglected area of price adjustment and the degree of market concentration (Chapter 14). However the main body of the book consists of a series of case studies of actual mergers. We have tried to look at the performance of a company post-merger to see whether there are gains to society that are worthy of the gift of market power that the merger bequeaths.

In Chapter 2 the formal theoretical framework for the pursuit of this question is presented. In Chapter 3 some attempts are made to isolate the effects of market power on economic welfare prior to the formal presentation of our measure of technical efficiency in Chapter 4. In Chapter 5 we proceed to look at a number of case studies concentrating on the efficiency of companies post-merger and where possible looking at any effects arising from the abuse of market power. Continuing the case study approach we investigate in Chapter 6 mergers in the engineering industry, comparing the success of GEC to the failure of British Leyland; in Chapter 7 we turn to the brewing industry and look especially at product quality; in Chapter 8 we concern ourselves again with GEC, but concentrate on the employment effects of merger activity; and in Chapter 9 we close the study of horizontal mergers by looking at the computer industry and technological progressiveness. Chapter 10 looks at Courtaulds and the textile industry as an important example of vertical merger activity, and Chapter 11 turns to an investigation of aspects of diversified mergers. Chapter 12, reporting on structure–performance relationships, continues in part the theme of diversification, but also looks at the links between market structure, price–cost

6 Müller (1976) finds that for West Germany the 50% figure is a good estimate.

margins and technical progress. In Chapter 13 we close our investigations with a study of price adjustment under different market structures.

In Chapter 14 we draw together our various results and attempt to assess whether on balance mergers have been beneficial in social welfare terms. In the light of these conclusions various suggestions about public policy will be made.

References

Aaronovitch, S. and Sawyer, M. (1975a), 'Mergers Growth and Concentration', *Oxford Economic Papers* (March).

– (1975b), *Big Business*, London: Macmillan.

Department of Trade and Industry (1970), *A Survey of Mergers, 1958–1969*, London: HMSO.

Econtel Research (1969), *Conglomerates*, London: British Industry Series.

Gribben, J. D. (1974), 'The Operation of the Mergers Panel since 1965', *Trade and Industry* (17 Jan. 1974), 70–3.

Hannah, L. (1974), 'Mergers in British Manufacturing Industries 1880–1918', *Oxford Economic Papers* (March).

– (1976), *The Rise of the Corporate Economy*, London: Methuen.

Hannah, L. and Kay, J. (1977), *Concentration in Modern Industry*, London: Macmillan.

Hart, P. E., Utton, H. A. and Walshe, G. (1973), *Mergers and Concentration in British Industry*, Cambridge: Cambridge University Press.

Meeks, G. (1977), *Disappointing Marriage – A Study of the Gains from Merger*, University of Cambridge DAE Occasional Paper No. 51, Cambridge: Cambridge University Press.

Müller, J. (1976), *The Impact of Concentration, a study of eleven W. German Industries*, mimeo.

Prais, S. J. (1976), *The Evolution of Giant Firms in Britain*, Cambridge: Cambridge University Press.

Utton, M. A. (1969), 'Diversification, Mergers and Profit Stability', *Business Ratios*, 24–8. (November), 42.

– (1971), 'The Effect of Mergers on Concentration', *Journal of Industrial Economics* (November), 42.

Walshe, G. (1974), *Recent Trends in Monopoly in Great Britain*, Cambridge: Cambridge University Press.

2

The welfare framework

2.1 Horizontal mergers: the welfare trade-offs

The primary focus of this book is on horizontal mergers, which account for the majority of merger cases. Horizontal mergers are often defended on the grounds that they permit efficiency gains via the exploitation of scale economies and so forth. On the other hand they raise seller concentration, and hence enhance opportunities for the exercise of market power. In a well-known, later revised, paper Williamson (1968, 1976) has put forward a procedure for netting out the social welfare gain or loss involved.

Williamson's trade-off model utilises the partial-equilibrium welfare framework of neoclassical economics, and follows in the tradition of the earlier analysis of monopoly welfare losses by Harberger (1954).[1] The general principles can be outlined with the aid of Figure 2.1. DD' is the demand curve for a commodity and c_1 is the average and marginal cost curve prior to the merger. (Average and marginal costs are assumed constant for simplicity of exposition.) Total social welfare is defined as the sum of the consumers' and producers' surpluses and is maximised when price equals marginal cost (in which case all the gains accrue to consumers since with constant average costs producers' surplus is zero).

Suppose, now, there is a merger which permits cost savings but also raises market price. Figure 2.1 illustrates two cases. In 2.1(*a*) pre-merger price equals average and marginal cost (no pre-merger market power). After the merger costs fall from c_1 to c_2 but price rises from p_1 to p_2. Figure 2.1(*b*) depicts the situation where the merger effects are the same, but where some market power existed prior to the merger ($p_1 > c_1$). In both cases there is a resource saving shown by the shaded area A_2, which is the welfare gain. However, the fall in output resulting from the price increase reduces the consumers' surplus by the shaded area A_1. Under the assumptions of partial-equilibrium welfare analysis the areas A_1 and A_2 measure the value of the social loss and gain respectively. Hence, the

1 See also Appendix A.2 and the following chapter.

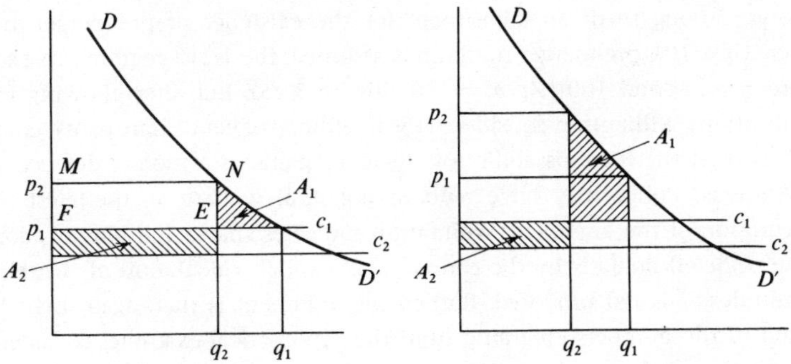

Figure 2.1 *(a) No pre-merger power. (b) Pre-existing market power*

net social gain or loss is $A_2 - A_1$ and the criterion for accepting mergers is simply $A_2 > A_1$.

Williamson derived operational formulae with which to apply this criterion in the following way. If the demand curve is linear,

$$A_1 = \tfrac{1}{2}(p_2 - p_1)(q_1 - q_2) = \tfrac{1}{2}(\Delta p)(\Delta q)$$

and

$$A_2 = (c_1 - c_2)q_2 = [\Delta c]\, q_2$$

Dividing through by $p_1 q_1$ and substituting $\eta \Delta p/p_1$ for $\Delta q/q_1$, where η is the elasticity of demand, we may write the criterion $A_2 > A_1$ as

$$\frac{\Delta c}{c_1} - \tfrac{1}{2}\eta \frac{q_1}{q_2}\left(\frac{\Delta p}{p_1}\right)^2 > 0 \qquad (1)$$

so long as $p_1 = c_1$ (no pre-merger market power). If pre-merger price exceeds cost, the equivalent expression to (1) is:

$$\frac{\Delta c}{c_1} - \left[\tfrac{1}{2}k\left(\frac{\Delta p}{p_1}\right) + (k-1)\right]\eta \frac{\Delta p}{p_1}\frac{q_1}{q_2} > 0 \qquad (2)$$

where $k = p_1/c_1$.

The main thrust of Williamson's argument was that, under 'reasonable' assumptions concerning the likely values of η and Δp the gains can easily exceed the losses. To show this he set (1) and (2) equal to zero and solved for Δc – the required cost savings needed to just neutralise the merger price effect – for given values of η and Δp. Table 2.1 records these values for the 'naive model'. Regarding $\eta = 2$ as a 'reasonable upper bound' and a 10% margin of price over cost as the normal maximum, Williamson concluded: 'a merger that promises non-trivial economies (say greater than two per cent) will generally yield a net allocative efficiency gain' (Williamson, 1968a). This conclusion was qualified in a number of ways, among them an adjustment for the existence of pre-merger market power. (If a 10% pre-merger mark-up is assumed, the 1.21% required cost saving where $\eta = 2$, and $100\ [Ap/p] = 10$ rises to 3.26). But after allowing for all qualifications Williamson considered the likelihood of net welfare gains remained great, so that the inadmissability of efficiency gains as a merger defence under US Antitrust Policy may have reduced potential welfare. In the latest (1976) presentation of the argument Williamson indicates that a 'full blown' adoption of the trade-off analysis by the courts – i.e. explicit calculation of the relevant magnitudes – is not proposed. Rather, the argument is that, against the background of the numbers emerging from the hypothetical examples considered, a case can be made for the US Courts to take account of certain, presently disregarded, kinds of argument on the nature and magnitude of expected efficiency gains when coming to a decision. In the UK the legislation already requires decisions in merger cases that take account of both benefits and detriments to the public interest. The relevance of the trade-off model to the UK situation, and to our analysis, is that it provides a useful conceptual framework within which to consider two basic welfare aspects of horizontal mergers, and yields formulae which permit assessment of the net welfare effect of the two mutually offsetting forces. Before proceeding to the empirical analysis, however, we raise a number of questions concerning the comprehensiveness of the trade-off model in dealing with the full range of welfare considerations that arise in merger cases, and the restrictiveness of the assumptions on which the model and numerical examples are based.

2.2 Qualifications and extensions of the trade-off model

(i) Reliability of the numerical estimates

Although the policy question to which the trade-off model was addressed is not an issue in the UK, the embodied estimates of the minimum cost savings required to offset market power effects are of interest. For practical purposes it is very useful to have some feel for the magnitudes of cost savings below which disadvantageous effects will predominate or, to put it the other way about, above which market power effects can be safely ignored.

But Williamson's conclusion that economies need be only 'non-trivial' depends critically on the chosen values of demand elasticity and price increase. Thus, from Table 2.1, if we take 3 and 20% respectively instead of 2 and 10%, the required saving rises tenfold to over 10%, and this figure would be even higher in the presence of pre-merger market power.

The choice of $\eta = 2$ as an upper bound may be an underestimate. Wenders (1967) preferred a value of 3, basing his view on an early survey of Hirsch (1950). The 10% maximum post-merger price–cost margin may also be too low. In defending this figure Williamson cited the early theoretical and empirical litera-

Table 2.1 *Required cost savings (%) to offset price effects of mergers: hypothetical cases*

100 $[\Delta p/p]$	η			
	3	2	1	$\frac{1}{2}$
5	0.44	0.27	0.13	0.06
10	2.00	1.21	0.55	0.26
20	10.32	5.76	2.40	1.10

Source: Williamson (1976, p. 12).

ture on limit-pricing, in particular the work of Bain (1968). In this static analysis price is set independently of demand elasticity, so as to forestall the entry of potential competitors. More recent, dynamic limit-price models feature an optimal price which is a function of demand elasticity and other variables (e.g. Modigliani (1958)). More generally Spence (1974) has argued that pricing is independent of entry conditions.

If the interdependence of the price- and cost-effects of the merger (via the demand elasticity) is recognised, the required cost savings in the welfare trade-off model increase dramatically. Essentially this is because much higher price–cost margins are now expected. In the extreme case of short-run monopoly pricing post merger, the price–cost margin is the reciprocal of the elasticity of demand:

$$\frac{p-c}{c} = \frac{1}{\eta} \tag{3}$$

Thus, if $\eta = 2$, $(p - c)/p = 50\%$. Looked at in this way, the maximum mark up of only 10% assumed by Williamson implies an elasticity of demand of 11.

De Prano and Nugent (1969) recalculated the required cost savings under the trade-off analysis, taking the interdependence of the price and cost effects and demand elasticity into account. Rearranging (3) they obtained:

$$p = \frac{\eta}{\eta - 1} c \tag{4}$$

so that

$$\frac{p_2}{p_1} = \frac{\eta c_2}{(\eta - 1)c_1} \tag{5}$$

In the case where pre-merger competition (i.e. $p_1/c_1 = 1$) gives way to postmerger monopolisation of the industry ($p_2/c_2 = \eta/(\eta - 1)$), they showed that the required savings exceed 30%, 40% and 81% respectively for $\eta = 2$, $\eta = 1.5$ and $\eta = 1.1$. Again these figures increase if there is pre-merger market power. The authors admit that complete monopolisation will not always come about, but in view of the very large savings required, especially when demand elasticity is low, drew the conclusion that a valid economies defence would be a rare event.

Thus the estimates of the cost savings required to neutralise merger price effects are sensitive to the value of η and to the choice of theoretical model of price formation.[2] The conclusion that only 'non-trivial' economies are required depends on rather restrictive assumptions in this regard. Without necessarily going to the extreme of full monopolisation after the merger, it seems more appropriate to conclude that quite substantial economies may be needed before market power effects can be safely assumed to be outweighed.

(ii) First-best considerations

Subject to certain reservations discussed in the following subsection, the maximum social welfare that is attainable under post-merger technology and demand conditions is neither the pre- nor the post-merger equilibrium illustrated in Figure 2.1, but the 'first-best' situation where post-merger price equals post-merger marginal cost ($p_2 = c_2$). Thus, deciding merger cases by comparing the pre-merger situation (with less market power, but foregoing any efficiency gain) with the post-merger situation (with increased market power but some cost savings) involves a choice between two 'second-best' outcomes. Obviously, the highest total welfare is generated if the benefit of the cost savings is secured and market power is simultaneously eliminated. Moreover, a very different distribution of the welfare gains is then achieved, all benefits accruing to consumers.

On the other hand, posing the policy options in terms of the second-best, pre- and post-merger choices only, has the merit of recognising institutional reality. The UK Monopolies Commission, in common with most antitrust agencies, has powers only to recommend that a merger be allowed to proceed or be blocked. It cannot under existing legislation impose some other solution of its own choosing, such as the first-best outcome. Even if the alternatives open to the Commission were expanded by legislation to include other options, securing the first-best outcome would face practical problems. This would require either some form of post-merger public regulation of price or profit or, *in extremis*, nationalisation and the imposition of marginal cost pricing. Both would be politically controversial, and encounter incentives problems in the firms affected. In

2 Other contributors to the debate have explored the consequences of employing alternative concepts of demand elasticity (O'Dwyer (1972), Slater (1974)). The estimated required savings do not, however, change dramatically on this ground alone. De Prano and Nugent (1969), O'Dwyer (1972) and Jackson (1970) also emphasised the inadequacy of Williamson's original treatment of pre-merger market power, which is corrected in the later versions (1972, 1976). See also Williamson's (1969) reply to De Prano and Nugent (1969).

particular, the risk would be that potential cost-savings through merger would never come to light if the 'penalties' of merger, in the firms eyes, were too severe. And antitrust agencies are not well placed to detect potential efficiency gains which firms are not anxious to reveal.

Yet the first-best problem remains, at least in theory, and recognition of its existence reveals a potential inconsistency in competition policy towards mergers on the one hand, and dominant firm monopoly on the other. In effect mergers are judged in terms of the *direction of change* of welfare: whether it is raised or lowered. Monopolies, however, are looked at in terms of the *level* of social welfare they generate, in relation to the 'competitive' alternative. If the latter is defined as (approximately) the first-best outcome (in which market power is neutralised but cost conditions are at least as good as those the monopolist achieves) a less stringent test is applied to mergers than to monopoly.

Policy implementation apart, the question is whether the loss of potential first-best welfare gains is large enough to matter in practice. The Williamson model can be easily extended to tackle this question, and a formula derived to show the magnitude of (forgone) first-best welfare gains, in relation to the net benefit (if any) of a merger under given assumptions about the magnitudes of cost savings, price effects, and demand elasticity. The exercise is carried out in the appendix to this chapter, in which there is a table showing the surplus of first-best over *the better of* pre- or post-merger welfare (whichever is the higher), all expressed as a proportion of pre-merger revenue. That is, the table reports the surplus S:

$$S = \frac{W_f - W_m}{R}$$

where W_f = first-best welfare level, for given demand elasticities, price to cost mark-ups, and cost-reductions from merger.

W_m = pre- or post-merger welfare level (whichever is higher) under the same conditions.

R = pre-merger revenue.

Most values of S reported are quite small, some trivially so. However, first-best losses equal to between 5 and 15% of pre-merger revenue can occur under elasticities in the range 2 to 3, price—cost mark-ups of 10 to 20% and merger cost savings of up to 20%. We suggest that it is against a background of potential losses of this magnitude that the asymmetry between merger and dominant-firm monopoly branches of competition policy should be considered, bearing in mind that the policy is more needed in more extreme situations of abuse of market power than in 'normal' circumstances.

(iii) The general second-best problem

As is widely recognised in the economics literature, the correction of individual departures from optimality leaving others untouched may not raise welfare and can even reduce it (Lipsey and Lancaster (1956)). Thus the piecemeal removal of monopolies does not guarantee an improvement until all monopolies are gone, and all other conditions for optimality met: a wholly improbable situation. The implication for the trade-off model is that an increase in the mark-up of price above marginal cost in a particular case can conceivably raise welfare rather than lower it, from a strictly resource-allocative point of view (but with distributional implications).

Whether or not an individual adjustment of price towards marginal cost raises welfare depends on substitutability and complementarity conditions among commodities (Dixit (1976)). Lowering the price of a particular commodity will raise welfare if the existing distortion for that commodity is proportionately greater than for other commodities with which it is a close substitute, and proportionally smaller than for any close complementary good. Thus, in the absence of close complements, piecemeal policy will have beneficial effects if the most severe cases of price elevation above marginal cost are dealt with first, as is hopefully the case in the competition policy area.

(iv) Spillover effects: weighting and incipiency

The case-by-case, partial equilibrium approach may understate the full effects of a merger if a price rise by the merging firms is matched by other firms, or if one merger initiates a chain reaction of others. Williamson referred to these external effects as weighting and incipiency respectively. The difference between the welfare effects as assessed and the full effects will depend in part on whether the spillover effects occur equally in the market-power and the cost-savings dimensions. In the case of weighting it is presumably only the price effect which carries over, since if the other firms do not merge there is no reason to expect any cost saving. Hence the full welfare effect is less beneficial than appears in the appraisal of the initial merger. In the case of incipiency much depends on the source of cost savings. If the knowledge necessary for securing the economy is confined to the firms in the initiating merger, or if for any other reason the resource saving is peculiar to these firms, then any subsequent mergers will tend to have only adverse welfare effects, which again should be added to those of the original merger. The subsequent mergers in these circumstances will presumably be undertaken to restore the earlier relative size structure amongst the leading firms in the industry, but with an overall increase in the level of concentration. If, on the other hand, both cost savings and price effects carry over equally to subsequent mergers, the estimated net benefit arrived at for the initial merger will hold valid for all individual mergers in the chain. But, taking the sequence of mergers as a whole, there will have been an overall increase in the opportunities for collusive behaviour.

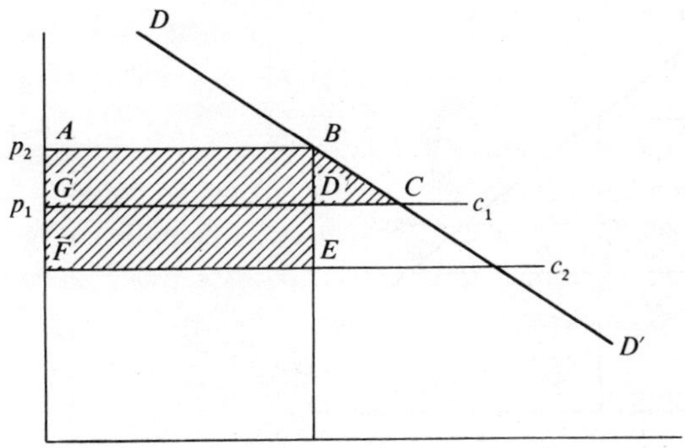

Figure 2.2

(v) Competition for monopoly gains

Posner (1975) and Tullock (1967) have argued that monopoly loss estimates of the Harberger–Williamson type understate the full resource misallocation effects because they ignore competition amongst firms for the prizes that monopoly power brings. For instance there will be competitive lobbying to secure exclusive rights to lucrative transportation routes, or competitive advertising to establish reputation monopolies for certain products.

The resource costs are non-negligible, they are incurred by both the successful and unsuccessful competitors and they are additional to the allocative distortions which occur *after* the monopoly position is established. Since the competition relates solely to the distribution of expected monopoly rents there is no net welfare gain. Hence *all* the associated real resource costs are deadweight losses; they represent resources which are diverted away from various forgone, welfare-producing alternative products that could have been supplied if no monopoly gains existed to be competed for.

Posner has explicitly criticised the merger trade-off model on these grounds. He argues that, if there is perfect competition in the bidding for monopoly positions, and risk neutrality, the competition will continue until the total costs incurred equal the value of the monopoly rent which is at stake. Thus, in Figure 2.2 the total social cost of a merger in the Williamson model is $ABEF$ + BCD, according to Posner, which must exceed the cost saving $GDEF$ made possible by it. (Strictly speaking, one should add, unless price falls.)

However, it is debatable whether the total expenditures to obtain or preserve a monopoly position will in practice equal the total monopoly profit. Information about monopoly opportunities is not widely available, and *less* expenditures would be committed under the more appropriate assumption of imperfect competition for monopoly gains. Moreover, as Mueller (1975) argues, many of the relevant

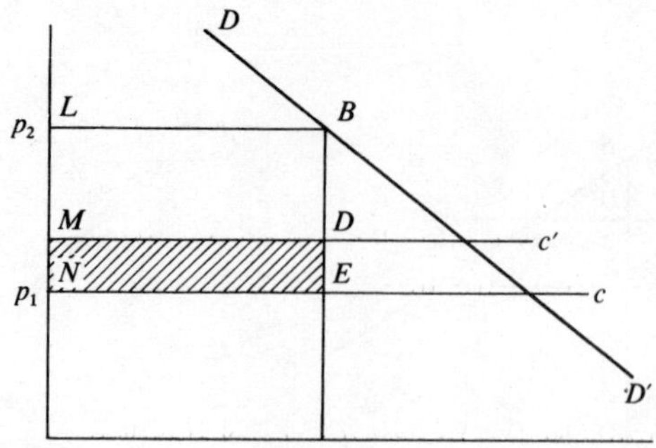

Figure 2.3

costs are included in reported company accounts: advertising, lawyers fees, public relations expenses, etc. For the successful firm these appear in the total cost rectangle rather than as dispositions of profit. Thus in Figure 2.3, which illustrates a simple monopoly situation, the successful monopolists' costs include the rectangle *MDEN*, which are costs he himself incurred in securing the monopoly. The monopoly rent rectangle *LBDM* measures the costs incurred by other, unsuccessful competitors for this same monopoly position *only* under the implausible assumption of perfect competition in the scramble for monopoly.

In sum, the Posner–Tullock arguments draw attention to an important, often neglected aspect of the social costs of monopoly. The implications for policy and for empirical analysis are twofold. First, a monopolist's costs include not only production costs but also the transactions costs of securing and maintaining his position. This issue is explored further in the following sub-section and in Chapter 3. Secondly, the social costs of a particular monopoly include a further element not captured by the traditional, partial equilibrium approach, namely the costs incurred by firms which were unsuccessful in securing the monopoly in question.

(vi) Cost levels under monopoly

The trade-off model, like the traditional welfare-loss model, employs an assumption that the observed cost curves reflect cost-minimising behaviour in the usual micro-theoretic sense. The full allocative impact of monopoly and merger is therefore missed if costs as well as prices tend to rise above their competitive levels as market power increases. Possible causes for such a tendency to exist include the considerations raised by Posner and Tullock, as previously discussed; the possibility of technical inefficiency arising where competitive pressure is weak (i.e. failure under a given technology to secure the maximum output from given input quantities); and pursuit of non cost-minimising policies (e.g. involving excessive staff expenditures, perquisites, discretionary investment

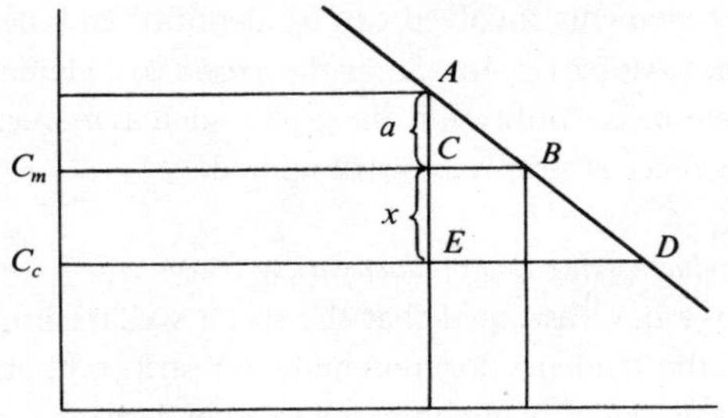

Figure 2.4

and growth) in furtherance of managerial objectives, inasmuch as product market power is a necessary but not sufficient condition for discretionary expenditure.

The degree of understatement of the welfare losses on this ground may be large. Comanor and Leibenstein (1969) illustrate the simple monopoly case as in Figure 2.4. Whereas the estimated loss is the area *ABC*, the true loss is *ADE*, to which must also be added the rectangle C_mCEC_c. In the linear demand curve case a simple relationship holds between *ABC* and *ADE*:

$$\frac{ADE}{ABC} = \left(1 + \frac{x}{a}\right)^2$$

where a is the price–cost margin, and x measures the cost elevation due to monopoly. Where x is large relative to a the understatement is clearly serious. For instance if $x = 3a$ the true welfare loss is *sixteen times* the estimated loss. Moreover the rectangle C_mCEC_c will also involve a relatively large additional welfare loss, because the losses arise not from marginal distortions of the output level, but from an element of excess average cost on all units produced.

Carrying these considerations over to the merger trade-off model raises problems similar to those affecting the choice between first- and second-best policy options, discussed earlier. Thus there are two approaches. One is to accept the pre- and post-merger cost levels as they are, without enquiring into their position relative to the cost-minimising ideals, and test for whether the claimed cost savings (assumed to be the net magnitude of the merger cost savings offset by cost increases associated with market power) exceed the disbenefits. This approach applies the more lenient, second-best type of merger criterion, giving much weight to institutional constraints and practicalities. The more ambitious alternative is to first purge the pre- and post-merger cost data of excess cost elements, before applying the trade-off criterion to the adjusted data. But this requires that the excess cost elements involved can be identified and measured within the necessary tolerance. Moreover, insofar as the excess cost elements are present because they generate direct utility for one group, such as management (Parish and Ng (1972)), the effect is simply redistributional.

(vii) Advertising, product quality and product variety

Up to this point we have assumed that the social welfare impact of monopoly relates simply to the tendency for monopoly to restrict output below the social optimum. We now need to turn our attention to other decision variables of the monopolist, namely advertising and product differentiation. In the case of advertising, Dixit and Norman (1978) have demonstrated that monopolies will tend to over-advertise, even in the absence of an entry threat. Within the standard, partial-equilibrium welfare framework advertising leads to benefits insofar as it raises the output of the monopolist, but these gains are moderated by the price increases resulting from advertising. Given these assumptions, there is a second-best optimum level of advertising which is greater than zero; second-best (or third-best) since the first-best solution would involve the elimination of the monopoly and therefore the elimination of advertising. It should be noted that if price falls with advertising, advertising in such cases would be unambiguously beneficial within the orthodox welfare framework so long as the benefits exceeded the resource costs of advertising. Conversely if advertising were to lead to an increase in price and a reduction in quantity there would be no trade-off – advertising would be unambiguously bad.

It could be argued that most advertising is not providing information on price and conditions of sale, and therefore is unlikely to create a more elastic demand for the product and hence a lower price. But the question of whether or not advertising is excessive becomes an empirical one and any suggestion for control can be fairly easily rebutted. This type of analysis can divert attention from the basic objections to advertising, that the flow of 'information'/persuasion will always be biased to the extent that the objectives of the corporation and the consumer are in conflict. Nor is it simply a matter of bias in the flow of 'information' embedded within advertising itself, but also the inevitable bias in communications in general when large areas of the media become dependent on advertising revenue.

Insofar as we are comparing a pre-merger competitive industry with a post-merger situation in which market power has been created the Dixit and Norman result indicates that under the conditions of the merger trade-off (i.e. where $\Delta p > 0$) the advertising implications of merger imply an additional detriment, and therefore a stronger case against merger where market power is created. However, in assessing a merger resulting in the acquisition of additional market power, where market power and advertising already exist, the implications are more ambiguous. Dixit and Norman have demonstrated the intuitively plausible result that oligopoly will tend to over-advertise to a greater extent than monopoly. Thus there can be some cases where mergers eliminating rivals will also eliminate excess advertising, not simply from the profit viewpoint but also in terms of the social optimum. It all depends on the pre- and post-merger locations relative to the interior maximum on the relationship between the difference of the socially optimal advertising rate from the actual advertising rate and the degree of monopoly. It is interesting to note that under second- (or third-) best conditions the socially optimal rate of advertising increases with the degree of monopoly (since output distortions are monotonically increasing) but the actual level of advertising has an interior maximum somewhere in the oligopoly range.

Turning to product differentiation there have been conflicting results in the literature. Until recently the prevailing view was that the question of the introduction of new products had nothing to do with monopoly. The monopoly problem remained in its traditional form as a problem of the restriction of supply in quantitative rather than qualitative terms. If consumers were sufficiently interested in new products[3] or new versions of old products, then they would be made available under monopoly, but of course subject to the usual monopoly restrictions on the rate of output (see, for example, Swann (1970)).

The crucial assumption, however, is the constant cost one. Under such conditions a monopolist will supply an infinite range of products so long as consumers are willing to pay a price at least equal to marginal cost. This assumption, in the case of the introduction of new products, is clearly untenable. We would normally expect that new products would introduce non-trivial setting-up costs and therefore it would be advantageous for the monopolist to restrict the variety of products on offer, especially if these had either zero or very limited revenue consequences. Under these cost assumptions, Lancaster (1975) has demonstrated that monopolists will tend to restrict the range of products to less than the social optimum since their policy will be dictated solely by fringe consumers and therefore not at all by the body of consumers who remain perfectly inelastic in their demand for the firms' products despite the fact that their preferred products (i.e. combinations of characteristics) are unavailable. The beer industry may provide an example of such behaviour. Fringe consumers in this case might be women and young people who, being brought up on soft drinks, may prefer a rather light, bland beer. The inveterate beer drinker, usually adult male, can be relied on to continue to drink beer despite the fact that his favourite variety is suppressed by the monopolist. The same example will suffice for another important Lancaster result; monopolies, as well as restricting the range to below the social optimum, will also pick a socially sub-optimal specification for the varieties it actually chooses to offer – for the same reasons.

3 'Sufficiently interested' here means that their demand function for the new product must intersect with the average cost function for that product.

Thus mergers which intensify market power will create the conditions under which it can become profitable to restrict product variety below the social optimum, and to offer products with specifications which do not satisfy the conditions of the social optimum.

(viii) Dynamic considerations

The trade-off model is a timeless analysis which neglects both the time-sequence in which the static costs and benefits of merger as opposed to alternatives accrue, as well as any effects which merger may have on the course of technical progress over time. With respect to the former Williamson acknowledged the problem that significant economies will eventually be realised through internal expansion if not by merger. Thus although a merger might pass on the static trade-off criterion, the eventual welfare effect could be negative if the cost savings could have been secured via the longer route of internal expansion, attenuating the deadweight losses due to the merger. Responding to this problem Williamson showed that the internal expansion alternative would have to be realised fairly quickly – say within 3–5 years – for a merger to be disallowed on this ground alone (1968a, p. 25). However, his calculations assumed instantaneous realisation of both the social costs and benefits due to merger (and involved questionable magnitudes of cost savings). If in practice the merger price-effects come about ahead of the cost savings this conclusion might no longer hold. In any event, some assessment of the time sequence of events should ideally be made when appraising individual cases.

The possibility of merger affecting technical progress arises because mergers affect market structure, which in turn has alleged effects on progressiveness, as argued by Arrow (1962), Schumpeter (1943) and Galbraith (1957) among others. However the alternative theoretical arguments conflict over the expected sign of the relationship between market power and progressiveness. The empirical evidence has been surveyed by Kennedy and Thirlwall (1972) and Kamien and Schwarz (1975) among others, and is further discussed in Chapter 12 below. Incorporating dynamic effects of this second type is easier when evaluating mergers that have occurred, than by assessing proposed mergers. Even in *ex post* analyses the problems are very great, on account of the complexity of the discovery process and the difficulty in attributing a particular breakthrough to a specific event such as merger. In practice the most that can be hoped for is a balance of probabilities, which must necessarily be struck more by reference to apparent tendencies across merger cases as a whole than to the particularities of individual cases.

(ix) Distributional considerations

Following as it does in the tradition of orthodox welfare analysis, the trade-off model is neutral towards transfers of welfare, e.g. from consumers to producers. But as Figure 2.1 shows, the welfare gains and losses are wholly unequally shared. The deadweight losses A_1 are suffered exclusively by consumers, who also lose out by the transfer of what was consumers' surplus prior to the merger and becomes monopoly profit after it (rectangle *MNEF*). Moreover, even the benefit of the cost-savings A_2 also accrues in the form of profit. Distributional considerations also add importantly to the seriousness of failing to consider the first-best outcome $p_2 = c_2$. Under this outcome the asymmetry of distribution of the gains is reversed: all gains accrue to consumers and only normal profits are earned.

But these are only the immediate distributional impacts. The ultimate effects depend upon how the extra profit is used: perhaps as expenditures to maintain the monopoly position; perhaps as socially beneficial R & D expenditure; or as dividends to shareholders; and so on. Thus the final redistributive effect is extremely hard to assess. To estimate the distributive consequences of monopoly is one thing, and a recent study in the US has suggested this is large (Comanor and Smiley (1975)). It is a very different matter to attempt an assessment of the contribution of individual, monopoly-increasing mergers to the overall result. At the same time, as Williamson admits, attaching only a slight weight to income distribution effects can significantly affect the outcome emerging from the trade-off criterion. And in practice social and political concern may be greater over the distributive than the allocative consequences of merger and monopoly.

(x) Politico-economic power considerations

Some mergers, especially those undertaken by the very largest firms in the economy, may alter the distribution of politico-economic power in society. In the UK this aspect of mergers has to be seen against a situation where the share of manufacturing controlled by giant companies is high and continuing to rise rapidly. Thus in 1970 the top 100 firms controlled 46% of manufacturing net output, compared with only 16% in 1909 (Prais (1976)). The effects of such power shifts are not amenable to inclusion in the trade-off analysis, since they are concerned with 'the quality of life in a democracy' (Williamson (1968a) p. 29) which cannot readily be expressed in efficiency (net value product) terms. Hence politico-economic power considerations have to be treated separately in the relevant cases, which might be defined as involving the top 50, 100 or 200 largest firms, depending on one's judgement as to where the threshold lies above which such considerations become important.

The important implication is that the trade-off analysis is an incomplete welfare guide in some cases. Irrespective of market power consequences, mergers involving large corporations should not be presumed unambiguously beneficial even where the economies defence under the trade-off analysis prevails. In this context, it should be noted that the attractiveness of mergers to the firm increases with firm size, on account of a non-linearity in the relationship between size and political influence. Thus a doubling of firm size for an already large firm has a bigger impact than occurs when, say, two corner shops are combined.

2.3 Vertical mergers: the welfare effects

Vertical merger brings into focus the whole question of the firm in a market economy. To what extent should the market handle transactions between economic agents supplying capital and labour, or, from the other point of view, to what extent should the firm, by internalising transactions, assume the co-ordinating role of the market. If efficiency considerations prevail, firms will continue to grow and extend their operations so long as extensions to the 'hierarchical' economy (intra-firm) give rise to increases in efficiency, and therefore profits, compared with the alternative of using the market (Coase (1937)). Oliver Williamson (1971) explores in some detail the possible sources of such efficiency gains, which revolve around the elimination of prolonged conflicts, informational economies, together with any technological links which may promote efficiency.

As far as the acquisition of market power is concerned, it has become the conventional wisdom to assume that a monopoly position at any stage of production would allow any excess profits within the whole chain of transactions to be appropriated by the monopolist. Thus a vertical extension of ownership could be explained only on grounds of efficiency and not by the pursuit of market power (see, for example, Needham (1974)). But this position can be sustained on only the most restrictive of assumptions. In the static case the analysis is correct only in the case of fixed proportions. If this is not descriptive of, say, the technology of the product to which the monopolist sells an input, then firms will substitute away from the monopolised input as its price is raised above marginal cost. By merging *downstream* the monopolist can avoid such input distortions and thereby appropriate the maximum monopoly rent. However, it is interesting to note that so long as the initial monopoly position is accepted then the vertical merger, by reducing distortions, raises the level of welfare (see, for example, Vernon and Graham (1971)). Nevertheless the outcome can still be an increase in price which raises the general trade-off problem. This situation can arise due to the fact that the extension of vertical control can imply an extension of control over additional inputs (see Warren-Boulton (1974)).

In the dynamic case the position is somewhat more worrying. A vertical extension can allow barriers to the entry of new firms and new products to be created and can also allow effective price discrimination to take place. More generally, in the oligopoly case, the vertical extension of any firm can have market power effects in both a static and dynamic sense (these aspects will be explored in Chapter 10). We are therefore left with a similar trade-off to the one we have described in the case of horizontal merger and therefore the framework we have developed can also be useful in this new context.

2.4 Diversifying mergers

The trade-off analysis may also be extended to diversifying mergers, since these too can give rise to the relevant kinds of cost savings and market power effects. While plant-level production economies are unlikely, various economies of firm size are potentially available, e.g. from the use of computers in managerial control; from lower transactions costs in raising large-scale finance, e.g. via share flotations; and so on. On the other side of the account, two kinds of anti-competitive effect of diversifying mergers have received most attention (particularly in the US where antitrust policies now preclude nearly all non-conglomerate mergers): potential competition and reciprocity. Potential competition can be reduced by diversifying merger if an existing competitor acquires and so eliminates a probable *de novo* entrant. Alternatively the acquiring firm may be the probable new entrant and so disappear from the schedule of potential entrants after the merger. Turner (1965) enumerated two necessary conditions to be fulfilled for a significant anti-competitive effect to be present: the acquired (or acquiring) firm must be perceived as the most likely entrant, with entry barriers for others significantly higher, and the market entered must have an oligopolistic structure, with actual price well above the competitive level. Steiner (1975, p. 263) has added a third condition, that actual price prior to the merger must be significantly less than the monopoly price. The anti-competitive effects from reciprocal buying arising from mergers are also described by Steiner (1975, pp. 219–22). Essentially, they arise if there is a deepening of monopoly power for the acquiring firm: if the effect in the acquired firm's market is designed as a predatory tactic and/or deterrent to entry there; or if by increased sales and/or profits in the combined firm there is an increase in influence in other markets, including the capital market.

There is, however, a fairly widely held view that these economies and anti-competitive effects of diversifying mergers, *free of significant horizontal and vertical side effects,* are likely to be relatively small. This is more likely to be true in the UK, where competition policy does not preclude horizontal and vertical mergers to the extent that it does in the US. Thus there is less pressure on UK firms to realise non-strictly-diversifying objectives (such as the realisation of firm-level size economies), or to pursue market power in relatively indirect ways, via conglomerate expansion. In this situation the strictly diversifying aspects of diversifying mergers – e.g. those associated with risk-pooling and the effectiveness of capital transfer – may be more likely to be seen.

Overall risk is reduced by merger whenever there is imperfect correlation between the profit streams of the two firms. Post-merger returns are the weighted sum of the two earnings streams:

$$Z = wx_1 + (1 - w)x_2 \tag{6}$$

where w, $(1 - w)$ are the relative sizes of the two firms and x_1 and x_2 are their profits. The expected post-merger return (u_z) is:

$$u_z = wu_1 + (1 - w)u_2 \tag{7}$$

with total variance (σ_z^2):

$$\sigma_z^2 = w^2\sigma_1^2 + (1 - w)^2\sigma_2^2 + 2w(1 - w) \operatorname{cov}(x_1 x_2) \tag{8}$$

As long as there is imperfect correlation between x_1 and x_2, the total post-merger variance is lower than the simple sum of the individual variances. With negative correlation, variability of post-merger profit is much reduced. As long as synergistic effects are not present, however, the mean post-merger profit does not increase: the gain is solely in the reduced variance associated with a given mean.

However, the reduction in risk is not a social gain in a perfect capital market, since shareholders already have the opportunity to hold shares of the companies in the ratio $(1 - w):w$ (Levy and Sarnat (1970)). The emergence of a social benefit therefore depends on the existence of capital market imperfections. For instance, a social benefit could arise where shareholder portfolios are small (e.g. on transactions costs grounds) since diversifying merger permits indirect investment in a larger number of individual profit sources. Alternatively, risk-pooling merger might reduce the risk of bankruptcy in a way that shareholder diversification cannot, and so permit some individually risky activities to take place that would otherwise not be undertaken, in the absence of this mechanism for shifting risk.

The choice between 'hierarchy' and market as a mechanism for allocating capital raises once more the question of the role of the firm in a market economy that was discussed earlier in the context of vertical mergers. The case for the corporate (hierarchical) system has again been put by Williamson (1970, 1975). In his analysis the 'appropriately organized' (multi-division or M-form) firm has advantages over the external capital market as a funds-metering mechanism in respect of access to internal information; ability to make marginal adjustments; and displacement costs. There is, however, an offsetting disbenefit. As the FTC (1972) has argued, one consequence of the development of diversified firms, publishing consolidated accounts, is that public information on the financial performance of individual industries is impaired or, in extreme cases, ceases to exist.

In putting this affirmative case for conglomerates on grounds of efficient capital transfer, Williamson treated corporate boundaries as for the most part fixed. But with inflexible corporate boundaries a globally optimal allocation of capital is unlikely. For the very factors which confer advantages on the M-form firm as an allocative instrument also give rise to a bias towards internal investment, whereas for a global optimum capital transfer across as well as within corporate boundaries is required. Thus, if it can be shown that diversifying mergers *per se* take place mainly or partly as a form of corporate search for new investment opportunities, as mooted by Cable (1977), and if Williamson's arguments are accepted, then such mergers generate a welfare gain by mitigating the discrepancy between the set of locally optimal and the globally optimal allocations of capital resources within the economy.

The welfare effects arising via risk-pooling and capital transfer can be incorporated into a welfare trade-off framework, but only in a rather loose sense. Because the effects are felt at an aggregated, systems level, affecting the operation of the economy as a whole, they are not easily apportioned for inclusion in trade-off calculations for individual merger cases.

2.5 Conclusions and implications for empirical work

This chapter has attempted a broad survey of the welfare effects that may be expected from mergers. The empirical work reported in later chapters has necessarily been more selective, focussing on what we judge to be the more important issues in different cases. The aim in writing the present chapter has been to provide an analytical background against which to set the individual pieces of evidence and the case studies which follow.

In the course of the chapter we have seen that the welfare trade-off model provides a basis for netting out the balance of social gain or loss arising from two of the most conspicuous aspects of horizontal mergers: their potential for saving costs and for raising price. However, the model does not embrace all the welfare effects that are likely in such cases, and the assumptions required to derive the net loss or gain from the considerations which are covered are restrictive, particularly with regard to distributional consequences. Our empirical work on horizontal mergers therefore does not adhere strictly to a rigid application of the trade-off model.

Although the model is most readily applied to horizontal merger cases, we have seen that it can also be extended to vertical and diversifying mergers. In both cases, however, some of the welfare issues arise at the level of the economy as a whole, in particular those concerning the basic choice between firms and markets as allocative and co-ordinating mechanisms.

The next chapter, Chapter 3, aims to assess the significance of monopoly power in the economy. It will thus serve as a bench-mark for the analysis of further merger activity resulting in enhanced monopoly power. Subsequently, in Chapter 4, an operational model is constructed by which we can assess empirically the consequences of merger for technical efficiency. The following chapters are largely concerned with estimating the magnitude of such efficiency gains and providing specific evidence on market power effects in a series of case studies.

Appendix A.2 The welfare trade-offs: a formal treatment[4]

Total welfare (W) is defined as social benefit minus cost:

$$W = TR + S + R - TC \tag{1}$$

where TR and TC are total revenue and production costs; S is consumers' surplus; and R denotes the intra-marginal rents accruing to producers. Under constant returns $R = 0$ so that:

$$W = \Pi + S \tag{2}$$

where $\Pi = TR - TC$.

Let p = price, c = unit cost (assumed constant) and assume iso-elastic demand: $q = Ap^{-\eta} =$ quantity.
Clearly,

$$\Pi = (p - c)q$$

and

$$S = \int_p^{\bar{p}} Ap^{-\eta}\, dp$$

where $\bar{p}$ is some arbitrarily high level of price (and $\eta \neq 1$). Hence, for given price and cost,

$$W = \int_p^{\bar{p}} Ap^{-\eta} dp + (p - c)q$$

$$= K + Ap^{-\eta}\left[p\frac{\eta}{\eta - 1} - c\right] \tag{3}$$

where $K = A\dfrac{A\bar{p}^{1-\eta}}{1 - \eta}$ is a constant. The Harberger, Williamson and first-best welfare comparisons can all be expressed in terms of (3).

The Harberger model

Harberger measured the welfare loss due to monopoly by subtracting monopoly profits from the aggregate decline in consumer welfare. On the present approach we compare the monopoly welfare level W_m with that under competition W_c with the aid of (3). Under competition $p_c = c$, so that:

$$W_c = K + Ac^{-\eta}\left[c\frac{\eta}{\eta - 1} - c\right]$$
$$= K + Ac^{1-\eta}\frac{1}{\eta - 1} \tag{4}$$

In monopoly, price exceeds cost by some mark-up $k = p_m/c$. Hence

$$W_m = K + Ap_m^{-\eta}\left[p_m\frac{\eta}{\eta - 1} - c\right] \tag{5}$$

4 We are grateful to Avinash Dixit for suggesting the approach adopted in this appendix and deriving the basic measure of welfare in equation (3).

Table A.2.1 *Monopoly welfare losses: illustrative cases*

η	k			
	1.05	1.10	1.20	$\eta/(\eta - 1)$
2	0.0024	0.0083	0.0336	0.50
3	0.0066	0.0141	0.0533	0.28

$$= K + Ac^{1-\eta}k^{-\eta}\left[k\frac{\eta}{\eta - 1} - 1\right]$$

As a proportion of total revenue, the monopoly welfare loss L may be written as $(W_c - W_m)/p_m q_m$. Therefore

$$L = \frac{K + Ac^{\eta}\left[c\dfrac{\eta}{\eta - 1} - c\right] - \left\{k + Ac^{1-\eta}k^{-\eta}\left[k\dfrac{\eta}{\eta - 1} - 1\right]\right\}}{Akc^{1-\eta}}$$

$$= \frac{1 - k^{-\eta}[(k - 1)\eta + 1]}{(\eta - 1)k^{1-\eta}} \qquad (6)$$

In this equation L is a rising function of both k and η. Harberger assumed $\eta = 1$, $k = 1.10$. The assumption that k and η are independent implies limit-pricing behaviour, for in the absence of an entry constraint the monopolist sets price so that $MR = c$, in which case $k = \eta/(\eta - 1)$.

Illustrative values of L are set out in Table A.2.1. Elasticities in the maximum plausible range are chosen (Hirsch 1950, Wenders 1967). Under unconstrained monopoly-pricing behaviour the losses are very large.

The Williamson trade-off model

Utilising (3), pre-merger welfare W_1 may be written:

$$W_1 = K + Ac_1^{1-\eta}k_1^{-\eta}\left[k_1\frac{\eta}{\eta - 1} - 1\right] \qquad (7)$$

where k_1 denotes the pre-merger price–cost ratio p_1/c_1. Similarly, post merger welfare W_2 is:

$$W_2 = K + Ac_2^{1-\eta}k_2^{-\eta}\left[k_2\frac{\eta}{\eta - 1} - 1\right] \qquad (8)$$

where $k_2 = p_2/c_2$, the post-merger price-cost ratio. *Ex hypothesi* the class of mergers under discussion is defined such that $k_2 > k_1$ and $c_2 < c_1$. The trade-off criterion asks whether $W_2 > W_1$, in these circumstances. From (7) and (8) this requires:

$$\left(\frac{c_2}{c_1}\right)^{1-\eta}\left\{k_2^{-\eta}[(k_2 - 1)\eta + 1] - k_1^{-\eta}[(k_1 - 1)\eta + 1]\right\} > 0 \qquad (9)$$

Table A.2.2 *Values of S_1 for selected cost reductions and price–cost ratios*

Post-merger price–cost ratio	Pre-merger price–cost ratio	Percentage cost reduction 5	10	20	30	Post-merger price–cost ratio	Pre-merger price–cost ratio	Percentage cost reduction 5	10	20	30
		(a) $\eta = 2$						(b) $\eta = 3$			
1.05	1.00	(0.2)	(0.3)	(0.3)	(0.3)	1.05	1.00	(0.4)	(0.4)	(0.5)	(0.7)
1.10	1.00	(0.9)	(0.9)	(1.0)	(1.2)	1.10	1.00	(1.3)	(1.4)	(1.8)	(2.4)
1.20	1.00	(2.9)	(3.1)	(3.5)	(4.0)	1.20	1.00	(4.1)	(4.6)	(5.8)	(7.6)
1.30	1.00	5.3	(5.9)	(6.7)	(7.6)	1.30	1.00	5.4	(8.3)	(10.6)	(13.8)
$\eta/(\eta - 1)$	1.00	5.3	11.1	25.0	(35.7)	$\eta/(\eta - 1)$	1.00	5.4	11.7	(20.3)	(26.5)
1.05	1.05	(0.3)	(0.3)	(0.3)	(0.3)	1.05	1.05	(0.4)	(0.4)	(0.6)	(0.7)
1.10	1.05	(0.9)	(1.0)	(1.1)	(1.2)	1.10	1.05	(1.4)	(1.6)	(2.0)	(2.6)
1.20	1.05	(3.1)	(3.2)	(3.6)	(4.2)	1.20	1.05	(4.5)	(5.0)	(6.4)	(8.3)
1.30	1.05	5.8	11.9	(7.0)	(8.0)	1.30	1.05	6.3	(9.2)	(11.6)	(15.2)
$\eta/(\eta - 1)$	1.05	5.8	11.9	26.5	(37.5)	$\eta/(\eta - 1)$	1.05	6.3	13.3	(22.3)	(29.2)
1.10	1.10	(0.9)	(1.0)	(1.1)	(1.3)	1.10	1.10	(1.6)	(1.7)	(2.2)	(2.9)
1.20	1.10	(3.2)	(3.4)	(3.8)	(4.4)	1.20	1.10	(5.0)	(5.5)	(7.0)	(9.1)
1.30	1.10	(6.2)	(6.5)	(7.3)	(8.4)	1.30	1.10	7.9	(10.1)	(12.8)	(16.7)
$\eta/(\eta - 1)$	1.10	6.7	13.1	28.4	(39.3)	$\eta/(\eta - 1)$	1.10	7.9	15.6	(24.5)	(32.0)
1.20	1.20	(3.5)	(3.7)	(4.2)	(4.8)	1.20	1.20	(5.9)	(6.6)	(8.3)	(10.9)
1.30	1.20	(6.7)	(7.1)	(8.0)	(9.1)	1.30	1.20	(10.8)	(12.0)	(15.2)	(19.9)
$\eta/(\eta - 1)$	1.20	9.6	16.7	33.3	(42.9)	$\eta/(\eta - 1)$	1.20	13.1	22.2	(29.2)	(38.1)
1.30	1.30	(7.3)	(7.7)	(8.7)	(9.9)	1.30	1.30	(12.7)	(14.1)	(17.8)	(23.3)
$\eta/(\eta - 1)$	1.30	13.8	21.4	39.4	(46.4)	$\eta/(\eta - 1)$	1.30	20.6	(27.0)	(34.2)	(44.5)
$\eta/(\eta - 1)$	$\eta/(\eta - 1)$	(52.6)	(55.6)	(62.5)	(71.4)	$\eta/(\eta - 1)$	$\eta/(\eta - 1)$	(32.3)	(36.0)	(45.6)	(59.5)

In the special case where competition prevails prior to the merger (Williamson's 'naive model') $p_1 = c_1$ so that $k_1^{-\eta}\{(k_1 - 1)\eta + 1\} = 1$.

First-best comparisons

The first-best situation is where $p_2 = c_2$ so that first-best welfare W_f is defined as

$$W_f = K + Ac_2^{1-\eta}\frac{1}{\eta - 1} \tag{10}$$

The surplus of first best over the higher of pre- or post-merger welfare, $(W_f - W_m)/R$ is therefore:

$$S = \frac{\left(\dfrac{c_2}{c_1}\right)^{1-\eta} - k_j^{-\eta}\{(k_j - 1)\eta + 1\}}{(\eta - 1)K_j^{1-\eta}} \tag{11}$$

where $j = 1$ if $W_1 > W_2$ (unfavourable mergers) and $j = 2$ if $W_2 > W_1$ (beneficial mergers).

Table A.2.2 reports values of S for cost reductions of between five and thirty per cent and for selected values of k_1 and k_2 between the competitive and monopoly levels. Entries above the heavy line in each subset of the table relate to cases where price falls as a result of the merger. Bracketed entries denote cases where the comparison is between W_f and W_2 (beneficial mergers). The table shows that if price–cost ratios of 1.2 or 1.3 are possible, and cost reductions up to 20 per cent, potential first-best losses equal 8 per cent of pre-merger revenue when $\eta = 2$ and 15 per cent when $\eta = 3$.

References

Adelman, M. A. (1961), 'The Anti-Merger Act, 1950–60', *American Economic Review*, **51**, 236–44.

Arrow, K. J. (1962), 'Economic Welfare and the Allocation of Resources for Invention' in R. R. Nelson (ed.) *The Rate and Direction of Inventive Activity*, Princeton University Press.

Bain, J. S. (1968), *Industrial Organisation*, Second Edition, Wiley, New York.

Blair, J. M. (1958), 'The Conglomerate Merger in Economics and Law', *Georgetown Law Journal*, **46**, 672–700.

GB Board of Trade (1969), *Mergers: A Guide to Board of Trade Practice*, HMSO.

Cable, J. R. (1975), 'Economies as an Anti-Trust Defence: Does the First Best Matter?' IIM Preprint 1/75–79.

– (1977), 'Searching by Merger and the Transfer of Capital', *Recherches Economiques de Louvain*, **43**, no. 3 (September 1977), 225–42.

Coase, R. H. (1937), 'The Nature of the Firm', *Economica*, **4**, 386–405.

Comanor, W. S. and Leibenstein, H. (1969), 'Allocative Efficiency, X-Efficiency and the Measurement of Welfare Losses', *Economica*, **36**, 304–9.

Comanor, W. S. and Smiley, R. H. (1975), 'Monopoly and the Distribution of Wealth', *Quarterly Journal of Economics*, **89**, 177–94.

De Prano, M. E. and Nugent, J. R. (1969), 'Economies as an Antitrust Defense: A Comment', *American Economic Review*, **59**, 947–53.
Dewey, D. (1961), 'Mergers and Cartels: Some Reservations about Policy', *American Economic Review*, **51**, 256–8.
Dixit, A. K. (1976), 'Welfare Effects of Tax and Price Changes', *Journal of Public Economics*, **4**, 103–23.
Dixit, A. K., and Norman, V. (1978), 'Advertising and Welfare', *Bell Journal of Economics*, **9**, 1–17.
Federal Trade Commission (1972), *Economic Report on Conglomerate Merger Performance*, US Government Printing Office.
Galbraith, J. K. (1957), *American Capitalism*, London: Hamish Hamilton.
Harberger, A. (1954), 'Monopoly and Resource Allocation', *American Economic Review*, **44**, 77–87.
Hirsch, W. Z. (1950), 'A Survey of Price Elasticities', *Review of Economic Studies*, **19**, 50–8.
Jackson, R. (1970), 'The Consideration of Economies in Merger Cases', *Journal of Business*, **43**, 439–46.
Kamien, M. I. and Schwarz, N. L. (1975), 'Market Structure and Innovation', *Journal of Economic Literature*, **13**, 1–37.
Kennedy, C. and Thirlwall, A. P. (1972), 'Technical Progress: A Survey', *Economic Journal*, **82**, 11–72.
Lancaster, K. (1975), 'Socially Optimal Product Differentiation', *American Economic Review*, **65**, 567–85.
Levy, H. and Sarnat, M. (1970), 'Diversification, Portfolio Analysis and the Uneasy Case for Conglomerate Mergers', *Journal of Finance*, **25**, 795–802.
Lintner, J. (1971), 'Expectations, Mergers and Equilibrium in Purely Competitive Securities Markets', *American Economics Review*, **61**, 101–11.
Lipsey, R. G. and Lancaster, K. (1956), 'On the General Theory of the Second Best', *Review of Economic Studies*, **24**, 11–32.
Modigliani, F. (1958), 'New Developments on the Oligopoly Front', *Journal of Political Economy*, **66**, 215–32.
Monopolies Commission (1969), *Reports* on the 'Unilever/Allied Breweries' and 'Rand/De La Rue' Proposed Mergers, HC 297 and 298, HMSO.
Needham, D. (1974), *Economic Analysis and Industrial Structure*, London: Holt, Rinehart and Winston.
Mueller, D. C. (1975), 'The Social Costs of Monopoly and Regulation: Comment', IIM Preprint 1/75–72.
O'Dwyer, M., (1972), 'Estimating the Welfare Effects of Mergers', unpublished MA dissertation, University of Warwick.
Parish, R., and Ng, Y. K. (1972), 'Monopoly, X-Efficiency and the Measurement of Welfare Loss', *Economica*, **39**, 301–8.
Posner, R. A. (1975), 'The Social Costs of Monopoly and Regulation', *Journal of Political Economy*, **83**, 807–27.
Prais, S. J. (1976), *The Evolution of Giant Firms in Britain*, Cambridge University Press.
Ross, P. (1968), 'Economies as an Antitrust Defense: Comment', *American Economic Review*, **58**, 1371–2.
Rowley, C. K. (1973), *Antitrust and Economic Efficiency*, London, Macmillan.
Schumpeter, J. (1943), *Capitalism, Socialism and Democracy*, London: Allen and Unwin.
Slater, M. (1974), 'Economies as an Antitrust Defense: Yet another Comment', mimeo, University of Bristol.

Spence, M (1974), 'Entry, Capacity, Investment and Oligopolistic Pricing', Technical Report 131, The Economic Series, Institute for Mathematical Studies in the Social Sciences, Stanford University (April).

Steiner, P. O. (1975), *Mergers: Motives, Effects, Policies,* Ann Arbor: University of Michigan Press.

Swann, P. (1970), 'Market Structure and Technological Progress: The Influence of Monopoly on Product Innovation', *Quarterly Journal of Economics,* **84**, 627–38.

Tullock, G. (1967), 'Welfare Costs of Tariffs, Monopolies, and Theft', *Western Economic Journal,* **5**, 224–32.

Turner, D. F. (1965), 'Conglomerate Mergers and Section 7 of the Clayton Act', *Harvard Law Review,* **78**, 1313–95.

Vernon, J. M. and Graham, D. A. (1971), 'Profitability and Monopolization by Vertical Integration', *Journal of Political Economy* **79**, 924–5.

Warren-Boulton, F. (1974), 'Vertical Control with Variable Proportions', *Journal of Political Economy,* **82** (July/August), 783–802.

Wenders, J. T. (1967), 'Entry and Monopoly Pricing', *Journal of Political Economy,* **75**, 77–760.

Williamson, O. E. (1968a), 'Economies as an Antitrust Defense: The Welfare Trade-offs', *American Economic Review,* **58**, pp. 18–36. Reprinted with author's corrections in *Readings in Industrial Economics* (Charles K. Rowley, ed.), London: Macmillan (1972), 111–35.

– (1968b), 'Economies as an Antitrust Defense: Correction and Reply', *American Economic Review,* **58**, pp. 1372–6.

– (1969), 'Economies as an Antitrust Defense: Reply', *American Economic Review,* **59**, pp. 954–9.

– (1970), *Corporate Control and Business Behaviour,* Prentice-Hall, NJ.

– (1971), 'The Vertical Integration of Production', *American Economic Review,* **61**, 112–23.

– (1975), *Markets and Hierarchies: Analysis and Antitrust Implications,* The Free Press, NY.

– (1976), 'Economies as an antitrust defense revisited', University of Pennsylvania, July 1976.

3

Welfare loss due to monopoly: a benchmark

This chapter aims to measure the welfare consequences of product market power in the UK.[1] Given that merger has been responsible for much of the observed increase in concentration within the UK we can attribute whatever consequences we are able to determine at least partially to previous merger activity. It is especially important to develop such estimates since (a) the conventional wisdom has it that welfare loss due to monopoly is insignificant and (b) no previous empirical estimates for the UK are available. The empirics will be restricted to the top 102 firms in the UK during the period 1968/69 and 1970/74. In the context of this chapter we will assume that the creation of monopoly allows for no gains in efficiency. The later chapters, giving empirical results for a wide array of actual merger cases and for industries with substantial merger activity, will provide information on likely gains in efficiency but it should be kept in mind that the first-best requires both optimal pricing and efficiency in the technical sense (see Chapter 2).

3.1 Theoretical analysis

If we accept that the conditions of contemporary capitalism are consistent with the existence of positions of monopoly power, and arguably conducive to it (Cowling (1978)), then it would seem unreasonable to rule out the question of monopoly power on *a priori* grounds. And yet this is exactly what has been done in most previous estimates of monopoly welfare loss going back to Harberger (1954). This has inevitably led to the conclusion that the social cost of monopoly is trivial. If, instead, we start out with the assumption that monopoly positions will be fully exploited we come, perhaps not surprisingly, to quite different conclusions.

Taking an orthodox, partial equilibrium view of social welfare, welfare loss

1 The chapter is based on Cowling and Mueller (1978) which reports on welfare loss estimates for the US and the UK. In this chapter we report only on the UK and give more complete information on the 102 firms in the sample.

(ΔW) due to monopoly (assuming linearity) can be written as:

$$\Delta W = \tfrac{1}{2}\Delta p \Delta q \quad (1)$$

with Δp being the change in price from competition to monopoly and Δq being the change in quantity.

Assuming constant costs, monopoly profits will be

$$\Pi = q_m \Delta p \quad (2)$$

where q_m is monopoly output.
Assuming profit maximising behaviour, and given linear demand and constant cost, monopoly output will be one half of competitive output and therefore

$$\Delta q = q_m \quad (3)$$

Substituting from (2) and (3) into (1) gives the result

$$\Delta W = \tfrac{1}{2}\Pi \quad (4)$$

Welfare loss from monopoly equals one half of monopoly profits. It is interesting first to contrast this with the Harberger derivation:

$$\Delta W = \tfrac{1}{2}pq\eta t^2 \quad (5)$$

where $t = \Delta p/p$, and η is the price-elasticity of demand. He then *assumed* $\eta = 1$ and, since he observed $\Delta p/p$ to be quite small (assuming constant costs this will be the ratio of profit to revenue, Π/R), the inevitable conclusion is that welfare loss is minimal. The crucial step he makes in generating this result is to assume that the change in price and the change in quantity are independent of each other. In contrast, if we assume monopoly pricing behaviour then low price-cost margins are inconsistent with a low price elasticity of demand. Harberger and others have therefore assumed away the monopoly problem by observing low mark-ups and *assuming* low elasticities.

In measuring monopoly profit we have tried to avoid two other sources of bias present in previous studies. The obvious measure of monopoly profit is the excess of actual profits over long-run competitive returns. Harberger (1954) and all subsequent studies have based their monopoly profit estimates on the deviation between actual profit rates and the mean rate and therefore their estimates are biased down to the extent that the mean rate includes elements of monopoly rent. We have instead made use of estimates of the cost of capital due to Flemming et al. (1976). Again, all previous studies, except Worcester (1973) have used industry data at a fairly high level of aggregation which can result in two sorts of downward bias. First, the aggregate industry measure will be biased down to the extent that some firms may be earning negative economic profits reflecting a position of short-run disequilibrium. Our position will be that the monopoly profits of some firms cannot be offset by the transitory losses made by others.[2] A second aggrega-

2 This point is developed at some length in Cowling and Mueller (1978).

tion bias is introduced when measured welfare loss is based on Harberger's derivation (equation (5)), since in such case the profit margin appears as a squared term. Again a downward bias is introduced with variation in the profit margins across firms within the industry. Clearly this is not a problem with our own derivation.

The above discussion has focussed simply on procedures for obtaining accurate estimates of the size of the welfare loss triangle. However, as discussed in Chapter 2, Tullock (1967) and Posner (1975) have argued that previous studies understate the social costs of monopoly by failing to recognize the costs involved in attempts to gain and retain monopoly power. These costs could take the form of investment in excess production capacity, excessive accumulation of advertising goodwill stocks, and excessive product differentiation through R & D.[3] Efforts to obtain tariff protection, patent protection and other types of preferential government treatment through campaign contributions, lobbying or bribery are parts of the social costs of the existence of monopoly as defined by Tullock and Posner. To the extent that these expenditures enter reported costs in the form of higher payments to factor owners and legitimate business expenses, firm costs in the presence of monopoly exceed costs under perfect competition. Estimates of welfare loss based on those profits remaining *net* of these expenditures *under*estimate the social cost of monopoly in two ways: first, by understating monopoly rents they understate the distortions in output monopoly produces; second, by failing to include these additional expenditures as part of the costs of monopoly.

Three adjustments to the usual welfare triangle measure of monopoly welfare loss are made to account for the additional expenditures to redistribute monopoly rents monopoly power induces. First, advertising is added to monopoly profit in calculating the welfare triangle loss to allow for the understatement of monopoly profit expenditures of this type produce. Second, the whole of advertising is added to the welfare loss. This takes the extreme view of advertising as merely an instrument for securing market power. To the extent advertising provides useful information to consumers, this measure overstates the cost of monopoly.[4] Third, all measured, after-tax profits above the competitive cost of

3 See Spence (1974). It is interesting to note that this type of activity generally dominates the entry-limiting pricing response. Entry limiting pricing can be thought of as having extra capacity because of potential entry and actually using it to produce output. Thus the profits associated with restricting output are lost. From this viewpoint we cannot accept Posner's position that the elimination of entry regulation would eliminate waste. As the probability of entry increases so would the optimal degree of excess capacity. Monopoly pricing would be maintained but social waste would still occur.

4 There will always be an inherent bias in the information provided given the interests of the agent doing the advertising so the argument for advertising as a provider of information should not be taken too seriously. Even if we base

Table 3.1 *Alternative definitions of social cost*

b	ΔW^b_{CM}	ΔW^b_H
1	$\Pi/2$	$(R/2)(\Pi/R)^2$
2	$(\Pi + A)/2$	$(R/2)[(\Pi + A)/R]^2$
3	$A + (\Pi + A)/2$	$(R/2)[(\Pi + A)/R]^2 + A$
4	$\Pi' + A + (\Pi + A)/2$	$(R/2)[(\Pi + A)/R]^2 + A + \Pi'$

where
Π = before tax profit
Π' = after tax profit
A = advertising
R = total revenue.

capital are used as the estimate of the expenditures incurred by others to obtain control of these monopoly rents. Obviously this estimate is but a first approximation. It is an underestimate, if the firm has incurred expenditures in the acquisition and maintenance of its monopoly position, which are included in current costs. It is an overstatement if actual and potential competitors can successfully collude to avoid these wasteful outlays. This type of argument can always be rebutted, however, by carrying the Tullock/Posner analysis one stage back and positing expenditures of resources to enter the potential competitor's position, and so on. The arguments that after-tax profits underestimate the additional costs associated with monopoly seem at least as reasonable as those suggesting overestimation.

3.2 **Empirical estimates**

We provide two sets of estimates, one based on our assumptions (ΔW^b_{CM}), the other based on Harberger-type assumptions (ΔW^b_H), both measured at the firm-level. For each approach we give a range of four estimates defined in Table 3.1.

Thus for $b = 1$ we define two alternative estimates of the welfare triangle, the one (ΔW^1_{CM}) based on interdependence of Δp_i and Δq_i, the other (ΔW^1_H) based on the Harberger methodology. ΔW^1_H is included for comparison with previous results. For $b = 2$, the same calculations are performed but for Δp_i, advertising expenditure (A_i) is deducted from cost. For $b = 3$, we add in advertising expenditure as a social cost and for $b = 4$, we also add in monopoly profits *after tax* as a further element of social cost. It should be noted at this point that in calculating Δp_i the appropriate profit measure is *before tax* profit since the price and quantity choice of a monopolist should not be affected by a tax on profits. Thus, in contrast to most previous studies, we use before tax profits to measure the

our welfare measures on post-advertising preferences it is still possible to demonstrate that monopolies (and *a fortiori* oligopolies) invest in too much advertising (see Dixit and Norman (1978)).

distortion between price and costs under monopoly (the ΔWs for $b = 1, 2, 3$). However it is *after tax* monopoly profits which provide an inducement to additional expenditures to gain monopoly, and it is these that are added in to obtain our fourth measure of welfare loss.

To estimate monopoly profits, we used the pre-tax cost of capital as calculated by J. S. Flemming et al. It may be argued that because of inflation we are under-valuing capital. Given that inflation in the UK in 1968/69 was substantial, although very much less than in the 1970s, we have corrected our data at the company level by the difference between the average rate of return at historic and replacement cost as calculated by Walker (1974). To the extent that our capital measure at the company level departs from a historic cost measure we will bias our results. We may expect this bias to lead to a systematic overestimate of capital since (a) revaluations generally take place at merger, when acquired assets are given a current market valuation, and most of the top 100 firms have been heavily involved in merger activity during the 1960s, and (b) revaluations, of land and buildings especially, do take place periodically, their frequency being related to the rate of inflation. Given that our estimate of capital will tend to be biased up, our measure of excess profits, and therefore of welfare loss, will tend to be biased down. The cost of capital measure used was the forward-looking, pre-tax measure which was estimated at 8.15% for the period 1968/69, Flemming et al. (1976).

The firms in our sample include companies operating in both intermediate and final goods markets. To justify the addition of triangular type measures of welfare loss for final and intermediate products, we must assume that the demand schedule for an intermediate product represents a derived demand schedule as in traditional Marshallian analysis. Under this assumption, triangular measures of welfare loss calculated from intermediate product demand schedules fully capture the loss in consumer welfare that monopoly distortions in the intermediate markets cause, as Wisecarver (1974) has recently demonstrated. Assuming advertising and other efforts to obtain monopoly power are as wasteful when undertaken in intermediate markets as in final goods market, the formulae presented in Table 3.1 can be applied to both intermediate and final goods producers. Our estimates refer to the top 103 firms in the UK for the periods 1968/69 and 1970/74.[5] Over the periods in question these firms were responsible for roughly one third of GNP. The time-periods used have been dictated by the availability of data. The basic source has been EXTEL cards but advertising expenditure was estimated by aggregating up from the brand level, using estimates of press and TV advertising contained in MEAL. We can therefore expect that our advertising expenditure figures will be biased down by the amount of non-media advertising. Table 3.2 gives the results for 1968/69, with firms being ranked by ΔW_{CM}^4. The two major oil companies, BP and Shell, dominate the table. The

5 The top 100 varies somewhat over time.

social cost associated with BP alone is roughly a quarter of one per cent of GNP. The other members of the Top Ten are industry leaders plus British American Tobacco. Two interesting features are the high ranking of Rank Xerox despite its size (explained presumably by its UK patent rights) and the low ranking of motor-car manufacturers (absent from the Top Twenty in 1970/74). We have computed estimates of welfare loss for the 1970/74 period, but we have not reported these results here. It is well known that the early 1970s was a period of very rapid inflation in the UK and this undoubtedly raises problems such as how to adequately account for stock appreciation and the revaluation of capital. Despite these problems, it is somewhat reassuring to note that the 1970/74 results look very much like the 1968/69 results except that the oil companies became even more dominant.[6]

The average estimates of welfare loss for ΔW^{b}_{CM} range between 3.9 and 7.2 per cent of gross corporate product (GCP) (value added) for the 1968/69 period. The estimate for ΔW^{1}_{CM} is almost identical with that for the US but in each of the other cases the value for the UK is well below that for the US.[7] The obvious and important difference between the two sets of results is the apparent greater expenditure on advertising in the US. Taking direct account of advertising quadruples the welfare loss estimate for the US but in the case of the UK welfare loss goes up by only about 40% (compare ΔW^{1}_{CM} with ΔW^{3}_{CM}).[8] Using the Harberger approach estimates of welfare loss vary between 0.2% and 3% of GCP in the same 1968/69 period.

It may be argued that it is unreasonable to assume monopoly price/output behaviour since industrial structure in the UK is essentially oligopolistic in character and although collusion is possible, perfect collusion is unlikely. This view would imply that one half of monopoly profits simply defines the upper bound on monopoly welfare loss for a specific firm – true welfare loss may be quite different. We can establish a lower bound on welfare loss, assuming that oligopoly output is independent of entry, by replacing equation (3) with the Cournot prediction. However this obviously depends on the number of firms in the industry in question, or where firms are of unequal size, on the Herfindahl measure of concentration. We have a real problem at this point since there is no

6 Indeed, comparing the results for the two periods indicates the large extent to which oil companies have benefited from the recent 'oil crisis'. However, this inference has to be qualified by the problems raised for the measurement of profit by stock appreciation during a period of rapid inflation of oil prices.

7 See Cowling and Mueller (1978).

8 This does not of course mean that advertising implies no additional social costs since profit-margins and the level of excess profits may both be partly determined by advertising insofar as elasticities of demand and entry barriers are influenced by the level of advertising in monopolistic industries. We should also note that in some cases our direct adjustment for advertising is very significant (e.g. Unilever, Imperial Group, and Beecham Group).

Table 3.2 *Monopoly welfare losses by firm (£m): 1968/69*

Company		ΔW^1_{CM}	ΔW^2_{CM}	ΔW^3_{CM}	ΔW^4_{CM}	ΔW^1_H	Company ΔW^2_H	ΔW^3_H	ΔW^4_H
1	British Petroleum	74.06	74.42	75.13	82.72	5.07	5.12	5.84	13.42
2	Shell Transport & Trading	49.43	50.82	53.62	53.62	2.15	2.28	5.07	5.07
3	British American Tobacco	26.78	27.03	27.53	49.09	1.02	1.05	1.55	23.11
4	Unilever	2.83	11.28	28.19	29.00	0.015	0.244	17.15	17.96
5	ICI	17.63	18.79	21.10	27.87	0.48	0.544	2.85	9.63
6	Rank Xerox	13.94	14.01	14.15	27.48	3.37	3.41	3.54	16.88
7	IBM (UK)	11.12	11.19	11.31	21.87	2.20	2.23	2.35	12.91
8	Great Universal Stores	9.57	10.05	11.02	21.60	0.495	0.547	1.52	12.09
9	Beecham	6.17	8.88	14.29	20.36	0.611	1.26	6.67	12.75
10	Imperial Group	2.78	8.55	20.08	20.08	0.014	0.137	11.67	11.67
11	Marks & Spencer	9.77	9.79	9.82	18.64	0.598	0.600	0.64	9.45
12	Ford	7.21	7.75	8.81	16.64	0.203	0.234	1.30	9.12
13	F. W. Woolworth	7.25	7.42	7.75	15.92	0.346	0.362	0.69	8.87
14	J. Lyons	0.00	0.74	2.84	14.16	0.000	0.009	2.111	13.425
15	Burmah	5.26	5.46	5.86	13.94	0.239	0.257	0.66	8.74
16	Distillers	5.62	6.12	7.12	13.40	0.170	0.202	1.20	7.49
17	Rank Organisation	11.45	11.66	12.07	12.53	1.19	1.23	1.65	2.10
18	Thorn	5.59	6.09	7.10	12.49	0.282	0.335	1.35	6.73
19	Cadbury Schweppes	1.82	5.02	11.44	12.30	0.036	0.283	6.70	7.56
20	Reckitt & Colman	2.91	4.69	8.25	10.41	0.113	0.293	3.85	6.02
21	Gallagher	2.24	4.18	8.05	10.26	0.023	0.082	3.96	6.17
22	British Leyland	6.53	7.43	9.24	9.84	0.091	0.118	1.93	2.52

23	Rio Tinto Zinc	9.20	9.20	9.20	9.20	0.538	0.538	0.54	0.54
24	GEC	3.87	4.19	4.82	8.24	0.086	0.101	0.73	4.15
25	Courtaulds	4.83	5.31	6.25	7.43	0.096	0.116	1.06	2.24
26	Esso Petroleum	4.73	5.62	7.41	7.41	0.083	0.117	1.91	1.91
27	Boots	3.25	3.52	4.06	7.19	0.113	0.133	0.67	3.81
28	Spillers	1.74	2.96	5.40	7.08	0.041	0.120	2.56	4.24
29	RHM	2.33	3.58	6.08	7.04	0.033	0.078	2.57	3.54
30	Arthur Guinness	2.61	3.18	4.33	6.87	0.091	0.135	1.28	3.82
31	Associated Br. Foods	3.75	4.34	5.51	6.77	0.062	0.083	1.26	2.51
32	Brooke Bond Liebig	1.86	3.13	5.68	6.71	0.035	0.100	2.65	3.68
33	Rowntree Mackintosh	0.487	2.46	6.40	6.40	0.005	0.127	4.07	4.07
34	Tesco Stores	2.51	2.73	3.18	5.86	0.077	0.091	0.54	3.22
35	Rothman's International	1.34	2.57	5.04	5.68	0.029	0.107	2.58	3.22
36	EMI	3.11	3.43	4.08	5.67	0.129	0.158	0.81	2.40
37	Allied Breweries	2.63	3.27	4.55	5.16	0.043	0.067	1.35	1.95
38	Lucas (Industries)	2.90	2.98	3.13	5.10	0.072	0.076	0.23	2.20
39	Consolidated Gold Fields	3.40	3.40	3.40	5.03	0.144	0.144	0.14	1.78
40	Dunlop Holdings	3.04	3.64	4.85	4.85	0.039	0.056	1.26	1.26
41	UDS Group	2.03	2.19	2.53	4.69	0.074	0.087	0.42	2.58
42	Plessey	2.54	2.56	2.61	4.67	0.075	0.076	0.12	2.19
43	GKN	3.20	3.32	3.56	4.52	0.043	0.047	0.28	1.25
44	Dickinson Robinson	2.19	2.25	2.37	4.11	0.081	0.086	0.21	1.94
45	Coats Paton	3.06	3.22	3.53	4.05	0.078	0.086	0.40	0.92
46	Metal Box	2.17	2.19	2.22	3.87	0.056	0.057	0.092	1.74
47	Sears Holdings	1.20	2.58	3.74	3.74	0.032	0.053	1.22	1.22
48	C. T. Bowring	2.28	2.29	2.31	3.55	0.043	0.044	0.062	1.30
49	Unigate	1.23	1.49	2.02	3.54	0.010	0.015	0.54	2.06

Table 3.2 *Monopoly welfare losses by firm* (£m): *1968/69*

	Company	ΔW^1_{CM}	ΔW^2_{CM}	ΔW^3_{CM}	ΔW^4_{CM}	ΔW^1_H	Company ΔW^2_H	ΔW^3_H	ΔW^4_H
50	Reed International	—	1.04	3.36	3.36	—	—	—	—
51	Johnson Matthey	1.65	1.65	1.65	3.09	0.044	0.044	0.046	1.49
52	George Wimpey	1.41	1.47	1.59	2.90	0.020	0.021	0.14	1.45
53	Thomas Tilling	1.56	1.85	2.44	2.83	0.028	0.039	0.63	1.02
54	Lonrho	2.68	2.68	2.68	2.81	0.112	0.112	0.11	0.24
55	British Electric Traction	1.01	1.15	1.41	2.39	0.024	0.031	0.30	1.28
56	Bass Charrington	–	0.361	2.33	2.33	—	—	—	—
57	Scottish & Newcastle Br.	1.13	1.28	1.58	2.14	0.023	0.029	0.33	0.88
58	Tube Investments	1.02	1.39	2.14	2.14	0.006	0.012	0.76	0.76
59	BICC	2.11	2.11	2.13	2.13	0.024	0.024	0.036	0.036
60	British Aircraft Corpn	1.31	1.32	1.33	1.72	0.020	0.020	0.032	0.43
61	Turner & Newall	0.79	0.85	0.96	1.68	0.012	0.013	0.13	0.85
62	Carrington Viyella	0.78	0.90	1.13	1.65	0.020	0.026	0.26	0.77
63	House of Fraser	0.53	0.75	1.17	1.60	0.005	0.011	0.44	0.87
64	Tarmac	1.16	1.17	1.20	1.60	0.024	0.025	0.053	0.45
65	Tootal	0.96	1.01	1.11	1.36	0.016	0.018	0.12	0.36
66	Assoc. Portland Cement	1.12	1.18	1.31	1.31	0.018	0.020	0.15	0.15
67	Grand Metropolitan	0.64	0.67	0.74	1.22	0.021	0.023	0.093	0.57
68	Ready Mixed Concrete	1.01	1.01	1.01	1.17	0.016	0.016	0.017	0.18
69	Fitch Lovell	0.49	0.54	0.64	1.14	0.004	0.004	0.098	0.61
70	British Oxygen	1.07	1.08	1.10	1.10	0.016	0.016	0.036	0.036
71	Whitbread	0.057	0.39	1.04	1.04	0.000	0.002	0.66	0.66

72	Harrison's & Crosfields	0.53	0.53	0.53	1.03	0.005	0.005	0.005	0.51
73	J. Sainsbury	0.33	0.40	0.53	0.97	0.001	0.002	0.14	0.58
74	Delta Metal	0.88	0.88	0.89	0.89	0.009	0.009	0.017	0.017
75	W. H. Smith & Son	0.38	0.43	0.55	0.73	0.003	0.004	0.12	0.30
76	Cavenham	—	0.22	0.72	0.72	—	—	—	—
77	Booker McConnell	0.37	0.43	0.55	0.55	0.004	0.005	0.13	0.13
78	Gill & Duffus	0.44	0.44	0.44	0.53	0.002	0.002	0.002	0.10
79	Inchcape	0.37	0.39	0.43	0.43	0.002	0.002	0.042	0.042
80	Amalgamated Metal Corpn	0.32	0.32	0.32	0.38	0.001	0.001	0.002	0.061
81	Guinness Peat	0.30	0.30	0.30	0.37	0.002	0.002	0.002	0.077
82	S. & W. Berisford	0.27	0.29	0.32	0.34	0.001	0.002	0.033	0.056
83	Wood Hall Trust	0.29	0.29	0.29	0.32	0.002	0.002	0.002	0.038
84	Mitchell Coutts	0.28	0.29	0.30	0.30	0.002	0.002	0.015	0.015
85	Trafalgar House Invests	0.22	0.22	0.22	0.22	0.003	0.003	0.003	0.003
86	Consolidated Tin Smelters	0.05	0.07	0.10	0.10	0.000	0.000	0.035	0.035
87	Pilkington Bros.	—	—	—	—	—	—	—	—
88	Bowater Corpn	—	—	—	—	—	—	—	—
89	Tate & Lyle	—	—	—	—	—	—	—	—
90	John Laing	—	—	—	—	—	—	—	—
91	Trust Houses Forte	—	—	—	—	—	—	—	—
92	Dalgety	—	—	—	—	—	—	—	—
93	Babcock & Wilcox	—	—	—	—	—	—	—	—
94	FMC	—	—	—	—	—	—	—	—
95	Debenhams	—	—	—	—	—	—	—	—
96	Philips Electronic	—	—	—	—	—	—	—	—
97	Vickers	—	—	—	—	—	—	—	—
98	ICL	—	—	—	—	—	—	—	—

Table 3.2 *Monopoly welfare losses by firm* (£m): *1968/69*

Company	ΔW^1_{CM}	ΔW^2_{CM}	ΔW^3_{CM}	ΔW^4_{CM}	ΔW^1_H	Company ΔW^2_H	ΔW^3_H	ΔW^4_H
99 Albright & Wilson	—	—	—	—	—	—	—	—
100 Mobil	—	—	—	—	—	—	—	—
101 Chrysler (UK)	—	—	—	—	—	—	—	—
102 P. & O. Lines	—	—	—	—	—	—	—	—
103 Texaco	—	—	—	—	—	—	—	—
Total all firms (103)	385.8	435.0	537.4	719.3	21.4	24.2	118.8	304.4
Total ÷ gross corporate product	0.0386	0.0436	0.0539	0.0720	0.0021	0.0024	0.0119	0.0305

Number of firms with $\Pi > 0 = 82$
Number of firms with $\Pi + A > 0 = 86$

systematic source of unbiased estimates of these Herfindahls. The general formula of welfare loss in the Cournot case is simply $\Pi/2N$ where N is the number of equal size firms. In the case of unequal size firms the formula is $\frac{1}{2}\Pi H$, where H is the Herfindahl measure of concentration. A symmetric duopoly would therefore imply welfare loss equal to one half of that for the monopoly case, and a symmetric triopoly one third of the monopoly loss.[9] It is interesting to note that the Herfindahl would have to fall to 0.1 (e.g. ten equal-size firms) for the estimates to approximate the value of the UK estimates based on the Harberger methodology. Since it would seem that Herfindahls as low as this would not be descriptive of most UK markets,[10] and recognising also that these are lower-bound estimates, the inference must be that Harberger type estimates understate the true value of welfare loss.

We must conclude that our evidence suggests significant welfare loss due to monopoly power. One other point is also brought out particularly by the UK results (e.g. in the case of the oil companies) and that is the international distribution of these social costs. Monopoly power held by UK companies in foreign markets may be advantageous to the UK economy whilst being disadvantageous in the global sense. Thus the issue is a distributional one and adds an international dimension to the distributional issues already implicit in our analysis. In any national evaluation of the social costs imposed by the actions of a particular company, the international distribution of these costs would presumably gain some prominence.

3.3 Implications and conclusions

Previous studies of the social costs of monopoly have generally (and often unconsciously) assumed that 'monopolies' set prices as if they did not possess market power, that the only important distortions in output are brought about through the deviations in one firm's market power from the average level of market power, that the losses of some firms (perhaps incurred in unsuccessful attempts to obtain monopoly power) legitimately offset the monopoly rents of others, and that all of the expenditures made in the creation and preservation of monopoly positions are part of the normal costs which would exist in a world without monopolies. With the problem so defined, it is not surprising that most of these studies have found the welfare losses from monopoly to be small.

Since we know from general equilibrium analysis that monopoly allocation distortions may be offsetting, the conclusion that partial equilibrium analysis yields small welfare loss estimates has seemed all the more impressive. Yet each

9 In the case of a symmetric duopoly $\Delta q = \frac{1}{2}q$ and in the triopoly case, $\Delta q = \frac{1}{3}q$. Thus in the two cases ΔW is, respectively, $\frac{1}{4}\Pi$ and $\frac{1}{6}\Pi$.

10 For an array of UK markets on which unbiased estimates of the Herfindahls can be calculated, the values varied between 0.1 and 0.65 (Cowling et al. (1975)).

of the studies that has come up with low estimates has done so in large part because it has made assumptions (e.g. demand elasticities equal to 1.0, monopoly profits are deviations from mean profits) that can be rationalised only as *ad hoc* attempts to answer the general equilibrium question. In contrast, the present study defines a procedure for estimating the costs of monopoly that is consistent with a partial equilibrium analysis that assumes market power does (or may) exist. Our results reveal that the costs of monopoly power, calculated on an individual firm basis, are on average large. The conclusion that 'even' a partial equilibrium analysis of monopoly indicates that its costs are insignificant no longer seems warranted.

Do we in fact overstate monopoly's costs? We have certainly made some assumptions which arguably might overstate the case (e.g. the full offsetting of monopoly profits through the competitive pursuit of monopoly power and the partial equilibrium framework). But we have also ignored important sources of bias in the other direction. These possible biases are present in the measurement of profits and thus enter the estimated magnitudes of both Δp_i and Π_i itself. We have already emphasised that reported profits understate true profits to the extent that firms compete for monopoly power by investing in excess plant capacity, advertising, patent lawyers, and so on. But much of the competition for *control* over monopoly rents may take place within the firm itself among the factor owners. Such competition will lead to an understatement of actual monopoly rents both through the inflation of costs that wasteful competition among factor owners brings about, and through the inclusion of part of the winning factor owners' shares of monopoly rents as reported costs. A large literature now exists on the variety of objectives managers have and the way in which these objectives are satisfied through their discretionary control over company revenues. To the extent that managerial control over firm revenues is the reward for successfully competing against other factor groups and potential managers, reported profits understate the true profitability. By ignoring these possibilities we err in being conservative when estimating the social cost of monopoly.

In this respect, it is useful to note an alternative, aggregative approach to the question. Phillips, in an appendix to Baran and Sweezy (1966), isolated several categories of expenditure, dependent on the existence of 'Monopoly Capitalism' (e.g. advertising, corporate profits, lawyers' fees). Their sum came to over 50% of US GNP. Although the assumptions upon which these calculations were made are rather extreme, they do suggest both an alternative method of analysis and the potential magnitude of the problem. Here too, it should be noted that our approach has been essentially micro-oriented and neoclassical in that we have taken the returns on corporate stocks as our cost of capital. From a more aggregative view it could be argued that profits are not required at all to generate the savings required to sustain a given rate of growth, since alternative macro policies are available. From this perspective, all profits are excess profits and our estimates of social cost are too conservative. Still further weight would be added against the position that monopoly power is unimportant, if the link between the distribution of income and wealth and the distribution of political power were considered.

What policy implications can be drawn from our results? First, the relative size of the welfare losses indicates that the static costs of monopoly power should no longer be regarded as necessarily small. Our monopoly welfare loss estimates by firm indicate the most significant contributors to these losses. The tops of our lists of the largest welfare losses by firm are logical starting points for intensified enforcement of antitrust policy. Our figures and supporting analysis further demonstrate that 'the monopoly problem' is broader than traditionally suggested. A large part of this problem lies not in the height of monopoly prices and profits *per se*, but in the resources wasted in their creation and protection. These costs of monopoly should be considered when selecting targets for antitrust enforcement.

One might argue that the high profits of some firms reflect economies of scale advantages, and, therefore, these firms should not be the victims of antitrust policy. This argument points to some form of regulatory or public enterprise solution to the monopoly problem. With respect to this type of policy, our estimates of the losses from monopoly represent a still further understatement of their potential magnitude. If a policy were adopted forcing the most efficient size or organisational structure upon the entire industry, the welfare loss under the existing structure would have to be calculated using the profit margin of the most efficient *firm and the output of the entire industry*, rather than the profit margins of the individual firms and their outputs.

Of course, any public policy has its own sets of costs and inefficiencies. For Tullock–Posner reasons a concerted effort to apply or strengthen the antitrust laws induces large, defensive expenditures on the part of business. Price and profit regulation leads to efforts to change, influence, or circumvent the application of the rules. The public enterprise solution raises the same sort of problems, with members of the bureaucracy participating in the competition for monopoly rents. Thus it might be that any alternative for dealing with existing monopoly power would involve higher costs than the monopolies themselves create. The present study does not answer this question. What it does do is dispel the notion that it need not even be asked, since the costs of monopoly within the present environment are necessarily small. The question of what the costs and benefits from alternative antimonopoly policies are still seems worth asking.

Appendix A.3

Data: definitions and sources

All the data on individual firms with the exception of advertising, have their origin in the data tabulations of the Exchange Telegraph Statistics

Service (EXTEL). Most of the relevant data in a summarized form was available in various issues of *The Times Review of Industry and Technology.* In the case of advertising the firm data had to be estimated via a process of aggregating estimates of press and TV advertising of the various products produced by each firm. These data were extracted from various issues of MEAL (*Advertisers Annual Analysis of Media Expenditure*) and, in the case of 1968, from the *Statistical Review of Press and T.V. Advertising,* Legion Publishing Company. *Who Owns Whom* was used in the process of aggregation.

Each firm's capital was measured as total tangible assets less current liabilities (excluding bank loans, overdrafts and future tax). Profit was measured before interest and tax and then adjusted for the estimated cost of capital (taken from J. S. Flemming, et al. (1976)).

References

Baran, P. and Sweezy, P. (1966), *Monopoly Capital,* New York: Monthly Review Press.

Cowling, K. (1978), 'Monopoly, Welfare and Distribution', in M. Artis and A. K. Nobay (eds.) *Contemporary Issues in Economics,* Association of University Teachers of Economics Conference Papers, 1977, London: Croom-Helm.

Cowling, K., Cable, J., Kelly, M., and McGuiness, T. (1975), *Advertising and Economic Behaviour,* London: Macmillan.

Cowling, K., and Mueller, D. (1978), 'The Social Costs of Monopoly Power', *Economic Journal* (December).

Dixit, A., and Norman, V., (1978), 'Advertising and Welfare', *Bell Journal of Economics* (Spring), 1–17.

Flemming, J. S., Price, L. D. D., and Byers, S. A. (1976), 'The Cost of Capital, Finance and Investment', *Bank of England Quarterly Bulletin,* **16** (June), 193–205.

Harberger, A. C., (1954), 'Monopoly and Resource Allocation', *American Economic Review,* **44** (May), 77–87.

Posner, R. A. (1975), 'The Social Costs of Monopoly and Regulation', *Journal of Political Economy,* **83** (August), 807–27.

Spence, M., (1974), 'Entry, Capacity, Investment and Oligopolistic Pricing', Technical Report 131, *Institute for Mathematical Studies in the Social Sciences,* Stanford University.

Tullock, G., (1967), 'The Welfare Costs of Tariffs, Monopolies and Theft', *Western Economic Journal,* **5** (June), 224–32.

Walker, J. L., (1974), 'Estimating Companies' Rate of Return on Capital Employed', *Economic Trends,* November, xx–xxix.

Wisecarver, D., (1974), 'The Social Costs of Input–Market Distortions', *American Economic Review,* **64** (June), 359–72.

Worcester, Jr, D. A. (1973), 'New Estimates of the Welfare Loss to Monopoly: U.S. 1956–69', *Southern Economic Journal,* **40**, 234–46.

4

Measuring changes in the efficiency of firms

4.1 **Introduction**

For public policy purposes there is a wide range of considerations to be taken into account in assessing the consequences of mergers. These include such broad questions as changes in the nature of our political and financial institutions, the redistribution of income, and possible inflationary effects. In addition there may be local effects such as the disruption of the labour market, increases in monopoly power and, of course, changes in the organisation of the firm. These aspects are considered in various places in this report, notably in the case studies. The relative significance of these issues varies considerably from case to case, and it is one of the virtues of the case study approach that the emphasis can vary where necessary.

However, one of the central concerns of our research was to find a way of measuring the static welfare effects arising from price changes and changes in the firm's productive efficiency. This chapter is about estimating the latter.

By efficiency we mean efficiency in the process of turning given inputs into given outputs. The conventional wisdom in favour of mergers in the later 1960s was based on two types of efficiency improvement which were thought likely to result.

The first type of improvement is due to economies of large-scale production. The existence of such economies in a number of industries has been documented (from engineering studies) by Pratten (1971). (However, the notion that *as a general rule* large firms are generally more efficient than small firms is cast in some doubt by studies such as those of Samuels and Smyth (1968) which find a significant negative correlation between size and profitability.) The second source of improved efficiency is the application of superior management skills to a larger organisation. Although in logic this is a kind of economy of scale it is not susceptible to the same kind of engineering analysis as is the production process.[1]

1 Also in this category one might include economies of scale in distribution and marketing.

Instead it is based largely upon a faith in the organisational capabilities of such men as Mr Jim Slater, Sir Arnold Weinstock, Lord Stokes, and a regiment of less well-known figures.

This rules out one possible approach to the measurement of efficiency improvements, that followed by Pratten, which would be to examine changes in production technique which occurred as a result of merger and ask engineers who knew the process to assess the changes in input use that would result. 'Super-managers' do not simply devise new and better production processes (if they do it at all), or ensure that economies of scale are fully exploited. They may close factories, change the research budget or redesign organisational structures and procedures. The separate effect of each of these changes is not measurable with any accuracy. In our case studies we did look for evidence of rationalisation and policy changes but from this alone it would be very difficult to deduce a reliable overall measure of efficiency change. One British study using an approach similar to this has been carried out by Newbould (1970), who questioned the managements of 38 firms which had merged, and analysed the motives behind the mergers and the consequences that ensued. He found that market dominance for one reason or another (including self defence) was the most important single motive in merger. Technological reasons such as the ability to exploit economies of scale came a long way behind this, and this is reflected in the failure to carry out much rationalisation following the merger. For example, twenty-one firms did not shut down any plant and thirty of the thirty-eight firms shut down less than 5% of their plant of any particular type. The general picture that emerges from Newbould's work is certainly not one of massive reconstruction or rationalisation of British industry by bold captains exploring new frontiers, and his findings may go some way to explaining why many mergers do not improve profitability.

Hart, Utton and Walshe (1973) also looked for evidence of improved efficiency. They managed to examine forty-two cases but, unlike Newbould, did not appear to adopt a systematic approach to the problem. Since they do not make a serious attempt to calculate efficiency changes their conclusions relate more to the issue of concentration than to efficiency.

An alternative is to ignore what is going on inside the 'black-box' of the firm and simply take profitability as a measure of efficiency change.

One advantage of this method is that it is easy to apply on a large scale. Most studies of this sort have used US data and they have usually found that taking over another firm is as likely to be unprofitable as profitable. If anything, the average tendency appears to be towards unprofitability. These findings have been summarised by Meeks (1977) and by Utton (1974), who have also carried out some calculations for British firms. In comparisons of merger-intensive firms with their industry average, Utton found more (but not significantly more) than half with profitability below the median for their industry. In a comparison with non-merger-intensive firms with similar growth rates he found the merger-intensive firms to be significantly less profitable in the following years. This confirmed Singh's (1971) earlier finding for the 1950s that in the majority of cases firms had a decline in relative profitability following a merger, and this decline was not reversed when longer periods after the merger were taken. Meeks (1977) in another large-scale study on similar lines found, on the average, a significant decline in post-merger profitability for the five years following the merger. This decline, although of the same order of magnitude, was not, however, found to be significant in years six and seven following the merger. This may well be because the size of his sample was smaller for these comparisons. (For the year of the merger itself Meeks finds a significant improvement in profitability, a result he dismisses as due to distortions.[2]) He makes adjustments for accounting bias due to the revaluation of the merged firm and for external influences by measuring a firm's profit rate relative to its industry. He concludes that since the market power of merging firms is unlikely to have declined the decline in profitability can be taken to indicate a decline in efficiency.

The major objection to this for our present purposes is that it does not really give any useful measure of the extent of the change in efficiency. Indeed, until we know what has happened to the price of output (and the cost of inputs to the firm) no firm conclusions can be drawn about changes in efficiency. Where comparisons with non-merging firms in the same industry have been made the industry has usually been defined very broadly (for example 'food' would be one industry.) There is very little to guarantee that the prices relevant to pairs of merging and non-merging firms in the same industry (thus defined) would move in the same direction, and is open to the possible claim that mergers are frequently a response to increased competition, so a decline in profitability would be expected anyway.

It would be possible in principle to meet this objection by using a less aggregated industry definition for profitability comparisons. But frequently there is no firm for which figures are available in the same narrowly defined industry as our merging firm, and we did not want to rule out the possibility of including monopolies in our study. Furthermore, one of our purposes was to look for efficiency changes as such, in order to complement the relative profitability approach.

Our minor reservations about using profitability as a measure of efficiency are compounded into major objections when it comes to the use of stock market measures (such as bid premiums and share price movements before and after the merger) for assessing efficiency gains. Failure to take into account market power effects is a criticism here also. More fundamentally, this method assumes that shareholders can and do successfully assess the future profitability of the combined enterprise. The obvious response to this is that if this is what shareholders

2 For instance, one of the firms frequently has an effective financial year of 15–18 months in order to bring the two accounting periods into line.

try to do the evidence of the profitability studies shows that they do it very badly. This method also ignores the large short-term speculative element in share price which, as readers familiar with Keynes' comparison of the stock market to a newspaper beauty competition (*General Theory*, pp. 156–7) will be aware, makes fashion an important element in share prices. In a period when mergers are fashionable this will be reflected in a higher price–earnings ratio for merger-intensive firms, a result found, for example, by Kelly (1967) for the US stock market and Kuehn (1975) for Britain. The only studies to conclude that mergers are beneficial include some element of share price valuation in their measure of the gains from merger (see Meeks (1977), Table C.A). For example Franks et al. (1976) conclude from share price data that brewing industry mergers have led to efficiency improvements. For a good discussion of the rationality of share prices in this context see Firth (1976) especially Chapter 2.

Another approach to the measurement of efficiency change is to examine labour productivity or output per man. This has the advantage of being fairly objective and easy to calculate but it also has a major deficiency. Direct labour is typically only one of many factor inputs such as raw materials and components, machinery, fuel, and packaging. Factor substitution or a change in the extent of vertical integration would make output per man an unreliable measure of total factor productivity.

What is really needed is to measure every factor used in the production of output and to add them up. Adding up diverse factors will, of course, require a set of prices to use as weights. In addition, since relative prices vary somewhat over time, there are bound to be index number problems in any such comparisons of efficiency.

Although such a measure of efficiency, measuring the use of all factors, comes closer to the ideal, its information requirements are immense. With the data sources available it would be possible to do it for every Census of Production for each MLH industry as a whole. However, it would be difficult to apply to individual firms on an annual basis.

The method actually used in our study corresponds to the 'dual' of the one just proposed. Instead of using prices as weights in an index, we use quantities. Efficiency changes are deduced from changes in prices and expenditures, rather than quantities. The effect on prices of changes in market power can also be deduced with this method, the details of which are given below.

Although we have criticised some alternative methods of deducing efficiency changes, we do examine such statistics as rates of return in the case studies. Their main weakness, which is usually that they only present a partial picture, is also their strength. Rates of return, labour productivity, details of firm reorganisation and associated cost estimates, each give a different insight into what happens when two firms merge and may be considered complementary. But none of them measure efficiency change.

4.2 The method employed to measure efficiency

To understand our method it is useful to think of the firm as a 'black box', purchasing certain inputs and using them to produce certain outputs. We define an increase in efficiency as a reduction in the ratio of inputs used to outputs produced.

The direct way of measuring this change in efficiency would be to list the inputs used up in every period and compare this list with the outputs produced. However, such detailed lists are only available for certain years, those in which a Census of Production was taken, and these lists do not give details on individual firms.

However, provided that either (i) the proportion in which inputs are used and outputs produced or (ii) the relative prices of inputs and the relative prices of outputs do not fluctuate greatly from year to year, the required information on inputs and outputs can be deduced from a knowledge of

(a) expenditure on inputs and their prices

(b) revenue from sales of outputs and their prices.

Revenue and expenditure figures can be obtained from published company accounts, and price data are available from a number of different sources.

In common with all methods of measuring efficiency certain assumptions are made, and it is useful to make some of these explicit. This will make clear the direction of various biases that are likely to creep in and alert the reader to the reasons for certain adjustments that are made. It should also provide the basis for deciding what conclusions can and what cannot be drawn in interpreting a particular series of measures.

Consider a production process that produces one output and uses N factors of production, denoted by the subscript i.

Let C = total cost of production

f_i = quantity of factor i consumed

p_i = unit price of factor i

Q = number of units of output produced

Π = total profits from production

P_0 = revenue from unit of output

R = total revenue from output produced

The following identities are implied:

$$\Pi \equiv R - C \quad (1)$$

$$R \equiv P_0 Q \quad (2)$$

$$C \equiv \Sigma f_i p_i \quad (3)$$

$$\Pi = P_0 Q - \Sigma f_i p_i \quad (4)$$

Assumption (1) The factors of production are consumed in fixed proportions to one another. This can be written

$$f_i = k a_i Q \quad (5)$$

a_i, assumed constant, is the relative quantity of factor i required to produce one unit of output. k is a measure of the total factor requirement per unit of output. It may vary with the scale of production, technical progress, or the efficiency with which a particular technique is used. Since the a_i are only relative quantities they are only defined up to a factor of proportionality and need normalising in some way. In practice this is done by choosing a value of $k = 100$ for a particular observation, say on the eve of merger. Then unit factor requirements appear as if they were measured relative to this observation. Only relative values of k between different observations are important, and not the absolute magnitudes.

If we substitute equation (5) into equation (4) we obtain the following

$$\Pi = P_0 Q_0 - \sum ka_i Qp_i$$

$$\text{i.e. } \Pi = P_0 Q_0 - kQ \sum_{i=1}^{N} a_i p_i \tag{6}$$

Now $\sum_{i=1}^{N} a_i p_i$ is the correct form for a fixed-weight price index of inputs, which we can call P_I

$$P_I \equiv \sum_{i=1}^{N} a_i p_i \tag{7}$$

Substituting (7) into (6)

$$\Pi = P_0 Q - kQP_I \tag{8}$$

whence it follows that

$$k = \frac{P_0}{P_I}\left(1 - \frac{\Pi}{P_0 Q}\right) \tag{9a}$$

$$= \frac{P_0}{P_I}\left(1 - \frac{\Pi}{R}\right) \tag{9b}$$

If our assumption of a single output of fixed input proportions is correct this formula will give us an exact measure of the change in unit factor requirement from observation to observation. Unit factor requirement, of course, is inversely proportional to 'efficiency' as we have defined it. The extension of the argument to a multiple output produced in fixed proportions is trivial. P_0 then becomes a price index of output rather than a single price.

A common sense interpretation of it may be made in the following way. $P_0[1 - (\Pi/R)]$ is simply average unit cost. When this is deflated by P_I we have average cost after allowing for a change in input prices: specifically, after allowing for a change in the price of a given factor combination represented by the weights a_i.

It may be illustrated graphically as in Figure 4.1. IQ_1 is the isoquant for a unit of output in the initial period and IC_1 is the associated isocost line. IQ_2 is the isoquant for the same output in the subsequent period. The slope of the ray $ODEF$ represents the assumed factor proportions, and the distance along that ray is proportional to the cost of using the factors in those proportions. IQ_2 represents a

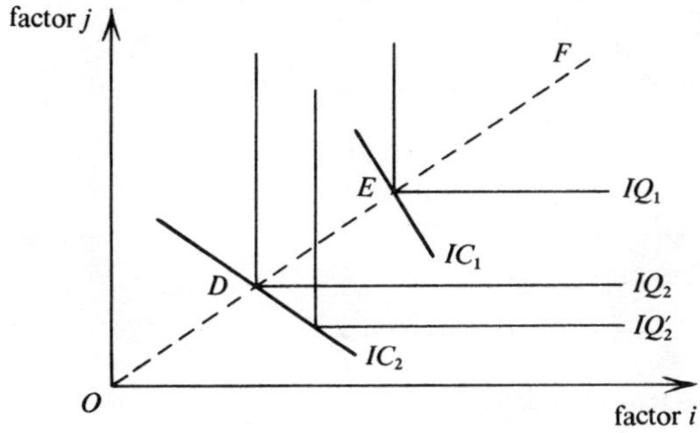

Figure 4.1 *Fixed factor proportions. Neutral and biased efficiency gains*

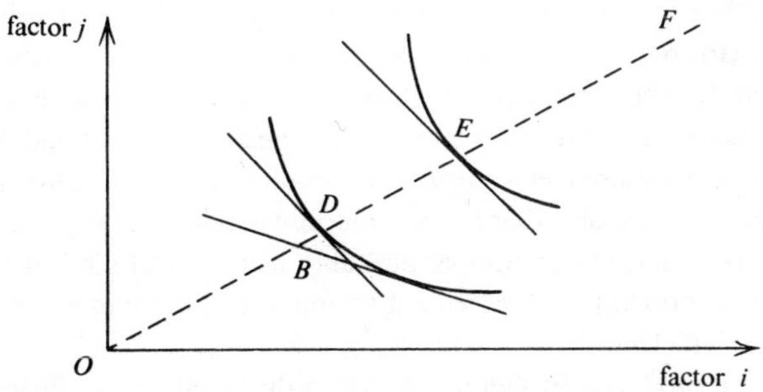

Figure 4.2 *Substitution of factors induced by relative price changes*

more efficient process because the cost of producing the same output is smaller. The relative value of total factor requirements before and after the change is given by OE/OD.

In comparing two time periods actual costs would of course depend on the price of the factors so it is necessary to deflate actual costs by a price index. That is why P_I appears in the denominator of equation 9.

As long as the factors are consumed in fixed proportions it does not matter if the relative prices of factors move divergently. If factor proportions change, however, as in the case where the new isoquant is IQ'_2 then an element of arbitrariness will be introduced into the measurement insofar as the measured gain in efficiency will be affected by relative factor prices.[3]

One reason for changes in factor proportions to take place is a change in factor prices which might induce the substitution of one factor for another. In this case the isoquants are better represented by curves than right angles. This case is illustrated in Figure 4.2. Since k measures total costs, assuming the fixed proportions represented by the ray OF, the calculated value of the ratio of factor require-

3 This problem arises whenever index numbers are used.

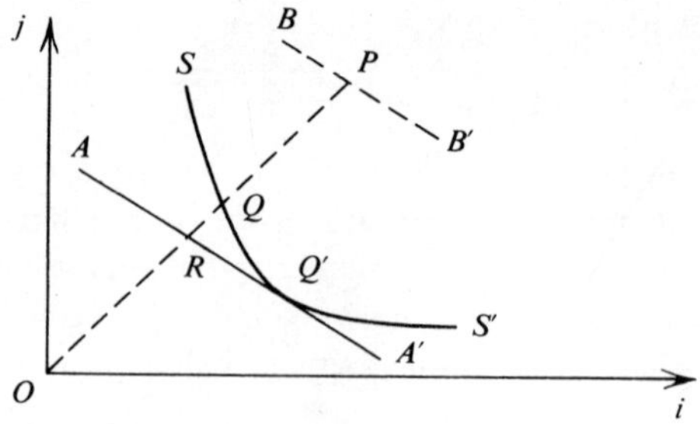

Figure 4.3 *Farrell's measure of efficiency*

ments before and after the change, k_1/k_2, will correspond to OE/OB. True technical efficiency differences would be captured by OE/OD. If this is regarded as the 'true' ratio of factor requirements then k_1/k_2 will overestimate the savings in factor requirements by the ratio OD/OB. (However, there are grounds for claiming that the efficient substitution of relatively cheap factors should be counted as part of any measured efficiency gain. Insofar as prices represent value in alternative uses it is desirable that firms economise in relatively expensive factors. Such 'allocative efficiency' is just as desirable as technical efficiency.)

The astute reader will notice that $1/k$ bears a strong resemblance to Farrell's measure of productive efficiency.[4]

Farrell's diagram is reproduced in Figure 4.3. SS' is the isoquant for efficient production of the output in question, using factors *i* and *j*. *P* is the actual factor combination employed. This is inefficient in two respects. First, it is technically inefficient because production is not on the isoquant. Farrell's measure of technical efficiency is OQ/OP.

P is also inefficient because the wrong factor combination is used. AA' is an isocost line and its slope represents the relative prices of *i* and *j*. Farrell uses the term 'price efficiency' for the ratio OR/OQ. The product of these two types of efficiency is OR/OP. It corresponds to the ratio of expenditure on factors in the efficient cases to expenditure in the actual case.

Although *k* is theoretically very similar to Farrell's measure of efficiency it differs in a number of respects. A trivial difference is that *k*, the total unit factor requirement, is the reciprocal of an efficiency measure. Secondly, no absolute standard of efficiency is assumed in the computation of *k*, since the objective is merely to compare two alternative situations. Farrell uses several different observations to deduce the most efficient production possibilities by the construction of an envelope representing the efficient isoquant. To do this he plots quantities of factors used per unit of output. He is faced with the difficulty that it is difficult

4 This was pointed out by Paul Stoneman. See M. J. Farrell (1957).

to construct such an envelope in more than two or three dimensions. Instead, we employ the 'dual' of Farrell's approach, concentrating on prices and expenditures rather than physical quantities. This allows us to consider many more factors of production. It also allows us to obtain estimates in the case of multiple outputs. P_0 is then simply a suitable index of output prices. If the composition of output varies significantly there may be some index number problems arising from the arbitrariness of the weights used in the construction of the price index, but this is bound to be a problem with multiple outputs and is not a result of the method of computation of k.

4.3 **Data requirements**

The input and output price indices involved in calculating k need a set of weights. The required weights for the input series are available at the MLH level and sometimes at the sub-MLH level for Census of Production years, such as 1963 and 1968. The latter is particularly useful since many of the mergers took place in the period 1967–69 and so the weights from the 1968 census were most appropriate in comparing the pre-merger to the post-merger situation. Details of the calculation of the input prices index are given at the end of this chapter.

The output price series (wholesale) are often obtainable at the MLH level, and information on individual firms' prices are frequently available from published sources including trade journals, and occasionally from the companies themselves.

The only other data requirement is the ratio of profits to revenue. Profits are measured before interest so k does not depend on the firm's financing method. Profits and revenue are available from the published company accounts, but the revenue figures sometimes do not go back beyond 1967 and in those cases it was necessary to ask the firms in question to supply the missing information. Another problem, particularly in diversified companies, is that of making sure that the profits and revenue figures correspond to the goods to which the input and output price indexes relate. Fortunately even quite large errors in the measurement of profits/revenue do not badly affect the accuracy of year-to-year comparisons of k, provided that the errors do not themselves fluctuate greatly. The term $[1 - (\Pi/R)]$, which is used in the formula for k, typically fluctuates far less than Π/R itself.

In summary, the method proposed is a practical method of estimating changes in efficiency, as the term is used by economists. It uses objective available information, and the biases it is subject to are mainly of the usual index number type.

4.4 **Sources of bias in** k

Let us consider the direction of this index number bias for a typical study, where the merger takes place in 1968, the year of the Census. To keep things simple, assume that the ratio profits/sales, the level of the output, and the

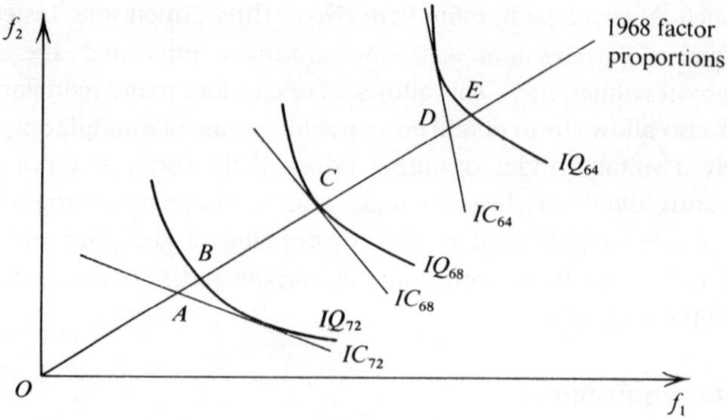

Figure 4.4. *Isoquants and isocost curves for the same output over time*

output price remain constant, despite an increase in the input price index. (Alternatively, assume that any changes in these have been corrected for.) The case is illustrated in Figure 4.4.

Factor proportions in 1968 are given by the tangency of the 1968 isocost line with the 1968 isoquant. Improvement in technical efficiency is occurring since the isoquants are moving towards the origin. Factor 1 is becoming cheaper relative to factor 2 and substitution is occurring.

The actual reduction in factor requirements between 1964 and 1968 is represented by the distance *CE*. But the apparent decline in factor requirements is only *CD*. This is because 1968 factor proportions are used in the comparisons. The consequence is that efficiency improvements before 1968 will tend to be underestimated. Conversely efficiency improvements after 1968 may tend to be exaggerated. The reduction in factor requirements for the same technique of production is *BC* but is actually measured as *AC*. The greater the degree of factor substitution, and the greater the degree of divergence of different factor prices, the greater will the bias be. Conversely, there are two ways in which the size of the bias will be small. If factor proportions do not vary the bias will disappear. Equally, if the relative prices of factors stay constant the measurement of factor requirements is independent of the factor proportions assumed and again the bias will disappear. In general we do not observe very large fluctuations in either factor proportions or relative prices in the course of a few years, so that we expect the size of this bias to be small. However, it is as well to be aware of the direction of this bias.

It is sometimes argued[5] that accounting measures of profitability are apt to

5 For an extreme view, see Harcourt (1965). For a more balanced perspective, see Gordon (1974). John Kay (1976) in a paper examining National Income accounts, concludes that in practice the differences between accountants' and economists' estimates may be quite small.

be misleading to economists. The principles of double-entry bookeeping do ensure some sort of consistency, however, and the major difference between accountants and economists appears to be over the time period in which something is declared as income (or 'profit'). The accountant adopts a principle of conservatism and in the early years of a project tends to count some of what the economist would call income as depreciation. Thus in any one year the economist and the accountant will disagree on the measurement of both income and the value of capital. It is not surprising that, when the ratio of these two quantities is taken, as in measurements of the rate of return on book value, weird and wonderful things can happen. The magnitude and direction of the disagreement between the economist and the accountant over the rate of return vary during the life of a single project, as a number of writers have discovered. However, the total income of a firm over its lifetime is agreed upon by the two professions. The consequence of this is that a bias in one direction in one year is offset by biases in the opposite direction in succeeding years. In addition, since we are not using book values of capital and are quite happy with accountants' measurement of revenues, we do not have the problem of biases in both the numerator and the denominator of a ratio.

A more basic problem which affects the interpretation of k as a measure of total factor requirement is that since our profit figures are taken from company accounts they do not represent pure economic profit, but contain an element which represents part of the cost of capital.

The terms 'capital' and 'cost of capital' are frequently used ambiguously, and this gives rise to some confusion. In simple textbook formulations capital services, and labour are the only two factors of production. The word capital serves as shorthand for the sum of all non-labour inputs, including

(i) materials and fuel,

(ii) tools and machines that are treated as current expenses by accountants,

(iii) the services, tools and machines whose cost is amortised over a few years, and

(iv) the services of capital assets such as buildings and cash holdings.

Accounting profits will generally reflect the *interest* component of the cost of all of these inputs.[6] If this element of cost as a proportion of total costs remains the same our measure of k will not be affected. However, if there is a substitution of this type of capital for other inputs generally, that is for machinery, materials and labour, the apparent cost of production as measured by k will decline due to an increase in accounting profits necessary to cover the interest cost. In other words, this will result in a downward bias in the trend of k over time. Our qualitative

6 Although only that proportion of assets financed by debts shows an explicit interest charge. Dividends on equity are an implicit interest change.

evidence on the type of changes usually made following merger suggests that the magnitude of this bias would be very small but the possibility should be borne in mind when interpreting our results.

Finally, we should also note the possibility that, following merger, the combined firm may increase its prices relative to the rest of the industry, although oligopoly theory suggests that the main effect of the increase in concentration will be a rise in the industry prices, and not just of the merging firm. To the extent that there is a relative price change an output price index based on industry prices will be biased down and lead to further downward bias in the estimate of post-merger factor requirements.

Our measure of factor requirement is designed with horizontal mergers in mind, and this is the predominant category in our case studies. If there is an element of vertical integration intermediate sales disappear from the denominator of Π/R but the profits of the two firms will be aggregated. This effect will lead to a downward bias in the change in k during the merger year. In addition the weights in the price indexes may alter considerably and this may be a source of further problems if relative prices vary. However, k can still be calculated provided account is taken of these complications.

Another consideration that should be borne in mind in considering the resultant estimates is that k may vary through changes in the degree of utilisation of productive capacity. To some extent this is a reflection of the firm's efficiency in production planning, and it is perfectly reasonable that k should incorporate this. On the other hand, perfect planning is not always possible, particularly in industries which are subject to large shifts in demand through the trade cycle. When demand falls capacity utilisation and hence productive efficiency will also fall. This can usually be allowed for satisfactorily by comparisons with other companies and by averaging over the trade cycle, but in the cases of bricks and machine tools we decided that the problem was sufficiently serious to require explicit correction.

4.5 A perspective on *k*

We have taken some care to spell out the possible biases and imperfections in k as a measure of factor productivity because an understanding of these issues is important when reading the case studies. Taken out of context, without regard to the issues raised in this chapter, comparisons of k can be dangerously misleading. Despite this we feel that it is a very useful descriptive statistic when taken in context. If one single measure of efficiency change did have to be chosen k would be preferable to more obvious measures such as accounting rates of return or labour productivity, which have more basic flaws and do not even begin to face up to any of the problems considered here.

Our examination of the sources of bias in k suggests that we will usually be overestimating the efficiency gain from merger, and this is very useful information.

If we find (as we do) that efficiency gains are typically fairly small our knowledge of this bias strengthens our conclusion that mergers typically do not result in large gains in efficiency.

Appendix to Chapter 4

Sources of output and input price indices

We obtained output price data from various sources. For example in many cases it was possible to use wholesale price indices (WPI) constructed by the Department of Industry and Employment. The Department of Industry maintains a large number of continuous price series, including import prices. These WPIs are calculated at commodity and MLH levels of aggregation. The indicators are free of value added tax (or purchase tax before its abolition) and represent price quotations by a number of manufacturers. For Fletton Bricks we were able to make use of a very detailed Monopolies Commission report. In the BMC–Leyland merger price series were calculated by one of the researchers from published sources on individual models, and adjusted for quality change. For the BICC–Pyrotenax merger a price series for mineral insulated cable was derived from *Laxton's Building Price Book.* In most cases the prices of separate firms in the same (narrowly defined) industry moved together so that the differences in the unit factor requirement cross-sectionally only reflect differences in $[1 - (\Pi/R)]$.

For the input prices series, P_I, the data requirement was extensive and much of it was previously unavailable from published sources. Consequently, a considerable part of the data was generated from basic sources with assistance given by the Department of Industry Wholesale Prices Section, which is gratefully acknowledged.

One series required was the Price Index of Materials and Fuel (PIMF). This index has been published for some time by the Department of Industry but relates to a rather high SIC order level of aggregation. It was felt that these series could not be used without the risk of major inaccuracies in the statistical analysis, and consequently a new set of PIMFs was constructed at MLH level of aggregation.

These indicators were constructed as follows. The first requirement was a breakdown of commodities purchased by each industry for purposes of production. This information was obtained from the Census of Production Tables. Consider the commodities purchased by industry j for production purposes in 1968. We define S_{ij} as the amount of commodity i purchased by industry j. In effect, the Census tables give an array of such purchases, as laid out below. Dividing the value of each commodity purchase (S_{ij}) by the total, we obtain a form of input–output coefficient, i.e. $\hat{a}_{ij} = S_{ij}/T_j$. These input–output coefficients were used as weights in deriving the PIMFs. In compiling these weights we adhered to the

	Value (£'000)
Purchases of commodity 1	S_{1j}
Purchases of commodity 2	S_{2j}
....	...
Purchases of commodity n	S_{nj}
Total value of input purchases	T_j

Department of Industry's practice of deriving the weights on a net sector basis. This means that intra-industry transactions, i.e. S_{jj} are netted out. In most industries these flows were of relatively small magnitude.

The price index of materials and fuel was then calculated as the weighted average, in period t, of the price indices of individual commodities purchased where the weights were the $\hat{a}_{ij}$s. Thus we have:

$$PIMF_{jt} = \frac{1}{\sum_i \hat{a}_{ij}} \quad WPI_{1t}\hat{a}_{ij} + WPI_{2t}\hat{a}_{2j} + WPI_{3t}\hat{a}_{3j} + \cdots + WPI_{nt}\hat{a}_{nj}$$

where $PIMF_{jt}$ is the price index of materials and fuel for industry j in period t and WPI_{nt} is the wholesale price index of commodity n in period t. Extending this calculation for all t we derived a continuous series for each PIMF covering the entire estimation period (1963–74).

Since each industry purchases up to sixty individual commodity inputs, the calculations involved in constructing the PIMF series were too extensive to be carried out manually. These calculations were therefore performed by computer once an appropriate program had been devised.[7]

The Census Tables do not cover all purchases made by industries. Some purchases cannot be identified and they are lumped together under a 'miscellaneous' heading. In extreme cases this category comprised 25% of total purchases. Where possible the Department of Industry investigated the broad composition of purchases within this category in consultation with the Business Statistics Office, in order to reduce the size of this category in the weighting pattern. What remained of the miscellaneous component was used to derive its weight and was included in the PIMF with a composite price index of materials constructed by the Department of Industry. This index reflects the overall trend in the price of industrial raw materials and is used by the Department of Industry in the construction of the broad sector PIMFs.

Since the weights used for calculation purposes were obtained from the 1968 Census of Production, we were implicitly assuming constant input proportions throughout the period (1963–74). Although this assumption may be thought somewhat contentious, there is no alternative source of input purchase informa-

7 This program was written by Mark Partridge whose help is gratefully acknowledged.

tion except for the 1963 Census of Production. However, some experiments with input–output coefficients in the Netherlands (see Tilanus, 1966) suggested that the majority of sizeable coefficients changed little over the 1948–60 period.

Another data requirement was an index of labour costs. The series used was the Index of Average Earnings by industry groups which is published by the Department of Employment. The series goes back to 1963 and comprises gross remuneration including overtime payments, bonuses, and commission. The index includes remuneration of manual and non-manual staff.

However, information on average earnings, which was used as our labour cost index, is only continuously available at SIC-order level of aggregation, i.e. for broad sectors of industry. Whilst this deficiency could lead to errors of measurement, it is not implausible that earnings in broadly defined industrial sectors would be promptly brought into uniformity through union pressure for earnings parity. Indeed, earning differentials for similar skills are not likely to be significant between MLHs within an SIC order class, and they will certainly not display the variance which might be expected with material input proportions.

References

Farrell, M. J. (1957), 'The Measurement of Productive Efficiency', *Journal of the Royal Statistical Society*, CXX, Series A, 253–66.

Firth, M. (1976), *Share Prices and Mergers*, Farnborough, England: Saxon House.

Franks, et al. (1976), *An Industry Study of the Profitability of Mergers*, London Graduate School of Business Studies Institute of Finance and Accounting Discussion Paper IFA-15-75. Presented at the Conference of the European Finance Association, London (Sept. 1976).

Gordon, L. A. (1974), 'Accounting Rate of Return vs. Economic Rate of Return', *Journal of Business Finance and Accounting*, **1**, 343–56.

Harcourt, G. C. (1965), 'The Accountant in a Golden Age', *Oxford Economic Papers*, **17**, 66–80.

Hart, P. E., M. A. Utton and G. Walshe (1973), *Mergers and Concentration in British Industry*, Cambridge: Cambridge University Press.

Kay, J. (1976), 'Accountants too could be happy in a Golden Age: the Accountant's Rate of Profit and the Internal Rate of Return', *Oxford Economic Papers*, **28**, 447–60.

Kelly, E. M. (1967), *The Profitability of Growth through Mergers*, Pennsylvania State University.

Kuehn, D. A. (1975), *Takeovers and the Theory of the Firm*, London: Macmillan.

Meeks, G. (1977), *Disappointing Marriage: A Study of the Gains from Merger*, London: Cambridge University Press.

Newbould, G. D. (1970), *Management and Merger Activity*, Liverpool: Guthstead.

Pratten, C. F. (1971), *Economies of Scale in Manufacturing Industry*, London: Cambridge University Press.

Samuels, J. M. and D. J. Smyth (1968), 'Profits, Variability of Profits and Firm Size', *Economica*, **35**, 127–39.

Singh, Ajit K. (1971), *Takeovers*, London: Cambridge University Press.

Tilanus, C. B. (1966), *Input-Output Experiments: The Netherlands 1948–61*, Rotterdam: Rotterdam University Press.

Utton, M. J. (1974), 'On Measuring the Effects of Industrial Mergers', *Scottish Journal of Political Economy*, **21**, 13–28.

5

Case studies of specific mergers

5.1 Introduction

In the earlier sections of this study we have presented a basic framework in which mergers and their effects can be analysed. In the widest terms this framework offsets the efficiency gains realised from mergers against the potential welfare losses that arise from the consequent increase in monopoly power. If the former offset the latter we may judge the merger as socially desirable. In this, the core of our study, we use the case study method to try to quantify the efficiency and market power repercussions of a series of specific large mergers. In Table 5.1 the participants in and dates of these mergers are detailed. As can be seen the mergers considered are all horizontal. The key factors determining their choice were:

(a) The merger was submitted to the Mergers Panel between 1965–70. British Celanese/Courtaulds as a merger falls outside this period, but this arose as a by-product of the study of Courtaulds in a later chapter.
(b) The merger was industrial rather than in the service sector, although we look at the effect of the Thorn–Radio Rentals merger on the television rental sector. This was a choice conditioned mainly by data problems.
(c) Data problems also led us to choose companies quoted on the UK stock exchanges.
(d) Finally we preferred to look at companies where the combined market share exceeded 30% and where the merger led to market share increasing by at least 25%.

The selection of companies that results gives us a wide spread, e.g. some mergers have already been looked at by the Monopolies Commission, some were promoted by the IRC, and yet others involved neither. If anything comes from these studies it is that there is no such thing as a typical merger. We do not have any reason to believe however that these mergers are not typical of many, or that our results are biased in any one direction because of our selection procedure.

Following on from this chapter there is a case study of two industries which

Table 5.1 *Mergers Studied*

Companies merged	Date	Product	Merged company
London Brick Co. Marston Valley Brick Co.	1968	Bricks	London Brick Co.
Courtaulds British Celanese	1969	Cellulosic fibres	Courtaulds
Ransome & Marles Co. Hoffman Manufacturing Ltd Pollard Ball & Roller Bearing Co. Ltd	1969	Ball and roller bearings	Ransome, Hoffman & Pollard Ltd.
British Insulated Callenders Cables Ltd Pyrotenax	1966	Mineral insulated cables	BICC
Tube Investment Ltd Coventry Gauge & Tool Co. Ltd	1969	Machine tools	Tube Investments
Berger, Jenson & Nicholson British Paints Ltd	1969	Paint	Berger, Jenson & Nicholson
Rowntree John Mackintosh	1969	Confectionery	Rowntree Mackintosh
H. & R. Johnson Ltd Richards Campbell Co. Ltd	1968	Glazed tiles	Johnson-Richards Ltd
Thorn Radio Rentals	1968	Television manu-facture and rental	No change

were transformed by a series of mergers, the electrical engineering industry and the motor car industry. We then report on a variety of cases which highlight particular facets of the impact of merger such as product quality effects, labour market effects and the implications for technological change before looking at vertical integrating and diversifying mergers. Although these aspects are discussed here, in the present study the majority of the effort has been expended in the search for efficiency effects. As for market power effects, it soon becomes obvious in this study that there are in general very few efficiency gains actually realised. Thus there is nothing to be traded off against the potential losses implicit in the monopoly positions created and so the demonstration of the abuse of such positions becomes less of an issue. It should of course also be realised that finding evidence of this abuse is no mean task and thus our results are thin on the ground; but in those cases where evidence of abuse (or non-abuse) has been gathered we specifically note it. The efficiency measure on which we rely is 'k', the derivation of which has already been detailed, but one should only read and interpret our estimates in the light of the detail presented in the text. To do otherwise is to deny the utility of the present exercise.

The studies are not the work of one person. This gives us a variety of approaches and a variety of stresses, each investigator in his search for effects being conditioned by the feel of the evidence and the nature of the important questions in each case. In the final section of this chapter we have made an attempt to discuss the generalities that arise from the wealth of detail thus produced and to draw some conclusions on the impact of merger.

5.2.1 Companies: London Brick Company and Marston Valley Brick Co.
Date: Second quarter, 1968.
Product: Fletton building bricks.

Mainly as a consequence of merger activity, the London Brick Company is now the sole supplier of fletton bricks. Approximately 90% of bricks produced are of clay, and something over 40% of the total, those including calcium silicate and concrete, are of the type known as fletton. The fletton sector, which is based on a particular clay known as Oxford clay, enjoys a substantial natural cost advantage over non-flettons because this clay has a high carbon content and therefore requires less fuel for firing. Oxford clay is only found in a belt which runs from Bletchley to Peterborough. The total monopolisation of the fletton sector is in complete contrast to the non-fletton sector, which in 1974 was made up of 153 mainly small producers (the seven largest accounting for 35.9% of non-fletton deliveries).

The merger between the London Brick Company (LBC) and the Marston Valley Brick Company took place in the second quarter of 1968. According to the Chairman's Statement in the 1968 Annual Report, LBC had been encouraged in the merger by the National Board for Prices and Incomes. They had said that 'since increased size in fletton manufacture lowers cost' LBC should not be deterred from merging for fear of falling within the provisions of the Monopolies Act. At the time approximate market shares for flettons were as shown (Monopolies and Mergers Commission (1976)): London Brick, 72%; Marston Valley, 14%; Redland, 8%; Whittlesea Central, 4%; Flettons Ltd, 2%. Flettons Ltd ceased production in 1970 and between 1968 and 1973 LBC acquired Marston Valley (1968), the fletton brickworks of Redland (1971) and those of Whittlesea Central (1973). The latter were owned by the National Coal Board. In each case the approach was made by the other party but as the Monopolies Commission report puts it 'LBC saw the acquisition of these works as a sensible and logical step'. Whatever the motives of LBC the result was a monopoly and in 1973, shortly before the last purchase, the government ordered the Monopolies and Mergers Commission to investigate and report on 'the supply of building bricks', which it did in 1975. The report was finally published in 1976 after a delay of over seven months.

5.2.2 The industry background

The demand for bricks depends on the level of activity in the construction industry. Nearly 70% of LBC's brick output is used in new housing (Annual Report (1967)), and this shows considerable fluctuations. In addition there are seasonal fluctuations in demand, but it is easier to allow for these by variations in stock rather than output.

Fletton and non-fletton bricks are for most purposes[1] interchangeable, but producers of flettons have a substantial natural cost advantage over non-fletton producers, which is only offset by transport costs. The exact extent of this advantage will vary with the price of fuel and the efficiency of the kilns used. The product mix will also affect the average value of this advantage. In non-flettons, facing bricks seem to require substantially more fuel than commons. The Monopolies Commission report (p. 51) suggests that although fuel savings may be very important in reducing the costs of fletton production, there are also major savings in labour requirements, the costs of raw materials and administration, selling and general expenses. Some of these savings can be attributed to the superior properties of Oxford clay, but probably a major additional cause is the substantially larger scale of production in flettons.

The question of scale economies is obviously crucial to the evaluation of LBC's position. In flettons the basic kiln used has an annual capacity of 62.5m bricks, but there are savings from linking up to four kilns together. To quote the Monopolies Commission:

> All things considered, a modern 250 million a year works is probably the minimum efficient size for fletton brick-making with the possibility of small capital savings, but not labour savings, beyond this size. A 250 million a year works represents 8.3 per cent of total fletton deliveries in 1973, when demand was strong, and 12.2 per cent in 1974 when demand was weak [para. 72].

Thus, as far as production economies of scale are concerned there appears to be no advantage from having a sole supplier of fletton bricks, and there seems little reason why LBC should not be split up into up to eight separate companies. However, LBC claim that there are other economies of large scale. For example, they claim that an output of 2,000m bricks per year is necessary to justify their own engineering facilities. The saving they claim from making their own equipment being 'due to the fact that no commercial profit is included in the value which LBC puts upon the engineering department's services' (Monopolies Commission, para. 132). However, this backward vertical integration may well be a major

1 For the advantages and disadvantages of flettons see the Monopolies Commission report, para. 109. Flettons are lighter and more uniform in dimension than non-flettons, but are generally less resistant to severe weather conditions.

source of barriers to entry into the industry. The minimum scale of 2000m bricks which it would imply is more than 2/3 of LBC's peak output.

LBC also claim economies of scale in Marketing and Research and Development. Their sales force has not increased since 1967 during which time they have increased their production capacity by 36% by acquisition. Their marketing organisation accounts for 2% of ex-works costs. Spreading the same costs over an organisation 36% larger would save £126,000 in 1973.[2]

£180,000, or roughly $\frac{1}{2}$% of sales revenue, was allocated directly to Research and Development in 1973, but additional work took place in the transport and engineering departments. LBC has made a number of achievements in recent years, such as the development of the self-stack equipment for brick handling[3] and improvements in production machinery. Research into kiln design and fire control has reduced the time spent by green bricks in the kiln by 'up to 50 per cent'. A new range of facing bricks has been introduced, allowing greater flexibility in the division of output between commons and facing bricks. 'New generation' works incorporate all these technical improvements. A 'fletliner' system of delivery by rail to certain locations has also been introduced. There seems to be, however, no evidence to show that the present size is required to support this R & D effort.

There are three more possible sources of economies in multi-plant firms producing flettons: transport, pecuniary economies in purchasing and variations in capacity utilisation.

The case is fairly weak for substantial economies arising out of a firm providing its own transport and maintenance organisation. LBC's own transport has the disadvantage that it cannot take advantage of return loads. It is possible, however, that there are offsetting gains in reliability from having some vehicles of one's own. About half the company's road haulage is undertaken by private contractors in normal trade conditions. The company has a fleet of over 600 vehicles, but considers the minimum optimal scale of own transport operations to be between 50 and 150 vehicles (Monopolies Commission (1976) para. 133). Thus the firm could be split into four with no loss on this account.

LBC claim that the size of the company enables it to secure large discounts. Discounts quoted are of 39 per cent for a conveyor belt 31 per cent for coal and 10 per cent for derv. This does not represent a gain in efficiency, however,[4] so much as a transfer of income to London Brick from its suppliers.

2 Based on a total ex-works cost of £23.88 m in 1973 for bricks. 2% × 23.88 × 36/136 = 0.126.

3 Mechanical handling systems here also have been introduced by other brick makers.

4 Except insofar as it improved the allocation of resources within London Brick by bringing the price of its supplies in line with marginal cost.

The final source of multi-plant economies arises when the level of demand falls below full capacity. It may be more efficient to close an old or obsolescent plant completely and keep a modern one running at full capacity rather than reduce the intensity of capacity utilisation of all plants. The principal reason for this is that there are many costs, including fuel and some types of labour, that have to be borne at the same level independently of output. It makes sense therefore, to have each firm in control of several kilns. It should be remembered, however, that one optimum works consists of four kilns, so the number of optimum sized works required to achieve optimality in this dimension is probably not more than two. This would leave room for at least four firms in the industry taking advantage of this source of scale economies.[5]

We argue therefore in total that the economies of scale are such that there is no economic rationale for there to be a sole producer of flettons.

5.2.3 Market structure and pricing behaviour

Dating from at least 1950, LBC has been the dominant firm in the fletton industry. Non-flettons cannot compete with flettons except in those market areas removed from the Oxford clay belt, where flettons have to bear large transport costs. In the 1960s LBC was worried about the threat from industrialised building methods, but alternatives to common bricks, in the form of lightweight concrete blocks, are probably the more serious competitors.

A profit maximising monopolist, faced with different elasticities of demand for its products in different market areas, would engage in price discrimination. In areas where competition was stronger, such as distant regions where transport costs are enough to wipe out the natural advantages of flettons, and in the case of common bricks, where closer substitutes were available, price would be set close to long-run marginal cost. In areas of less severe competition, such as facing bricks and market areas close to the Oxford clay, there would be a bigger mark-up on marginal cost. Price discrimination of this kind is objectionable because it distorts the allocation of resources away from the optimum.[6] Too few resources are employed in the production of goods for the market segments with less competition and high mark-ups. Furthermore, if the monopolist is a maximiser of sales rather than profits too many resources will be devoted to marginal sales, which would be more efficiently supplied by competitors. LBC has engaged in price discrimination. The Monopolies Com-

5 Since Oxford clay is reasonably consistent between works there would be no problem of loss in variety, since all types of brick can be produced at each works.

6 We are not referring to the perfectly discriminating monopolist who manages to discriminate between different intra-marginal units of consumption by a single consumer.

mission found that the price of facings was too high relative to commons; and that the price of bricks for distant markets was too low relative to near markets. The Monopolies Commission, however, did not find the average price level for bricks too high. They considered that LBC's target figure of 20% return on capital was acceptable. This seems high to us, however. The average for 1969–74 was 22.2% compared with 14.4% for UK quoted companies in manufacturing (Monopolies Commission (1976) Table 23). This is a premium of over 50%, which is not justified by the riskiness of the enterprise, for even in the worst year, with an unexpected fall in demand of 29% (1974), the company earned a comfortable 9.1%. For new works, the profit rate is even higher. From the Monopolies Commission report, Table 30, we can deduce that the rate of profit (after depreciation) on the New Saxon works was 38½% in 1973, a year when it was not even fully operational.

5.2.4 The effect of the merger between Marston Valley and LBC

Between 1955 and 1965 the company always earned a rate of return between 22% and 30%. LBC was already the dominant supplier by 1968 and was able to control the price level of bricks. Its market power was established and there is no particular reason to suppose that the firm would want to increase prices even further after the merger. Despite Redland's complaint of unattractively low prices there is no evidence that LBC used the low end of its price spectrum to drive its fletton competitors into its embrace.[7] In fact, London Brick have said that Marston Valley charged more for some bricks prior to the merger. These prices were brought into line with London Brick's. On this evidence, the immediate effect of the merger on price was to reduce the average level.

Against this, there are two considerations. Marston Valley, who did most of its trade through merchants, gave larger discounts than LBC. Following the merger these discounts were reduced. It is not known what the net effect of these two adjustments was, but the Monopolies Commission did receive 24 complaints, some of which referred to elimination of competitive price quotations. The other consideration is that, in June 1970, LBC awarded a 20% pay increase and then applied to the NBPI for an increase in price to cover this. It appears that the Government stepped in and granted this increase. The Prices and Incomes Board did not seem too happy about this. They thought the price increase rather more than necessary to cover the cost of the wage settlement. Furthermore, it was clearly inflationary and the NBPI suggested that the Monopolies Commission look into the question of market power and inflation in the brick industry. The Commission's evidence is summarised in their Appendix 10. This shows that the average level of pay is higher for London Brick. This can be

7 See Monopolies Commission (1976), para. 190, although in para. 191 LBC deny that price affects demand more than marginally.

interpreted as the gains to workers from working in a modern, well equipped firm or alternatively as the proceeds from sharing in the monopoly profit. One implication of this is that reported profits will understate the extent of monopoly profits. However, the level of wages is only one aspect. By themselves high wages are not inflationary. It is the timing of increases which is crucial. The table shows that London Brick tended to award increases ahead of the non-fletton sector. We consider that this does indicate that companies like LBC (with the power to raise prices to cover wage increases) may unwittingly initiate an inflationary spiral.[8]

With the exception of the occasion when the firm managed to circumvent the NBPI by obtaining government permission directly, the various price control institutions seem to have had some success in holding down price increases below the rate of increase of wages and fuel and raw materials prices. The firm's long-run profitability has not suffered, however, as they have managed to improve their efficiency somewhat. (The low profit rate of 9.1% for 1974 was due to the very severe decline in sales.) Table 5.2 shows what has been happening to unit factor requirements over the years.

Interpretation of these figures is not quite straightforward. The main problem is variation in capacity utilisation which affects the brick industry more than most. A low rate of utilisation is inefficient and increases unit factor requirement (see 1973 to 1974 when demand fell drastically). Some idea of the size of this effect can be obtained by reference to Figure 5.1 where unit factor requirements are graphed against output. It is apparent that, after allowing for output variation, a big shift in efficiency occurred between 1969 and 1973. Over this period there was a 20% reduction in inputs per unit of output. The performance post-merger also seems to be a considerable improvement over the pre-merger values for k for the two firms (as shown in Table 5.2).

This improvement was brought about in a number of ways. In June 1969 the first stage of the 'new generation' King's Dyke plant was opened. The second stage followed in June 1971. Its final total capacity (in 1975 when the last stage was completed) was 250m bricks a year, i.e. the theoretical minimum efficient scale. Another works, New Saxon, with a capacity of 125m bricks a year, was built between 1971 and 1973 at a cost of between £1.55m and £1.60m. Together, however, these represent less than 13% of total capacity and so their substitution for older works could not account for the total observed efficiency increase. Even a 50% reduction of total factor requirements in these plants would have saved only $6\frac{1}{2}$% of the firm's *total* requirements.

Of the £10 million spent on modernisation between 1964 and 1974, less than half must have been on these two new generation works. The rest of the money was spent in modernising and mechanising older works, including Ridgmont,

8 See Chapter 13 below.

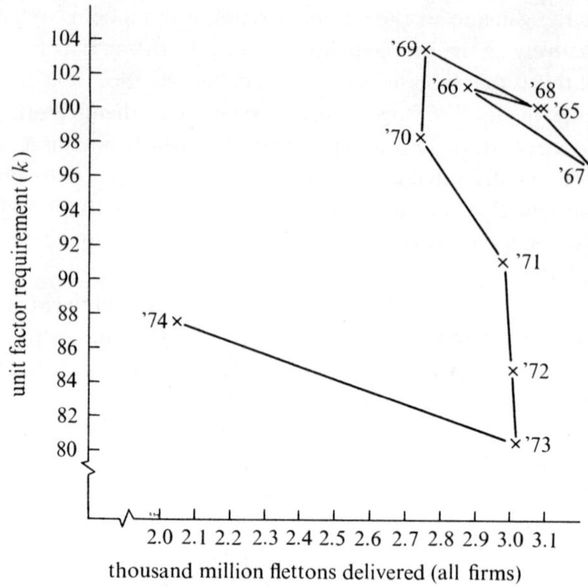

Figure 5.1 *Unit factor requirement plotted against aggregate production of fletton bricks 1965–74*
Sources: *k* – Table 5.2 above; production – Monopolies commission (1976) Table 9

one of the two works operated by Marston Valley. Their other, smaller works, was considered too costly to convert and was closed. Ridgmont produced 406 million bricks in 1973, but it is unlikely that the savings here could have approached 50%. Without allowing for depreciation, production costs are estimated to be 50% higher than at King's Dyke (Monopolies Commission (1976) Table 71). If mechanisation saved 25% of all costs at Ridgmont this would amount to $3\frac{1}{2}$% spread over the entire firm. The total saving on King's Dyke, New Saxon and Ridgmont would then be of the order of 10%.

This leaves half of the 20% saving in factor requirements to be accounted for by the modernisation of other existing works and savings in overheads as the firm expanded. LBC, in their meetings with the Monopolies Commission staff, drew attention to their ability to spread the costs of their marketing organisation – amounting to 2% of ex-works cost – over a bigger firm since their mergers. The increase in sales from the merger amounts to almost 30% of total sales. Therefore the saving of total factor requirement from this source is 0.6%, which is very small when compared to the sort of savings that can be derived from investment in modern plant.

After the Marston Valley merger the engineering, personnel, estates, purchasing and transport departments were integrated, and the Marston Valley technical

Table 5.2 *Unit factor requirements: bricks*

Year ended 31 December	Output price / Input price 1968 = 100	London Brick profit / revenue (%)	Unit factor requirement: London Brick	Unit factor requirement: London Brick[a] and Marston Valley pre-merger
1963	115.9	n.a.	n.a.	n.a.
1964	110.8	n.a.	n.a.	n.a.
1965	105.0	20.0	99.7	101.4
1966	101.2	15.7	101.2	103.9
1967	98.3	17.4	96.3	98.0
1968	100.0	15.7	100.0	—
1969	97.5	10.6	103.4	—
1970	96.5	13.6	98.9	—
1971	93.8	18.2	91.0	—
1972	88.0	18.8	84.7	—
1973	84.7	19.9	80.5	—
1974	79.7	7.5	87.5	—

[a]This series indicates values of k generated by combining the profit and revenue of the two firms prior to the merger (standardized to make 1968 value of k for the joint firm = 100).

department shut down. No figures are available on the savings from these sources, but they are probably smaller than the economies in the marketing side. Other sources of savings were the rationalisation of the facing brick range, with the elimination of close substitutes, and the transport of unburnt bricks, mechanically loaded and unloaded, to sites where more efficient kilns were operating. It would seem that savings from such sources were quite small, and that most of the efficiency gain was due to new investment. Some idea of the potential savings from this source can be gained by examining the wide spread in production costs between new generation and other works. This information is presented by the Monopolies Commission (Table 17), and even after allowing for depreciation and interest new works show substantial savings. (The Monopolies Commission provide adjusted profit rates for the New Saxon works.) Also LBC closed down eight works in 1974. According to the Monopolies Commission (para. 221) these were typically works which could not generate the same level of surplus profits as the newer works.

These data on the new works are interesting for another reason. They show that in 1973 price was 23.9% higher than long-run marginal cost in the most efficient works even assuming a cost of capital of 20% p.a. This is not reflected in LBC's profit figures apparently because the firm continues to operate plants that are not the most efficient. Taking the updated 1974 capital costs the table indicates that if only best practice works were used prices could be 14.5% lower and still yield 20% return on capital invested. These figures support the view that the major cause of the gain in efficiency of London Brick since 1969 was investment in modern techniques. This investment consisted principally of the mechanisation of production. In Chapter 4 we argue that in such cases some of the apparent reduction in factor requirements might be due to a substitution of capital for other inputs. We investigated this possibility by calculating the capital–output ratios for the years 1968–74. This showed a *falling* trend. This series is biased since capital is valued at historic cost and output at current prices. However, much of the firm's capital was revalued for the 1968 accounts and some current purchasing power (CPP) figures are given for fixed assets in the 1976 accounts, so we were able to make a more reasonable comparison for these two years. The capital–output ratio still showed a substantial decline. We therefore consider that our figures do not contain an undue bias.

5.2.5 An evaluation of the merger

Investment could in principle have taken place without a merger. LBC's expertise probably contributed something to the gains from that investment, and there probably were some gains arising from spreading the use of modern techniques of management over a larger area of operations. The mechanisation of production, though, is not an arcane discipline. In the absence of merger it would in principle have been possible for Marston Valley to have mechanised their Ridgmont works and to have closed the other one. Indeed, failure to do this would have demonstrated gross incompetence by the Marston Valley management. Without LBC's expertise the return on this investment may have been lower. Also, in the absence of any mergers since 1965 selling expenses in the industry may have been higher by 0.6% of ex-works costs.

The gains from multi-plant operation have not been quantified. The biggest advantage is increased flexibility over the trade cycle, since it is probably cheaper to shut down some plants completely rather than reduce output at others. Many of these advantages can be enjoyed by a multi-kiln operation, however.

In summary, it seems that the gains in efficiency from the merger itself could have been at most 2–4% of Marston Valley's sales or 0.33–0.65% of the combined firm. No evidence is available of any sources of decline in efficiency following the merger. Neither is there any evidence of any direct price or 'market power' effect of the merger. This is not surprising in view of the London Brick Company's dominant position before it bought Marston Valley. In addition, price control may have mitigated the effects of LBC's increase in monopoly power.

We are not so sanguine as the Monopolies Commission about the *level* of LBC's profits. On average they have earned at least 50% more than the market rate. This level of profitability had already been reached by the time of the merger. But the inference that the merger did not have any market power effects should not be drawn too readily. The elimination of LBC's competitors means that new entry into fletton production is made more difficult. Further, we do not know what the course of brick prices would have been in the absence of the Price Commission.

5.3.1 **Companies: Courtaulds and British Celanese**
Date: April 1957
Product: Cellulosic fibres

The story of Courtaulds' dominant position in the cellulosic fibres industry (but not the story of Courtaulds itself) begins in 1904 when Courtaulds bought the UK patents for the manufacture of artificial silk (rayon).[9] Courtaulds did not discover the process in question–they simply acquired by purchase a UK monopoly for the new product. Their monopoly position was substantially extended in 1909 when they bought the US patent rights. The UK patents expired in 1920, there was substantial entry but until the end of the 1920s the production of rayon remained a profitable activity, partly because there was a corresponding substantial increase in world demand for the product. Things got more difficult after 1929 and many recent entrants left the industry. In 1933 there were protests by surviving firms about the predatory pricing activities of Courtaulds. This activity was made possible by the continuing profitability of the US division of Courtaulds, where the slump in demand had started some years later. In 1936 Courtaulds put forward an abortive scheme to monopolise the industry, but was able to organise and sustain a variety of price fixing arrangements. The position remained relatively stable over the next twenty years, but by the early 1950s it was left with one substantial rival, British Celanese. One may thus consider the previous half century as one in which Courtaulds tried to retain something like the dominance initially afforded by the granting of patent rights relating to the process of producing rayon, in the face of natural tendencies leading to its elimination. We now seek to identify the underlying tendencies which led to the 1957 merger with British Celanese.

Throughout the Second World War, the early post-war period and into the Korean War there was no lack of demand for fibre. Difficulties began to appear after 1951 when cotton prices fell sharply with the ending of the Korean War and cotton started to erode the market for rayon in, for example, dress manufacture.[10] This tendency was increased by innovations in cotton (e.g. treatment resulting in improved crease resistance) which increased its competitiveness. At the same time the market for rayon was also being eroded from another direction – nylon was beginning to replace rayon in some of its uses.[11] These changes

9 Much of the discussion and analysis of this merger is based on the report by the Monopolies Commission (1968a).

10 The price of American cotton yarn (32's weft) fell from 74.75 d per lb in 1951 to 53.32 d per lb in 1955.

11 It should be noted however that the two major shareholders in British Nylon

in the fibre market created a situation in which it became increasingly difficult for Courtaulds to secure cartel-like arrangements. In 1956 the Restrictive Practices legislation also came into force. Courtaulds' reaction, to merge with its major rival, can be seen as a replacement of an existing arrangement with the ultimate in collusive agreements. It was once again a move to maintain the degree of monopoly against the natural tendencies making it fall.

The merger with British Celanese was completed in early 1957 and this left only a fringe of very small firms also producing cellulosic fibre. Harbens was acquired in 1959, British Enka in 1961, Kirklees in 1962 and Nelson's and Lustrafil in 1963.[12] Thus Courtaulds emerged in a very dominant position in the UK market for cellulosic fibre. But how dominant? There was foreign competition with the expectation that this would increase with the advent of EFTA in 1960.[13] There were the newer synthetic fibres and there was cotton. Competition from these different sources might be thought to considerably circumscribe the monopoly power of the new Courtaulds. This was certainly the view advanced by Courtaulds in their discussions with the Monopolies Commission. On the basis of the evidence, however, it is difficult to sustain.

In the case of foreign competition it can be seen in Table 5.3, that the degree of protection afforded to Courtaulds in the UK market was very considerable.

There remained the possibility that the advent of EFTA could act as a brake on the monopoly power assumed by Courtaulds. The investigation of the Monopolies Commission revealed that Courtaulds adopted tactics to minimise the impact of this threat to its position in the UK. This involved the acquisition of shareholdings in some firms and the establishment of franchise arrangements with others. By these means Courtaulds was able to maintain its monopoly position in the UK in face of reductions in tariff barriers. If a reduction in tariffs was seen to be a pro-competitive policy the aims of such policy were clearly subverted by the reaction of a dominant firm in a particular UK market. This sort of reaction must have clear implications for the effectiveness of tariff policy generally where the UK market in question is dominated by a powerful corporation quite capable of modifying the international environment in which it has to operate. It must be seen as a further factor to be taken account of when assessing the social desirability of merger and the resulting creation of private power. Such behaviour also raises a further issue of welfare. Public policy reducing barriers to the entry of

Footnote 11 continued
Spinners, the major UK producer, were Courtaulds and ICI. Thus any switch from rayon to nylon was not entirely disadvantageous to Courtaulds. Again a position had been gained by which dominance in a now more diversified market for artificial fibre had been maintained. The threat of the new synthetics had been reduced by acquiring a direct interest in them.

12 This left only Lansil which was finally acquired by Courtaulds in 1973.

13 Tariff rates were progressively reduced from 1 July 1960 and were removed entirely on 31 December 1966.

Table 5.3 *Tariff rates on man-made fibres (%)*

	Continuous filament yarn	Staple
1954	47	60
1955	47	60
1956	47	60
1957	41	60
1958	41	60
1959	41	65
1960	41	65
1961	40	65
1962	40	65
1963	32	50

Source: Computed on the basis of Board of Trade data reported in Appendix 4 in Monopolies Commission (1968a).
Method: The tariff on Continuous Filament Yarn included a tariff per lb (t^1) and an *advalorem* rate (t).

Since the import price (P_M) was unknown it was assumed that after adjustment for tariff it was equal to the Courtaulds price (P_C). Thus $P_M + t^1 + tP_M = P_C$, and therefore $P_M = P_C - t^1/1 + t$. The tariff rate is then $P_C - P_M/P_M$.

In the case of staple Fibre there was no *ad valorem* tariff so that the tariff rate is simply $t^1/P_C - t^1$.

foreign firms into the UK market may not only give little benefit in terms of greater competition but also imply waste in that dominant firms like Courtaulds are forced into policies, which they otherwise would not seek to adopt, of restricting entry into the UK market. One aspect of this will involve a transfer of income between UK and foreign firms but also we can envisage there will be real resource costs involved in both achieving and sustaining these arrangements. This is simply a special case of the general problem posed by the regulation of monopoly power, an issue discussed in Chapter 3.

Evidence of the effectiveness of Courtaulds' international arrangements was provided by both overseas producers and by UK fibre users (Monopolies Commission (1968a) p. 123). Overseas producers claimed that fear of retaliation by Courtaulds, in their own home markets or on other export markets of importance to them, prevented them undercutting Courtaulds in the UK. Thus an effective collusive solution is obtained. Fibre users claimed that reductions in EFTA duties had not brought about the expected competition. They claimed that this was due to (i) arrangements made by Courtaulds with Swedish and Austrian producers, (ii) the Norwegian producer supplied wood pulp to Courtaulds and would not compete in the fibre market, (iii) the Finnish producer agreed not to compete in exchange for know-how from Courtaulds. In the case of Svenska Rayon, where Courtaulds had acquired an interest, prices formerly lower than Courtaulds were raised as the tariff-rate fell. In the case of Lenzing (another company in which Courtaulds had acquired an interest) supplies were withdrawn. It was also claimed that some of Courtaulds UK customers were unwilling to buy imported fibre for fear that Courtaulds would retaliate by refusing to supply. Two companies reported that in times of excess demand they were informed by Courtaulds that any application for remission of import duty on imported fibre would be opposed.

The evidence in the Monopolies Commission Report demonstrates clearly that Courtaulds was able to effectively insulate itself from foreign competition in the market for cellulosic fibres. There remains the question of the degree of competition provided by nylon and cotton. In the case of nylon the threat to Courtaulds had already been countered. Courtaulds had a 50% stake in British Nylon Spinners, the major UK supplier, and picked up a further stake with the takeover of British Celanese. The ICI bid for Courtaulds in 1961 could be seen primarily as an attempt to monopolise the nylon industry. The bid failed but subsequently the substantial ICI shareholding in Courtaulds was obtained by Courtaulds in return for the stake in British Nylon Spinners, plus a cash settlement. By this time however Courtaulds had developed an independent capability in nylon production.

In the case of cotton it could be argued that the pricing of this fibre would limit the degree of monopoly achievable by Courtaulds in the cellulosic market, insofar as they are substitutes. However, cotton and rayon are clearly not perfect substitutes for each other, and, moveover, in many uses they are not close substitutes at all. In fact in many uses the question arises as to whether they should be regarded as complements rather than substitutes. This issue will be addressed again in a later chapter (Chapter 9) where we consider the vertical integration of Courtaulds into the textile industry. However over the period 1954/63, that is for the period immediately before and after the British Celanese merger, Courtaulds was not heavily involved in the cotton textile industry and thus its monopoly power may have been to some greater or lesser extent circumscribed by the pricing of cotton. To determine the significance of this would require estimates of the cross-price elasticity of demand for the two types of fibre. The Monopolies Commission report raised this question but reported no estimates of the relevant elasticity. In checking the literature there is very little econometric evidence on this point. However Lewis (1971) obtains results which indicate gross complementarity between cotton and man-made fibres in the period 1949–64. However the results relate only to cotton equations and the coefficients are of doubtful significance. However, a complementary relationship between cotton and rayon was suggested by Markham (1952) who argued that this would be expected, at least in the early development of rayon, since both fibres opened up new end-uses for each other. If true then monopoly pricing in the rayon industry will not be constrained by low prices for cotton. But the evidence is weak and we should simply conclude that cotton can be regarded as either a substitute or a complement for rayon, and thus there is no presumption that competition in the market for cotton precludes the existence of considerable monopoly power in the rayon market. Of course even if substitutability was high, lower marginal costs in the production of rayon would still ensure a substantial degree of monopoly for Courtaulds.

Having established that the preconditions exist for the exploitation of considerable market power in the case of Courtaulds we have now to look to the evidence as to whether this power was in fact exploited. However before looking at the evidence it would be difficult to explain the behaviour of Courtaulds over this period if it were not anxious to exploit the market power it had so assiduously cultivated, protected and maintained. This may not of course be reflected in profits since the benefits of monopoly may be taken in ways which ultimately raise costs as well as revenues. We will proceed by reporting first on practices which imply the exploitation of monopoly power and then we will report evidence relating to prices, profits and efficiency.

The Monopolies Commission investigation revealed cases of price discrimination practised by Courtaulds. Courtaulds discriminated in favour of firms who were mainly exporters. This is as one would expect since exporters will generally be faced with a more elastic demand for products. Thus their derived elasticity of demand for inputs will itself be more elastic and the optimal price for a monopolistic seller of inputs will therefore be lower, provided transaction with third parties can be controlled. Interestingly other complaints by Courtaulds' customers cast some light on the conditions for effective price discrimination. Some of these firms appeared to have persistent rationing problems with their fibre supplies from Courtaulds (Monopolies Commission (1968a) p. 116). This is inexplicable as a long-term phenomenon unless Courtaulds was seeking to maintain a discriminatory price structure. By determining both price and quantity Courtaulds was trying to determine the user of the fibre sold as well as the initial purchaser. This can be seen as a way of bolstering the very stringent terms and conditions of sale which Courtaulds attempted to enforce. One of these conditions was a prohibition of the reselling of yarn without Courtaulds' consent (Monopolies Commission (1968a) p. 116).

The other instance of price discrimination was in the case of linen where from 1965 onwards it was alleged that Courtaulds discriminated in favour of Lancashire (where Courtaulds had acquired substantial interests) and against the linen industries of Northern Ireland and Scotland (Monopolies Commission

(1968a) p. 121). Further discussion of this issue will be reserved for the later chapter concerned with vertical integration.

A further interesting and related phenomenon was reported by the Monopolies Commission. Following the Suez crisis price increases made by Courtaulds in the case of viscose and acetate yarns and viscose staple fibre (all cellulosics) exceeded those made in the case of nylon and acrylic fibres. This would appear to be an example of a more rapid rate of adjustment of prices to changes in cost in the monopoly case, given that in equilibrium we would expect the elasticity of price with respect to marginal cost to be unitary in all cases where the degree of monopoly is unchanged. In a sense, therefore, this represents another way in which a monopoly position can be and was exploited. Further discussion of this issue is reserved for the chapter on 'Mergers, market structure and the rate of price adjustment' (Chapter 13).

5.3.2 Impact of the British Celanese merger

We have already established that there are grounds for believing that Courtaulds has been able to achieve and maintain a position of considerable market power within the UK over the last half century. We now seek to examine the behaviour and performance of Courtaulds immediately before and after its merger with British Celanese. We will focus our attention on:

(i) the prices of the main products made by Courtaulds which could be expected to be influenced by the British Celanese merger;
(ii) the ratio of output price to input price indices for Courtaulds;
(iii) the ratio of profits to revenue for Courtaulds and British Celanese;
(iv) the efficiency measure as developed in Chapter 4 which is a composite of the previous indicators.

The period studied will be 1954 to 1963 inclusive. With the merger taking place at the beginning of 1957 this will give us a span of years before and after the merger but avoiding the Korean War period in the early 1950s, and the period in the 1960s when Courtaulds was rapidly extending through into textiles. This period of vertical integration is examined in a later chapter (Chapter 9).

(i) Courtaulds fibre prices

Table 5.4 reports the data on fibre prices as reported by the Monopolies Commission. Their source was Courtaulds but the same pattern of prices is revealed for the UK as a whole by the *Board of Trade Journal* and by *EXTEL Supplementary Cards*, 'British Industries'. The most remarkable feature about the prices of the viscose and acetate textile yarns is their great stability both before and after 1957 but with a marked discontinuity in 1957, with prices going up by more than 10% in that year. An inspection of the monthly data reveals that the price increase took place in January/February whereas the merger was finally consummated in April. This should not preclude the existence of a unified

Table 5.4 *Courtaulds' fibre prices*

	Viscose textile yarn (d per lb)	Acetate filament yarn (d per lb)	Viscose tyre yarn (d per lb)	Viscose staple fibre (d per lb)
1954	54.0	70.0	47.0	24.0
1955	54.0	70.0	50.0	24.0
1956	54.0	70.0	49.0	24.0
1957	60.0	78.5	49.0	24.0
1958	60.0	78.5	49.0	24.0
1959	60.0	78.5	49.0	23.06
1960	60.0	78.5	46.0	22.75
1961	61.5	77.5	46.0	22.75
1962	61.5	77.5	46.0	22.75
1963	61.5	77.5	44.0	22.75

Source: Derived from data reported in Table 3 of the Appendix to the Monopolies Commission Report, pp. 92*A* and 92*B*.

front as far as prices were concerned prior to the actual sealing of the merger. Clearly negotiations were going on well in advance and the expectation of merger could easily lead to a coordinated view about the appropriate price level. This evidence on the prices of these important products of both Courtaulds and British Celanese makes it a little difficult to understand the Monopolies Commission view that there was no evidence of increased prices as a result of the merger. It is not that they examined this sharp discontinuity and found alternative satisfactory explanations but they simply presented the evidence in an appendix and concluded *without comment* in the main body of the report that there was no evidence for price increases.

In the case of tyre yarn and staple fibre there is no evidence for a change in price at the time of merger and indeed in the 1960s these prices have fallen slightly. However if staple fibre was an intermediate product within Courtaulds then this price series may not be very meaningful. In the late 1960s the same problem arises in the case of textile yarns since in that period Courtaulds became its own best customer.

If we now examine the price behaviour of other fibres over this period the evidence is quite revealing (see Table 5.5). The price of cotton yarn fell continuously until 1960, and even then did not achieve the position it held in 1956. In the case of nylon yarn its price fell from 1954 to 1956, remained constant until 1960 and then fell again. Thus rayon yarn (viscose and acetate) stands out as the only case of a price increase, and a very substantial one at that, in the late 1950s. This is consistent with the view that Courtaulds, via its merger with British Celanese, was able to re-establish its position and its market power in at

Table 5.5 *Other fibre prices*

	Cotton[a] American yarn (d/lb)	Nylon[b] yarn (shillings/lb)	Nylon[b] staple (shillings/lb)	Terylene[b] staple (shillings/lb)
1954	52.13	42.08	10.25	—
1955	52.37	38.79	10.25	—
1956	51.93	35.92	10.25	10.50
1957	50.88	35.92	10.25	10.50
1958	49.65	35.92	10.25	10.50
1959	45.26	35.92	10.25	10.50
1960	50.39	31.07	10.25	9.84
1961	52.38	28.50	10.18	9.17
1962	48.21	28.50	9.42	9.17
1963	47.16	25.07	9.42	7.50

[a]Source: *Board of Trade Journal*
[b]Source: EXTEL: *Supplemental Cards 'British Industries'.*

least some of the markets in which it was operating. In the case of staple fibre it can be seen that the pattern of prices for nylon and terylene staple approximated very closely the pattern for rayon staple – complete stability in the late 1950s followed by some limited price reduction in the early 1960s. This evidence is therefore consistent with the view that the merger did little to change Courtaulds' competitive position in these markets.

(ii) Ratio of output prices to input prices

We have up to this point simply observed the movement, or lack of movement, in the prices of the various fibres produced by Courtaulds. However inferences about changes in market power must be qualified since changes in input prices and productivity have not yet been examined. Thus although we observed a sharp change in the price of some of Courtaulds products in 1957 this may be ascribable to a sharp change in the price of inputs. Equally well, however, we would not expect that output prices could keep pace with changes in input prices given that it is frequently alleged that it is the science-based industries like man-made fibres where we can expect the most rapid rates of productivity growth. Table 5.6 reports output and input prices indexes which relate to the fibre products produced by Courtaulds and British Celanese. Both the fixed-weight and the chained index of output prices show an increase of about five per cent in 1957 with a subsequent tendency to fall over time. The materials and fuels price index P_{IMF} shows a similar pattern but the change from 1955 to 1956 is less than one per cent. Labour earnings (P_L) obviously show a continuous tendency to rise, from 100 in 1954 to 162 in 1963, but it should be

Table 5.6 *Estimated k for Courtaulds and British Celanese*

	(1) P_0^1 1958 weights	(2) P_0^2 chained	(3) P_{IMF} materials and fuels	(4) P_L labour earnings	(5) P_I 1958 weights	(6) P_0^1/P_I	(7) $(\Pi/R)_C$	(8) $(\Pi/R)_{BC}$	(9) $(\Pi/R)_{C+BC}$	(10) $k_{(C)}$	(11) $k_{(BC)}$	(12) $k_{(C+BC)}$
1954	94.9	100.0	100.0	100.0	100.0	0.949	0.390	0.272	0.362	0.579	0.691	0.606
1955	92.6	101.2	101.9	105.1	102.6	0.903	0.400	0.218	0.358	0.542	0.706	0.580
1956	95.8	99.6	103.6	111.3	105.3	0.910	0.358	0.160	0.312	0.584	0.764	0.626
1957	100.0	105.0	104.7	113.8	106.7	9.937	—	—	0.242	—	—	0.710
1958	100.0	100.0	103.5	119.5	106.9	0.935	—	—	0.294	—	—	0.709
1959	97.7	97.7	100.6	126.6	106.2	0.920	—	—	0.229	—	—	0.709
1960 (Feb.)	96.4	98.8	100.5	135.5	108.1	0.892	—	—	0.341	—	—	0.588
1961	96.7	100.3	100.3	149.3	110.9	0.872	—	—	0.297	—	—	0.613
1962	96.7	99.9	97.5	153.5	109.6	0.882	—	—	0.266	—	—	0.648
1963	95.9	99.2	97.1	161.5	111.0	0.864	—	—	0.340	—	—	0.570

Notes:

(i) P_0^1, P_0^2 are weighted indexes of the prices reported in Table 5.2. The weights are derived from the quantities reported in Table 3 of the Appendix to the Monopolies Commission Report. The indexes are intended to be representative of Courtaulds and British Celanese, before and after the merger. In order to achieve this, acetate yarn production for 1954, 1955, 1956 is assumed equal to production for Courtaulds in 1957 (i.e. 48.4 million lbs) since British Celanese was primarily an acetate producer, but we have no record of its production prior to the merger.

(ii) P_{IMF} is derived from estimates provided by the Department of Industry (see Chapter 4 for details).

(iii) P_L is an index of the average hourly earnings of male, manual workers working in the production of man-made fibres. Source: *Statistics of Incomes, Prices, Employment and Production*, Ministry of Labour, No. 1, April 1962 – No. 29, June 1969.

(iv) Π/R is the ratio of net profit before tax *in total* to sales revenue *for fibres*. This ratio was taken because of the lack of profit data for fibres only and the lack of total revenue data for the firms in question.

(v) k is the efficiency measure proposed in Chapter 4.

noted that labour costs as a share of total costs are quite small in this industry and show a tendency to fall over time (21.6% of labour, materials and fuel cost in 1958, falling to 20.5% in 1963). The aggregate input price index (P_I) shows a fairly steady tendency to increase over time leaving the ratio of output price index to input price index (P_0/P_I) moving down from a high level in 1954 but rising again in 1957, subsequently showing a gentle decline. In fact from 1957 to 1963 the ratio falls by about 8% – not a very remarkable fall for a six year period having in mind that a high rate of productivity growth might be expected. Certainly this observation would be quite consistent with an increasing divergence between price and marginal cost if we assume a productivity growth rate of more than $1\frac{1}{2}$% p.a., which is itself well below the national average.

(iii) The ratio of profits to revenue (Π/R)

The ratio of profits to revenue is a further indicator of market power. If we assume constant costs then it is equal to the Lerner index of monopoly. However when we are observing its variation over time, particularly in an industry like man-made fibres, we can expect that a large part of any change could be due to variation in the degree of capacity utilisation. Thus we can really only check for any apparent trend in the variable. In fact the empirical work is made very difficult by the paucity of data. Total revenue data for the two companies was not available for the time-period in question but it was possible to synthesise the sales revenue each company received from its various fibre interests. Courtaulds revenue was derived directly from the quantity and price data reported by the Monopolies Commission and British Celanese revenue was estimated from data on total UK production for each fibre, data on Courtaulds production and data on the capacity of British Celanese and the other much smaller producers of rayon. Ideally we would then take the ratio of profits, from the various rayon interests of Courtaulds and British Celanese, to these estimates of their revenue from rayon. However, this was unavailable for this period and so we have a ratio of profit, from all activities, to revenue from only rayon activities. The ratio as calculated is obviously quite inaccurate but so long as the share of rayon in sales revenue remains roughly constant and the ratio of profits to revenue in other activities also remains roughly constant, then the estimate of Π/R may give a guide to the changing market power and/or efficiency of Courtaulds in the UK rayon market. These estimates are reported in Table 5.6. The only comparisons which should be made are down a particular column. Courtaulds and British Celanese cannot be directly compared since Couraulds appeared to be more diversified than British Celanese. Thus the Courtaulds profit–revenue ratio will be expected to be larger than that for British Celanese. The magnitude of the merger, with reference to the rayon market, comes across from our estimates of sales revenue. Although British Celanese was much smaller than Courtaulds in terms of assets our estimates suggest that its sales revenue in the rayon market was almost one third of that for Courtaulds (e.g. in 1956 £15.8m compared with £50.8m). Thus it is apparent that in terms of that market the merger was indeed a potentially significant one.

Looking down column (9) our estimates indicate a decline in the ratio of profit to revenue for the initial post-merger period followed later by a return to something like the pre-merger position.

(iv) Estimates of efficiency (k)

These estimates combine the information provided by the ratio of output to input prices with the ratio of profit to revenue with the aim of isolating any changes in the efficiency of resource use following from the merger. We see that following the merger the efficiency of the combined enterprise tended to fall and only succeeded in re-establishing the pre-merger position after three years had elapsed. This would suggest that there were real transitional costs but that these were not rewarded by subsequent efficiency gains. There are no indications of the cost savings which were argued for by Courtaulds in its submission to the Monopolies Commission. Obviously it can be argued that the data is not very accurate and also that changes in k can be ascribed to cyclical movements. Nevertheless any significant change in efficiency should show through over the period in question. It must also be pointed out that although it is unlikely that the bias in comparisons over time will be severe since it was only in the period after 1963 that Courtaulds became significantly involved in the textile industry.

5.3.3 **Courtaulds and the state**

The case of cellulosic fibres was referred to the Monopolies Commission in 1965. In 1968 the Monopolies Commission reported and made various recommendations. Essentially the Commission's view was that the 'monopoly of production had to be accepted' since size brought substantial benefits but that regulatory policies be adopted which would modify the behaviour of Courtaulds. They recommended:

(i) reductions in tariffs (to 10% for staple fibres and 15% for yarn);
(ii) price discrimination should be ended;
(iii) Courtaulds' franchise arrangements with EFTA producers should be ended, and
(iv) further acquisitions in the textile and clothing industries should be stopped where Courtaulds share of capacity or sales in that sector exceeded 25%.

Our results cast doubt on the premise underlying this policy prescription and suggest that a structural solution to this monopoly problem might be followed with little fear of efficiency losses. This inference is also supported by evidence provided by Courtaulds to the Commission regarding its own policy on production. Courtaulds apparently decided that the production of staple fibre should be divided between two separate factories (this was in the late 1960s), with the larger factory being organised as a series of small flexible units, and that the production of yarn be divided between several small factories. Since apparently scale economies at the plant level do not justify concentration in single large plants the alleged economies must be at the firm level and are not linked with being a large cellulosic fibre producer. In terms of technological progress the argument could go either way but Courtaulds' record does not look promising. It bought the initial patent rights to rayon and it bought into the production of nylon, the two major discoveries over the previous sixty years.

Nevertheless the recommendations relating to behaviour were fairly stringent and might be expected to have an impact on Courtaulds position. The then Board of Trade reacted to the Commission's findings by asking for Courtaulds comments, and fifteen months later came up with a rather watered-down set of proposals. Courtaulds had agreed to end price discrimination and its EFTA arrangements but the Board of Trade had decided that no change in tariff policy was necessary and the textile acquisitions recommendation lapsed. It should be noted that there was no suggestion that Courtaulds holdings of shares in EFTA companies should be sold.

5.3.4 Conclusions

The merger between Courtaulds and British Celanese should be seen as an attempt to preserve the degree of monopoly in the cellulosic fibres industry in the face of tendencies which were leading to its reduction. Indeed the history of the cellulosic fibres industry in the UK can be seen as a sequence of acquisitions of monopoly positions by Courtaulds followed by a variety of changes leading to its expected demise, followed in turn by vigorous and effective action by Courtaulds to re-establish its former control. Thus it is an excellent example of both the direct social costs of monopoly, via loss in consumer surplus and the indirect social costs implicit in the attempts by capital to both secure and maintain monopoly positions. There were no indications of cost savings following the merger.

5.4.1 Companies:
Ransome and Marles Co. Ltd
Hoffman Manufacturing Ltd
Pollard Ball and Roller Bearing Co. Ltd
Date: June/July 1969
Product: Ball and roller bearings

Bearings are required whenever two moving metal surfaces are in contact. There are two basic types, with different uses, plain bearings such as are found in the 'big ends' of an automotive engine and roller bearings. We concentrate on the latter. In 1975 there were approximately 15,000 basic types of roller

Table 5.7 *Profit and turnover (£m), pre-merger: Ransome, Hoffman & Pollard*

	Ransome & Marles		Hoffman		Pollard	
	Turn-over	Profit before tax	Turn-over	Profit before tax	Turn-over	Profit before tax
1962	n.a.	1.4	n.a.	1.7	n.a	0.2
1963	12.5	1.2	9.4	1.3	n.a.	0.5
1964	13.6	1.4	10.5	1.3	8.6	0.7
1965	13.8	1.5	10.8	0.9	8.8	0.4
1966	13.6	1.3	11.2	0.8	8.7	0.5
1967[a]	13.5	1.3	10.8	0.6	8.4	0.5
1968	14.4	1.5	11.5	0.4	9.5	0.6
1969	15.8	1.7				

Source: EXTEL.
[a]Sales prior to 1967 supplied by RHP.

bearings made in the UK (Laing & Cruickshank (1976)), in three classes:

(i) ball – steel balls moving in a machined groove (52% of 1975 market)

(ii) roller and needle – cylindered rollers differing only in dimensions, the latter having a diameter of under three inches (29% of the market)

(iii) tapered roller – tapered in order to be able to withstand a thrust in any direction (19% of the market).

Prior to the merger Ransome and Marles produced a large proportion of its output for the automotive industry (the major user of bearings). Hoffman was a leading supplier of aero engine and precision bearings, and Pollards had its major strength in the production of self-lubricating bearings and automobile fan and water pump spindles. (It also had a small subsidiary in industrial fasteners). In Table 5.7 the pre-merger profit and turnover figures are presented. These companies ranked two, three and four in the size league for bearing manufactures taking 14.4%, 11.5% and 9.5% of the total market respectively. Shefko (Swedish) had 17.8%, British Timken, Torrington and Fafnir (US owned) had 5.3%, 5.0% and 4.0% of the market respectively.[14] This left about a dozen others with a total turnover of £0.8m. Total sales, imports and exports are detailed in Table 5.8, the foreign trade position showing a market deterioration over our study period.

5.4.2 The efficiency of the bearing industry prior to the merger

The change in the unit factor requirement which will be discussed below will give some indication of how the merger affected the efficiency of the

14 Source: Harvard International Senior Managers Programme (1973) (HISMP).

Table 5.8 *Bearings: sales, imports and exports*

Year	Sales by UK manufacturers (£m)	Imports[a] (£m)	Exports[a] (£m)	% difference $\frac{\text{exports} - \text{imports}}{\text{imports}}$
1966	62.1	8.6	14.1	64.0
1967	64.9	9.2	15.0	61.9
1968	68.3	11.0	15.4	40.0
1969	78.0	13.3	18.2	36.0
1970	89.3	18.4	22.1	20.6
1971	96.2	19.7	27.1	37.5
1972	129.1	19.7	26.3	33.8
1973	146.8	29.1	32.6	11.9
1974	175.6	46.4	40.6	−12.6

Source: *Annual Abstract of Statistics*, for sales; imports/exports from *Overseas Trade Statistics*.
[a]Includes 'parts thereof'

merged companies but there does not seem any doubt amongst students of the industry that before the merger it was poor, even though competition was keen. This seems to be the opinion of the contributors to HISMP *Case Studies*, the technical press,[15] and the Industrial Reorganisation Corporation. As represented in the *Case Studies*, the IRC state that Hoffman 'had strong engineering skills, but its manufacturing facilities were antiquated and its management disorganised. Poor cost accounting procedures resulted in faulty records of operation costs and improper inventory control. In the opinion of the IRC to improve Hoffman's performance would require an almost total changeover in management ranks.' On Pollard a member of the IRC board thought that its financial accounts were '... suspect'. He suspected that the company had smaller profits than the report showed, large quantities of obsolete inventories, and inadequate pricing methods. Ransome and Marles who apparently escaped comparatively unscathed, were considered by the IRC to be 'relatively, the most sound'. However, by the normal standards applied to the general engineering sector of industry, its overall position would not have been considered strong. A statistic that appears in all the sources that have been mentioned in this section is that the productivity per worker of the constituent companies was in 1968 on average £2,000, at least a third less than that claimed to be the average in Europe. Our figures suggest that £2,400 was a more appropriate measure, but if productivity had been expressed in real terms the difference would have had greater significance. Problems of interpretation arise from possible different factor input ratios, but the message is reasonably clear.

15 E.g. the *Economist*, 18 October 1969.

Moreover, the consensus among the industry's critics was that the range of products offered was too large. Opinion differs as to the exact amounts, for instance 45,000 (*Financial Times*, 19 Feb 1974) combined total and 7,000 to 13,000 (*Engineer*, 5 March 1970) each have been quoted. The IRC agreed with the latter estimate for at least two of the companies and added that the three companies had over 5,000 products which each generated less than £1,000 sales per year.

5.4.3 **The merger of Ransome, Hoffman and Pollard**

The Industrial Reorganisation Corporation may be described as the moving force behind the merger. It carried out its study, it explained:

> because the ball bearing industry is a large sector of engineering technology, making up an essential input to major exporting sectors such as the motor and aircraft industries; secondly, compared with the industries in Western Europe and North America the structure of the UK based industry appeared *fragmented* [our italics] thus fell directly within IRC'S remit; and in the third place, the possibility of a merger between Ransome and Marles and Shefko Ball Bearing Co. . . . could mean that there might shortly be no viable British owned company in the industry.

When justifying an increase in concentration in the bearing industry the IRC claimed 'the necessity for volume production supported by advanced production engineering know-how'. It spoke of the 'identity of view in the industry' and that there were 'too many companies producing in sub-optimum manufacturing units an excessive range of bearings in too short-runs' and blamed the 'fragmentation' of the industry as partly responsible for the low productivity of British owned firms, and the deteriorating terms of trade for bearings. It considered that the three companies 'offer considerable scope for rationalisation and development'. The concentration displayed by European bearing industries was considered highly significant. In 1968, two companies in Germany, Skefko and Kugelfischer FAG, shared over 80% of the market. 70% of the French and Italian markets was supplied by Skefko which also dominated Scandinavian markets. The volume of sales and economies of scale resulting from rationalisation could be expected to 'generate a cash flow for new plant and machinery, for sustaining a strong development effort in advanced production engineering techniques and mounting an extensive overseas marketing effort'.

The actual reorganisation of the bearings industry did not proceed smoothly. Initially, the IRC had hoped that Skefko would be a participant in the proposed merger[16] – creating a virtual monopoly – but the negotiations faltered in early December 1968, because Skefko insisted on an absolute majority in the company

16 It already had a joint research and development scheme with Ransome and Marles and the two companies belonged to a consortium owning a factory in Australia.

rather than the 40% offered. However, after considerable reluctance on the part of Pollard, the IRC underwrote a merger with £9m to form RHP, independent of Skefko.

5.4.4 Efficiency of Ransome, Hoffman and Pollard since the merger

The consensus amongst the students of the bearings industry is that the merger which led to the formation of RHP has been a success; typical in sentiment, if rather hyperbolic, is 'RHP represents one of the few pockets of light in the general industrial gloom in the UK economy' (*Financial Times*, 11 Feb. 1975). The changes that have taken place in RHP may be categorised into:

(i) Reorganisation

At the inception of RHP, Mr D. King of Pollard left the company taking with him his senior staff, the new managing director was G. W. Barlow, previously the managing director of English Electric Computers. He brought with him former colleagues to head finance, personnel and administration. Barlow's plans involved drastic reorganisation. Traditionally, bearing companies based their divisions on their major product-lines and maintained large headquarters staff. The new divisions were to be based on the markets the company served and be responsible for design, manufacture and marketing. The headquarters staff would be kept to a minimum. Initially the divisions were General Bearings, Transmission Bearings, and Aerospace Bearings, and two subsidiaries – Dick Bearings, which supplied stockists, and Whitehouse Industries, which produced industrial fasteners. Since then the company has further reorganised into Automotive, Transmission, Aerospace, and Water Pump Bearings, and Whitehouse Industries; Dick Bearings has been sold to UDT.

(ii) Rationalisation

Since the merger, there has been a large reduction in the labour force; indeed, to quote from what was intended as a complimentary article 'the main claim to noteworthiness (of the merger) has been the sheer size of its redundancy' (*Financial Times*, 30 Oct. 1972). Table 5.9 indicates its extent.[17] Productivity per worker is sometimes claimed (see *Financial Times*, 30 Oct. 1972) to have reached £4,000 within two and a half years of the merger but in the case of UK workers this did not occur until 1973/74. For the group as a whole the claim might be justified. The increase in productivity expressed in current terms would seem significant. When account is taken of the change in the price of bearings, there

17 Not surprisingly Barlow is quoted as saying (*Business Administration*, December 1972) 'the single most important function in making a merger work ... is the personnel function'.

Table 5.9 *Labour force of RHP*

Year ending 3 Oct.	Total no. employed by the group—including overseas	Turnover per worker in current prices	Turnover per worker in 1970 prices	Number employed in UK	Turnover[a] per UK worker in current prices	Turnover per UK worker in 1970 prices
1970	14,833	2,705	2,705	14,456	2,414	2,414
1971	13,897	3,172	2,967	13,520	2,988	2,794
1972	12,355	3,383	3,021	11,992	3,110	2,777
1973	11,084	4,239	3,593	10,725	3,702	3,137
1974	10,659	4,889	3,564	10,302	4,378	3,192
1975	10,490	6,062	3,545	10,141	5,512	3,209

Source: Turnover and number employed from published accounts. The price deflator was that used in the *k* calculations – see below.
[a]Assumed to be equal to home sales + direct exports.

would still appear to have been a marked increase in productivity between 1970 and 1973 but there has been little or no increase in the last three years. It must be emphasised that productivity as measured does not allow for increases in other inputs.

It is unfortunately difficult to isolate the extent to which the labour force was reduced in response to the move to rationalise *ex post* the merger and the extent to which it was reduced as a result of deteriorating market conditions. The demand for bearings is highly responsive to changes in the trade cycle and 1971 to 1972 represented a trough in the bearing market as did 1975. A fall in demand might have spurred the constituent companies of RHP to rationalise but that must remain open to conjecture.

One of the most important aspects of RHP's rationalisation programme has been the concentration on the manufacture of a particular type of bearing in each one of its nine, now eight, plants. Associated with this is an agreement with FAG of Germany to fill gaps, when warranted by demand, in the other's product range (*Financial Times*, 7 May 1974).

RHP is clearly proud of its associated investment programme, claiming that, for its company's size, it is 'probably the largest undertaken in the British engineering industry'. Table 5.10 shows the extent. In 1976 RHP announced plans to spend £4.5m that year and £5.0m in 1977 (*Financial Times*, 22 Jan. 1976). For this it was to be assisted by special loan facilities from the Government of up to £4.9 million.

Table 5.10 *Capital investment of RHP*

Year ending 3 October	Capital investment (£m)
1970	1.3
1971	2.1
1972	2.4
1973	2.5
1974	1.9
1975	3.0

Source: RHP Press Notice, July 1975.

(iii) Reduction in the product range

Since the merger there has been a significant reduction in the range of bearings sold by RHP. This reflects not only the discontinuation of types of bearings which were manufactured by the constituent companies and which were in competition with each other, but also greater concentration on high volume, and by implication (but only by implication) high profit lines. In 1975 RHP manufactured approximately 12,000 (compared to approximately 45,000 by its constituents in 1968) different bearings of which 5,000 were included in regular production schedules and 7,000 were manufactured only in response to special orders.[18]

(iv) Diversification

In January 1976 RHP purchased MTE Ltd, a holding company for a group manufacturing electro-mechanical and electronic control devices, high voltage switchgear and motor starters. In 1975 its turnover was £63.6m and profits before tax £5.8m. Part of the rationale[19] behind the acquisition of this company was that sales of its products were believed to be six to nine months ahead of that of bearings in the trade cycle. This diversification may therefore be partly interpretated as an attempt to counterweigh the effects of the cycle.

The above gives some indication of the changes that took place in RHP. Our next task is to evaluate the effect. We start by looking at the amount exported by the constituent companies of RHP. Prior to the merger data have not been published. Since the merger, RHP's exports have been as in Table 5.11, but the performance of the industry as a whole (Table 5.8) has not been good. Although the change in the unit factor requirement will, in our opinion, provide the most reliable measure of how the merger has affected the efficiency of the constituent companies of RHP, we can first utilise some other relevant information.

18 Scherer (1975) cites this merger as 'most strikingly an example of increasing efficiency through the elimination of over-lapping product lines'.

19 According to Laing and Cruickshank (1976).

Table 5.11 *RHP Exports*

Year	Direct exports (£m)	Other exports[a] (£m)
1970	6.7	5.2
1971	9.4	3.7
1972	7.5	4.5
1973	8.9	7.3
1974	12.1	7.0
1975	12.6	7.7

Source: published accounts.
[a]Presumably this refers to sales of overseas subsidiaries.

(a) *Return on net capital employed.* This traditional measure of efficiency, calculated from EXTEL data, indicates what one would expect about the pre-merger situation – Hoffman was the least strong and was becoming weaker; Ransome and Marles had the highest return. The same return (14%) was not earned by RHP until 1974, whilst 1975 represents the most successful year when judged by the return on assets (20.6%).

(b) *Market shares UK.* It is not clear from where the contributors to the HISMP *Case Studies* derived the market shares they quote and thus a comparison between those in 1968 and those in 1972 might be of only limited value. But it would appear that RHP had not improved in the share its output represented of the total and it had indeed declined relative to both the total and to Skefko. Even more surprising than this, especially as it appears to have gone unremarked by any of the sources which have been quoted in this paper, is the apparent dramatic increase in the importance of British Timken.

(c) *World market.* It has not been possible to ascertain the shares of world sales enjoyed by the constituent companies of RHP. All that can be said is that in 1972 RHP was just outside the top ten of world producers as measured by their sales (HISMP). Naturally little can be concluded from this though no doubt some comfort will be afforded to those who view success in terms of a company's position in the World league table of size.

(d) *Capital expenditure.* The amounts spent by the competitors of RHP on new capital may only be inferred from occasional references in the press to specific projects and it has not therefore been possible to make a rigorous comparison with expenditure by RHP, although it would seem rather harsh on the latter to claim its 'investment to sales ratio is not far off the industry average' (*Financial Times,* 22 Jan. 1976). However, there does not seem any doubt that other companies in the bearing sector have carried out significant investment programmes. Skefko's has 'nearly matched' (*Financial Times,* 22 Jan. 1976) that of RHP since 1970 and plans to spend £4.7 million in the near future, whilst Fafnir was described, in 1975, as having 'hefty' investment plans of £3.5 millions (*Financial Times*, 11 Feb. 1975). British Timken planned to spend £1.5 million in 1975 and Torrington £500,000.

Comparing the efficiency of RHP's capital with that of competitors is even more difficult than comparing expenditure. The *Economist* (20 Feb. 1971) was scathing about the scope for mechanisation of even RHP's most modern plant, and stated that its productivity per man of £4,000 per annum compared badly with the £5,000–£6,000 of comparable European factories and £10,000 in the United States; this does not state the productivity of other companies in the UK which would have been more relevant. Other conclusions one may draw are however that the productivity per man in British Timken is approximately the same as in RHP and that the factory being built in Durham for NSK of Japan will be the most fully automated in the United Kingdom (*Financial Times*, 11 Feb. 1975).

5.4.5 The effect of the merger on the unit factor requirement of RHP

The major problem when assessing *k*s for bearing producers is that inputs into bearings, or the proportion they form of total cost, are not given in the Census of Production.[20] Fortunately, the greater part of the variable input into bearings consists of steel and labour. Opinion differs as to the proportions. A contributor to the HISMP *Case Study* writing circa 1973, gave a breakdown of costs for standard and special ball bearings and though the total cost differed, direct labour formed 6% of the total cost in each case, and by inference from their breakdown, 11% of variable cost. Laing & Cruickshank (1976) estimated that in 1975 labour represented 48% of total price, which would imply a higher proportion of variable cost. Given that during the intervening period between the dates of these studies there had been a substitution of capital for labour by the major companies it would seem difficult to reconcile the differing data. It would, moreover, be hard to believe in the light of the capital investment programmes undertaken by the major bearing producers and of the large degree of rationalisation carried out certainly by RHP, that the cost of labour could represent nearly half of the price. In any case, some validity is conferred on the HISMP *Case Study* estimates by the greater detail with which they are supported. Therefore, the weighted index of input prices used in the calculations to estimate *k* is based on the HISMP *Case Study* data.[21]

It is clear from Table 5.12 that in the years leading up to the merger the unit factor requirement of both Ransome and Marles and Pollard was declining,

20 Information on bearings is included under 'Other mechanical engineering' MLH 349/1.

21 The wage data (average earnings), are taken from *Department of Employment Gazette*.

Table 5.12 *Unit factor requirement of RHP*

	Hoffman	Ransome & Marles	Pollard
1963	107.5		
1964	107.9	110.2	113.9
1965	110.9	108.3	115.7
1966	110.5	107.8	111.6
1967	109.6	104.5	108.3
1968	110.8	103.1	108.0
1969		100.0	
1970		97.3	
1971		95.5	
1972		97.6	
1973		92.8	
1974		74.9	

Note: *k* set equal to 100 in merger year.

Table 5.13 *RHP, profits and prices*

	P_0/P_I	Hoffman	Ransome & Marles	Pollard
		$\frac{\Pi}{R}$	$\frac{\Pi}{R}$	$\frac{\Pi}{R}$
1963	100.00	13.88		
1964	98.75	12.49	10.60	7.64
1965	97.09	8.40	10.71	4.58
1966	95.29	7.16	9.41	6.24
1967	92.74	5.33	9.75	6.42
1968	92.30	3.89	10.53	6.26
1969	89.59	—	10.62	—
1970	81.73	—	4.69	—
1971	81.12	—	5.75	—
1972	80.33	—	2.73	—
1973	75.61	—	1.73	—
1974	63.37	—	5.32	—
1975	60.91	—	9.15	—

though not that of Hoffman, and that the average unit factor requirement of RHP since the merger is significantly lower than that of its constituent companies during the period being considered. Table 5.13 shows that k has fallen post-merger because P_0/P_1 has fallen, as also has Π/R for the larger part of the period. This movement in relative prices does not seem to indicate any abuse of monopoly power.

Table 5.14 *Unit factor requirement of competitors to RHP*

	Skefko	Torrington	FAG(UK)
1968	102.6		
1969	100.0	100.0	100.0
1970	95.6	87.9	90.1
1971	90.1	85.4	87.3
1972		87.0	85.1
1973		86.6	84.3
1974		70.7	69.9

Note: 1969 set equal to 100 for comparisons with RHP.

Before strong conclusions may be drawn about the benefits from the merger a comparison must be made with the trend in the *k* of other companies in the bearing industry. Unfortunately, data on British Timken is not published and that on three other bearing producers is only available for a few years. The evidence does, however, suggest (see Table 5.14) that the efficiency of Skefko was increasing 1968–71 and that of both Torrington and FAG (UK), a small subsidiary of the major German company, showed a greater improvement than that displayed by RHP since it merged. At best, therefore, it would appear that the merger allowed the constituent companies of RHP to be as efficient as their competitors.

5.4.6 The market for bearings since the merger

The most traumatic change that has occurred in the world market for bearings during the period covered in this study has been the emergence of Japan as a major exporter. Japan's share of UK imports rose from 0.9% in 1960 to 14% in 1973.[22] This pattern is reflected in other countries also.

The types of bearing the Japanese export is limited to those that are small sized but sell in high volume; apparently they supply only 45 sizes to the UK (Laing & Cruickshank (1976)). A memorandum[23] to the EEC Commission from the trade associations of the more important members claimed, 'In ball bearings, Japanese competition is concentrated in popular metric ball bearings up to 62 mm. outside diameter. In this sector which represents about 40% of all ball bearings by weight – and by volume 75% – their market share is about 40% and in some widely used sizes as much as 70%.' Similar claims were made about roller-bearings.

The memorandum was part of a campaign by the domestic producers of each

22 It should be noted that imports from West Germany represent the largest proportion of the total; since 1960 it has varied between 20 and 30%. Source: *Trade Statistics.*

23 *Low Priced Imports from Japan and State Trading Countries, The Threat to the EEC Bearing Industry* presented by the Bearing Associations of UK, France, West Germany and Italy, May 1976.

of the bearings imported from Japan. Its theme was the alleged unfair competition by Japan, claiming a dumping policy with prices 25—40%, and sometimes 60% below the European market price, which would not 'even cover the material costs of European manufacturers'. They also argue that Japanese increases have generally kept below the recent upward valuation of the yen and have not kept pace with inflation, 'so it is impossible to see how Japanese products can be selling profitably at these prices'. The press has sometimes been sceptical about these claims, attributing some of the Japanese success to the limited range in which they export bearings and to shorter and more reliable delivery dates.

The results of an earlier campaign than that in which the above quoted memorandum played a part, were, in 1971, a two-year 'voluntary' quota of Japanese bearings into the UK, a similar agreement with France, a total ban on Japanese bearings imports into Italy and the raising of tariffs on bearings into the United States.

NSK of Japan is currently building, with the aid of a £1.4 million development grant, a plant in Durham. The announcement of this project gave rise to a vigorous campaign from British bearing companies and, partly as a result of this, conditions[24] were laid on the Japanese being allowed to start.

The relevance of this challenge from the Japanese to the merger which formed RHP is two-fold: the increased absolute and relative size of RHP has raised its influence on government policy. It is significant that in the press-reports on the British bearing producers' fight against either Japanese imports or the building of the NSK factory, quotations from Barlow figure largely, for instance his claim that Japanese competition had resulted in the loss of 1,700 jobs (*Financial Times* 11 Feb. 1975). The difference that RHP's influence made to government policy is impossible to judge.

The other aspect of the increase in Japanese competition which is relevant to this study is that it provides a powerful check on the exploitation of the increase in its market-power by RHP and no doubt on the development of 'X' inefficiency. This chapter will not enter into a discussion of the merits of free-trade but the hostility displayed towards the NSK plant reflected a fear of a capital intensity greater than its British competitors as much as that it would, for reasons that were not specified, sell below its average total cost.[25]

24 (a) Half the output of the plant must be exported.
(b) Half the value must be added in the UK.
(c) The output from the plant must result in 'considerable substitution' of Japanese imports (*Financial Times*, 19 Feb. 1974).

25 In any case for NSK to carry out the latter policy, in order to force out competition and subsequently exploit a monopoly position, would require sufficient profit in Japan to bear the short-term loss and would require that, having ceased production, the British companies could not subsequently re-enter the market as the Japanese charged the monopoly price.

5.4.7 Summary and conclusions

The RHP merger, which transformed the bearing industry, was instigated by the IRC. Had it not taken place the Swedish SKF would have attempted to take over Ransome and Marles, the largest British-owned UK producer, and if this had been allowed by the Monopolies Commission, would probably have led to Hoffman, and perhaps Pollard, ceasing to produce non-speciality bearings. If the Commission had prohibited the SKF takeover, and it would have had excellent reasons for so doing, there is no strong evidence to suggest that either Ransome & Marles or Pollard, would have ceased to survive, though the same cannot be said of Hoffman. Much would have depended on the degree with which these companies could have matched the increase in the efficiency of their competitors.

It would also appear that at the time of the merger there was considerable scope for the participants to improve their efficiency and that this opportunity has been largely taken. Certainly the reorganisation carried out by the new management of RHP would seem to have been a success. At the same time, however, the efficiency of RHP's competitors has also been improving. It would seem that the merger has merely allowed RHP to keep up. On the crucial question, however, of whether the constituent companies of RHP would have been able to increase their efficiency to the same extent in the absence of the merger, it is, in our opinion, unlikely.

The failure to overcome the Japanese challenge is a disappointment. The silver lining however may be the limitations this force puts on the exercise of the substantial market power provided by the merger.

5.5.1 Companies: British Insulated Callender's Cables and Pyrotenax Ltd. Date: 1966 Product: Mineral Insulated Cable

The product in question, mineral insulated cable (MIC), consists of one or more metal conductors surrounded and separated from each other by an insulant. Standard cables comprised 90% of BICC's MIC sales in 1965 and 80% or Pyrotenax's sales in 1965/66. Prior to the merger Pyrotenax and BICC produced over 90% of the total UK market, the remainder going to Glynwed Ltd, with virtually no imports. As can be seen the merger created a virtual monopoly. The problem facing us is that MIC forms only a small proportion of total cable production in the UK and this leads to data problems. However, the Monopolies Commission report on this merger yields a wealth of information.

Pyrotenax was formed in 1936 to manufacture MIC, with total sales of £4½m in 1965/66. At the time of merger it had two factories, one at Hebburn-on-Tyne, Durham, producing copper MIC, one at Slough manufacturing aluminium MIC, and a subsidiary, Currie and Warner, at Birmingham, supplying accessories. It also had wholly owned subsidiaries in Canada, Australia, New Zealand, India, USA and Italy. Details of sales and profits can be found in the Monopolies Commission Report. BICC was formed in 1945 through a merger of British Insulated Cables and Callender's Cable Construction Ltd and claimed in 1966 to be 'the largest and leading organisation of its kind in the world', with total sales of £299m, the MIC division contributing only £4½m. In fact it only produced MIC post-1955, prior to which Pyrotenax was a monopolist.

In the ten years prior to the merger the MIC market grew from around 11½ million yards of standard cable per annum to 46m yards p.a. Given the ownership of foreign subsidiaries exporting was not extensive, the two companies exporting only £1.1m worth of MIC in 1965.

5.5.2 Pre-merger pricing policy

Pyrotenax, in its evidence to the Monopolies Commission (1967), claimed to aim for a predetermined profit per finished coil, though added that on several occasions the amount of profit had been reduced. BICC acknowledged Pyrotenax as price leader and as a result their prices were very similar. What price competition there was seems to have been confined to the discounts and rebates they offered. The MC considered that in 1965 'BICC was on average more generous to industrial users and contractors than Pyrotenax'.

Market power of the monopolist depends on the degree of substitution possible between MIC and alternative cables. The Monopolies Commission was satisfied that MIC 'has real technical advantages which make it at least highly desirable in certain situations'. As to an actual price comparison with substitutes, a series supplied by BICC to the Monopolies Commission, and published without comment, shows MIC prices rising from 100 to 116 between 1961 and 1966, with a representative PVC insulated cable rising from 100 to 151.2 (the biggest rise occurring in the last year).

5.5.3 The report of the monopolies commission on BICC/Pyrotenax

The Monopolies Commission was clearly uneasy about the merger – in its conclusion the Report states, 'the benefits are certainly not negligible but in view of the success and resourcefulness of Pyrotenax over the years, it cannot be assumed that continued competition in the production and supply of MIC would not have produced equally good results'. The reason for the merger was that ICI, the major shareholder in Pyrotenax, offered its shares to BICC; as the Report explains, 'nor ... was the reason for the merger that there were great improvements in efficiency to be gained in a radical change in the structure of the industry ... economies and other benefits are claimed but they appear to have been almost an afterthought'.

The grounds for the Commission's reservations were the paucity of the gains from synergy,[26] especially as these might have been gained through internal expansion by Pyrotenax, and the widespread fear amongst customers and competitors in other spheres, who might also be consumers of MIC, that BICC would exploit its monopoly position. There were obvious grounds for this fear when BICC announced its intention that 'Pyrotenax's pricing policy will come under the same control as that of the MIC Division and that the list prices and discount terms shall as soon as possible be made identical'. To allay fears on the exploitation of monopoly power the Commission insisted on a number of assurances by BICC as to their future behaviour. However no provision was apparently made for the monitoring of BICC's behaviour to consider whether the undertakings that BICC made were being observed.

5.5.4 The history of the MIC industry since the merger

As has been mentioned above, data are not published at a sufficiently disaggregated level to allow very much to be learned about the market for, and production of, MIC. Fortunately BICC has kindly provided the necessary information to estimate how the unit factor requirement has changed since the merger and to gain some understanding of developments in other areas. To go some way to completing the picture, consumers of MIC and a former competitor in this market have also been approached.

Before reporting the results of an interview with an executive from BICC some brief comments should be made on the value of such interviews in general. Reservations may be expressed about what may be gained from an interview with a manager on any topic and these should be particularly pertinent when the topic in question is as sensitive as his company's performance since a merger. An understandable unwillingness to admit, perhaps even to himself, the problems that have been caused by the merger, on the one hand, or to claim successes in controversial areas such as market-power and the size of the workforce,[27] on the other, might all serve to set definite limits on how much he will disclose. Added to this, managers may be genuinely mistaken, and given the passage of time that might have elapsed since a merger and/or that their expertise might not cover all of the topics on which they might be questioned, this would not be surprising. This all serves, however, to depict interviews in the worst light. Provided that these possible drawbacks are borne in mind interviews often prove to be a useful method of collecting information.

26 One should note that the Commission's discussion of the gains from the merger centre on gains to the combined companies rather than gains to the community from freed resources.

27 Managers might justifiably claim that on the redundancy resulting from a merger they are presented with the classic Morton's Fork: they are expected to rationalise but are unpopular if they sack workers.

Table 5.15 *Sales of MIC (millions of metres) 1965–74*

Year	Sales	Year	Sales
1965	35.3	1970	31.6
1966	38.1	1971	31.6
1967	31.9	1972	26.8
1968	27.2	1973	34.9
1969	26.4	1974	30.6

We interviewed an executive who was closely involved in BICC's application to the Monopolies Commission. He very readily provided the data for which he was as asked and answered all our questions apparently frankly and in full. His views indicate that since the merger 'very little' rationalisation had taken place, although some had in the production of special lines, but in general the wide range of types of MIC made production economies of scale difficult to realise. However, copper-tube and supplies of rod are now produced internally for Pyrotenax, and some economies in the purchase of PVC and accessories have been made possible. It was not possible to estimate the magnitude of these savings.

The merger had enabled greater coverage of export markets than Pyrotenax alone could have afforded. The overseas factories of Pyrotenax had been maintained. Direct exports had risen from £1.216m (the Commission's report put this at £1.218m) in 1965 to £3.136m in 1974, all in current terms, an increase of 158%. The ratio of exports to turnover had increased from 14% in 1965 to 19% in 1974.

A fall in output after the merger can be observed; this was partly because of strong competition from the manufacturers of other cables. The amount of MIC sold in total each year was as in Table 5.15.

Post-merger coordination of R & D was possible with respect to accessories and termination, but this apparently did not in general take place with respect to mineral insulated cables because their simple construction offered little scope for improvement.

During the interview the interviewee stressed that up to then BICC and Pyrotenax had continued to be autonomous units, each with its own sales force, and that representatives competed to attract business from specific authorities through the availability of stock and the quality of service. No competition took place in price. He did, however, mention that some changes were planned. During a subsequent discussion he explained that these would consist of the integration[28] of the two sales forces and ending of the separation of the two

28 This integration has now taken place.

companies in all respects except production. Finally, it seems, there had been no substantial changes in the terms offered to other manufacturers, but discounts have now increased to a top rate of 27% (the Commission reported the top non-quality discount as 24% by BICC, 23% by Pyrotenax).

These answers have been reported reasonably verbatim though in a form which would be acceptable to BICC. We do not attempt to defend the blandness of the answers. The definite conclusions that can be drawn are that the merger apparently did not result in production rationalisation, an increase in the level of sales, or, given their value was given in current terms, to the amount of exports. It has not proved possible from our discussions to ascertain if any of the undertakings made to the Commission have been broken but it should be noted that BICC informed the Commission of its intention to merge the respective marketing departments before doing so.

Glynwed ceased to manufacture MIC in 1969 and as far as we are aware, BICC now has a complete monopoly with respect to its supply. We thus approached Glynwed for comment. An interview was held with a spokesman for Wednesbury Tube, the subsidiary of Glynwed that operated in this field, and he suggested that the following statement accurately summed up that part of the discussions which were on the record:

> A spokesman for the Wednesbury Tube Company, was asked why his company had ceased to manufacture MIC. He replied that the decision was in fact taken by the holding company, Glynwed Ltd, primarily, he believed, because the view was held that there were more pressing problems within his company which were in need of the attention of its management than the improvement of the performance of the (relatively small) mineral insulated cable department.
>
> The immediate difficulties facing that department in 1969 were:
>
> 1. The need to produce a new range of cable to meet new British Standards in metric terms.
> 2. A lack of profitability arising from poor works efficiencies, which had resulted partly from a strike in the autumn of 1968.
>
> So far as he recollected there had never been any allegation that BICC had acted, with adverse effects upon his company, in contravention of its undertakings to the Monopolies Commission.

A member of the marketing department of Wednesbury Tube who had been responsible for MIC supplied a list of who had been his principal customers. Most of these had switched to BICC/Pyrotenax after Glynwed had ceased to produce MIC. This list was supplemented by wholesalers and electrical contractors in the Midlands area who were identified from the telephone directory. Initially we contacted a sample of customers by telephone and on the respondent's agreement, a questionnaire was sent. Of the twelve companies approached, only two replied and in both cases, they politely refused to provide information. Therefore, a telephone survey of the remaining ten in the original sample and two other wholesalers was carried out.

We can only state the obvious reservations about the value of such a study. The chief buyers who were interviewed usually were reluctant to discuss any aspect of the market in which they operate, and this especially applied to the terms of payment – nor could all remember, or had experience of, conditions in this market at the time of the BICC–Pyrotenax merger. Nor does the size or method of selection of the sample give grounds for expecting it to be reasonably representative.

At the very best strong discontent about either the terms offered to some customers, or the way these have changed since the merger, might have been reflected in their responses to the questions. No such feelings were evident. Those buyers who could remember conditions at the time of the merger did not agree to the leading questions that the terms they had been offered since had become less favourable and none of the respondents expressed dissatisfaction with their treatment from BICC.

5.5.5 The effect of the merger on the unit factor requirement *(k)*

Generally speaking the major problem with which we have been confronted when estimating *k*s for years before and after a merger has been that the value of sales before 1967 (the year of the Companies Act which extended the information which it was mandatory for firms to publish) may not have been published and/or the level of aggregation of sales and profit data may have been too high. In this study approximate profit and sales data for the early period is given in the Monopolies Commission's report and similar information on the period since has been provided by BICC.

A weighted average input price has been constructed from other information supplied by the company. Output price data are, however, not ideal. There is a wide range of types of MIC, each with its own price series and in the absence of a weighted average it is necessary to choose a 'representative' series. Matters are made worse by the absence of a price series for a period spanning many years both before and after the merger.

In the Commission's report the prices are given that BICC and Pyrotenax each charged for different types of 660 voltage cable; the index of its prices (though of precisely which type is not stated) is described in the report as being 'representative'. This *k*s which result from employing one of these series are shown in Table 5.16 (a), but when any others were used the pre-merger situation appears the same, i.e. between 1962 and 1966 the unit factor requirement of both companies fell, with that of BICC showing the biggest decrease.

In part (b) of Table 5.16 the *k*s have been estimated by using a price series for 440 voltage cable which spanned the pre- and post-merger periods but which has

Table 5.16 *Unit factor requirement, BICC and Pyrotenax*
(a) 1 × 660v, 4 × 0.025 cables

Year	Pyrotenax			BICC		
	$\frac{\Pi}{R}\%$	$\frac{P_0}{P_I}$	k	$\frac{\Pi}{R}\%$	$\frac{P_0}{P_I}$	k
1962	16.9	156.5	149.4	8.6	170.8	183.5
1963	16.4	157.8	152.0	9.2	172.3	183.5
1964	15.6	169.8	164.4	8.5	126.5	136.5
1965	13.9	98.5	97.7	12.2	104.5	108.2
1966	13.3	100.0	100.0	14.8	100.0	100.0

(b) 1 × 440v 2 × 0.002 cables

Year	Pyrotenax			BICC		
	$\frac{\Pi}{R}\%$	$\frac{P_0}{P_I}$	k	$\frac{\Pi}{R}\%$	$\frac{P_0}{P_I}$	k
1962	16.9	154.2	147.1	8.6	154.2	165.9
1963	16.4	152.5	146.0	9.2	152.5	162.4
1964	15.6	117.6	113.8	8.5	117.6	127.0
1965	13.9	111.1	110.3	12.2	110.0	114.1
1966	13.3	100.0	100.0	14.8	100.0	100.0
1967		120.1		10.7	120.1	128.2
1968		99.4		10.5	99.4	104.7
1969		93.1		10.8	93.2	101.2

(c) BICC prices

Year	$\frac{\Pi}{R}$	$\frac{P_0}{P_I}$	k^2
1970	10.5	100.0	104.7
1971	11.7	119.4	123.5
1972	10.4	113.4	120.0
1973	11.8	80.4	83.5
1974	6.5	81.4	89.4

$\frac{\Pi}{R} = \frac{\text{profits before tax}}{\text{turnover}}$

k = unit factor requirement

$\frac{P_0}{P_I} = \frac{\text{output price index}}{\text{input price index}}$

1. In parts (a) and (b) k is set equal to 100 for 1966.
2. Multiple used to adjust k (1966) for BICC to 100 in part (b), applied to k here.

not been published since 1969. The compilers of the source[29] apparently attempt to estimate average prices. The editors did not know whether both BICC and Pyrotenax had been approached for prices pre-merger but surmised it would have been only one. It will be noticed that the index 1961–66 has a closer resemblance to that of 660 voltage sold by Pyrotenax than that for BICC. If the price index of 660 voltage is indeed representative of indices for other types of cable it would seem more likely therefore that the index shown for 440 voltage refers to that of Pyrotenax. If this is the case the actual price charged by BICC would have been higher, as would its unit factor requirement, at the beginning of the period being considered.

What is interesting about the k indicated by part (b) is that it apparently rose in 1967, suggesting teething problems for the newly formed MIC Division, but that of the pre-merger companies was regained by 1969.

Since 1970 BICC has constructed a price index for MIC which it uses in the construction of an index for cable in total which it supplies to the Department of Employment. It is not possible to judge the accuracy of this index but it should be noted that the weighting for its components was changed in 1972 leading to the illusion that prices of the original 'bundle of goods' had fallen. The *ks* in part (c) of Table 5.16 have been calculated using this index. They would suggest that, compared to 1970, the efficiency BICC displayed when producing MIC was low in 1971 and 1972 but dramatically higher in 1973 and 1974. The reason for this is that whilst Π/R remained virtually constant 1970–73, P_0 had risen only 1% but P_I, 27%, and in 1974 P_0 was 29% higher but P_I, 58%. Given the distortion arising from the reweighting in 1972 the size of the decrease in k, especially as it occurred so rapidly, must be viewed with some scepticism. Nevertheless, it would appear that the unit factor requirement has dropped since the merger, and it would seem likely that BICC has now surpassed the efficiency of Pyrotenax at the time of the merger.

BICC has been shown our estimate of P_I and claims that we have underestimated its increase between 1970 and 1971 and 1971 and 1972, but overestimated for the 1972–74 period. In this case, therefore, it would appear that the increase in efficiency when producing MIC has been smoother but less dramatic than our figures suggest. BICC believe that efficiency has increased by about 3% per annum.

5.5.6 Summary and conclusions

To summarise, the merger of Pyrotenax with BICC was not undertaken with the expectation that significant rationalisation would be possible. Discussions with a manager from BICC have led us to believe that this has not, in fact, taken place. The trend in k since the merger, which suggests efficiency has

29 Laxton's Building Price Book (Kelly's Directories).

increased, is therefore somewhat surprising, although doubts on the quality of our data make one wary of reading too much into the estimates. We have not observed any attempt to misuse the market power generated by the merger.

5.6.1 Companies:
Tube Investments Ltd, Coventry Gauge and Tool Co. Ltd
Date: July 1969
Product: Machine Tools

The British machine tool industry experienced a series of mergers during the 1960s, during that decade the number of companies falling from 350 to 200. In 1960 the 20 largest companies produced ½ of total deliveries but by 1970 this required only the seven largest companies. Although our main concern here is with the Tube Investments – Coventry Gauge merger of 1969 we must, given this degree of activity, also look at the industry more widely.

The work proceeds initially by looking at the market conditions over the period in question in Section 2, in Section 3 we analyse changes in market structure, in 4 scale economies are discussed. In 5 the TI – Coventry Gauge merger is focussed upon, in 6 the performance of the industry in general is analysed and conclusions are presented in Section 7.

5.6.2 The market for machine tools

Machine tools is a generic name, often given the adjective metal-working that covers a group of products varying in technology from numerically or computer controlled machines down to the simplest lathes. These products are often categorised according to their function – boring, drilling, turning, lathes etc., but although it is feasible to divide products between the firms in the industry (see Department of Trade and Industry (1970) Appendix A), it is not as far as we are concerned, necessary or practical. We will thus consider metal-working machine tools as one group of products to be treated as a whole. Although the companies with which we deal do specialise to some degree, they all are involved in producing a wide range of machines.

The most noticeable and most commented upon characteristic of this industry is its fluctuations in demand. This is as one would expect in any capital goods producing industry. These fluctuations do not match perfectly internationally but international cycles are not so out of phase as to cancel each other out in aggregate. To indicate the market, in Table 5.17 a series on deliveries, exports, and imports, at current prices is presented. One should be a little wary of this data given changes in sources over time.

5.6.3 Returns to scale in machine tool production

Given the fluctuations in machine tool output we require to know how costs are likely to vary with short-term output levels before we can really

Table 5.17 *The market for metal working machine tools, Current prices*

Year	Deliveries					
	Total		Export		Imports	
	No. ('000)	Value (£m)	No. ('000)	Value (£m)	No. ('000)	Value (£m)
1951	109.0	48.6	34.7	16.8	6.8	13.5
1952	112.3	62.0	33.1	20.3	19.1	56.4
1953	95.2	66.2	27.5	20.8	11.0	43.4
1954	98.7	65.6	27.1	18.2	6.1	13.2
1955	99.7	75.4	23.3	18.6	7.3	13.9
1956	—	85.5	—	21.4	8.7	21.4
1957	—	95.2	—	24.4	7.7	17.6
1958	—	83.9	—	20.7	6.0	14.0
1959	—	78.8	—	18.6	7.7	12.9
1960	—	95.9	—	24.3	10.8	17.4
1961	—	115.7	—	28.6	13.3	26.9
1962	—	127.2	—	35.5	16.2	27.5
1963	—	114.2	—	39.2	12.5	25.5
1964	—	121.7	—	37.8	16.6	32.5
1965	81.0	141.3	—	43.9	18.1	32.7
1966	81.3	149.1	—	43.5	18.4	36.9
1967	74.9	171.2	—	45.7	20.5	53.2
1968	73.4	168.5	—	53.1	17.3	45.0
1969	73.1	189.1	—	57.6	19.1	40.6
1970	72.7	218.6	—	116.3	36.7	77.9
1971	—	207.7	—	129.6	—	69.2
1972	—	184.7	—	109.7	—	72.3
1973	—	213.2	—	121.5	—	103.5
1974	—	251.0	—	154.7	—	143.9
1975	—	301.1	—	—	—	—

Sources: Main body of data – Machinery & Production Engineering, *Machinery & Production Engineering Survey of Machine Tool Statistics 1951–1970*, value of deliveries 1967–75 from *Trade & Industry*, May 1976, export & import data post 1970 from *Business Monitor – Overseas Trade Analysed in Terms of Industries 1974*, Department of Industry HMSO 1975.

make any judgement upon the efficiency of firms. Moreover, as we wish to analyse the success of mergers we must also have information on any scale economies to be expected from the merger itself. For this information we turn to Pratten (1971).

Pratten identifies four main dimensions of scale for machine tool production: (a) the output of particular models, (b) the size of batches, (c) the size of factories, (d) the size of firms.

Table 5.18 *Output of model of machine tool and unit production cost*

Output per year	5	10	20	50	100	200	400	800
Size of batch for assembly	5	5	10	20	33	50	(flow assembly)	
Production costs per tool	100	95	91	86	83	81	78	77

Source: Pratten (1971) Table 17.4, p. 173.

As regards the effect on costs of short-run cyclical fluctuations in sales we can perhaps best consider Pratten's estimates of the effect of changing batch sizes on costs, for as he argues the size of batches is affected by demand. These estimates are presented in Table 5.18. As can be seen costs are likely to increase per unit as sales fall, i.e. as capacity utilisation falls costs per unit increase. If one moreover assumes a lag in reducing inputs as output increases one would expect further increases in unit costs as output falls.

With regard to the other economies Pratten suggests that there are economies in design and development costs and costs of patterns and special jigs as the production run of a model increases. These costs will vary from 6% to 29% of average production costs. Thus one would expect that merger would increase production runs and thus reduce these initial costs per unit. Pratten also suggests that there are economies to be derived from increased factory size, with some unquantifiable economies also coming from increased firm size. However, overall it is the economies of long production runs that are of greatest importance through the spreading of initial costs.

5.6.4 **Market structure**

Over the study period this industry has become steadily more concentrated. We can, however, give a more detailed picture of the merger activity in the study period. In Figure 5.2 we illustrate the history of Coventry Gauge and Tube Investments machine tool interests. In Table 5.19 we illustrate the merger activity of the other big 6 machine tool companies. The tendency to greater concentration is obvious. It might be asked however whether this is leading us to a position any different from other machine tool producing countries or are we just catching up. In Table 5.20 we present data on company and establishment size that illustrates that compared to other European companies the British industry was already made up of large firms prior to the merger wave of the second half of the 1960s, although as far as one can tell this was not matched by large establishments. Given Pratten's analysis of the availability of scale economies, i.e. that the spreading of initial costs is the main factor, this may be as one should expect.

1957	Coventry Gauge Ltd (inc. Coventry Gauge & Tool Co. Ltd, A. Lawrence & Co., Pneumatic Scale Ltd, Pitter Gauge & Tool Co. Ltd (acq. 1953))	Tube Investments (agency for Cincinnati Milling Co. of USA)
Oct. 1958	acq. Rockwell Engineers Ltd	
Sept. 1964	acq. Humphries & Son Ltd	
Feb. 1966		acq. Charles Churchill
Aug. 1968	acq. Kanduk Precision Instruments Ltd	
April 1969		acq. Vero Machine Tool
June 1969		acq. Cyril Bath of Ohio, USA
1970		acq. Joseph Bradbury acq. Crypton Triangle
1971		acq. Healy of Leicester
1973		agreement with Okuma Machine works of Japan
Oct. 1973		acq. Iwema (Sweden)
1976		

Figure 5.2 *History of Coventry Gauge and Tube Investments (machine tool division)*

5.6.5 The Coventry Gauge – Tube Investments Merger

The growth of the Tube Investments machine tool division has already been illustrated above, and although there were a few small acquisitions post 1969, the Chairman in his annual report for 1969 felt that the company had then reached the minimum viable size for a machine tool supplier. (In fact prior to the acquisition of Churchill in 1966 it had been little more than an agent for the Cincinnati Milling Co. of the USA.) One ought to note however that by 1975

Table 5.19 *Acquisitions in the machine tool industry*

Company		Acquisitions
Alfred Herbert	1966	BSA Machine Tools
Staveley Inds.	April 1965	Craven Bros. (Manchester) Ltd
	Mar. 1966	Asquith Machine Tool Co.
Cincinnati Milacron	None	
George Cohen	April 1966	W. E. Sykes Ltd
600 Group	Nov. 1966	F. J. Edwards Ltd
	Aug. 1967	J. A. Dicks Hldgs. Ltd
	Mar. 1970	Dickson Engineering Ltd
B. Elliot	Nov. 1965	Elliot-Wilson (formerly GWS Burdett & Co. Ltd)
	Feb. 1966	Elliott-Wilson (formerly Wilson-Machine Tools Ltd)
	June 1966	Butler Machine Tool Co. Ltd
	Oct. 1966	D. Mitchell & Co. Ltd
	Dec. 1966	S. Russell & Sons Ltd
	June 1968	Halifax Rack & Screw Cutting Co. Ltd
John Brown	n.a.	

Source: primarily EXTEL cards

the TI machine tool division had reduced output to its 1967 pre-merger level.

The first post-merger step of TI was to begin rationalisation. To this end Churchill's Hard Metals division was closed down and Coventry Gauge's smaller production units at Baginton and Yarmouth were closed. The Churchill factory at Bedford was closed leaving only four main production units – Blaydon, Coventry, Halifax and Southampton. In 1969 the rationalisation cost £400,000 leading to a loss for the division as a whole. During 1970 this rationalisation continued – a loss making German subsidiary was sold, and the factory at Southampton closed with its work transferred to Coventry. Churchill Tools & Services business was also sold. Another £212,000 was spent on this rationalisation. The rationalisation and a downturn in business in 1970 and 1971, meant a drop in numbers employed by 20%. Also in 1971 two factories at Woolwich and Godalming closed due to rationalisation. The Hyde factory of the recently-acquired Crypton Triangle was also closed. During 1972 the Churchill Redman factory at Halifax was closed and the work transferred to Blaydon. This closure is attributed to low sales and a desire for higher productivity. A further 20% reduction in staff was achieved. As far as one can tell the only new factory built is one for Iwema of Sweden in 1975 and Blaydon and Coventry are the only two big production units that survived the previous ten years of rationalisation.

Table 5.20 *Comparisons of firm size in machine tools*

Number of largest companies	Estimated average number of persons employed by largest companies				
	UK	France	Italy	Nether-lands	Belgium
	1963	1963	1961	1962	1962
4	3,572[a]	2,095	993	270	659
8	2,955[b]	1,531	772	216	566
20	1,859	967	530	138	284
50	971[c]	580	335	80	127

[a]for 6 largest companies.
[b]for 9 largest companies.
[c]for 55 largest companies.

Number of largest establish-ments	Estimated average number of persons employed by largest establishments				
	UK	France	Italy	Nether-lands	Belgium
	1963	1963	1961	1962	1962
4	n.a.	1,135	1,429	257	653
8	n.a.	973	1,012	196	561
20	n.a.	681	619	127	281
50	464[b]	467	381	77	126

[d]An imputed figure, probably an underestimate.
Sources: UK data from *Census of Production 1963*, Report 42, Table 3, European data from L. Phlips (1971).

The success of this rationalisation programme is yet to be analysed. Our main indicator is '*K*', the measure of efficiency discussed in Chapter 4. In an ideal world we would wish to calculate *k* for pre- and post-merger periods and see how it has changed over time. Unfortunately we cannot find data on both profits and sales prior to 1967. Thus we must see whether *k*, our estimate of inputs per unit of output has fallen over time since 1968, i.e. given the rationalisation that has occurred does TI machine tool division appear to have become more efficient? Our one main advantage in this exercise is that, as with most companies with machine tool interests, TI report profit and turnover data for the machine tool division independent of the rest of the group. For input and output prices however we must rely on industry data. In Table 5.21 the relevant data and computed *k*s are presented. A cursory glance at the relative prices of output to input shows that for the period 1967–73 the industry relative price was falling, but by 1975 nearly

Table 5.21 *Estimates of unit factor requirements; Coventry Gauge, Tube Investments (machine tool division)*

Year	$\frac{P_0^*}{P_I}$	Coventry Gauge		Tube Investments		
		$\frac{\Pi}{R}$%	k†	$\frac{\Pi}{R}$%	k†	$k_{C+T}^{\dagger\S}$
1967	97.4	6.97	100.8	4.5	103.4	102.6
1968	92.2	3.94[a]	98.5	2.9	99.4	99.2
1969	89.7	—	—	−0.2[b]	100.0	—
1970	89.1	—	—	−0.6[c]	99.7	—
1971	94.5	—	—	3.5	101.4	—
1972	90.7	—	—	−1.3	102.2	—
1973	84.6	—	—	4.3	90.0	—
1974	88.3	—	—	4.4	93.9	—
1975	96.4	—	—	5.7	101.1	—

Notes
[a] covers 62 weeks.
[b] covers 17 months and includes Coventry Gauge from 1.7.69.
[c] includes special provision for expected losses on Rolls Royce's collapse.
*The weights to generate P_I are 47 : 53 wages to raw materials. Wages are average earnings of manual employees. Weights from 1968 Census of Production.
† k adjusted to set 1969 value to 100.
§ k_{C+T} is the k value for an 'as if' firm of Coventry Gauge and Tube Investment together in the pre-merger years.
Sources: EXTEL, *Trade and Industry*, and *Department of Employment Gazette.*

all the previous fall had been made up. The movement over time does not appear to indicate any abuse of market power as regards prices.

In Table 5.22 we detail k values for other firms in the industry (in each case k is set equal to 100 in 1969), and a series on total output of metal working machine tools at constant 1966 prices. The two relevant points to make are:

(1) The efficiency estimates of all firms have similar cyclical patterns, this pattern being closely related to the time distribution of output.

(2) Realising that the only difference between these k estimates is the price-cost margins of each firm, the time patterns reveal increases in efficiency 1972–73, but in general lower efficiency in 1975 than 1969. On the price–cost margin side this is reflected in the heavy losses incurred by Alfred Herbert with lesser losses by Staveley Industries. The pattern shown by Tube Investments is thus reflected in the performance of its competitors.

Our observations lead us to believe that the short-term fluctuations in capacity utilisation will affect efficiency. Moreover, we have economies of scale in the industry. Between 1967 and 1975, TI's real output has remained almost

Table 5.22 *Output of machine tools and k values for major firms (machine tool interests only)*

Year	Output of machine tools 1966 prices (£m)	*k*				
		Cincinnati Milacron	Alfred Herbert	600 Group	John Brown	Staveley Inds.
1966	164.0	—	92.0	—	—	—
1967	163.0	—	98.9	103.4	—	—
1968	160.0	96.7	98.4	99.5	102.8	101.1
1969	172.2	100.0	100.0	100.0	100.0	100.0
1970	179.2	97.8	97.3	99.3	100.2	97.0
1971	153.9	102.7	115.6	104.9	109.0	104.3
1972	128.4	99.9	112.6	106.0	106.6	101.3
1973	137.4	96.1	99.7	95.7	100.1	92.6
1974	125.5	100.3	109.8	100.7	101.9	95.7
1975	114.8	—	135.2	104.9	111.7	103.6

Source: as for Table 5.21

constant (i.e. by 1975 in real terms the effect on TI's output of the merger is zero), thus we would not expect scale to affect a comparison of *k*s between these dates, and a total improvement of 4% is indicated. But the degree of capacity utilisation may well be different between these dates. Thus between 1972 and 1973 output (and thus probably capacity utilisation) rose by 7%, but efficiency rose by 12%. If as in Figure 5.3 we plot real output (at 1966 prices) against *k*, we see that in the immediate post-merger period *k* is maintained at the pre-merger level as output falls by nearly a half (with its consequent scale effects) but the 1972–75 experience indicates small changes in output leading to large changes in *k*. All the fall in *k* is gained between 1972 and 1973, but this is soon lost in the next two years. Comparing movements in *k*s of TI against other companies does not seem to get us very far either. In total, we cannot isolate any gains that can be clearly attributed to the merger.

If we get away from estimates of *k* we can look at two other performance indicators.

(a) Research and Development and technological progressiveness. It has not been possible to generate data on R & D expenditure of TI's machine tool division but the company Chairman stresses in his reports both the importance of R & D and their success in generating new products. There are doubts however on the strength of the R & D effect which we come to below. The company did however introduce a number of technologically advanced machine tools in the early 1970s.

(b) Export performance. Here the picture is also clouded but again from the company's reports, one can gather that exports represented 31% of sales in 1974

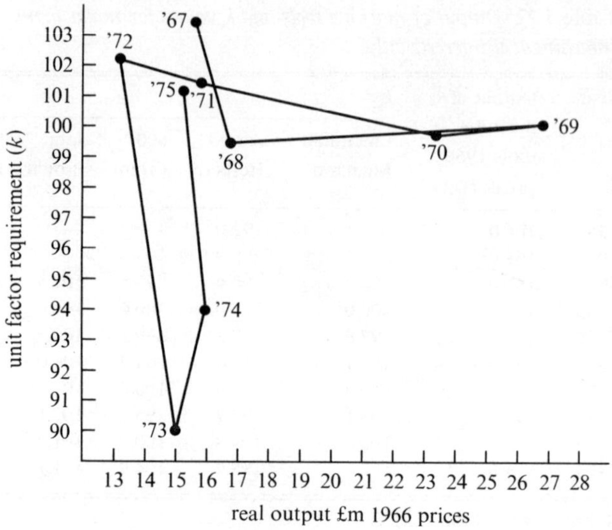

Figure 5.3 *Tube investments, unitfactor requirement* vs *real output*

but 52% of output in 1972. This is apparently a reduction over time and it would appear from Table 5.17 that 1972 was a bad year for exports for the industry as a whole. To add to this the Coventry Gauge part of TI has twice won Queen's Awards for export success.

5.6.6 The performance of the machine tool industry as a whole

In 1960 the Mitchell Report (Machine Tool Advisory Council (1960)) stated:

> We consider that as a generalisation it is safe to say that the performance of the U.K. industry in comparison with its Western competitors suffers from over concentration on the production of standard machine tools and that this accounts for its shrinking share of the increased world trade and for the high proportion of machines imported into this country.
>
> Basically this over-concentration on standard types springs in our view from the lack of a sufficiently intensive development effort.

The report considers that the 1960 level of R & D expenditure of £3m p.a. should have been increased to £8 m p.a. The Way report of 1970 indicates that there had been significant advances in the nature of machines produced in the previous decade, but the industry suffered from low capital investment and failed to expand in the 1960s. There appeared to be scope for increased output resulting from better management and improved design. They indicate that R & D as a % of

Table 5.23 *Machine tool industry R & D expenditure 1964–73*

Year	R & D carried out in private industry (£'000 current prices)	% of sales
1964/65	2,590	2.1
1966/67	5,397	3.1
1967/68	5,427	3.2
1968/69	5,246	2.7
1969/70	4,202	1.9
1972/73	1,600	0.75

Source: *Studies in Official Statistics. No. 21*, HMSO, 1974.

deliveries[30] rose from 2.1% to 3.7% in the years 1964/65–1968/69, as opposed to 1.7% to 2.3% for mechanical engineering as a whole.

To bring the picture up to date we can consider first the trade statistics in Table 5.17. Exports as a percentage of imports suffered a secular decline from 149% in 1970 to 107% in 1975 passing through 187% in 1971. There is no significant sign of improvements in export performance post the merger boom.

We do not have any data on investment in capital goods over the study period but one feels that the pattern of the 1960s was repeated. As for R & D expenditure the pattern is depressing. In Table 5.23 industry R & D expenditure is presented. Given the increase in costs over time the decline in this series would be all the more apparent in real terms. There is no sign here of increasing concentration leading to higher R & D expenditure, especially as a percentage of sales.

5.6.7 Conclusions

This industry is one suffering from continued fluctuations in sales that appear to dominate its performance. It is one where the biggest firm (Alfred Herberts) is in severe financial troubles, where R & D has fallen over time and imports gain ever more importance and where a wave of merger activity in the 1960s dramatically increased concentration. We have found, in the case of Tube Investments, rationalisation due to merger but cannot isolate any significant increases in efficiency. We have also observed an absence of efficiency improvements in other firms. It would seem apparent that size is not a cure for the industry's ills, even though scale economies would seem to exist ripe for exploitation.

To suggest a cure at the end of this investigation would be an impertinence but it would appear that a vicious circle of low profitability, low investment and low R & D needs to be broken. Further concentration does not appear to be the required policy instrument.

30 The different sources explain the non compatibility with data in Table 5.23.

5.7.1 Companies: Berger, Jenson and Nicholson and British Paints Ltd
Date: Second quarter 1969
Product: Paint

Berger, Jenson and Nicholson, one of the paint industry's five largest producers, was the product of a merger between Lewis Berger and Jenson and Nicholson in 1960. Following its acquisition of British Paints in 1969, BJN became the second largest paint producer, with only ICI Paints Division (Dulux) accounting for a higher level of paint sales. The other three large-scale producers comprise International Paints (owned by Courtaulds), Wall Paper Manufacturers (owned by Reed International) and Donald Macpherson. Altogether these five producers accounted for nearly 60% of all paint sales in 1969. Below these, seven companies accounted for about 15% of sales, with the remaining 25% being subdivided between more than 500 manufacturers of various sizes (*The Times*, 24 April 1970).

Although the company produces both industrial and marine paints, BJN are most prominent in the decorative field. In 1969 BJN earned an estimated £11 million out of a total of £17 million in sales of decorative paints (*The Times*, 24 April 1970). Following a battle between the German based chemical company, Farbwerke Hoechst and the American paint giant Sherwin-Williams, the former acquired BJN in 1970.

The historical development of the industry reveals a rapid post-war increase in concentration. At the beginning of the century the industry comprised approximately 400 small firms, the largest firm employing less than 3% of the total number employed in the paint industry. Since 1945 the growing dominance of a few large companies was fostered by several mergers and acquisitions. More recently two major waves of merger activities are discernible. Firstly, at the end of the 1950s when Pinchin Johnson was taken into the Courtaulds group and Lewis Berger merged with Jenson and Nicholson. Secondly, in the mid 1960s British Paints (later acquired by BJN) joined the American company Celanese and Wall Paper Manufacturers joined the Reed International group. All this activity has led to the existence of a fragmented industry structure, consisting of a small group of very large companies, a few medium-sized firms and a large fringe of small firms. In the decorative paint market alone the leading four firms account for more than 70% of retail sales (*Financial Times*, 10 May 1974).

5.7.2 Aspects of the paint market

Since 1958 sales of paint have grown fairly rapidly, with a boost post 1968. Up to mid 1960 the annual average was 3% growth. The level of paint imports is very low with imports (as a percentage of total UK sales) failing to reach the 3% level. In contrast the level of paint exports is fairly high, averaging about 10% of sales (1958–73) (see Table 5.24). This is a trend which has continued from

Table 5.24 *Exports and imports of paint*

Year	% of total sales	
	Exports	Imports
1958	11.6	0.6
1963	9.8	1.4
1968	10.9	2.8
1973	8.4	2.1

Sources: (i) *Annual Statement of Trade of the U.K.* (1958–1968)
(ii) *Business Monitor*
(iii) *Census of Production* 1963, 1968

the nineteenth century when British paint manufacturers supplied most of the Empire countries.[31] The value of the total output of the paint industry in 1968 was £174.6 million. Of this total exports accounted for £20.3 million, consumers (retail market) £37.5 million, and other industry (intermediate output) £112.2 million (*The Times*, 24 April 1970). Within the total of £112.2 million accounted for by other industries, the construction industry is by far the largest purchaser taking more than £50 million. The second largest 'industrial' purchaser of paint is the motor vehicles industry which accounts for £12.3 million of sales.

Since a large part of the sales to the construction industry involves direct sales from the paint manufacturer to the users – professional decorating and contracting firms as well as government and local authority buyers – large contracts are involved (*The Times*, 24 April 1970) Similarly, sales to motor vehicle manufacturers involve large contracts. All this suggests a significant level of buyer concentration facing paint manufacturers. This is counteracted to a certain extent by the paint manufacturers' ownership of many retail as well as merchanting and distributive outlets.

5.7.3 Barriers to entry in the market for paint

Although no figures for economies of scale in paint production are available, the market leaders appear to gain substantially from large-scale operations. Some economies of scale are obtained from the use of high speed stirrers and continuous sand (or bead) mills. Both are recent process innovations which, according to Armitage (1967), represent a real advance in paint-making techniques. Another source of production economies is the use of large storage tanks of up to 10,000 gallon capacity. Significant economies of increased dimen-

31 *Studies in Official Statistics No. 22* (1973, pp. 56–63), *Annual Statement of Trade of the UK, Business Monitor.*

Table 5.25 *Advertising/sales ratios for paint*

	Advertising (*A*) expenditures (£'000)	Sales (*R*) revenue (£'000)	*A/R* (%)
1963	3,048	127,303	2.4
1968	2,885	139,751	2.1
1973	4,997	250,346	2.0

Source: (i) *Statistical Review* (1963 and 1968).
(ii) Meal, *Monthly Digest* (Dec. 1975).
(iii) *Census of Production Reports* (1963 and 1968).
(iv) *Business Monitor:* Paint (1974).

Note: The figures quoted for advertising expenditure are very approximate and therefore may not coincide exactly in coverage with those for sales revenue.

sions are enjoyed by large-scale manufacturers from the use of such equipment. Other important sources of scale economies include marketing economies – bulk purchasing and distribution – as well as multi-plant economies which yield gains from the rationalisation of R & D and advertising etc.

Since the 1920s the industry has become increasingly based on scientific principles of manufacture and formulation and as Armitage stresses, the vast increase in types of paint produced requires specialist chemists and physicists for successful technical progress to be undertaken (*The Times,* 24 April 1970) Clearly only firms operating on a large-scale can afford to maintain the necessary large R & D departments. The industry's record in R & D is a good one compared with most other industries. According to Valentine most companies spend about 3% of their turnover on R & D, and on average 10% of all employees work in R & D laboratories. Although the government sponsors some of the industry's research associations, the bulk of R & D expenditure is accounted for by private industry. In 1969/70, of a total expenditure of £2.9 million, private industry accounted for £2.7 million with research associations spending the remaining £0.2 million. When the total expenditures are disaggregated by use of funds it can be seen that the bulk is spent on 'development' (HMSO (1973)). The results of these R & D outlays have largely comprised product innovations although some process innovations have also been introduced during the recent past.

Another important barrier to entry is the existence of strong brand loyalty especially in the market for decorative paints. Thus, the high level of expenditure on R & D is supplemented by heavy advertising outlays (Table 5.25). This is especially for the market leaders, for example, in 1971 the three leading decorative paint makers – ICI, BJN and Reed International (who account for more than 50% of all advertising) – together spent well over £2 million on television commercials alone. It is estimated that to launch nationwide a new decorative paint could cost well over £1 million (*Financial Times*, 20 June 1972). Together, therefore, the need for both heavy R & D and advertising expenditures creates a substantial barrier to the entry of new firms.

Finally a possible barrier to entry facing foreign paint manufacturers is the existence of fairly high import duties. These range from zero for commonwealth countries, to a maximum of either

(i) 14.4% of value, or

(ii) 7.2% of value, plus £0.225 per gallon – whichever is the greater.

Small firms can survive by supplying local contacts in the building and decorating trade. They offer a small specialised range of paints and have little need to engage in the search for new processes or products. Survival problems are greater for medium-size firms who are unable to compete with large firms. They cannot afford expensive R & D and advertising programmes, or supply the same range of products and command the same number of retail outlets nor can they rely on local contacts like smaller firms. It is perhaps for these reasons that the number of medium-size firms in the industry has fallen quite rapidly, many of them having been taken over by the largest firms. On the other hand it may simply be that medium-sized firms are more attractive takeover targets than the smallest firms.

5.7.4 **The merger and its consequences**

The merger which led to the formation of Berger, Jenson and Nicholson in 1960 seems to have been defensive in origin, possibly motivated by Courtaulds' purchase of Pinchin Johnson. At any rate, the constituent firms each went their own separate ways during the 1960s. No rationalisation seems to have taken place, and each plant made much the same product as before. This suggests that the arguments for scale economies were not really very strong. With the purchase of British Paints a critical point seems to have been reached. By this time the firm was producing nine different brands of decorative paints alone, obviously giving scope for economies in marketing by reducing the number of brands. Consequently a fairly simple scheme of rationalisation, requiring very little new investment, was carried out. No site was closed, but the production of industrial paint at Bristol was discontinued, and concentrated in Stratford, East London. The Bristol plant now specialises in decorative paints. Specialist paints (especially marine paints, and paints for the construction industry) are now produced at the Newcastle plant. This rationalisation had an impact on total employment. As Table 5.26 shows the numbers employed by BJN fell fairly sharply after the merger in 1969. By 1970 the workforce was reduced by about 8% and by 1973 the number employed had fallen by more than 20% (as compared with the 1969 level).

After its acquisition of British Paints, BJN became the centre of a takeover battle. Thus in late 1969 – early 1970, both the giant American paint company Sherwin-Williams and the large German chemical company, Farbwerke Hoechst

Table 5.26 *Berger, Jenson & Nicholson: no. of employees 1967–74*

1967	4,655	1971	4,894
1968	4,254	1972	4,488
1969	5,501	1973	4,392
1970	5,063	1974	4,561

Source: EXTEL British Co. Service (1975).

Table 5.27 *Unit factor requirement. The paint industry*

Year	$\frac{P_0}{P_I}$	Profit/ revenue % *BJN*	*Unit factor Requirement (k)* *BJN*	Craig & Rare	Blundell Permoglaze
1964	114.4				
1965	112.0				
1966	110.1				
1967	108.9	3.97	109.3	105.3	111.8
1968	105.2	4.78	104.7	101.5	107.2
1969	100.0	4.38	100.0	100.0	100.0
1970	98.4	4.37	98.4	97.0	95.0
1971	102.4	5.05	101.6	96.8	100.2
1972	104.2	6.45	101.8	95.7	98.6
1973	99.6	7.85	96.3	88.8	93.2
1974	94.0	5.95	92.4	83.7	90.1

Notes: Data are for year ending 31 December except input prices which are lagged one quarter.

Source: *Department of Employment Gazette* and EXTEL.

put in takeover bids for BJN. Eventually BJN was acquired by the German company, Hoechst, in 1970. It was suggested at the time of the takeover battle that such a move was almost inevitable in view of the price BJN paid for British Paints earlier in 1969. By enlarging the company's equity, the board's control of BJN fell to below 14% following its acquisition of British Paints. This laid BJN wide open to a takeover bid. Hoechst's acquisition of BJN appears to have been largely motivated by the possibility of gains from vertical integration. Indeed, by 1972, BJN were purchasing more than a tenth of their raw materials from their parent company Hoechst (*Financial Times*, 20 June 1972). In addition, the firm claims that there were important gains in expertise following this takeover, describing it as a 'two way traffic in technology', increasing the speed of technical development. The firm also claims that the financing of new developments is easier now than it was for the constituent firms.

Table 5.27 shows how these considerations have affected unit factor requirements according to our measurements. Unfortunately, the number of years observed is limited by the fact that published company accounts do not give sales figures before 1967. However, we do know that P_0/P_I fell by around 5% between 1964 and 1967. This was accompanied by a fall in profits from £1.69m to £1.52m so it appears that some of this came out of profits and to this extent was not due to a gain in productive efficiency. However, from 1967 the firm was able to increase output prices by less than the rise in input prices and increase profitability. The measured efficiency gain over these two years is around 9%. Following the merger, no significant gains in efficiency appear in our measurement until 1973 when there appears to be an increase in efficiency of 4% compared with the year of the merger. There is a further improvement in 1974, also of 4%.

Taking as a whole the six years following the merger, there appears to have been a smaller change in efficiency in this period than in the two years preceding the merger. If any conclusions about the merger can be drawn from these figures, it is that the merger did not produce rapid improvements in efficiency. Any efficiency effects there might have been were not felt until four years had elapsed. Moreover both the companies for which we have presented comparative estimates of k performed better over this period than BJN.

If the individual years' observations are taken literally, there were some small immediate benefits for BJN, possibly due to the rationalisation of production, but the small size of this gain is surprising, especially in view of the 8% reduction in work force achieved (see Table 5.26). The reason for this seems to be that in the paint industry labour costs are just less than 20% of total.[32] This would exactly account for the 1.6% gain between 1969 and 1970, but then we still have to explain why there was an apparent decline in efficiency in 1971 and 1972. The obvious answer seems to be that there was some dislocation following Hoechst's takeover of the company and subsequent reorganisation.

The company's profits were not affected by this decline in efficiency. Until 1970 there had been a steady downward trend in output price relative to input prices, made possible in part by increased efficiency. However, in 1971 and 1972 this price trend was reversed temporarily, enabling the firm to increase its profitability despite lessened efficiency.

5.7.5 **Conclusions**

Rapid technical progress has occurred in the paint industry in recent years with the development of ways of producing more cheaply paints that in many ways are of higher quality in terms of adhesion, ease of application, colour range, and so on. Under these conditions it is perhaps not surprising that the major contributions came out of the laboratory rather than the work study office.

32 Based on 1968 Census of Production

Changes as a direct result of merger activity seem to have played little part in the major gains made by this industry during the 1960s. Indeed, the scope for *production* economies of scale do appear to be limited, and so far BJN have not needed to close any plants. If the efficiency of research and development within the company has improved substantially as a result of the merger, the results of this improved efficiency have not had much impact on our efficiency measure to date. The only discernible impact is a temporary slowing down in the rate of efficiency improvement, and in fact a dropping behind other comparable firms.

We have already noted that the original merger which gave this company its name was purely defensive in origin, and led to no rationalisation at all. Newbould (1970) concludes that it is a common occurrence. Such mergers are unnecessary from the point of view of the economy, and would also be regarded as unnecessary by the management in a situation where mergers are more tightly controlled and the threat of takeover by hostile raider is more remote. Thus we may argue there may be many unproductive mergers purely as a consequence of a permissive merger policy.

5.8.1 Companies: Rowntree and John Mackintosh
Date: May 1969
Product: Confectionery

Confectionery is usually divided into chocolate confectionery and sugar confectionery. The two major types of confectionery have in the years immediately before and since the merger of Rowntree and Mackintosh, had reasonably constant market shares.[33] Per capita consumption in volume terms has also remained virtually static since at least 1960. Imports have risen but still take only a small proportion of the total confectionery market. Exports, however, have steadily risen during the period being considered.[34]

The Prices and Incomes Board (1968a) claimed that in 1967 the UK had the highest per capita consumption of confectionery in the world. Published data[35] shows that this was so in at least 1972 and 1973 and that in 1971 Belgium slightly led the UK in the per capita consumption of chocolate confectionery.

The UK confectionery market in the period before the merger (1960–69) may be described as large but static with respect to both the level of demand and to how demand was distributed amongst the major categories of confectionery. From this one might conclude that the only scope for an individual company to expand would be through:

(a) intensive marketing to increase brand shares;
(b) diversification;
(c) increasing export sales and production abroad;
(d) merger.

33, 34, 35. The Cocoa Chocolate and Confectionery Alliance *Annual Reports*.

5.8.2 Concentration in confectionery

The production of chocolate is much more highly concentrated than that of sugar confectionery. This can be seen from Table 5.28 to have been the case at least from 1961 to 1972. Published data do not allow it to be established whether since then conditions have markedly changed, though data in *Mintel*[36] suggests that in 1973 the three[37] firm concentration ratio in chocolate production was 78% and in sugar-confectionery production was 35% whilst the *IPC Marketing Manual* shows that between 1969 and 1973 'major user' demand was relatively more concentrated in the markets for the major types of chocolates than in those for most types of sugar confectionery. Table 5.28 also shows that concentration in both chocolate and sugar confectionery has been increasing with that for the latter displaying the bigger increase.

5.8.3 The companies in confectionery

Other than operating in the same industrial sector Rowntree and Mackintosh were similar in two important respects:

(i) The marketing policies of both companies were heavily biased towards the promotion of brand-names rather than the names of their companies. The principal brands of each are given in Table 5.29 and it will be noticed that their names do not usually include those of their manufacturers (the major exception is Rowntree's Fruit Gums and Mackintosh's Toffees).

This should be contrasted with products produced by Cadbury which tend to contain 'Cadbury's' in their name.

(ii) The companies had a similar ethos which was to some extent a result of the low-church – the Rowntree family being Quaker and the Mackintosh family Methodist – and apparently deeply held religious beliefs of their original founders.

The merger of Rowntree and Mackintosh brought together the second and fourth largest UK confectionery producers. At the time of the merger, according to *Retail Business*, Cadbury had an estimated 25% share of the market, Rowntree, 16%, the American-owned Mars, 14% and Mackintosh, 7%. The statistics, however, conceal the considerable variation in the shares these, and other companies, held of particular types of confectionery: in 1965 Cadbury dominated the chocolate bar and milk chocolate assortments, Rowntree, plain-chocolate assortments and fruit-gums, Mackintosh the 'twist' wraps and toffees (with Sharps), Mars the filled 'countline' bars and Bassetts, liquorice. The potential for the exploitation of market-power offered by the merger to a large extent depended

36 Mintel – *Market Intelligence Reports.*

37 The four firm concentration ratio, for sugar confectionery, as given by Mintel, was 41%. It does not give sufficient information to calculate a similar statistic for chocolate but *Retail Business* suggests it would have been 80%.

Table 5.28 *Concentration in UK production of confectionery for home market 1961–72; proportion of volume produced by largest firms*

	Largest firms								
	4	10	15	20	25	30	40	50	100
1961									
Chocolate	78.4	84.2	*N/A*	*N/A*	*N/A*	*N/A*	*N/A*	*N/A*	*N/A*
Sugar confectionery	15.1	35.8							
Total	46.9	60.1							
1963									
Chocolate	—	85.6	89.6	92.4	93.8	95.0	96.7	97.4	98.7
Sugar confectionery	—	41.0	49.9	57.3	63.5	68.3	75.8	81.8	91.2
Total	—	58.6	64.4	69.1	73.1	76.7	82.2	86.2	94.3
1966									
Chocolate	—	89.2	92.8	94.7	96.3	97.3	98.6	98.8	99.4
Sugar confectionery	—	42.4	51.9	60.1	66.0	70.8	77.5	82.4	91.8
Total	—	62.3	68.5	73.3	77.3	80.7	85.6	88.8	96.6
1967									
Chocolate	79.5	85.4	*N/A*	*N/A*	*N/A*	*N/A*	*N/A*	*N/A*	*N/A*
Sugar confectionery	22.5	45.9							
Total	54.1	67.8							
1969									
Chocolate	—	90.8	93.5	95.5	96.8	97.6	98.7	98.8	99.4
Sugar confectionery	—	49.1	58.8	65.5	71.3	75.6	82.4	87.1	94.4
Total	—	64.9	72.2	77.3	80.8	83.7	88.0	90.9	96.4
1972									
Chocolate	—	94.2	96.5	97.9	98.7	99.1	99.3	99.5	99.9
Sugar confectionery	—	59.3	68.4	74.7	79.0	82.7	87.9	91.2	95.0
Total	—	73.9	79.1	83.1	86.0	88.1	91.2	93.2	97.0

Source: *NBPI* (1968a) for 1961 and 1967; Cocoa and Chocolate Confectionery Alliance *Annual Reports* for remaining years.

Table 5.29 *Principal brands of Rowntree and Mackintosh*

Rowntree:	Kit Kat	Mackintosh:	Quality Street
	Black Magic		Rolo
	Smarties		Toffo
	After Eight		Weekend
	Aero		Toffee Crisp
	Dairy Box		Good News
	Walnut Whips		Fox's Glacier Mints
	Fruit Gums		Tooty Fruities
	Pastilles		Caramac
	Polo		
	Jelly Tots		

Source: Company Reports.

on the cross-elasticity between the products of Rowntree and Mackintosh. It will be noticed that Rowntree placed greater emphasis on chocolate confectionery and Mackintosh on sugar confectionery. It is hard to believe that there is no significant cross elasticity of demand for any two types of confectionery, regardless of whether one is a sugar confectionery and the other is chocolate, despite the claims by D. J. Barron (Chairman of Rowntree at the time of the merger) that there was virtually no overlapping between the markets in which their brands were sold (*Financial Times*, 3 April 1969).

5.8.4. **Background to the merger of Rowntree and Mackintosh**

Prior to the merger of Rowntree and Mackintosh in 1969 the confectionery industry had already seen the merger of Cadbury and Schweppes. We also have reason to believe that a number of suitors had been wooing Rowntree before their merger with Mackintosh. Thus, for example, General Foods made an attempt to take over Rowntree, apparently attracted by possible economies in joint promotions and purchasing (*Financial Times*, 10 June 1969). Rowntree Mackintosh deny emphatically that any such economies were available. The takeover was never realised.[38]

This General Foods bid came on the heels of interest shown by Cadbury in Rowntree (*Financial Times*, 11 June 1969). No formal bid was ever made and no merger took place.

We had an interview with senior managers from Rowntree Mackintosh, from which we gained the impression that discussions on an informal, low-key level had been held for some time about the possibility of merging Rowntree and Mackintosh and this confirms what Barron had said in a press interview held just before the merger took place (*Financial Times*, 3 April 1969). They denied in this interview, and in correspondence since, that the presence of other suitors for Rowntree or the bid by General Foods had any influence on the decision to merge. Nor do they agree that the possible enhancement of Cadbury's marketing ability arising from its merger with Schweppes was any spur to the merger process. We did consider that the merger, by increasing their size, could have made Rowntree less vulnerable to takeover by unwanted suitors. They deny this, however, arguing that a merger with another company, reducing the control formerly held by the Rowntree family charitable trusts could increase vulnerability to take over and a relatively minor increase in size of one third, arising from the merger with Mackintosh, could not deter any of the two dozen or more potentially 'predatory' giants like General Foods.

5.8.5 **Reasons for the merger of Rowntree and Mackintosh**

The evidence would strongly suggest that the expected gains from the merger were almost solely in marketing. This point was made in discussions

38 It should be noted that Rowntree employees, as reported in the Merger Panel report, opposed the merger.

with senior managers from Rowntree Mackintosh. Some of the views expressed then might be summed up by comments in a press report soon after the merger:

> One of the advantages of bringing Rowntree and Mackintosh together has been the formation of a group with expertise in every art of the confectioner from chocolate and toffee to chewing gum – and liquorice. This gives flexibility in responding to public taste, but what is probably more important, a full range of techniques for the development of new products.

The objective of achieving marketing economies does not preclude the possibility that it was also hoped that production-economies would arise. In Mackintosh's offer to shareholders the expected gains would come from 'the greater selling power and increased range of outlets provided by the merger, and improved sales in South Africa, Canada, Ireland,[39] Australia, New Zealand and and E.E.C.' 'Additional savings' would be possible in transport, distribution, purchasing, production and research and development in the medium term, and 'considerable other benefits', in the short term in marketing and selling. However one might expect on *a priori* grounds that companies which are reliant on a large number of brands would enjoy only limited gains to production from integration; e.g. where machines are specific to particular brands, and where the number of brands is not reduced post merger it is hard to see how capital scale economies can indeed be achieved, although it has been put to us by Rowntree Mackintosh that much of the machinery in the industry is non-specific. It should be noted that some capital economies were suggested by the findings of the NBPI report (1968a) which showed that whilst tons of confectionery per employee of the four largest firms was 21.8 and that of the next six largest was 19.7, investment per ton was £83.7 in the former but £99.4 in the latter. An inverted '*U*' shaped direct production cost (edible material, packaging and direct labour) curve is suggested by lines selling over 7,000 tons having such costs per ton of £205, 5,000–7,000 tons, £229, 2,000–5,000, £224, under 2,000 tons, £188.

5.8.6 The effects of the merger on Rowntree and Mackintosh

In Section 5.8.7 the change in the unit factor requirement of Rowntree and Mackintosh from the merger will be discussed. Here we focus on other effects of the merger. The impression gained through discussions with managers from Rowntree Mackintosh is that gains were largely of the sort anticipated before the merger. They emphasised that there had been no redundancies as a result of the merger and that the bulk of the gains had been to marketing. To some extent the latter represented conventional savings. Mackintosh did not apparently have a market-research department and was able to take advantage of excess capacity in Rowntree's. Some economies in specialist machinery for distribution had also

39 They already had a joint company in Ireland.

been possible. The major gains had, however, been derived from supplying a broader range of products than was the case for either company individually before the merger. The managers were, understandably, vague about the precise way this might be of benefit but we inferred that it would be analogous to the broadening of an investment portfolio into income-earners which would be most profitable at different stages of the trade-cycle, though in this case the hedge would be against fluctuations in consumer demand for particular products rather than macro-cycles. As was indicated above, such changes, if any, in consumer taste for confectionery that have recently taken place would appear to have been limited to within, rather than between, the major categories.

This impression as to the advantages to marketing which was gained from the said discussions is borne-out by newspaper articles appearing since the merger (e.g. *Financial Times*, 9 Nov. 1970) which stress the broad base of brands now offered by the combined company. Very little is said about economies in areas other than marketing. Significantly, a gain from Rowntree taking advantage of a new product, Junglies, initially developed by Mackintosh, was only effective because of the former's expertise in marketing pastilles and gum.

It is not easy to evaluate the advantages to marketing from the merger because of the obvious problems of estimating the counter factual. The shares of the chocolate market enjoyed by Cadbury and Rowntree Mackintosh in 1973 were 35% and 26% respectively, compared to 40% and 24%–27% (of Rowntree and Mackintosh combined) in 1967. Mars had increased its share from 7% to 18%. Therefore, at best the merger would appear to have allowed Rowntree and Mackintosh to have maintained their market shares with the successful challenge to Cadbury's dominance being mounted by Mars. Rowntree Mackintosh were the largest producers of sugar confectionery in 1973 with 17% of the market (*Mintel*), compared to Basset's 10% and Trebor-Sharpe's 8.5%, but it has not proved possible to establish market shares for earlier years.

As was suggested in Section 5.8.1, given the static nature of the UK confectionery market one might expect British manufacturers to attempt to expand their sales to overseas markets and it would certainly appear that this has been the policy of Rowntree Mackintosh. Since its inception the company has been talking about its plans, for instance to expand its organisation in Belgium (*Financial Times*, 6 May 1970) and its factory in Hamburg (*Financial Times*, 13 May 1970). This strategy would appear to have been successful as company reports show the proportion of sales represented by sales to overseas customers to have risen from 31% in 1969 to 45% in 1975 with a rise to other EEC members from 8% of total sales to 21%. This does not necessarily reflect the proportions of profits earned in overseas markets but according to K. Haslinger, Rowntree Mackintosh's then Chairman of their European Division, in 1970 sales to EEC members had become profitable only within the last two years, so that at least an increase in profitability of overseas sales had occurred.

Table 5.30 *Indices of confectionery exports (including sales of overseas subsidiaries) by company (current prices)*

Year	Rowntree Mackintosh	Needlers	Maynards	Cadbury[a]	Bassets	Mars[c]	Jamesons
1967	*n.a.*	79	72	*n.a.*	77	*n.a.*	*n.a.*
1968	83	102	83	89	92	*n.a.*	82
1969	100	100	100	100	100	100	100
1970	119	271	126	105	116	113	215
1971	138	263	185	106	120	133	294
1972	156	223	198	119	136	141[b]	573
1973	180	257	207	141	155	325	723
1974	238	357	278	267	191	*n.a.*	1,238
1975	284	305	511	239	275	*n.a.*	1,776

[a]Includes exports by Schweppes.
[b]In 1971 the accounting year was changed from 31 July to 31 December. No account has been taken on figures for 31 July–31 December.
[c]Mars is diversified into products outside confectionery.

A guide to what Rowntree and Mackintosh's export performance might have been had they not merged can be gleaned from that of other confectionery producers. Data on confectionery exports are detailed in Table 5.30.

The comparisons made will depend on the base years chosen. The 1969 base seems appropriate for comparing pre and post merger performance. Since the merger Rowntree Mackintosh exports have grown faster than Cadbury's (since 1974 the Cadbury figures include Schweppes exports). We only have data to 1973 for the other large company, Mars. It outperformed RM for those years but its figures include nonconfectionery products. The ranking of the large companies is thus open to doubt. Of the smaller companies, Bassett's exports grew more slowly than RM's, while those of Needlers, Maynards and Jamesons grew faster. However, Jamesons started from a very low base. Perhaps the fairest conclusion is that exports have shown extensive growth in the period covered, but there is no obvious indication that the merger has led RM to a performance that differs significantly from the industry average.

5.8.7. The change in unit factor requirements (k) for Rowntree Mackintosh

Sales and profit data has been published separately for Rowntree Mackintosh and Mackintosh since their merger and it is therefore possible to assess how the merger has affected the unit factor requirements of each of the partners. Prior to the merger Rowntree showed a rather more rapid improvement in efficiency than did Mackintosh but subsequent to merger both show a similar experience until 1974. Unit factor requirements for Rowntree Mackintosh showed an increase in the two years following merger but subsequently declined quite rapidly. For comparison we have included information on four other firms involved in the chocolate and sugar confectionery industry.[39a] Our results indicate that the increase in efficiency for Rowntree Mackintosh subsequent to merger was at least as good as that of other firms in the industry over the period in question. The apparent temporary reduction in efficiency in 1970/71 appears in the case of all the firms we have looked at and cannot therefore be assumed to indicate any transition costs associated with the merger.

5.8.8 Conclusions

The confectionery industry is large but stable as far as demand is distributed between major categories. This has led to fierce competition and confectioners are heavily orientated towards marketing. The gain to marketing was the principal reason for the Rowntree Mackintosh merger. Our results suggest that this merger has not involved any significant transition costs and efficiency gains have been at least as good as for comparable non-merging firms.

5.9.1 Companies: H. & R. Johnson and Richards Campbell Co. Ltd
Date: March 1968
Product: Glazed ceramic wall and floor tiles.

Glazed tiles[40] are listed in the Census of Production as being a sub-group of sub-division 21 of the pottery industry, which is classified as *MLH* 462 of the Standard Industrial Classification. All sections of the pottery industry are concerned with the forming, firing, decoration and glazing of clay, but the glazed tile section has some special characteristics which make it seem more suitable for production-line methods than domestic pottery. Gay and Smyth (1974) also claim that 'the manufacture of tiles dispenses with most traditional pottery skills and this encourages dispersion'. Hence the tile industry in Britain is less concentrated geographically than domestic pottery or sanitary ware.

Most of the kilns used for firing are tunnel kilns, through which tiles can be transported in a continuous process, each tile receiving the correct pattern of

39*a* We have in fact constructed indexes for all publicly quoted companies which we considered comparable in terms of their range of products. Given that the pattern of k values was very similar in all cases we have just reported our results for four of the firms. Except for Mars, which is itself quite diversified, all the companies are rather small in comparison with Rowntree Mackintosh. Ideally we would have wished to make comparisons with Cadbury, the other confectionery giant, but this is rendered impossible by the lack of data on their confectionery activities over this period.

40 We wish to thank those people in the industry who helped us with information for this report. Much of our background is drawn from Gay and Smyth (1974).

Table 5.31 *Unit factor requirement of UK confectioners*

Year	$\frac{P_0}{P_I}$	Unit factor requirement						
		John Mackintosh	Rowntree	Rowntre Mackintosh	Barker & Dobson	Jamesons Chocolates	Needlers	Mars
1963	100.0	103.1	107.6	—	109.1	—	—	—
1964	98.1	103.9	107.4	—	107.2	—	—	—
1965	99.6	105.1	108.0	—	106.1	—	—	—
1966	95.6	100.8	104.5	—	101.4	—	—	—
1967	95.1	102.6	105.1	—	101.9	—	99.4	—
1968	93.2	100.6	101.4	—	101.4	102.1	100.1	101.7
1969	91.6	100.0	—	100.0	100.0	100.0	100.0	100.0
1970	96.4	105.9	—	105.8	106.4	105.8	113.2	105.7
1971	97.0	104.4	—	105.0	105.8	101.7	110.0	106.3[a]
1972	93.5	99.8	—	100.7	100.5	96.6	104.8	99.5
1973	79.3	86.4	—	85.3	85.5	82.3	89.0	87.0
1974	79.5	89.1	—	84.7	86.6	87.6	90.9	—

[a] Accounting year changed in 1971: *k*. for July–December = 102.3.

temperature variation in the firing cycle, without the need for heating and then cooling the entire kilns. Tunnel kilns are large pieces of equipment and not very flexible, and so modern, efficiently designed, intermittent kilns also have their part to play.

Compared with the size of the industry, economies of scale in the production process are not very significant. Gay and Smyth, for instance, say that there are no fixed items of plant that would give rise to economies of scale provided a minimum size is achieved, but some marketing, commercial and financial economies are available. Large factories tend to operate a number of tunnel ovens, and the subject of this report, which is the dominant firm, operates a number of factories in nearly all stages of production.

The Italian tiling industry, which has a much less concentrated[41] structure than the British, dominates the world's production of tiles. In 1975 the major tile producing area had 257 factories with 27,000 employees. Almost half the employees work in factories concerned with decoration and glazing only. Of those, only seven per cent are in factories of over 200, and 47% are in factories of less than 100. The factories with the biggest 'productive efficiency' (measured as output per head) were those with factories with between 100 and 200 employees.[42] Even the theoretical productive efficiency does not seem to increase much beyond 200 employees.[43] This contrasts with over 4,000 employees in H. & R. Johnson—Richards Ltd, UK operations.

Whatever the size of the various possible economies of large size it is the installation of the most efficient productive processes which is crucial to economic efficiency in this industry, as, indeed, in many others (Salter (1960)). Many of the family firms in the pottery industry have disappeared because they were not suited to a climate of rapid technological change, requiring the adoption of new skills and technical knowledge on the part of management, and changes in the organisation of the firm.

The major firms in the tile industry that survived to the 1960s were all, by and large, adaptable in this sense. Some of the improvements in technology which occurred were pioneered by suppliers of raw materials and machinery to the

41 Market concentration that is – geographical concentration is quite high. Over 70% of output is produced in the District of Sassualo, in the region of Emilia–Romagna. Much of the passage that follows is based on 'The Ceramic District – Today and Tomorrow' produced by the Rotary Club of Sassudo–Casalgrande. Translation (mimeo) from the Italian by Mr R. Shipley to whom we are very grateful.

42 Ibid, Table 8.

43 Ibid. Table 9. Figures based on 'theses of Drs. Cervi and Canotti'. Theoretical output per head is $6\frac{1}{2}$% higher in the largest size category than in the under 200 employees range. This figure is likely to be biased upwards as a measure of *economic* efficiency because of the greater ratio of capital to manpower in larger factories.

industry, but the market leaders of the 1960s had themselves been involved in technical improvements, especially H. & R. Johnson Ltd. For example:

(a) A major innovation was the addition of limestone to china clay which resulted in tiles with much more accurate dimensions. This, together with the introduction of lugs for spacing, led eventually to the growth of the do-it-yourself market, since less skill is needed to fix an accurately made tile with built in spacers.

(b) The discovery that tiles could be made only 5/32 in. thick instead of 3/8 in. (a reduction of over 50%) meant a saving in raw materials and fuel, reduced firing times, easier packaging and reduced transport costs.

(c) Another innovation with important ramifications was the development of standardised colours, making it possible to match tiles produced in different batches. This enabled stockists to carry smaller inventories in the knowledge that colours could be matched in fresh purchases of stock.

As well as these industry-specific technical innovations, H. & R. Johnson was a firm noted for the introduction of well-tried mechanical methods (such as overhead conveyors, for instance) from other industries, for the first time in the pottery industry. As we shall see, the introduction of such best-practice techniques can have a more dramatic effect on efficiency than static gains in economies of scale.

5.9.2 The evolution of market structure in the tile industry

In 1935 there were 50 firms in Britain producing glazed wall and floor tiles. By 1958 this number had fallen to 25, by 1963 to 18 and in 1970 there were 14 firms. Only eight firms were making glazed wall and fireplace tiles in 1975, and there was some overlap with the seven firms producing unglazed floor tiles.[44] Johnson–Richards now probably have about 60% of the market, with much of the rest going to Pilkington's. At the time of the merger between H. & R. Johnson and Richards Campbell the market share of H. & R. Johnson was reckoned to be 33% and of Richards Campbell 23%. This merger was one of many in the glazed tile industry in the 1960s. Richards Campbell itself was the outcome of a merger in 1964 between Richards Tiles Ltd and the Campbell Tile Company. Pilkington's Tiles took over Carter Tiles Ltd and itself later became part of a conglomerate firm, Thomas Tilling Ltd; H. & R. Johnson acquired an interest in and subsequently bought out Malkin Tiles (Burslem) Ltd.

Meanwhile, however, some new entry did occur. Polycell, a subsidiary of Reed International started marketing plain tiles made, using a different process, by a separate firm. The latter firm has since ceased production. In addition, import penetration has increased significantly in recent years (see Table 5.32). However,

44 Business Monitor Report *Pottery*, 4th quarter, 1975

Table 5.32 *Imports of glazed wall and fireplace tiles*

Year	Imports as a % of home consumption
1968	4.2
1971	4.2
1972	6.9
1973	10.4
1974	14.0
1975	12.1

Source: Business Monitor Reports. 1975 figures subject to later revision.

these imports seem to be mainly high-priced decorative tiles, and there does not seem to be any real challenge to the major domestic producers in the biggest section of the market which is plain tiles at the bottom end of the price range.

Imports from such countries as USA and Japan have to bear an import duty of at least 17.4%; tiles from Common Market countries bear the EEC rate which is about 3% of value. Some of the strongest foreign competition comes from Italian industry, whose prices are somewhat higher in Britain than home-produced brands, but which offers a wider range of designs.

Entry barriers are probably greatest in the market for plain white or cream tiles, where product differentiation is minimal, and where a new entrant would have to offer a lower price to gain a reasonable market share. Most barriers to entry probably arise at the marketing stage in persuading retailers to stock the product rather than at the production stage. Entry barriers created by expenditure on advertising do not appear to be a problem.

5.9.3 **Price behaviour in glazed tiles**

The glazed tile industry is unusual in that it has been permitted by the Restrictive Practices Court to maintain an agreement on prices. They managed to achieve this by tying it in with an agreement limiting the range of tile sizes offered for sale, thus eliminating 'wasteful competition'. A high price penalty was levied on non-standard tiles. Industry discipline is aided by the high degree of concentration and the absence of low-priced imports or major cost differences.

The dominant figure in these agreements, Derek Johnson, does not appear to believe in short-run monopolistic profit-maximisation. For example, in one annual report he said: 'The establishment and maintenance of a substantial export trade depends, not on extracting the maximum yield in a period of short supply, but on establishing sound distribution, setting price levels which take full account of worldwide competition, and backing these up by first-class quality

Table 5.33 *Production costs and selling prices of tiles*

Italy	Average 1971	Dec. 1973	March 1974	June 1974	Sept. 1974	Dec. 1974	March 1975	May 1975
Production costs	72.3	100	115.5	122.6	141.8	141.3	145.1	147.7
Prices	70.2	100	111	125	134	119	111	109

and service.' The price of British tiles does, indeed, show stability through the trade cycle (although there have been some price rises in recent years which can be attributed to cost inflation). Table 5.33 shows the selling prices of tiles in Italy for 1971–75. In Britain tile prices do not tend to decline during a recession. Economists disagree on the desirability of such stability as seen in the UK; on the one hand it helps to keep firms viable in a recession and mitigates macro-economic effects, but on the other hand it may lead to some misallocation of resources in the short run.

Apart from the stability of the industry price, what about its level? The industry has been prevented from introducing the increases it would have liked by the Price Commission, so that for the year ending March 1975 the ratio of profits to sales fell to 8.44%. The figure aimed at seems to be 15% of sales if we look at what H. & R. Johnson were achieving before the merger took place in 1968, and again in 1973 and 1974 when the company had settled down following the reorganisation which took place after the merger.

A comparison with the other large firm, Pilkington's Tiles Ltd (Tables 5.34 and 5.35) indicates that the latter was making a poorer showing. Since selling prices are the same, and we can assume that both firms paid the same prices for inputs it appears that before 1968 Johnson's were more efficient than Pilkington's. This is partly because of the problems Pilkington's had following the merger with Carter Tiles Ltd in 1965. Gay and Smyth say that Mr A. N. Smith, the Managing Director of Pilkington's, pressed through a rationalisation programme when by the end of 1965 it was clear that something needed to be done. They comment that a merger 'takes a long time to bear fruit in this industry'. This fruit can perhaps been seen in the post 1970 gain in profitability on sales, by which time Pilkington's were part of a conglomerate. Their return on capital started creeping back up in 1968.

What can we conclude about the pricing policy of the industry? Although a target of 15% return on sales looks plausible when looking at H. & R. Johnson, it must be remembered that the price is set in a cartel arrangement, so it is alternatively possible that price is set so as to enable the least efficient firm to barely make a profit, extra profits going to Johnson's because of their greater efficiency. The exact rationale of the price is probably not straightforward, but it was such as

Table 5.34 *Ratio of net profit before tax to sales: glazed tiles*

	H. & R. Johnson[a] Ltd (year ended 31 March)			Pilkington's Tiles[b] (year ended 30 Sept.)	
Year	Sales (£m)	Profit before tax (£m)	Profit/revenue %	Year	Profit/ revenue %
1965	6.0	0.94	15.64		
66	6.6	1.09	16.58		
67	7.0	0.98	13.92	1967	4.64
68	8.4	1.23	14.60	68	5.80
69	15.8	1.35	8.56	69	8.33
70	16.9	1.07	6.31	70	8.14
71	18.0	1.66	9.17	71	10.81
72	21.1	1.92	9.12	72	11.19
73	26.9	4.32	16.06	73	11.00
74	33.2	4.69	14.14	74	8.40
75	36.0	3.04	8.44		

[a] Includes results of wholly-owned subsidiaries and after 1968 refers to H. & R. Johnson-Richards Ltd.
[b] After 1970 refers to tile and pottery division of Thomas Tilling Ltd which seems to coincide with the former Pilkington's Tiles (including Poole Pottery).

to give Johnson's a generous rate of return on capital and, incidentally, to make the less efficient firm ripe for takeovers.

These remarks should not be taken to imply that Richards Campbell were technologically backward. As one of the survivors to the 1960s, and taker-over of other firms, they were obviously not just a traditional pottery firm. They are reputed to have had some capable management, most of which is with the present company, and at the time of the merger they were attempting to introduce a 'once-fired' process which would eliminate a lot of the warehousing, organisation and handling costs involved in the traditional process.

5.9.4 The Johnson–Richards Campbell merger and its aftermath

Table 5.35 shows that, as far as the shareholders in Johnson's were concerned, there were no immediate benefits. Indeed, they had to wait five years before the firm regained its pre-merger level of profitability. The Chairman attributed this to the upheaval caused by the reorganisation of the enlarged group. Even in his 1968 report, he did not anticipate the benefits of the merger to be reaped before 1970.[45] Not only was there reorganisation following the merger, but there was also substantial new capital investment. In the period following the

45 Most of this section is based on the Chairman's statement in the company report.

Table 5.35 *Rate of return on capital employed: glazed tiles*

	H. & R. Johnson[a]		Richards Campbell[b]		Pilkington's	
Year	(31 March) Capital employed (£m)	Rate of return (%)	(31 Dec.) Capital employed (£m)	Rate of return (%)	(30 Sept.) Capital employed (£m)	Rate of return (%)[c]
1961	2.62	27.0	1.38	13.0	1.04	15.4
62	2.79	25.5	1.43	10.6	0.96	16.9
63	3.17	16.5	1.46	10.5	1.06	18.3
64	3.57	20.8	5.16	12.8	1.26	19.6
65	3.91	25.2	5.66	6.7	1.65	25.2
66	5.01	23.3	6.14	7.9	3.47	8.9
67	5.71	18.6	7.52	6.1	3.88	8.5
68	6.29	21.1			3.88	10.7
69	6.94	9.6	merged with		3.99	15.0
70	15.56	8.9	H. & R. Johnson		3.97	15.4
71	15.36	12.4				
72	15.16	13.7				
73	118.84	26.7				
74	20.27	23.5				
75	24.18	14.7				

[a] Including Richards Campbell from 1968 onwards.
[b] Figures refer to Campbell Tile Co. prior to 1964, when Richards Tiles Ltd was acquired.
[c] Figures not available for after 1970 because takeover by Thomas Tilling led to disappearance of separate asset figures for Pilkington's tiles.

merger £2½m was spent. A large new biscuit tunnel kiln, a spray drier for the production of clay dust and two new glost kilns were installed. Furthermore, seventeen tunnel kilns and their ancillary production lines were converted to completely new methods of operation. Given accountants' conventions in writing off investments this would tend to result in lower levels of profits being reported for these years in any case, but there does seem to have been some disruption to the firm. The Chairman's report of 1969 mentions problems of forecasting demand following rationalisation; until 1970 the firm was unable to meet all its demand. The major scope for rationalisation abroad was in Greece, in the sales force, and in the entire operation in Australia. Gay and Smyth say of the merger that it 'quickly produced rèsults. Production was concentrated in the best plants and old ones were eliminated. A new corporate image quickly appeared and the sales forces of the two firms were amalgamated. The contrast is marked with some of the mergers in the industry where rationalisation was achieved, if at all, only gradually.'

Of their labour relations Gay and Smyth say that a system of regular consultations appears to have developed more rapidly than elsewhere. According to people who know the industry, the redundancies that occurred appear to have taken

Table 5.36 *Johnson-Richards Workforce*

Year ending 31 March	H. & R. Johnson-Richards Ltd average no. of UK employees	Output per man deflated by price index of output at 1963 prices (£)
1968	1,979	3,556
1969	4,756	2,781
1970	4,471	3,164
1971	3,941	3,467
1972	4,243	3,101
1973	4,463	3,497
1974	4,533	4,067
1975	4,651	4,022

Source: EXTEL cards.

place humanely and amicably. Full discussions were held beforehand between management and the workforce. The extent to which the workforce has been trimmed can be roughly gauged by reference to Table 5.36.

The change from 1968 to 1969 is affected largely by the merger between Johnson's and Richards Campbell and also by the smaller takeover of Malkin Tiles Ltd. Some of the redundancies in 1970–71 can be attributed to shortage of demand and were temporary. The increase in gross value of output per man, although deflated by a price index for tiles, does not take into account the shift from plain to the more expensive decorative tiles, and so may be an overestimate of the productivity increase in physical terms. The drop in output per man from 1968 to 1969 is a combination of the effect of averaging Johnson and Richards/Campbell productivity, and the disruption caused by reorganisation.

A more satisfactory measure of the change in efficiency is, we believe, our measure of the unit factor requirement (k). Some of the elements for calculating this and the resultant values are given in Table 5.37. It can be seen that some of the reason for the decline in profitability in the years immediately following the merger was the failure to raise output prices in line with the rise in input prices. Some of this lost ground was eventually regained in 1972, and, judging by our calculated values for k, the firm appears to have also made up the lost ground by becoming more efficient. The observation for 1972 was heavily influenced by the coal strike in which the firm's British production facilities were shut down for $3\frac{1}{2}$ weeks and £800,000 output was lost. This represents 3.8% of the firm's output for the year. Another problem with the figure for this year is the fact that a large increase in price occurred during the year. Unfortunately our price index is based on annual observations (collected in August or September). If the price rise was

Table 5.37 *Unit factor requirement: glazed tiles*

Year ended March 31	Output price index[a] P_0	Input price index P_I	$P_0/P_I \times 100$	Unit factor requirement (k) Johnson-Richards	Pilkingtons Tiles[c]
1964	87.0	85.6	101.6	—[b]	
1965	87.0	89.6	97.0	95.8	
1966	93.0	93.9	99.0	96.7	
1967	98.0	96.8	101.2	102.0	
1968	100.0	100.0	100.0	100.0	100.0
1969	100.0	105.6	94.6	101.3	92.8
1970	100.0	112.5	88.9	97.5	86.1
1971	104.8	123.7	84.7	90.1	80.1
1972	133.7	135.5	98.9	105.2	92.8
1973	143.9	148.0	97.2	95.5	91.4
1974	150.3	167.5	89.7	90.2	84.3
1975	160.7	201.6	79.7	84.5	84.6

[a] Source: *Kelly's Guide to Building Materials*, various years, trade prices from wholesalers.
[b] Ratio of profits to sales not published. If a figure of 15% is assumed $k = 100.9$. From 1968 includes Richards Campbell.
[c] 1968 set to 100 for comparison purposes.

Mean values of k:				
(Johnson-Richards)	1965–68	$\bar{k} = 98.63$	1971, 1973–75	$\bar{k} = 90.08$
	1969–75	$\bar{k} = 94.90$	1969–71, 73–74	$\bar{k} = 93.2$
	1970, 71, 73, 74	$\bar{k} = 93.33$	1970, 71, 73–75	$\bar{k} = 91.6$

not in force for the whole year our price index is biased upwards. In addition, export prices may not have increased by as much. There is evidence from the Chairman's report that prices in Australia had to be reduced during this financial year because of increased competition. For these reasons the figure for 1972 is probably best regarded as an aberration. The decline in P_0/P_I for 1974 and 1975 is not entirely of Johnson-Richard's own volition. The Chairman complains that price increases were held down by the Price Commission.

Inspection of Table 5.37 reveals that we have some reason to believe that an increase in efficiency has occurred since the merger. If we simply compare the figure for 1968 with the latest available, an increase of efficiency of 15% could be claimed. This is even slightly greater than the increase in labour productivity given in Table 5.36. This is unexpected. It may be that, because of the intervention of the Price Commission, export prices have risen substantially faster than domestic prices. (The ratio of exports (from Britain) to total revenue is around 20%.) It is also logically possible, though not very likely, that the bulk of profits comes increasingly from the firm's overseas operations. This would tend to lead to some exaggeration in the measured efficiency increase. We do not believe however, that this could amount to a measured gain of more than one or two per cent.[46]

Given the substantial amount of investment that has taken place some of the fall in k might be due to substitution of capital for other inputs rather than, for instance, embodied technical progress. To test this proposition we calculated the ratio of net capital to sales for the years 1969–77. This figure showed a fairly steady decline from 0.80 to 0.62. This trend is biased downwards because the capital measure is based on historic cost whilst sales are in current terms. When inflation is accelerating this will produce a fall in the measured ratio even if the true ratio is constant. Taking into account the growth of the firm and the path of prices the fall in the measured capital output ratio seems consistent with a fairly constant real capital intensity.

Considering the type of bias that can creep in when measuring k it seems reasonable to regard 15% as an absolute upper limit of the efficiency gain in the years following the merger; if we ignore the two years after the merger, as the Chairman's statement at the time implies we should, and ignore the exceptional year of 1972, we have some reason to believe that the biases in the remaining years will tend to cancel each other out, and taking an average of the measured value of k for these years should give us a fairly reasonable picture. It would probably be most appropriate to compare Johnson–Richards as one company in these four years with the performance of the two firms as separate companies in the four years immediately preceding the merger. As we cannot do this because of data shortage we compare the mean value of k for the four pre-merger years for Johnsons (98.63) and for 1971, 1973, 1974 and 1975 for Johnson–Richards (90.08). This represents an improvement in total factor productivity of 8.7%. The t-value for the difference between these means is 1.74 which although not significant at the 5% level for a one-tailed test, gives us some reason to believe that the observed difference is not purely sampling variation. The question which now arises is, how much of this improvement in efficiency can be attributed to the merger?

The merger more than doubled the size of H. & R. Johnson Ltd, and added £4.9m to the book value of total assets. Rationalisation of sales operations in Greece, of factories in Australia and of many different operations at home including production, warehousing and accounting, took place. There was also a large investment programme of £2½m in the years immediately following the merger.

This was later followed by a plan to spend a further £3.3m (which was later trimmed to maintain the company's liquidity). We believe that it was this £2½m

46 Suppose that sales are equally divided between home and overseas, and that initially the profit on sales is 10% in each market. If, through greater monopoly power abroad, profits on these sales now increase to 14% and nothing else changes, efficiency will (mistakenly) be measured so as to imply an improvement of 2.22%.

investment, amounting to 25% of the value of the company, which made the rationalisation work. Some of the money went towards buying a new large biscuit tunnel kiln, a spray drier, and two new glost kilns. The rest of it seems to have gone mainly towards reorganisation of existing facilities. There was some reduction of managerial and sales force overheads and there are marginal economies of scale in the production of the body.[47] It is difficult to see how reduction of these overheads alone could have saved 8 or 9% of total costs.

What might have happened if the merger had not taken place? Johnson's could probably have done much of the modernisation that they did do, but it would have only affected their own output. Richards Campbell would have had to do likewise or gone under. Pilkington's had started their own programme of rationalisation at the end of 1965, and are now in quite good health. In fact they have managed to show similar gains to Johnson–Richards (see Table 5.37).

Gay and Smyth regard the merger we are studying as exceptional within the industry for the extent to which rationalisation was carried through. Moreover, one cannot help suspecting that the problems that Richards Campbell were facing in 1968 may have had their roots in the merger between Richards Tiles and the Campbell Tile Co. It will be recalled that Pilkington's had been in some difficulty as a result of its own takeover of Carter Tiles Ltd. If the earlier merger had not taken place the counter factual might be less optimistic. Each firm, not distracted by the problems of integration, might have been able to carry out its own modernisation, programme.

5.9.5 **Other aspects of the merger in glazed tiles**

As we have seen, shareholders had to forgo some profit in the years immediately after 1968, but consumers have less to complain of; under the industry's agreement prices were as high as the industry wanted anyway, and industry discipline was quite tight. In fact prices failed to keep pace with costs and this was one reason for the reduction in the rate of return which occurred after the merger. In the terms of our static model there were no market power effects, there was a gain in efficiency, and income was redistributed from shareholders to consumers.

We mentioned earlier that dynamic effects may be more important than the static effects on which we have concentrated so far. By dynamic effects we mean principally innovation in production methods, in product design, and extension of the market to other uses and other geographical areas. In production, Johnson–Richards seem more to be users of best-practice technique than innovators: although Richards Campbell had been experimenting with a once-fired process Johnson–Richards seem content to leave the pioneering of this to others. As far as

47 In Italy these economies are made consistent with a fragmented market structure by the lack of vertical integration.

Table 5.38 *Exports from the UK (current prices)*
H. & R. Johnson–Richards Ltd

Year ending 31 Mar.	(1) Exports (£m)	(2) Total group sales	(1) ÷ (2)%	Home sales (£m)
1968	2.39	8.43	35.2	5.9
69	4.89	15.83	30.9	11.5
70	5.29	16.94	31.2	11.9
71	5.03	18.04	27.9	12.8
72	5.08	21.06	24.1	13.8
73	5.41	26.88	20.1	14.0
74	6.24	33.13	18.8	15.1
75	7.94	36.00	22.1	18.4

Source: Company Annual Reports.

products are concerned, most of the basic research on tile properties and fixing aspects are covered by the research association. The firm mainly goes in for development work. The firm has been active in extending its range of decorative tiles, and is quite quick to respond to foreign innovations.[48] However the period of major innovations, which occurred in the 1950s and sixties, seems to be over, at least temporarily.

H. & R. Johnson–Richards Tiles Ltd has quite an active overseas policy. For example they have subsidiary or associated companies in Australia, Canada, Greece, India, New Zealand, South Africa, Sweden and Switzerland. They export both biscuit tiles for their overseas factories and finished tiles. Table 5.38 shows the size of the export trade. Despite an increase in total revenue from abroad, exports have declined as a proportion of group sales. This reflects the setting up or purchasing of production facilities abroad. The company is now the largest manufacturer of glazed tiles in the world.

5.9.6 Summary and Conclusions

The merger between H. & R. Johnson Ltd, and Richards Campbell Ltd was one in which the acquisition of market power in order to raise prices was not really an issue. The major motive seems to have been the personal desire of the Chairman of Johnson's to manage successfully a growing company. In terms of efficiency the merger can be termed a success. This is attributable mainly to the rationalisation and investment that took place following the merger. Much, though by no means all, of the modernisation and reorganisation which took place could have been done without the merger since scale economies are limited. It is

48 For example it took a year to respond to the introduction of a rectangular tile.

possible that Richards Campbell might not have had the will to modernise itself and might have eventually gone under but for the merger, but we have no real evidence of this. As things turned out benefits were realised from installing 'Johnson methods' into the firm of Richards Campbell. This can be regarded as spreading managerial talent over a larger company, which in turn might be thought of as a sort of economies of scale in management. Whether this is possible depends on the size and complexity of the firm – Johnson–Richards was not a large firm at the time of the merger and can still be regarded as of medium size.

From the point of view of merger policy the main lesson[49] to be learnt from this case is that even where production economies of scale are almost totally irrelevant rationalisation can be achieved by medium-sized companies. This so-called rationalisation may consist mainly of installing best-practice techniques of production. Such efficiency gains do not happen automatically but require the existence and implementation of a plan by the management. Merger is not really necessary in these cases, and an outright ban would probably do little harm. If such mergers are to be allowed there is a strong case for making them contingent on the existence of a plausible, detailed, rationalisation and investment plan by the new management.

5.10.1 Companies: Thorn and Radio Rentals
Date: 1968

Products: Television manufacturing and rental, and television colour tube manufacturing.

This study will focus its attention, especially regarding the effects of the merger, on television rentals. This is justified by the influence of the merger being in all likelihood most felt in this area but has anyway been necessitated by the lack of suitable data on television and colour tube manufacturing at a sufficiently disaggregated level.[50]

5.10.2 Background to the Thorn–Radio Rentals merger

Table 5.39 shows the numbers of TV sets produced between 1947 and 1974 and the number in use from 1970. Thorn had the largest share of the market, and the merger increased Thorn's market share by about a quarter to approximately one third of the total.

Significant features of television production are:

(i) television manufacturing is 'essentially a matter of assembling a number of components ranging in size from small transistors, resistors etc. to

49 Pilkington's Tiles Ltd is now a part of Thomas Tilling Ltd and seems fairly autonomous. The apparent success of this takeover seems to hinge on the subsidiary being left fairly well alone by the conglomerate parent.

50 Thorn has refused to co-operate with our study.

Table 5.39 *The number of TV sets produced and in use*

	Number produced (million)		Number in use (million)	
	Monochrome[a]	Colour	Monochrome	Colour
1960	2.1			
1961	1.3			
1962	1.5			
1963	1.7			
1964	2.2			
1965	1.6			
1966	1.4			
1967	1.2	0.03		
1968	1.8	0.14		
1969	1.8	0.14		
1970	1.7	0.49	18.1	0.7
1971	1.6	0.83	17.8	1.7
1972	1.6	1.35	16.8	3.3
1973	1.0	2.1	14.8	6.0
1974	0.7	2.0	13.6	8.0
1975	0.5	1.6	12.8	9.5

[a]Before 1967 monochrome statistics include those on colour.
Sources: for no. produced — *Annual Abstract of Statistics.*
for no. in use — Price Commission (1976).

larger parts such as picture tube and cabinet sections' (Monopolies Commission (1968b)).

(ii) At the time of the merger imports represented only 3% of the market but were expected to become a major threat to home producers. This pessimism arose from the planned conversion in 1969 of UK televisions from 405 lines definition standard to 625, the latter being almost universally used throughout Europe.

(iii) Televisions are consumer durables and might therefore be expected to confront producers with the possibility of a declining market as saturation is reached. However this is mitigated by the potential for growth afforded by colour television and by the development of portable television.

At the time of the merger colour tubes were maufactured by only three companies, Thorn, Mullard, (a subsidiary of the Dutch Company Philips) and RCA Colour Tubes, the last one-third owned by Radio Rentals and two-thirds by RCA Great Britain (a subsidiary of the Radio Corporation of America). Its future was uncertain with RCA(GB) having the option of buying out the Radio

Rentals share if ownership were transferred. In fact a new company was subsequently set up with Thorn taking 51% and RCA 49% of the shares. Colour tubes usually form about 40% of the cost of a set (*Guardian*, 21 October 1975).

The UK television rental industry is 'easily the best developed and most advanced anywhere in the world', according to *Retail Business* (1976). The NBPI (1968b) estimated that in 1968 nearly half of the TV sets in use were rented and of these 60% came from specialist rental companies. The non-specialist sector is currently dominated by Co-operative Societies, who supply approximately 400,000 sets, whilst other identifiable retail chains account for another 1–1½ million. The Price Commission (1976) estimated that at the end of 1975 there were a total of 3,100 specialist shops, supplying 6.95 million sets, whilst 2,500 non-specialist multiples and 3,400 independents accounted for 4.15 million sets. Similar information does not appear to have been published for the pre-merger period.

At the time of the merger, ten companies, each with over 100,000 sets, controlled four fifths (NBPI (1968b)) of the specialist market. The Monopolies Commission gave the number of specialist rental outlets (for 1968) controlled by Thorn as 490 and by Radio Rentals as 615, 15% and 19% of all such outlets. It maintained that Thorn had a total of 947,000 sets on rental from specialist outlets, 18% of the total from specialists, and 1,089,000 from all their outlets, 14% of all sets rented. The corresponding figures for Radio Rentals were 1.4 million (27%), and 1.5 million (18%).

The NBPI is usually quoted, as for instance by the Monopolies Commission, as finding the television rental industry 'highly competitive', but comments made in its report might make one think that this is an overstatement. Half of the consumers it sampled had not compared prices before renting and it found that some firms could have absorbed increases in Selective Employment Tax but, instead, passed these on to consumers who 'were in effect captive' (because they had entered into contracts). Further doubts are cast on the competitiveness of the industry by the NBPI's findings that rental charges differed considerably between companies and that 'rental charges are somewhat complex and imperfectly understood by customers. Even if initial weekly rents appear to differ little, total charges over a period of one, three or five years vary widely'; e.g. when *Which?* compared colour television rentals it showed that whilst the advertised rent charged by DER, Thorn's major television rental subsidiary, was 36s 11d and by Radio Rentals was 37s the amount of rent that would actually be paid to the companies over five years would be £468 and £405 respectively. Thorn provided the Monopolies Commission with a set of charges it thought was more representative and in this the difference between DER's charge and both that of Radio Rentals and the average, was smaller. Regardless of how much higher the rental charges for DER sets were than those of competitors, in particular Radio Rentals, there would seem no doubt that it was very difficult for consumers to compare prices. The market would seem to have been far from 'highly competitive'.

5.10.3 The companies prior to merger

Thorn was founded in 1928, as the Electric Lamp Company, by Jules Thorn and he would appear from press and company reports to have been the driving force throughout its development into 'one of Britain's most outstandingly successful companies' (*Financial Times*, 24 Nov. 1970), with a turnover in 1976 of £845 million. The company is currently active in a wide range of consumer durable and engineering markets, the latter beginning in the year before the merger with Radio Rentals. Turnover, in 1976, including that between divisions (giving a different total from above) was divided into:

Consumer durables	£394.7 million
Lighting	£195.7 million
Domestic appliances	£221.8 million
Engineering	£144 million

At the time of the merger 15.4% of group trading income was derived from specialist rental sections, 11.8% from television manufacturing, 7.7% from its retail shops and 65.1% from all other activities including tubes and valves and all overseas activities. Rentals account for 99% of the income from specialist retail sections and 31% of that of retail shops. In 1967, 15% of the monochrome sets it produced went to its own rental companies (in 1966 25%) and 21% of its colour sets. Retail outlets controlled by Thorn had been taking about 7–9% of Thorn's production. In 1967 the company exported approximately 12,400 sets, over 30% of the total UK exports of televisions.

Two further points should be made on the characteristics of the company:

(i) Thorn has apparently always preferred to maintain a smaller headquarters staff than would be normal for other companies of similar size; for instance at least as recently as 1970 the company had no industrial relations officer and data processing was non-executive, whilst its first industrial training officer was only appointed in 1969 (*Financial Times*, 25 Nov. 1970).

(ii) It has been alleged both that Thorn's policy from the outset has been to buy technological expertise through takeover and that this was precisely the aim with respect to colour tubes when the company merged with RCA's tube company (*Financial Times*, 24 Nov. 1970). It should, however, be noted that RCA had the option of buying all of Radio Rentals' holding and that at the time of the merger, at least as far as the Monopolies Commission was aware, it had not decided to do so.

Radio Rentals was formed in 1964 through the merger of two leading rental chains, Radio Rentals and Rentaset. According to the Monopolies Commission its trading income in the year ended 28 February 1967 consisted of:

Specialist rental sections –	UK	£29,536m
	Overseas	£2,288m
	Retail shops	£2,842m
Manufacturing sections –	Television	£3,613m
	Other products	£1,816m

In the nine months ending 30 November 1967, rentals accounted for 95% of the income of specialist rental sections in the United Kingdom and 64% of the income of the retail shops. Radio Rentals manufactured televisions through its subsidiary, Baird Television. In the year ended February 1969 Baird's disposals amounted to 140,000 sets of which ten thousand were colour. In 1967 Radio Rentals took about three quarters of Baird's output, a 'small number' were exported, and the remainder were taken by other UK distributors including some of the major rental companies (Monopolies Commission (1968b)).

5.10.4 **Reasons for the merger of Thorn and Radio Rentals**

Thorn and Radio Rentals told the Commission that the 'most important' reason, for the merger, was the expected advantage the combined company would have in meeting competition from overseas manufacturers in both the home and overseas markets. This competition would become fierce with the introduction from late 1969 of 625 lines standard, making the UK part of a large market comprising most European countries. It would not be too harsh, however, to assert that the companies were rather vague as to how the merger would actually enable them to meet this competition. They maintained that if the UK industry were to survive it would have to develop 'mass production and low cost, technically advanced, internationally orientated manufacturing units'; the expected cost savings from the merger would not in themselves be sufficient to ensure success against foreign competition, but it would be necessary to 'reduce costs further by making heavy capital investment in the most modern plant ... and to spend greater sums ... on research and development'. Colour tube production would particularly benefit from the introduction of heavy capital investment. It was, however, left to the Commission to infer both that all these improvements would be introduced and that they would not have been possible in the absence of the merger. Perhaps most revealing as to the expected gains to meeting foreign competition was the companies' claim that they would be 'encouraged' to 'increase' investment if they had an 'assurance of reasonable security in the home market and an even level of production'.

On the anticipated economies to manufacturing the companies reported that they 'had not consulted each other in detail' but expected 'substantial saving on

Table 5.40 *Total expected cost savings to TV rentals expected by Thorn and Radio Rentals*

Thorn	Radio Rentals
60 outlets closed saving £475,000 a year	100 outlets closed 'over a number of years' saving £650,000.
Improved use of field service engineers, saving a total of £25,000–£30,000	Improved use of field service engineers would save 'at least £400,000' for Radio Rentals alone.
Saving on the cost of central repair depots amounting to £250,000	No estimate.
Saving from the joint purchase of service materials – £125,000	No estimate.
Radio Rentals' use of Thorn's computer, saving – £398,000	This would save £250,000.
Centralisation of administration – £500,000	This would save £250,000.
Saving on the cost of distributing sets – £100,000	This had not been quantified but £70,000 would be saved in whole-saling to independents.

Source of data: Monopolies Commission (1968b).

the cost of producing components and television sets'. Radio Rental would benefit from Thorn's 'greater experience of larger volume production ... and from access to special machinery developed by Thorn for its own use' which Radio Rentals could not develop itself because it was a smaller manufacturer. It was Thorn's aim to avoid duplication and a common chassis would be introduced. The companies estimated that in March 1968 the cost of materials, direct labour and tools for Thorn was £4 lower than for Baird. The expected gains in TV rentals are detailed in Table 5.40.

The other expected gains from the merger would, for the most part, arise from the increase in vertical integration. '*Assured orders*' (our italics) would enable production to be planned further in advance, at a higher level, and more evenly, and cost savings would result from the increased scale of production and better use of resources.

5.10.5 **Developments since the merger**

(1) Tube manufacture

In the post-merger period the UK has ceased to manufacture monochrome tubes and only the Dutch-owned Mullard continues to manufacture colour tubes. Thorn stopped manufacturing tubes in 1975 with the closure of its Sunderland monochrome plant and Skelmersdale colour tube plant, the latter jointly owned with RCA. The latter closure resulted in the loss of 1,370 jobs.

It is pertinent to this study to examine whether the British-based monochrome and British-owned colour tube industries would have survived had the merger not taken place, particularly as the closure of the Skelmersdale plant led to a monopoly situation. Certainly Japanese competition has had a traumatic effect on these industries and British senior executives have been widely reported in the press as asking the government to seek voluntary export controls from the Japanese. Accusations were made of dumping but these appear to have been found to be unjustified (*Financial Times*, 6 Jan. 1976). Thorn admitted that Japanese competition was only part of the reason for its failure in tubes with its finance director reported as saying 'with the Japanese there is a ghastly problem, but even without the Japanese there would still be a problem' (*Guardian*, 5 Aug. 1975). There appears to have been a severe contraction in the demand for monochrome and colour televisons, the number of the latter sold falling from 2.0 million in 1974 to 1.7 million in 1975. The Skelmersdale plant alone had a capacity of almost a million tubes year. This is somewhat ironic[51] in that a frequent complaint of UK television and tube manufacturers was that frequent changes in tax and related mandatory conditions of sale[52] had made them reluctant to take advantage of booms in case they were short lived, and had consequently lost customers to foreign companies. Apparently Thorn and Mullard witnessed this happening in 1973 but when they decided to overcome their caution and expand, their worst fears were realised by the reintroduction of credit restrictions in December of that year and even more devastatingly, the introduction of 25% VAT in 1975.

It is impossible to draw any but the most tentative conclusions about whether Radio Rentals and/or Thorn would still be manufacturing colour tubes if they had not merged. Thorn took a gamble when it undertook its heavy investment programme at Skelmersdale and the gamble did not pay off. Presumably the possibility of realising economies of scale implied by the size of the Skelmersdale plant would have been denied to either Thorn or Radio Rentals separately. The corollary to this is that neither would have been committed to a high level of fixed costs when demand turned down. Possibly therefore, there would have been sufficent demand to justify a smaller plant owned by either Thorn or Radio Rentals. If the two companies had remained separate, moreover, there is

51 Further cause for irony is provided by Mullard apparently (*Financial Times*, 7 Jan. 1976), not being able, at least initially, to sell to Thorn because of 'technical differences'.

52 *Financial Times*, 6 Jan. 1976, reported that in 'recent years' the government had made 47 changes in purchase tax, VAT, HP and rental deposits on 31 occasions.

the possibility that Radio Rentals would have adopted a policy more appropriate for dealing with Japanese competition; this is probably what the minority report from the Monopolies Commission had in mind when it advocated 'leaving room for a variety of policies in development and design'. Some credibility for this is provided by reports that part of the reason for the failure of British tube manufacture lies in British television manufacturers not foreseeing the popularity of small screen colour sets (*Guardian*, 31 Oct. 1975). Radio Rentals might have anticipated this boom. Whilst this must remain as speculation, it can be stated uncategorically that the merger did not save British-owned tube manufacture.

(2) Television manufacturing

Since 1973 the UK television industry has experienced a slump. This is apparent from the tables above. The reasons for this would appear to be similar to those for the decline of the tube industry, though press reports have tended to lay greater stress on an early satiation[53] of the market than on the effects of the imposition of 25% VAT. The press and other commentators on the industry seem agreed that either through unpreparedness, or an initial caution that it would be shortlived, UK manufactuers were not able to meet the increase in demand which followed the relaxation of credit controls in 1973 and the shortage of supply was met from imports, particularly from Japan. Even Thorn was forced to do this (*Sunday Times*, 16 June 1974). The argument appears to be that having provided an opportunity for the Japanese to sell in the UK they were able to continue to do so even after UK producers were fully capable of meeting demand. The reasons for this would presumably be that brand loyalties had developed and/or the Japanese had developed an expertise for selling to the UK. But there would seem every likelihood that the Japanese would have been successful even if they had not been afforded this initial foothold. British manufacturers appear to have largely abandoned the manufacture of televisions at the upper and lower end of the range of screen sizes. In 1975 sales of '18 in and under' and '26 in and over' screen sizes each represented 17% of the market (*Electrical and Electronic Trader*, 22 Aug. 1975). Accusations of dumping do not appear to have been commonly made and as early as 1973 it was being claimed that Japanese and German sets were more expensive than British (*Financial Times*, 1 March 1973).

A decline in imports since 1973 may reflect Japanese agreements to restrict their television exports to the UK but it has been claimed that they had difficulty meeting even these limits (*Financial Times*, 1 Nov. 1974). A factor of some importance must be the direct investment by foreign companies in the UK. The examples most frequently cited are Sony's and Matsushita's factories in Wales, each of which had an initial potential of 5,000 sets a month.

53 This may be interpreted as the familiar cyclical model of the demand for a consumer durable; one would expect the initial peak and trough to be most marked immediately after the good's introduction.

Information on Thorn's performance in television manufacturing since the merger is particularly sparse. It has maintained the market share of the combined companies pre-merger (*Retail Business* (1976)) but its company reports give data at too aggregated a level to conclude whether its efficiency in manufacturing sets has changed. Similarly, little is given away on Thorn's record of television exports though it claimed in 1974 (*Financial Times*, 13 March 1974) to be planning to export 20% of its production which must be compared to 4% at the time of the merger (Monopolies Commission (1968b)). It has not been possible to ascertain whether this had anything to do with the merger. As with tube manufacturing, estimating the counter factual in television manufacturing has proved impossible. If Radio Rentals had remained independent it might have anticipated the increase in demand for very small and large sets but that must remain conjecture.

(3) Television rentals

Thorn/Radio Rentals has apparently maintained the pre-merger share of the total rentals market enjoyed by the constituent companies combined with 31% in 1976 against 32% in 1968 (*Retail Business* (1976)). Assuming that the share of the specialist market has similarly remained at the pre-merger level any developments within this sector must be considered to a large extent a reflection of the behaviour and/or performance of Thorn.

The Price Commission (1976) found that 'in a sample of 26 main shopping areas of cities and large towns at least four of the companies of the five main groups were represented in each. Thus it appears that there is plentiful choice in large towns'. It is therefore understandable that the Price Commission was surprised at apparent monopoly profits that were being earned. 'There is an argument that prices could well be lower, even if this would have to be at the expense of reduced profit margins. Normally one would expect competition to produce this result, but on the figures which emerge from this study, there is no evidence that it has.' The evidence that the Commission cited for excessive profits on the return of the specialist rental companies was:

1972	18.5%
1973	23.9%
1974	22.6%
1975	21.0%
1976	19.4%

The Commission was not explicitly concerned with the degree with which monopoly power was being exercised but it could well have drawn attention to the difference in the level of prices and their rate of change, between specialist and other outlets. Table 5.41 shows that between 1970 and 1976 it was usually cheaper to rent a monochrome from a multiple non-specialist than a specialist and invariably cheapest to rent from an independent dealer.

Table 5.41 *Average monthly TV rental charges (including VAT) to new subscribers*

Date	Specialist renters		Multiple non-specialists		Independent retailers	
	£	Index	£	Index	£	Index
			20 in. mono			
31 March 1970	2.30	100.0	2.26	100.0	2.19	100.0
31 March 1971	2.30	103.9	2.26	100.0	2.24	102.3
31 March 1972	2.53	110.0	2.40	106.2	2.29	104.6
31 March 1973	2.66	115.7	2.61	115.5	2.34	106.8
31 March 1974	2.66	115.7	2.78	123.0	2.44	111.4
31 March 1975	2.78	120.9	2.78	123.0	2.48	113.2
30 June 1975	3.24	140.9	3.19	141.2	2.91	132.9
30 September 1975	3.29	143.0	3.17	140.3	2.98	136.1
31 December 1975	3.43	149.1	3.27	144.7	2.99	136.5
13 February 1976	3.47	150.9	3.27	144.7	3.01	137.4
			22in. colour			
31 March 1970	7.02	100.0	7.10	100.0	7.21	100.0
31 March 1971	7.08	100.9	7.10	100.0	7.29	101.1
31 March 1972	6.97	99.3	6.89	97.0	7.24	100.4
31 March 1973	7.04	100.3	6.99	98.5	7.28	101.0
31 March 1974	7.10	101.1	7.21	101.5	7.46	103.5
31 March 1975	7.28	103.7	7.49	105.5	7.58	105.1
30 June 1975	8.46	120.5	8.60	121.1	8.79	121.9
30 September 1975	8.59	122.4	8.61	121.3	8.83	122.5
31 December 1975	8.81	125.5	8.60	121.1	8.90	123.4
13 February 1976	8.87	126.4	8.60	121.1	8.91	123.6

Source: Price Commission (1976).

Unless there are diseconomies of scale[54] the price–cost margin when supplying monochrome sets is therefore higher for specialist than non-specialist renters. This assumes that the quality of rental service is not higher from specialists than non-specialists. There is no evidence to suggest that either specialists sell different, let alone superior, sets than non-specialists, nor that they provide better maintenance service. With colour sets it would appear that specialists usually charge the lowest rents. Given economies of scale this might be expected. As the extent of these economies is not known it is not possible to draw any conclusions about differences in the level of the price–cost margins when supplying colour sets between specialists and non-specialists. It is however significant that since 1970 the price increase has been higher for specialist renters than for either multiple non-specialists or independents, which, assuming costs have not risen at a faster rate for the former, would suggest an increase in the price–cost margins for specialists.

One would have predicted that after their merger the rental charges of Thorn and Radio Rentals would have come into line and this is precisely what appears to have happened. In 1968 *Which* reported that the approximate total rent that would be paid to DER for a 25 inch colour set would be £288 by the end of the third year and £468 by the end of the fifth; the corresponding figures for Radio Rentals would be £270 and £405; the ratios of these prices would be 1.1 and 1.7 respectively. When a similar comparison was made in 1975 of the total rental over five years of a 22 in., Thorn charged £422 and Radio Rentals £410, a ratio of 1.01.[55]

5.10.6 Thorn–Radio Rentals unit factor requirement (k)

Data on the sales and profits that Thorn earns from television rentals is not published. Similar data is, however, available on Radio Rentals from 1966 and after the merger. It is therefore possible to make some estimate of how k has changed for Radio Rentals but this need not be any indication of any change to the unit factor requirement of the DER rentals division.

A weighted average input price for television rentals is not constructed by the Department of Industry. The major inputs, at a highly aggregated level, are given by the NBPI (1968b) for 1962–66, and in the Price Commission (1976) for 1971–76. It has been assumed that the proportions in 1966 are relevant until

54 It is perhaps more accurate to talk of economies and diseconomies of specialisation rather than of scale. The tone of the Monopolies Commission's and Price Commission's Reports is that the two are synonomous. Conceivably, however, a non-specialist chain, especially the Co-op, could operate on a larger scale than a specialist.

55 Curiously when *Which* (July 1970) compared 19 in. colour set rentals in 1970 it found no difference between Thorn and Radio Rentals over three years and only £3 difference (£348 to £345) over five years.

1968. The incorporation of depreciation presents a major problem in the construction of P_I and it has been assumed that Radio Rentals changed from its pre-merger policy of writing off sets over seven years to Thorn's policy of writing off over five by 1970. The index of depreciation costs in any year is simply an average of the previous five or seven observations on television retail prices.

Table 5.42 shows the change in k for Radio Rentals and a sample of other television rental companies. Of crucial importance is the fall in P_0/P_I. The rental of sets has remained stable[56] as have the retail prices of televisions, but the prices of labour, fuel and 'other materials' have all risen. The last may not be an appropriate index as it refers to the price of miscellaneous materials purchased by the industrial, not retail sector.

Table 5.42 shows a significant drop in Radio Rentals' unit factor requirement, over 35% between 1966 and 1974. Some words of caution are, however, warranted. Firstly the accuracy of P_I particularly in its treatment of depreciation,[57] must be considered as less than in the series elsewhere. Secondly P_0 was supplied by the Department of Industry and reflects changes in the rental charged by the industry as a whole. As Table 5.41 shows, the rentals charged by the specialist sector have increased at a faster rate than those of the non-specialist. Thirdly, given that Radio Rentals is a wholly-owned subsidiary, data in its published accounts should be treated with some caution. Given this however, the movement in k over time since the merger follows a very similar pattern to that of the other companies, except that Granada managed to reattain its 1968 efficiency earlier than the other companies following a general rise in unit factor requirement in 1969 and 1970, and Rediffusion have gained greater increases in efficiency than Radio Rentals over the study period. Any benefits that can be attributed to the merger do not seem obvious.

5.11 **Conclusions and implications**

The objectives that have been attributed to managers or firms in economic theory are numerous and diverse. The classical profit maximisation approach has been supplemented by sales maximisation, growth maximisation, and utility maximisation, the latter capable of being extended to cover such aspects as power, the easy life or status. No one approach is generally held to be superior to any other. Thus when it comes to asking 'why do firms merge?', we are

56 Table 5.42 compares the increase in rents inclusive of VAT of specialist and other rental companies. Rentals of colour televisions exclusive of VAT have remained fairly stable for specialists which implies a fall in the rentals of non-specialists. Rentals of monochrome rose by 22.2% between March 1970 and February 1976 for specialists.

57 The dramatic apparent increase in efficiency immediately after the merger (1967–68) may well be a reflection of an inadequate treatment of depreciation. It would seem unlikely that the effect on efficiency could have been so immediate.

Table 5.42 *The unit factor requirement*[a] *of Radio Rentals and a sample of specialist rental firms*

Date	P_0/P_I	Radio Rentals		Granada		Rediffusion		Telefusion	
		Profit/ turnover (%)	*k*	Profit/ turnover (%)	*k*	Profit/ turnover (%)	*k*	Profit/ turnover (%)	*k*
1966	100.0	13.7	116.5						
1967	99.5	14.1	115.3			18.3	103.6	13.9	102.6
1968	96.4	23.2	100.0	13.8	100.0	17.5	100.0	12.3	100.0
1969	97.7	21.4	103.6	9.1	105.3	16.3	102.9	11.2	102.6
1970	102.4	22.8	106.6	9.6	109.8	15.0	109.4	9.6	109.4
1971	97.6	19.8	104.9	13.2	99.9	11.0	108.5	10.3	102.8
1972	93.9	19.9	102.1	17.6	92.1	15.7	100.0	10.5	99.8
1973	87.9	22.1	96.3	18.8	88.0	21.2	90.6	10.1	97.2
1974	71.9	20.5	85.4			21.3	78.7	7.9	86.6

[a] In each case k is set equal to 100 in 1968.

immediately faced with a problem. Fortunately, however, we are not concerned whether firms have managed to undertake successful mergers with success defined with respect to their own objective functions. We have attempted in earlier chapters to define success in social welfare terms with the arguments in the social objective function being deadweight monopoly welfare loss (with a negative coefficient) and real resource saving or increases in productive efficiency (with a positive coefficient). To illustrate how the conflict of firm and social objectives operates consider the case of a profit maximising firm that generates higher profits after merger than did the two individual companies prior to merger. If the extra profits are generated through real resource saving the social and private judgements of the merger are the same – it is beneficial. If however the profits arise from the exercise of market power the improvement in the firm's performance relative to its objectives is not reflected in the social judgement – in social terms the merger is not a success.

In our introductory section to this chapter we have already made clear that there is a wide diversity of experience in the performance of firms after merger, and that to attempt generalisations is rather ambitious, but it seems incumbent upon us to draw some conclusions from the material presented in the case studies above. A warning is however merited here, for in drawing these conclusions we cannot add all the provisos that are included in the text of this chapter, and thus to just read these conclusions out of context of the whole chapter may be misleading. We would particularly advise that before any inferences are drawn with respect to any particular merger using material from this section, that reference is made back to the individual case study where all the relevant evidence and conditions are presented. This statement carries extra weight when it comes to interpreting the values of k (our unit factor requirement measure) presented below. Given this, we can start by looking at the efficiency aspect of our welfare trade-off framework, for that is the area where most of our results lie and where most of our effort has been expended.

Our starting point is to consider why mergers are expected to lead to efficiency gains. The usual arguments cover three factors:

(1) a merger enables the joint company to reap the benefits of economies of scale;

(2) the merger will involve the application of better management to one of the merged firms;

(3) there will be undefined gains from 'synergy'.

The reasons for expecting benefits from mergers that have been put forward by the participants vary: lowering costs due to increased size (London Brick); the 'necessity for volume production supported by advanced production engineering know how' (RHP); gains to marketing (Rowntree Mackintosh); the expected advantage the combined company would have in meeting competition from overseas manufacturers in both the home and overseas markets (Thorn/Radio

Rentals). In certain cases the gains to be expected are very unclear and ill defined, especially when the merger is a defensive one. In other cases one suspects that no efficiency gains are to be expected and that the merger is purely a means of retaining market power when it would otherwise be diluted. For our purposes however we shall concentrate on the three possible resource-saving factors above.

The reaping of the benefits of scale economies requires first that such benefits should exist, i.e. the technology is such as to involve scale economies; second that the resultant firm size and plant sizes should match the technological optimum; and third that post merger the firm and plants should be integrated and rationalised to form a coherent whole. Consider first plant scale economies. On London Brick we have argued that the technology does involve increasing returns to scale, but the optimum size plant did not require one firm to be the sole supplier. Courtaulds' behaviour is not consistent with reaping the benefits of plant scale economies, but with RHP such economies did exist and have apparently been realised through a great reduction in the product range. In BJN there are a number of plants suggesting that the firm is greater than is necessary for the exploitation of plant scale economies. In the glazed tile industry quite a small scale seems optimal. Thus, although the reaping of the benefits of plant scale economies may be important in certain cases, as a reason for expecting efficiency gains it is not very pervasive on this evidence.

Firm level economies are also argued to exist. One has to distinguish here between gains to the firm at another firm's (or customer's) expense and true savings in real resources. Apart from benefits to R & D, management usage, or political power, all matters to which we refer below in this or later chapters we have not really observed any great gains to the firm or society arising from or expected from such firm level economies.

The spreading of better management as a reason for expecting gains from merger is our next category. The idea carries a number of implications – better management should enable greater output to be derived from the same input, it should involve the introduction of the latest technology and it should enable what scale economies are available to be realised. We have one case where this factor has been at work (Johnson-Richards) and in another (RHP) it must be one of the reasons for the increases in productivity realised. In our study of engineering (Chapter 6) the matter is stressed more forcibly. What we feel however on the present evidence is that rather than better management being a reason to expect gains from merger, a more appropriate statement would be that effective management (in some general sense) is a prerequisite of achieving real resource savings after a merger.

Our third category is a catch-all term labelled 'synergy', i.e. that the whole is greater than the sum of the parts. This seems to be very much the reason for expecting gains from the BICC/Pyrotenax and Rowntree–Mackintosh mergers, but by its nature leaves vague exactly what is implied. It may be used to include gains from vertical integration (which was to yield small benefits to BICC and Thorn), and in the Courtaulds study (Chapter 10) we inspect this concept more closely. But in general we have not observed any obvious gains that can carry this label.

Consider now the measure of efficiency on which we have concentrated, the unit factor requirement, k. Given that resource savings may arise for a number of reasons, have we been able to isolate any savings that can be attributed to the merger and its effects? In Table 5.43 we present the estimates of k generated in the text. In each case k is standardised to 100 in the merger year, and for the years prior to merger we have calculated k from the joint profit and revenue of the two firms as if they were one. We ought here to repeat our warning on the interpretation of k. To look at these figures in the absence of the detail presented in the case studies may be misleading; thus, for example, the figures on Johnson-Richards for the years before the merger are constructed using an assumption of constant market shares and may therefore be unreliable. Also, as we have stated elsewhere, year to year variations in k should not be taken as implying a great deal – only the trends really mean much. Given this however, we can draw some conclusions.

Our starting point is to define a performance norm with which to compare the actual performance of the firms after merger. We consider that it is appropriate to argue that

(1) if efficiency has not risen faster than at an annual rate of increase of $1\frac{1}{2}$% p.a. then the merger is not a success. This rate seems a reasonable expectation of performance without merger in most industries, although from many one might expect a greater rate of increase.

(2) if the efficiency of the firm has not improved faster than that of non-merging competing firms then the merger is not a success. Although it may be argued that competing firms may increase their efficiency in response to the improvement in the merging firms we consider this an unlikely occurrence, and even if it did occur it would illustrate that firms were capable of increasing efficiency without merger.

Using the data in Table 5.43 our first comparison is between merger year efficiency and the lowest value of k attained in any of the post-merger years. Such a comparison would tend to bias the results in favour of mergers. From the table it is clear that in nearly every case the lowest value of k appears in 1973 or 1974 and that k falls dramatically in nearly every case post 1972. We have no explanation for this behaviour except that it may be due to increased capacity utilisation arising from an expansion in output in 1973. Once again however this will tend to bias our results in favour of merger. In these terms there have been some significant absolute increases in efficiency (London Brick, 20% in 6 years; RHP, 25% in 6 years; Johnson-Richards 10% in 4 years). Given the unreliability of the BICC and Radio Rentals figures, and thus ignoring these cases, we find that the

Table 5.43 *Unit factor requirement*[a]

Year	London Brick/ Marston Valley	Ransome Hoffman & Pollard	BICC/ Pyrotenax[b]	Tube Investments/ Coventry Gauge	BJN/ British Paint	Rowntree/ Mackintosh	Johnson/ Richards Campbell[c]	Thorn/ Radio Rentals[d]	Year	Courtaulds/ British Celanese
1963	—	—	131.0	—	—	106.8	—	—	1954	85.4
1964	—	—	118.8	—	—	106.7	—	—	1955	81.7
1965	101.4	—	80.4	—	—	107.5	100.0	—	1956	88.2
1966	103.9	109.7	79.5	—	—	103.8	100.5	116.43	1957	100.0
1967	98.0	107.3	100.0	102.6	n.a.	104.6	104.0	115.33	1958	99.8
1968	100.0	107.1	97.0	99.1	n.a.	101.4	100.0	100.0	1959	82.8
1969	103.4	100.0	93.7	100.0	100.0	100.0	101.3	103.6	1960	86.3
1970	98.9	97.3	97.0	99.7	98.4	105.8	97.5	106.7	1961	91.3
1971	91.0	95.5	114.5	101.4	101.6	105.0	90.1	104.9	1962	80.3
1972	84.7	97.6	111.2	102.2	101.8	100.7	105.2	102.1	1963	—
1973	80.5	92.8	77.4	90.0	96.3	85.3	95.5	96.3	1964	—
1974	87.5	74.9	82.8	93.9	92.4	84.7	90.2	85.5	1965	—
1975	—	—	—	101.1	—	—	—	—	1966	—

[a] In this table we present estimates of the unit factor requirement as follows (a) in the post-merger period for the joint firm, (b) for the pre-merger period as if the merging firms were one. The merger year is shown by a line breaking the series. All figures are standardised to 100 in the merger year.

[b] For fuller details see text. The series is derived from non-continuous sources.

[c] Pre-merger figures constructed on an assumption of constant market shares.

[d] Radio Rentals only. The dramatic fall in k 1967–68 is probably due to a change in accounting practice. See the detail in the case study above.

N.B. (a) These figures are not reliable out of their case study context.
(b) Only trends in k carry reliable information.

three companies above plus Tube Investments, Rowntree Mackintosh and Courtaulds all achieve efficiency gains greater than $1\frac{1}{2}$% p.a. Thus BJN does not pass the $1\frac{1}{2}$% rule even on this most favourable comparison of these 'successful' companies, Tube Investments has by 1975 returned to an efficiency level below that in the merger year and the Courtaulds figures give a false impression in that the value of k for the merger year was considerably higher than its pre-merger historical average. Compared to pre-merger efficiency it only achieved an 8% advance in 7 years. The only mergers therefore that can satisfy the $1\frac{1}{2}$% criterion are London Brick, RHP, Johnson-Richards and Rowntree Mackintosh.

Using our second criterion to look at these four most successful mergers we have non-merging competitors for RHP and Rowntree Mackintosh. In the RHP case, both Torrington and FAG (UK) have managed to attain increases in efficiency in excess of 30% over 6 years, a greater rate than RHP. However Rowntree Mackintosh appears to have made gains at least as great as those of its competitors. Taken together it would seem that even these successful mergers do not yield gains that differ greatly from those achieved by non-merging rivals.

One further point that has to be made is that there are transitional costs associated with merger. If we compare our estimates of k in the years immediately post-merger to the merger year figure we see that Tube Investments, BJN, and Thorn/Radio Rentals all experienced increased unit factor requirements. In the text of this chapter we have seen that these 'transitional costs' were not mirrored in the estimates for competing firms. In other cases (BICC, Courtaulds) the merger year value of k was also above the pre-merger figure, implying further costs (the fall in k immediately on merger by Radio Rentals we argue is due mainly to changes in accounting practices with respect to depreciation, but the fall in k for RHP may well reflect efficiency gain).

Overall we have three findings.

(a) Four of the cases show efficiency gains exceeding $1\frac{1}{2}$% p.a.;
(b) No case shows extensive gains in efficiency relative to non-merging competitors;
(c) Positive transitional costs are often associated with merger activity and these costs are not incurred by competing firms.

The combination of (b) and (c) on this reading of the evidence (which is biased towards favouring merger) must imply that society has not attained any extensive resource savings as a result of these mergers over what could have been achieved without them.

There is one further point of note. Three of the most successful mergers (London Brick, RHP and Johnson-Richards) were followed by extensive programmes of investment. We do not consider this to be purely coincidental.

As a further indication of efficiency of one industry or a firm a fairly reliable estimator is the extent to which that industry or firm manages to maintain its market share in a world context. Thus in a number of case studies we have looked at export performance. For the UK economy the results are disappointing. In those industries where there is considerable trade, e.g. machine tools, televisions, ball bearings, a surplus of exports over imports prior to the merger has turned into a deficit. In the case of Courtaulds the figures are difficult to interpret because performance on the world market has been heavily influenced by market restrictions. In the Rowntree Mackintosh case exports increased but so did those of competing firms. So in general it seems as if merger does not lead to improved export performance. There is however another side to this issue. A merger may yield market power in a domestic context but that power may be considerably weakened in the world context. This may be one reason for finding that market power realised by merger has not led to increased profitability. This is part of the wider question that is the second part of our efficiency/market power trade off.

All the mergers we have looked at, primarily because of our selection procedures, have involved the resultant company obtaining significantly increased market power. In general the granting of this power is in itself undesirable if no efficiency gains are realised. As we have argued that such gains have not been realised it is not really necessary for us to establish that the increases in market power have led to welfare losses, just the potential for such losses is sufficient. However, although our results are not extensive and there are problems in identifying welfare losses, we have attempted to draw some conclusions on this issue. To start we can refer back to the estimates of deadweight welfare loss presented in Chapter 3 – for a number of companies studied there are also included in our case studies here. We must initially realise that we have only looked at some of the activities of each of these companies, but even so, our earlier estimates show that Thorn, Courtaulds, Rowntree Mackintosh, Tube Investments and BICC have all generated significant monopoly welfare losses. When we turn to the actual exercising of the increased market power resulting from the mergers studied our conclusions are as follows:

(1) We have observed high levels of the rate of return on capital for a number of the merged companies. Thus in the case of London Brick the Monopolies Commission detailed a 22% rate of return. We have argued however that there was no increase in this consequent to the merger and that the firm had considerable market power prior to merger. In Johnson-Richards quite a high rate of return has been achieved but this has depended largely on a prices agreement maintained in the industry that has been judged desirable by the Restrictive Practices Court. In television rentals the Price Commission has pointed out that high rates of return are being attained. In each of these three examples, however, apart from the basic problem of attributing these profits to market power, there is no evidence that the gains arise from the merger studied.

(2) When we look at price levels the evidence is a little more informative. We

have argued for example that there is a suspicious history of prices in the cellulosic fibre industry;

(a) Two months prior to the Courtaulds–Celanese merger rayon yarn prices were increased by 10%, being stable for a long period before and after.

(b) In the post-merger period prices of the more competively supplied cotton and nylon yarn fell, but rayon yarn prices did not.

(c) In the six years after the merger, output prices for Courtaulds rayon yarn relative to input prices fell by 8%. This is very little in an industry where annual productivity growth of *at least* $1\frac{1}{2}$% could be expected.

In the majority of the cases we have studied output prices relative to input prices have fallen considerably over time, and in some cases we have been able to suggest that market power was not being used to increase profitability, although we have not established this rigorously as, e.g. in the BICC/Pyrotenax case, customers were reasonably happy with post-merger pricing, and in fact some discounts were increased. In general, therefore our evidence does not give strong support to a view that market power was being used to increase prices although there is evidence that it has been in some cases. But the potential is always there.

(3) We have found cases of undesirable price discrimination. The Monopolies Commission state that London Brick have discriminated in their pricing policy, and Courtaulds are believed to have acted similarly in favour of exporters.

Although these results are not extensive, given the conclusions drawn with respect to efficiency change we do not need to proceed any further. We have brought together a set of results relevant to our prime question – the market power/efficiency trade off, but prior to drawing some final conclusions we have a few other aspects of performance on which to comment.

(1) It is often argued that increased firm size and concentration favour technological progressiveness. We can make a few observations on this from our cases. On the question of R & D expenditure, London Brick have argued for scale economies arising in this area, but there seems no evidence that their present size is required to support this R & D effort. In the machine tool industry we actually observe significant reductions in the R & D/sales ratio over time. On the question of innovation and the diffusion of innovations the evidence is not very extensive. However, observations on k discussed above do not indicate many gains in productive efficiency being realised. Although we note new products and processes in Tube Investments, British Paints and London Brick, among others, no obvious improvement over the pre-merger performance is illustrated. Given however that much innovation is embodied in new capital goods this may explain why those industries with high investment levels have experienced the greatest gains in efficiency.

(2) The variety of products available to consumers is another factor that may be influenced by merger, but there is a conflict here. The savings in resources achieved by RHP were largely attributed to a reduction in the product range, but to assess the net welfare effect requires a balancing of the savings in resources against the loss in welfare. In this case the initial range was generally considered excessive. In Rowntree Mackintosh the gains to marketing may well imply some loss of choice, but here the possibility of a judgement is less. This is a question considered again (in Chapter 7) where also product quality is further discussed.

(3) A third factor worthy of mention is illustrated well by the Courtaulds case. Merger is not the only way to attain or retain market power; it can be manipulated by cross-firm agreements, and especially in the international context by protective tariffs. This latter approach requires the firm to hold considerable political power. The costs of maintaining international agreements and promoting protective legislation should be considered as important as any other costs. In fact one can gain the impression that in certain cases the main expected gain to the firm of the increased size resulting from merger is to give it greater political voice.

The mergers that we have studied in this chapter have involved a number of government institutions at one stage or another. Primarily we note the role of the IRC, the Monopolies and Mergers Commission, the National Board for Prices and Incomes and its present equivalent, the Price Commission. We have noted in some of the cases that price legislation has alleviated any price increases that might have been observed, and have little further comment to make on this institution. The role of the IRC is further illustrated in later chapters and if one were to anticipate those results and draw some conclusion, the most favourable one would be that the IRC did not always, or even very often, back winners. It is however the Monopolies Commission for which we must reserve our major comment. Of the companies considered here the Monopolies Commission has investigated London Brick, Courtaulds, BICC, and Radio Rentals. Only London Brick has really been at all successful in efficiency terms – a sufficiently loaded comment. We are concerned however that when conditions are imposed on companies either as a prerequisite to merger or as a protection against the exercising of market power there is no mechanism for ensuring adherence to them, and that the conditions imposed by the Commission may well be subject to extensive political wrangling between the government and the company (see the Courtaulds case).

To summarise briefly, efficiency gains from merger are in general not found. Market power has been enhanced and we have some specific indications of its use. The judgement must therefore be against merger. The institutions that exist to regulate merger and market power, moreover, have not, on this evidence, shown themselves to be effective in promoting and protecting the public interest.

References

Armitage, F. (1967), *The British Paint Industry,* Pergamon Press.

Department of Trade and Industry (1970), *The Machine Tool Industry,* London: HMSO.

Gay, P. W., and Smyth, R. L. (1974), *The British Pottery Industry,* Butterworth.

Harvard International Senior Managers' Programme (1973), *Case Studies on RHP and its formation,* Cambridge, Mass.

HMSO (1973), *Studies in Official Statistics,* No. 21, London: HMSO.

Laing & Cruickshank (1976), *Background to the UK Roller Bearing Industry,* Stockbrokers Report.

Lewis, K. A. (1971), 'Multimarket Demand Functions in the Presence of Supply Constraints: International Demand Functions for Cotton and Wool', *Southern Economic Journal* (October), 210–18.

Machine Tool Advisory Council (1960), *The Report of the Sub-Committee (The Mitchell Report),* London: HMSO.

Markham, J. A. (1952), *Competition in the Rayon Industry,* Cambridge, Mass.: Harvard University Press.

Monopolies Commission (1967), *British Insulated Callenders Cables Ltd. and Pyrotenax Ltd., A Report on the Proposed Merger,* London: HMSO.

– (1968a), *Man Made Cellulosic Fibres: A Report on the Supply of Man Made Cellulosic Fibres,* London: HMSO.

–(1968b), *Thorn Electrical Industries Ltd. and Radio Rentals., A Report on the Proposed Merger,* London: HMSO.

Monopolies and Mergers Commission (1976), *Building Bricks,* London: HMSO.

National Board for Prices and Incomes (1968a), *Report No. 75; Costs and Prices of the Chocolate and Sugar Confectionery Industry,* London: HMSO.

–(1968b), Report No. 52; *Costs and Charges in the Radio and Television Rental Relay Industry,* London HMSO.

Newbould, E. (1970), *Management and Merger Activity,* Liverpool: Guthstead.

Pratten, C. (1971), *Economies of Scale in Manufacturing Industry,* Cambridge: Cambridge University Press.

Price Commission (1976), *Television Rental Charges,* Report No. 19, London: HMSO.

Phlips, L. (1971), *Effects of Industrial Concentration,* Amsterdam: North Holland.

Retail Business (1976), *Report No. 2, UK Television Market,* London.

Scherer, F. M. (1975). *The Economics of Multiplant Operation,* Cambridge, Mass.: Harvard University Press.

Salter, W. E. G. (1960), *Productivity and Technical Change,* Cambridge: Cambridge University Press.

6

Mergers in the engineering industry

6.1 Introduction

This chapter examines two of the most well-known mergers in our study. First, the merger forming the British Leyland Motor Corporation Ltd, which took place in 1968. Second, the mergers in 1967 and 1968 to form the General Electric Company Ltd. The mergers are of interest for a number of reasons, and have been grouped together to highlight the differences which caused the first to be a commercial failure and the second to be a commercial success. The obvious reason for contrasting these mergers is, of course, the different outcomes, but there are other factors to bear in mind. Both occurred in the engineering industry and both firms have been hit by economic recessions. Both mergers were sponsored by the Industrial Reorganisation Corporation (IRC) and their dominant personalities, Lord Stokes and Sir Arnold Weinstock, were held in esteem by the IRC as well as the Government. Finally, the mergers were the culmination of earlier mergers and were heralded by the news media at the time as likely to provide the solution to the problems facing the respective sectors.

The question to which an answer is sought, therefore, is what are the distinguishing features of these mergers which marked one out for success and one for failure? In an attempt to answer this question, case studies of British Leyland and GEC are presented separately with conclusions about the merits and demerits of each merger. Finally a concluding section re-emphasises some of the points made in the text of each case study, in an attempt to isolate distinguishing features.

6.2 The merger between Leyland Motor Company Ltd and BMH Ltd

This merger led to the formation of British Leyland, then the second largest motor manufacturer outside the United States and the fifth largest non-nationalised company in Britain.[1] Apart from the size of the company which resulted, this merger is interesting for a number of reasons:

(i) There was substantial encouragement from politicians, namely Anthony Wedgwood-Benn and Harold Wilson and from the Industrial Reorganisation Corporation. Although the decision of whether to merge was left to the managers of the companies concerned, it seems doubtful whether the merger would have taken place were it not for this encouragement (see Turner (1971) pp. 116 ff., pp. 164–7).

(ii) The takeover seemed to represent a part of the Government's industrial policy, the rationale of which was that if a well managed company (which Leyland was considered to be – the IRC code word for it was 'mustard') took over a badly managed company (which BMH – code word 'cress' – was considered to be) the badly managed company could be transformed. This theory seemed to be shared by the stock market at the time of the big merger boom and, possibly, also by the mergers panel.[2]

(iii) Each of the parties to the merger already had substantial experience of mergers and takeovers. BMH was the result of the merger in 1952 of Nuffield (Morris) and Austin and the takeover of Pressed Steel Fisher and Jaguar in 1966. Leyland had previously purchased Albion Motors and ACV (both commercial vehicle manufacturers) and Standard-Triumph and Rover Cars. Whilst making it difficult to isolate the impact of a single merger, the history of Leyland gives many insights into the motivation behind mergers and the consequences that ensue.

(iv) There is, furthermore, a great deal of information available about this company, and this is partly because it has been subject to much public scrutiny in recent years. The psychological impact of the well publicised failures of the hopes for British Leyland may well have been the most important factor in changing public attitudes to merger as a cure for an ailing firm.

6.2.1 The market for cars and commercial vehicles

The major division of the market is between cars and commercial vehicles (CVs) although some small vans and pick-up trucks are really variants

1 See Turner (1971). A great deal of the information on the circumstances surrounding this merger comes from this excellently told story of the formation of British Leyland, based on the Company's own intimate records. Excellent background information is to be found in Rhys (1972a). *The Minutes of Evidence* and the Fourteenth Report from the Expenditure Committee, HMSO 1975, provide interesting comments from people very involved in the industry. The Central Policy Review Staff (CPRS) report, *The Future of the British Car Industry*, also contains some illuminating tables and international comparisons. The other major report in this area is to be found in Ryder (1975) (The Ryder Report) which details the proposed new structure of British Leyland (as of 1976).

2 Since there was no requirement to show any benefits from a proposed merger it is possible that the panel thought mergers had no effect at all.

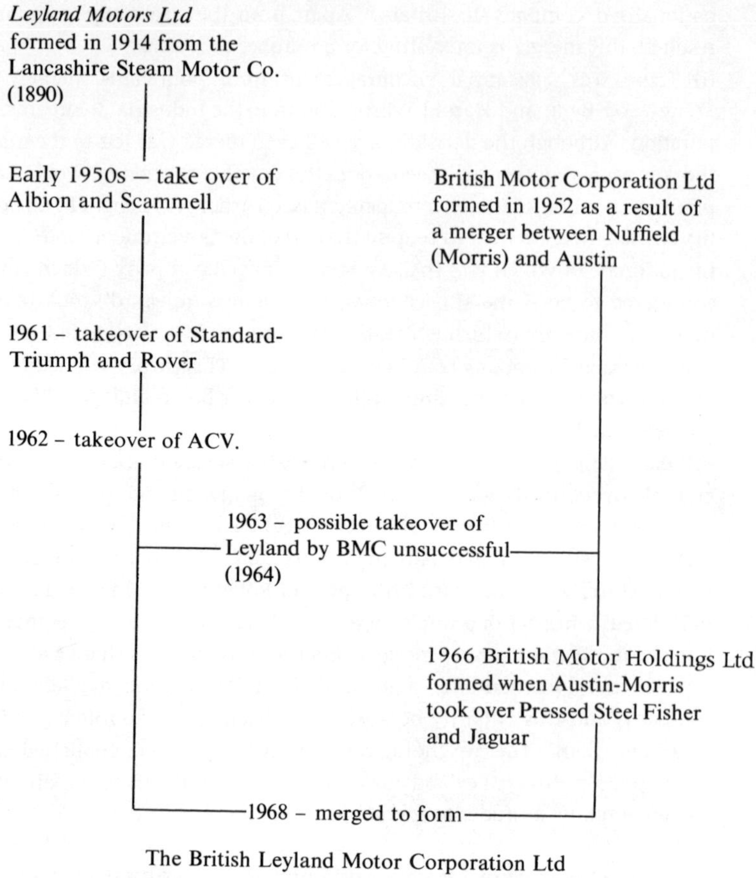

Figure 6.1 *Events leading to the merger of the Leyland Motor Co. Ltd with British Motor Holdings Ltd*

of cars. The major distinction from the manufacturing point of view is that most post-war cars are of unitary body shell construction, i.e. there is no separate chassis and the body shell provides the rigidity which supports the engine, transmission, steering etc. This, combined with the fact that it is the shape and size of the body which is the major source of product diversity in cars, means that body panel production dominates the economics of car production much more than is the case with commercial vehicles. In the latter there is a great deal of product diversity according to the varied needs of industrial customers. Even buses tend to be made much more to individual specifications than cars. In both cars and commercial vehicles there is room for the specialist producer, taking advantage of the lack of vertical integration in the industry and large-scale production by component manufacturers.

The production of motor vehicles has grown dramatically since the immediate post-war years – by a factor of four or five for cars, somewhat less for CVs. Until about 1960 the major constraint on sales was productive capacity. This applied throughout the world, and the government put pressure on the industry to export. The consequences are spelled out by Rhys (1972a) p. 379:

> The all-out drive to produce cars for world markets meant that production was primary and quality secondary. During the period 1946–56 the poor reputation gained by the British car industry, especially in Europe, as producers of second-rate and unreliable vehicles proved long-lived. Only in the late 1960s was the industry able to start erasing this reputation from the minds of overseas dealers and customers.

He also points out that the emphasis on volume led to a deterioration of labour relations and to the failure to build up a good sales and service network overseas to support the export markets. In the meantime, however, good profits could be made without being very efficient or overtly profiteering. The shortage of cars was such that until the mid 1950s second-hand prices were above new car prices. Imports were discouraged by a tariff of 33.3% reduced to 30% in 1962. The tariff came down in stages to 17.5% in 1969 and 11% in 1972.

At the start of the 1960s the period of excess demand was over, except for periods at the peak of economic activity. Increased costs and improvements in specification were not reflected in increased prices and profit margins fell. In 1956 and 1966 the major car firms achieved similar trading profits of around £30m. In 1956 this was achieved on sales of 708,000 cars whereas in 1966 it took sales of 1,606,000.

One of the major problems continually facing the industry is the fluctuation in demand for its products. In the past, the Treasury has tended to use hire purchase rules and purchase tax rates on cars to regulate the level of effective demand in the economy. In addition, since both cars and commercial vehicles are durable goods they tend to be subject to accelerator effects, causing demand to vary far more than in other industries. This has made investment planning difficult and has contributed to the financial weakness of motor manufacturers, as well as aggravating problems of labour–management relations.

6.2.2 The evolution of market structure

In cars, British Leyland and Ford dominate the domestic industry with Vauxhall and Chrysler some way behind. Table 6.1 gives shares in total production by number of vehicles produced for the major companies in Britain. The market share figures suggest a surprising degree of stability. In cars, BMC firms showed a slight post-war decline. Ford's secular growth seems to have

Table 6.1 *Percentage shares in production (numbers) of cars and commercial vehicles for British firms*

Year	1947	1954	1967	1969	1971	1973	1974	1976	1977 Jan.–Oct.
Cars									
Firm									
Austin-Morris (BMC)	40.1	38	34.7	37.7	38.2	38.6	36.6	51.7	48.7
Specialist cars	17.5	14.2	12.0	11.8	12.7	11.7	11.2		
Total BL	57.6	52.2	46.7	49.5	50.9	50.3	47.8	51.7	48.7
Ford	15.4	27	28.4	29.4	21.0	26.0	25.0	28.7	30.7
Chrysler (Rootes)	10.9	11	11.7	10.5	16.2	15.2	17.1	10.8	12.2
Vauxhall	11.2	9	12.7	11.0	11.4	7.9	8.9	8.2	7.9
Others	4.9	0.8	0.5	0.4	0.6	1.1	0.9	0.6	n.a.
Total	100.0	100.0	100.0	100.8	100.1	100.5	99.7	100.1	100.0
Commercial vehicles									
*BMC (Nuffield-Austin)	27.9	35	25.7	12.9	17.6	13.8	13.0	23.5	n.a.
*Rover	–	9	8.8						
Leyland (Trucks & Buses)	2.2	4		26.9	20.6	19.0	17.9	8.8	n.a.
Albion	1.3		5.8						
ACV	2.9	2							
Total BL	34.3	50	40.4	39.8	38.2	32.8	30.9	32.3	30.4
*Ford	22.9	15	26.4	29.4	26.4	32.9	32.6	38.1	38.1
*Chrysler-Dodge-Rootes	7.9	9	6.6	6.9	5.7	6.3	6.2	3.9	4.0
*Vauxhall-Bedford	20.3	21	23.8	22.0	27.7	25.7	27.9	23.2	19.1
Others	14.6	5	2.7	1.9	1.9	2.3	2.4	2.6	n.a.
Total	100.0	100	100.2	100.0	99.9	100.0	100.0	100.1	100.0

Source: Rhys, *The Motor Industry* for 1947, 1967, 1968, 1969; SMMT for 1971, 1973, 1974, 1976, 1977.
*Denotes mass-producers – tend to produce more standardised and less 'heavy' vehicles. (Heavy vehicles have larger unit value.)

halted in the mid 1950s. Chrysler has also gained sales, principally in the 1970s. The small-scale producers declined drastically up to the 1960s and then recovered slightly. Since 1954 (and, indeed, before that) the major factor increasing market concentration has been merger activity. The most important horizontal mergers have been the formation of BMC from Austin and Nuffield, Leyland's purchases of Standard-Triumph and Rover, and BMC's purchase of Jaguar. (The latter was in part a consequence of BMC's vertical merger with Pressed Steel. See Turner (1971), p. 108.) Finally, in 1968 came the formation of British Leyland.

The table does not include imports. Until about 1968 these were negligible, and dominated (as in other countries) by the VW Beetle. The two main reasons for this were the post-war lack of productive capacity abroad relative to booming home markets, and high tariffs. Capacity eventually increased enough to supply export markets and the Kennedy Round led to reductions in tariffs. Thus it was almost inevitable that imports should rise drastically in the 1970s. It was also inevitable that Britain's share of the world export market should decline as other countries' ability to produce increased. The effect of these changes on the car market has been to reduce effective concentration. Since there is no longer chronic excess demand, competition in the car industry is now fiercer than it was in the 1950s when there were more domestic producers.

In commercial vehicle production the situation is complicated by the wide variety of commercial vehicles – buses, vans, light trucks, 'light' heavy, 'medium' heavy and 'heavy' heavy trucks, and special purpose vehicles. The post-war growth, especially in the light-heavy market, meant that large-scale production methods became economic in that range.[3] Some firms in this category successfully moved up the weight scale; others left the industry, mainly because of difficulties in overcoming consumer loyalty to traditional, heavy-heavy producers. The small firms manage to survive by meeting special needs. For instance, the vehicles made by the small firms using labour-intensive methods tend to be more durable and may have better fuel consumption. This will make it worth while for high-mileage operators to pay the extra for the specialist vehicle. This explains why the share of the small producer has halted its decline.

The heavy commercial vehicle market has not suffered the slumps that have affected cars. A cautious attitude on the part of producers and the need for skilled labour have put a restriction on the rate of growth of capacity to produce heavy CVs. Excess demand with waiting lists in excess of a year has been the normal state of affairs. This shortage of capacity allowed some foreign heavy vehicle producers to enter the UK market. In 1974 CV import penetration was 13.76% and in 1975 dropped back to 11.17% in response to the fall in total demand

3 This passage draws heavily on D. G. Rhys (1972b).

The bus market is less dependent on specialists than the heavy CV market, since there is more scope for standardisation. This is mentioned by Rhys:

> As the majority of vehicles are bought by large undertakings requiring batches of anything up to 200 vehicles a year and as requirements are relatively similar there is more scope for larger volume production although not necessarily for mass-production. As a result, of the 13,000 or so large 'buses made in the U.K. annually some 8,000 are made by Leyland-AEC, about 1,000 by Daimler and about 800 by Bristol. Nearly all the remainder are made by the mass-producers, Bedford and Ford, utilizing components and techniques used for truck production. In fact only Seddon among the independents competes in the market for large 'buses [Rhys (1972b) p. 251].

In 1975 imports accounted for only 4.9% of new registrations of coaches, buses and taxis. Thus imports are not such a threat in this market.

In summary, the motor vehicle market is quite fragmented. Even within the separate markets of cars and commercial vehicles there are many divisions and sub-divisions, the identity of customers in different sub-divisions being quite different. Because of this, brand loyalty is probably very much restricted to specific sub-divisions within the total market. The type of marketing needed is probably quite different in different areas. There is some overlap in techniques of production, but it is not clear how this would benefit an integrated producer of the whole range of commercial vehicles.

6.2.3 The production process and economies of scale

British Leyland is active in producing a very wide range of motor vehicles, from small family saloons to luxury cars and from mass produced light vans to specialised, heavy commercial vehicles. These products have in common the internal combustion engine and all the parts necessary to transform the engine into a controllable vehicle (transmissions, brakes, steering, etc.). This in turn implies some common elements in the production techniques.

According to Rhys (1972a), scope for economies of scale exists only in certain production processes such as engine block manufacture where the optimum level of output appears to be one million per year. However, no individual model achieves sales of this size. Only by incorporating the same engine in different models could demand for engines move production into the 'technically efficient' range for the engine manufacturers.

The area of operations with most unreaped economies of scale is in the production of body panels. Optimum output would appear to be around two million a year. This number however, is larger than the total output of British cars and so this optimum is purely theoretical. The big danger in standardising basic engines and body panels across a range of car models is of course that sales will be lost to competitors, because customers no longer find the variety they want, so it is always possible that product rationalisation may achieve nothing more than a shrinking market share as brand loyalty decays and consumers find what they want elsewhere. There is probably less resistance to standardisation of cabs on commercial vehicles (see Rhys (1972a) pp. 106–8), but on the other hand the cab represents a much smaller proportion of total costs for CVs than the body shell does for cars.

The optimum scale for assembly is much lower than for production of engines or body panels and is in the region of 200,000 to 250,000 units a year. This is well within the range of most car manufacturers, and both BMH and Leyland had such a production level. Although most individual models fell short of this optimum, it is possible to change the variety and model on a production line with hardly any disruption. With the exception of light vans and other car variants there are no very great complementarities in the production of cars and CVs.

Non-production economies of scale are frequently used as justification for a merger when it is obvious that there are no production economies of scale. They are very difficult to quantify and so their existence is nearly impossible to refute or confirm. They can be categorised as managerial, marketing and financial economies. The replacement of the existing senior management by a more competent set through merger is sometimes called the exploitation of managerial economies of scale. The theory is that the good management has some spare capacity and so can manage a larger firm without any loss in efficiency.

Managerial economies might also be said to occur if the costs of managerial overheads do not increase proportionately to output. For example, if one wages clerk can pay twenty people as easily as ten this is a source of 'managerial' economies. One can almost always think of cases where an existing management department is not at optimum scale. Unfortunately, changing the size of firm to make these departments optimal may move other departments away from optimality. Furthermore, against managerial economies have to be set the disadvantages of control loss and attenuated lines of communication. As we shall see, there are grounds for supposing the latter predominated in the case of BL.

The major sources of marketing economies seem to be: overheads in setting up sales and service organisations abroad, brand loyalty, and the demand by dealers for a range of vehicles to show clients.

The impact of overheads on average marketing costs can be reduced by increasing total sales. This can be achieved either by selling larger numbers of a few models or by selling a wide range of models, each with limited sales. Overheads will generally be greater the wider is the range of models offered, both because of the need for larger stocks of vehicles and spare parts and greater complexity of organisation, so that there will be a trade off between extra sales and extra overheads.

Since some brand loyalty is a feature of the car (and probably CV) market it can be exploited by providing a range of vehicles. Clients' needs change but they may be happy to buy the same brand as they bought before if there is a suitable model available. Again there will be a trade off between extra sales generated and larger overheads.[4] In practice, since markets and dealer networks are different we conclude there are no significant marketing economies to combining in one firm the following three categories of volume cars, prestige cars, and trucks and buses.

Financial economies of scale can in theory be achieved because of the larger cash flow through a larger firm, and because of improved access to the capital market. Increased cash flow means cushioning for risky projects that fail. In the long run these are supposed to be balanced by risky projects that succeed. In practice it may simply give poor managements a longer time to hide their incompetence.

In summary the significant sources of economies of scale could have been exploited by the formation of three separate companies, each specialising in one particular type of product. Even without a merger there was still plenty of scope for rationalisation within BMC, which had not taken much advantage of the opportunities offered by the earlier merger between Nuffield and Austin.

One complication was the somewhat inappropriate ownership by BMC of Jaguar. This was a consequence of the unfortunate takeover by BMC of Pressed Steel, which made Jaguar nervous about its supply of bodies.[5]

The central justification for the BMH/Leyland merger was probably concern about the viability of the Austin-Morris division of BMC. Economies of scale, therefore, were really only incidental to the main hope that a more ruthless and effective management would be able to solve the problems of the largest component of the new firm whilst still managing to keep the commercial vehicle and prestige car divisions running efficiently. In our assessment of the merger, therefore, we concentrate on car production to see whether these hopes have been fulfilled.

6.2.5 The merger and its consequences

As early as 1963 the possibility of a kind of takeover of Leyland by BMC was discussed. The talks fell through in 1964 because demand was running at record levels and both firms felt prosperous.

In the years following, the balance of advantage shifted to Leyland. Demand fell away and so did profit margins, especially on cars. On top of this the new Austin 1800 was a commercial failure. During the negotiations which eventually led to the merger, BMC's financial position deteriorated considerably and this

4 For an empirical analysis see Leech and Cubbin (1978).

5 Incidentally, this purchase made things a bit more difficult for Rootes (Chrysler) who were forced to ship bodies to Coventry from Scotland.

enabled the Leyland management to secure control of the board of the new Company, British Leyland. Sir George Harriman, Chairman of BMC, was forced to resign and the bitterness engendered by the negotiations led to the resignation of Mr Joe Edwards, who had started the belated rationalisation of BMC. Sir Donald Stokes of Leyland became Chairman of the newly formed company, with the support of the Industrial Reorganisation Corporation.

Apart from scale economies the major sources for potential efficiency change were thought to be the reduction of overmanning, improved cost control and the replacement of obsolete methods of production. Before changes could be made it was necessary to set up an organisational structure to control the mammoth enterprise. We consider the organisational changes and their side effects first, and then examine the extent to which these sources of efficiency improvement were exploited.

Organisation

The task facing Sir Donald Stokes was a difficult one. In effect, he had to integrate eight public companies since previous mergers had not resulted in any appreciable rationalisation, and there was a legacy of distrust and hostility among them to overcome.

The intent at the time of the merger, declared in a document signed by Sir Donald Stokes and Sir George Harriman, was that the Corporation should not be a holding company with largely autonomous subsidiaries, but an integrated organisation. This was attested to by Mr John Barber in his evidence to the Expenditure Committee (1975), when explaining the detailed study made of the Corporation after the merger.

However, the basic structure of the firm remained unchanged until the two reorganisations of 1974. As Ryder (1975) points out:

> It is generally accepted that there were conflicting schools of thought within the Corporation – some working towards full integration and others hoping to preserve the independence of the old company structure. The present organisation is largely the result of these historical factors. The large Austin Morris/Pressed Steel operation has been broken down into separate divisions but the Rover Triumph and Jaguar Divisions remain mostly unchanged except for the loss of their parts and KD ('knocked down') activities to the newly created Parts KD Division. The other main feature of the past few years has been the building up of a large corporate staff, [Ryder Report, p. 44].

The last sentence illustrates one of the dangers inherent in the taking over of a large company. The new management may know little about the complexities of the day-to-day running of the firm and may be tempted to install staff at headquarters to monitor and control the activities of the separate divisions. In consequence, according to one ex-middle manager of British Leyland 'every function (was) duplicated by a Central Staff Department situated either in London or in the Midlands'.[6]

Part of the problem was a lack of delegation by Lord Stokes. The Ryder Report says that he had too many people reporting to him (21 directors and managers) and Salmon (1975) claims that without Stokes's personal authority no activity could be initiated. Salmon is worth quoting:

> Parkinson's Law . . . proceeded to have a field day. Managers at the factories viewed the growth of new central staff with astonishment and disbelief. Although it was originally envisaged that the manning of these new departments would be covered by transfer without any replacement from the factories, on the mistaken basis that the responsibilities themselves would go with the staff, only a few moves proved possible for it was found that the functions had to be duplicated. The expansion of the new departments was mushroom-like, and such transfers as were made were often possible only because the factories offered managers to head office whom they themselves were happy to release. In the event, therefore, many new senior staff were perforce recruited from other companies, some quite unconnected with the motor industry.

Salmon suggested the solution, later to be endorsed by the Ryder Report – the need for a manager at plant level able to take the initiative in decision making. 'No one – certainly not at the factories – any longer felt solely responsible for anything, and consequently no one could be held accountable for the inevitable errors.' British Leyland in addition suffered from frequent changes of staff, and morale was low as a result.

Salmon also criticised 'the attenuated lines of communication and responsibility that are endemic in the organisation, and the disappearance of any coordination at the five major factories'. He suggests that each company within the corporation 'must have a managing director who possesses full authority, with policies in the formation of which he also has a say . . . After all, each of the companies was autonomous before, and most of them consistently made profits'.

It was only in November 1977 that the standard treatment for managerial diseconomies of scale was finally adopted. The new Chairman, Mr Michael Edwardes, removed from the Board the managing directors of the operating divisions, making them responsible for profits in their own area.

Overmanning

According to Turner (1971) Sir Harold Wilson had expected Lord Stokes to cut his labour force following the merger. However, British Leyland did not wish to do this for a number of reasons. Paramount among these must have been

6 See Salmon (1975).

the bad publicity GEC received when it closed the AEI telecommunications factory in Woolwich (even though AEI planned to close it before the takeover went ahead). On the positive side, Lord Stokes wanted to expand production sufficiently to justify BLMC's surplus manpower.

Graham Turner himself[7] on BBC Television News, had predicted 30,000 redundancies. Stokes felt he had to deny the report and it is claimed (Turner, p. 181) that this set back the process of rationalisation eighteen months – some might say much longer. Whatever the reasons, it is apparent that the problem of overmanning was not really tackled. Indeed, we have already seen how the problem got worse with the duplication of staff in the factories at headquarters. If Stokes hoped to buy good labour relations with this policy he did not succeed.

Another problem relating to the labour force and one that has grown more complex as a result of the large size of the firm, is the large number (thirty-five) of separate collective bargaining agreements, the negotiation of which takes up a great deal of central management's time. The difficulty of simultaneously reducing the number of bargaining agreements and moving to wage parity among plants without giving away large pay awards grows at an increasing rate with the number of component parts of the firm. Nine years after the merger little progress had been made in dealing with this problem. With separate firms the question of parity would probably not have arisen.

Cost control, rationalisation, and modernisation

More success was attained in adopting a business-like attitude to cost control in the design stage with some possible detriment to the traditional Longbridge attitude that 'designing cars ought to be fun'. The Marina, first new British Leyland high volume car, did undergo a cost reduction exercise even though it 'was not, like that of the first Cortina, a fairy tale of clockwork planning', and there was a feeling that 'it was – in the final analysis – the car which planners wanted and not the car which an out-of-control production machine had delivered to them' (Turner (1971) p. 207). The Marina also provided the opportunity to replace obsolete plant and equipment at Cowley for body manufacturing and assembly. Table 6.2 gives a summary of the rationalisation and modernisation between the merger and the Ryder Report. It also gives some idea of the size and complexity of the company even though it only mentions a fraction of the 55 main manufacturing plants left by the end of 1974.

The new firm was not particularly striking in demonstrating the economies of producing in large firms. It must be admitted that organising the firm to take advantages of being large could most easily be done over a period of many years as models were replaced in such a way as to ensure a greater proportion of

7 Author of *The Leyland Papers* and at the time the BBC Industrial Correspondent.

Table 6.2 *Summary of main items of rationalisation and modernisation carried out by British Leyland 1968–74*

Category	
Products	Riley marque discontinued.
	Morris Minor, Morris Oxford, Austin 3 litre facilities closed down.
	Minor and A55 vans abandoned.
	Several new products introduced including buses, tractors, trucks and cars. The latter sometimes demonstrating the attempt to produce a large number of variants with the minimum number of body panels e.g. Marina, Allegro.
	Number of Austin-Morris marques reduced from 24 to 12.
	Number of specialist car marques reduced from 15 to 12.
Plant closures, relocation, etc.	Fisholow Products Ltd sold off.
	Daimler bus production moved to Leyland.
	Jaguar parts and service moved out of Browns Lane, Coventry.
	Closure and clearance of Adderly Park West and Coventry Tool and Gauge plant.
	Number of plants reduced from 70 to 55.

New investment, modernisation of plant	Modern body-manufacturing and assembly facilities for producing Marina at Cowley.
	New plant at Liverpool for Triumph range.
	Extra facilities at Bathgate for production of own cabs for CVs.
	Extension of Jaguar production facilities.
	Substantial improvements to Swindon press shop.
	Rebuilding and re-equipment of north engine shop at Longbridge.
	Modernisation in production of vans at Common Lane, East Birmingham.
	Installation of most modern assembly plant in Europe at Solihull (Rover production).
Distribution system	Establishment of regional sales offices.
	Reduction of number of dealerships in Britain.
	Formation of BL International. Some rationalisation abroad.
Industrial relations	Replacement of old payments systems.
Management overheads	Building up and strengthening of central staffs.
	New research and service centre at SU carburettor.
Organisation	Truck factory at Bathgate transferred to Truck and Bus Division.
	Coventry Climax transferred from Jaguar and Special Products division.
	Jaguar transferred from Austin-Morris to Specialist Cars.

Source: Mainly company reports.

common parts. Some progress was made with the Marina. A wide range of variants was produced using the minimum number of different body panels.[8] (This contrasts with the previous BMC policy of producing versions with distinct panels.) However, this could have been achieved without merger. In assessing the merger the relevant question is whether advantage has been taken of the comprehensive model range to achieve economies of scale in internally-produced components.[9] By 1971 Donald Stokes was claiming that the number of model variants produced had been reduced from 39 to 24 – 12 of the 15 deletions coming from the Austin-Morris division, and that plans were 'currently under development' to eliminate 'unnecessary competition between British Leyland models' (1971 Annual Report). However, this had not been achieved by 1974, and in fact the Ryder Report recommendations were based largely on a planning document originating inside British Leyland.

The rationalisation which did take place consisted of scrapping the more luxurious variants of basic models which could equally have been accomplished by the constituent firms in BLMC, although possibly the merger between Rover, Jaguar and Triumph would have been needed for the rationalisation of specialist cars. Indeed, it is difficult to find in production economies any rationale for one firm to produce the whole range of cars, trucks and buses. For example, the Expenditure Committee say

> Ford management were optimistic about their ability to achieve most scale economies in the UK. This suggests that BLMC's problems are not those of scale and can be solved by product rationalisation and plant modernisation. Mr. Beckett told us that specialised units such as light diesels for commercial vehicles and specialist cars such as the Capri required joint production with Ford (Germany) in order to spread tooling and design costs sufficiently [p. 71].[10]

It seems that, as far as production economies are concerned, little advantage has been taken of the fact that BLMC is an integrated firm producing the whole range of cars, trucks and buses. It was not until the Board became accountable to the government that any really integrated view of the company was formed. True, Austin-Morris truck production was transferred to the Truck and Bus Division and one overseas marketing division was formed (the International Division). So far, however, only a limited use has been made of the International Division (Expenditure Committee, p. 97) and British Leyland seem reluctant to

8 It will be recalled that body panel production is the area of most scope for scale economies in production.

9 Externally-produced components can be rationalised without the necessity for merger. The component manufacturers have had some success in persuading the assemblers to do this.

10 It also suggests that two separate firms or operating divisions, Austin-Morris and Rover-Triumph-Jaguar, would also be viable from a production economy point of view.

divulge the extent of rationalisation of the truck and bus operations. The available evidence suggests that whilst senior executives have worked hard at rationalisation there is scope for much more. (See p. 28 of the Ryder Report (1975).)

None of the official reports gives any indication of why the production of trucks, buses and cars by one firm should be desirable. Indeed, the conflict between the remarks of Mr Barber (in evidence to the Expenditure Committee, see below) and Sir Don Ryder can be seen as arising out of the problems of such an integrated firm. The Ryder plans were based on the belief 'that British Leyland should be run, as far as possible, as four separate businesses – British Leyland cars, British Leyland Trucks, British Leyland Special Products and British Leyland International' (Ryder Report, p. 40). This represents a reversal of the original policy of the firm's management. One of the problems of BL as an integrated firm is the tendency of the car side, which accounts for 70% of the business, to dominate the concerns of the whole company – and for the car side itself to be dominated by the ailing Austin-Morris component.

Finally, we may note that little scope has been found in retrospect for either marketing or financial economies of scale unless one defines as a financial economy of scale the fact that, beyond a certain size, the government is very likely to intervene with financial support to stop liquidation of the company and the loss of jobs.

Evaluation of the merger

Since the government's intervention in 1974, British Leyland has been very much in the public eye. The publicity afforded the company has been mostly unfavourable, with emphasis on labour disputes, production problems, and reliability vis-à-vis certain foreign makes. Given the importance of the industry and the taxpayer's financial involvement this scrutiny is understandable. However, it may be that public impression of the company is an unbalanced one. It is the purpose of this section to look at some objective measures of performance.

One much publicised figure is Leyland's share of the home market (Table 6.3) especially in months where there have been production difficulties. Column (i) gives some indication of the remarkable fall in market share. Yet when allowance is made for the increase in import penetration, BL's share appears remarkably stable (column (ii)). Thus the company appears to be doing as well (or badly) on average as the other firms located in Britain in maintaining its share against the rising tide of imports. If we look at total production (Table 6.1) the story is similar. Contrary to the impression frequently given by journalists, a great deal of the increased import penetration can probably be attributed to variation in consumers' tastes and requirements that could not be met economically purely from British sources, combined with the low level of protection afforded the British industry. Having said this, there is no doubt that some of the import penetration might have been prevented had the British firms been more efficient.

Table 6.3 *British Leyland's share of UK new car registrations (by volume)*

Year	BL share (%)		(iii)
	(i) Including imports	(ii) Excluding imports	Import penetration (%)
1968	40.57	44.23	8.30
1969	40.25	44.94	10.43
1970	38.11	44.47	14.28
1971	40.16	49.74	19.28
1972	33.12	43.29	23.51
1973	31.87	43.92	27.42
1974	32.74	45.41	27.90
1975	30.88	46.23	33.22
1976	27.43	44.21	37.94
1977	24.33	44.54	45.38

Source: SMMT

Some estimates of efficiency changes are presented in Tables 6.4 and 6.5, in the form of estimates of *k*. It will be recalled that the measure takes into account changes in input prices, output prices and profitability. It is an unfortunate effect of mergers that separate profit figures for different divisions are not disclosed. Although it is known that the car division was less profitable than the truck and bus division, it is not known by how much, or whether there was a difference in the trend over time. Accordingly the measures of factor input requirement for cars and commercial vehicles are based on the assumption that profitability in the two divisions moved similarly from year to year. If profitability declined faster in cars than in trucks or buses our measure will overstate the gain in efficiency in car production, and understate it for trucks and buses, and vice versa. At the time of writing, however, we have not managed to obtain divisional profit and sales information. It is known that profitability from volume cars is much more volatile than from commercial vehicles. For instance, Austin-Morris made a loss of nearly £16m in 1970.

Table 6.4 shows estimates of unit factor requirements for cars, and compares the constituent companies of British Leyland with Ford. All firms show an improvement in productivity over time, but the most striking is that shown by BMC between the first period (1956–61) and the second (1962–67). The measured gain here is 16.8% as against Ford's 11.5%. (Note that there were no significant mergers that can explain this.) Even so, BMC were still not as efficient as Ford by the late 1960s. From the table, it would appear that Leyland was more efficient than Ford in this second period. However, at this time Leyland produced only a very limited range of cars and its profit figures are very heavily influenced by their commercial vehicle operations, so the two series are not really comparable. Similar problems make comparison difficult between BMC and Leyland.

Table 6.4 *Unit factor requirements – cars*

Year	Output price index / Input price index: British Leyland	Ford	Unit factor requirement (k): BMC		Leyland				Ford	
1956	134.6		133.8							
1957	136.1		133.3						125.3	
1958	131.4		127.6	E =					119.6	G =
1959	131.6		127.7	126.4					117.3	116.6
1960	114.6		112.9						104.5	
1961	121.7		124.1						116.1	
1962	110.6		112.4		111.1				107.9	
1963	108.0		107.8		105.9				101.3	
1964	102.0		101.3	B =	97.0	A =			99.4	C =
1965	101.6		101.4	105.2	95.9	100.9			103.5	103.1
1966	96.3		98.9		92.9				98.7	
1967	104.2		109.5		102.47				108.0	
1968	100						100.0		95.2	
1969	97.5	96.1					97.1		93.1	
1970	94.9	95.5					98.6	D =	96.0	F =
1971	92.3	92.4					93.6	97.1	101.5	96.5
1972	97.0	99.3					98.7		97.5	
1973	93.2	98.6					93.6		95.6	

Notes: Output prices are adjusted for quality change. Separate prices were calculated for Ford and British Leyland after 1968. Prior to this differences in k represent merely difference in profitability. Means of grouped years are denoted by letters A–G.

Tests of significance

Comparison	$\bar{x}_1 - \bar{x}_2$	% difference	t	degrees of freedom
A–B	4.35	4.1	1.22	10
A–D	3.79	3.8	1.26	10
B–D	8.14	7.7	3.33*	10
E–B	21.17	16.8	4.81*	10
C–D	6.59	6.4	2.32*	10
C–G	13.42	11.5	3.75*	9
C–F	6.6	6.4	2.61*	10

*Indicates significance at 5% level.

The efficiency improvement between 1962–67 and the third period, 1968–73, is much less. The most direct comparison can be made for Ford, which shows an improvement of 5.9%. Does the figure for British Leyland for the same period represent a greater or smaller improvement than this? To answer this question

Table 6.5 *Unit factor requirements – commercial vehicles*

Year ended 30 Sept.	Output price index / Input price index	Profits / Revenue	Unit factor requirement (*k*)	
1963	107.5	6.0	105.1	mean = 99.6 (1963–67)
1964	104.6	8.8	99.2	
1965	102.5	9.5	96.6	
1966	100.5	7.5	97.7	
1967	101.7	5.8	99.7	
1968	100.0	3.9	100.0	
1969	98.2	4.4	97.7	mean = 98.9 (1969–73)
1970	96.5	0.4	100.0	
1971	99.9	2.8	101.1	
1972	97.5	2.5	98.9	
1973	96.2	3.3	96.8	
1974	89.2	0.1	92.7	

Notes: Based on wholesale price index numbers and financial results of Leyland and British Leyland. Mean 1969–74 = 97.9. The *t*-value for the difference between the 1963–67 and 1969–74 means is 1.04. It is not significant.

we need to consider what the observed figure for British Leyland would have been if both the Leyland components had improved efficiency by the same amount. In 1967 BMC and Jaguar produced something over four times as many cars as Standard-Triumph and Rover. If both parts of British Leyland had improved efficiency by 5.9% the weighted value for *k* would be 97.5. The observed figure of 98 is 0.5% higher than this. This is not a large or statistically significant difference.

When one considers that BMC had further to go than Ford in the direction of efficiency improvement one must conclude that the evidence fails to support the hypothesis that the merger accelerated the increase in efficiency in car production.

A similar conclusion follows from the calculations for unit factor requirements for commercial vehicles (Table 6.5). Even if the most favourable post-merger period (1969–74) is taken the difference in factor requirements is not statistically significant. The percentage reduction is much lower than for cars. This supports the qualitative evidence which failed to find enough sources of gains to offset the problems of managing a larger firm.

Tables 6.4 and 6.5 also give an indication of how the consumer has fared over the years. The price of cars and commercial vehicles has declined relative to the cost of purchases required for their manufacture. This has been achieved partly by efficiency improvements but also by reductions in profit margins following the ending of the post-war period of excess demand and by the lowering of barriers to international trade. The reluctance of firms like British Leyland to pass on cost increases in price increases has also played its part in the reduction of output prices relative to costs, but this may have happened anyway with increasing international competition. In short, we cannot attribute to the merger any detrimental effects of market power on price.

It can be argued that the reduction in the number of models, by restricting the choice of consumers, has been and will be detrimental. This is a complex question and this is not the place to discuss it at length, but the point is raised as a note of caution against assuming that a reduction in the number of varieties offered is a good thing as long as it increases profits. Such assumptions seem implicit in some of the views expressed in the Ryder and CPRS reports. In the present case it seems as if the reduction in varieties was made up for by an increase in the number of imported models. For an empirical analysis of the rise in import penetration see Leech and Cubbin (1978).

6.2.6 **BL/BMH merger: conclusions**

It would be an over-simplification to attribute everything that has happened to British Leyland since 1968 to the merger betweeen Leyland and BMH. In particular, the financial difficulties of 1974 and 1975 owed something to the world recession brought on by the sudden increase in oil prices, inflation and bad industrial relations created over many years of conflict and insecurity. However, the fact that the giant firm of British Leyland was unable to cope with the situation without help from government funds has probably brought home to the few remaining enthusiasts that mergers are not a very effective general cure for industrial ills. Indeed, there are strong grounds for believing that the problems were more intractable because of the very size of the firm.

Over the years the motor industry has been the subject of fairly heavy merger activity. As we have seen, British Leyland was the outcome of several mergers. Some of these, such as the Austin-Morris merger, seem to have been carried out cynically and almost entirely for the purpose of reducing competition, the result being a firm divided against itself which only managed to show profits as long as it did because of high import duties and the post-war excess demand for cars.[11] Others, such as the merger between BMC and Jaguar to form BMH and several within the commercial vehicle sector, can be thought of as defensive mergers. In Jaguar's case, they were worried about their supply of bodies following the BMC acquisition of Pressed Steel. Thus, mergers often prompt other mergers for which there would otherwise be no commercial or economic rationale.

The formation of British Leyland was conceived and executed during the

11 There was fairly rapid rationalisation of engines and gear boxes but in other respects the firm was like two separate entities. For example, until 1966 Austin and Morris had separate boards of directors and kept separate books. In 1966 Joe Edwards started trying to carry out some long overdue reform. He left the company during negotiations over the Leyland merger because he was offered only a subordinate position.

period when merger mania was at its height. The IRC believed that the Leyland management team would ginger up the BMH management. The BMH team seemed to be motivated by a desire to respond to the wishes of politicians.

The merger did not have the magic results hoped for by the IRC. Senior management, including Lord Stokes, seem to have worked hard at rationalisation. The main problem seems to have been that they were spreading themselves over a very large company, the major component of which had suffered from years of neglect. Much of the rationalisation that occurred could have happened without the merger. BMC could have sold its truck interests to Leyland and Jaguar, Triumph and Rover could have been organised as a separate company. If the managements of these three separate companies had then worked as hard at efficiency improvement as the British Leyland management perhaps more would have been achieved.

It seems very difficult to justify the present large size of British Leyland. Product rationalisation could have occurred in smaller companies, and there is evidence that it was starting to happen in BLMC anyway. There probably were some small marketing advantages in being a horizontally integrated motor vehicle manufacturer. But these seem to be outweighed by the difficulties of finding a suitable organisational form for a company so heavily dominated by cars. The difficulties that middle management might have to face in a large corporation appear to have occurred in BLMC (see Salmon (1975)). Trade unionists giving evidence to the Expenditure Committee also felt that problems arose because of the lack of flexibility afforded to local management in a large corporation.

The dominance of the more glamorous car divisions has led some observers to suspect that commercial vehicle operations have been neglected as a result of the merger. This view is supported by figures showing a decline in the market share of British Leyland commercial vehicles and apparently very small recent gains in productivity compared with cars.

Finally, the most important aspect of the formation of British Leyland was political. With the benefit of hindsight, we can see the merger as a prelude to nationalisation. Even without eventual government intervention, the merger would have represented a substantial increase in the centralisation of an important sector of the economy. Since the merger cannot be justified retrospectively on efficiency grounds, the final judgement must be a political one, beyond the scope of this chapter.

6.3 The mergers of GEC with AEI and English Electric

This case study will be concerned with the background to the mergers of GEC with AEI and EE within the context of the engineering industry, the effect of the mergers on GEC and the implications for the industry. The early history of the British electrical engineering industry and the three major companies which dominated the industry until the mid 1960s has been adequately covered elsewhere (Jones and Marriott (1970), Latham (1969), Counter Information Services (1973)). Besides the interesting insights into the role played by American firms such as Westinghouse and GE of America, such sources show the progress of AEI, GEC and English Electric, from being firms established in the first twenty years of this century to firms who dominated their industry at the beginning of the 1960s. Part of this growth was due to merger and takeover of smaller firms, particularly in domestic consumer products, and partly due to internal growth in an expanding market. These firms were the British electrical giants involved in all sectors of the industry, whereas most of their rivals' productive capacity was concentrated in subsectors of the engineering industry. In terms of the size of individual contracts, the electrical machinery industry and telegraph and telephone apparatus are the most important subsectors. In these markets the firms faced monopsonists, the Central Electricity Generating Board (CEGB) in the first industry and the Post Office in the second. It has always been considered that there was sufficient countervailing power in these sectors for increases in concentration to pass by without comment, but the evidence presented below may lead to a reappraisal of such an attitude.

6.3.1 The changing environment of the electrical engineering industry

In the early years this industry was covered by cartel agreements at both national and international level and by restrictive practices which boosted profits and restricted competition, particularly during times of recession when there was always the danger of greater competitive pressure on prices due to producers' excess capacity. The most famous of these agreements was the lamp ring dating back to the Phoebus Agreement of 1924 and the International Electrical Association (IEA) agreement of 1934.

In the middle of the 1950s, the passing of the Restrictive Trades Practice Act (1956) outlawed the legally enforceable restrictive agreement: in future all restrictive agreements had to pass the scrutiny of the Restrictive Practices Court and actively benefit society in some way. It is not surprising that firms within the electrical engineering industry should have found such agreements attractive, for it is a highly capital intensive industry, which implies high unit costs when capacity is not fully utilised and demand tends to be 'lumpy'. In such a situation a cartel or agreement would seem a simple method of maintaining profit levels.

The 1956 legislation hit the industry hard; also, about the same time (1957), the Monopolies Commission recommended that both the national restrictive agreements and the IEA's agreement should terminate and that in future UK manufacturers should not enter into such agreements. The industry itself was also under inspection from the Monopolies Commission in respect of lamps, electronic valves and cathode ray tubes and electrical machinery. Of all the restrictive agreements pertaining to the industry only one survived intact: The

Telephone Apparatus Manufacturers' Agreement (TAM) which was protected by being a Crown Agreement with the Postmaster General. A full appreciation of the extent and importance of these agreements to the industry is only obtained when it is realised that they covered all areas of production and were signed by all the main producers. (For a full account see Dutton (1978).)

The ending of the official agreements did not mean that firms stopped making any agreements. It is difficult to estimate how many secret agreements are likely to exist in this industry, but the Monopolies Commission's recent investigation into the cable industry forced the cable makers to admit to a secret restrictive agreement operational from 1965 to the end of 1974 (see below).

The industry, under attack from legislation designed to encourage competition, began to strive for a new mode of behaviour. Unfortunately for them by the middle of the 1960s the industry had other troubles. Over-capacity was a major problem. No one had anticipated a turndown in demand, least of all AEI. Their Chairman, Lord Chandos, had expanded the capacity of the firm particularly on the heavy side of electrical engineering (turbines, generators, switchgear, etc.) which not only put the firm into serious financial difficulties but aggravated other problems of the industry. In fact the three major companies, AEI, English Electric and GEC all had their problems at the beginning of the 1960s. English Electric, aware of its over-commitment to the heavy side of the industry, tried to merge with GEC in 1960 but talks collapsed. GEC was not in a particularly strong financial position at this time. It was after the collapse of the negotiations with English Electric that, while looking round for profitable investments it bought Radio and Allied, owned by Mr George Sobell and Mr Arnold Weinstock (his son-in-law), and Weinstock (later Sir Arnold) came to GEC (see Figure 6.2). AEI was in trouble; having raised a lot of capital quickly and committed it to long-term growth, the returns did not materialise. Unfortunately, neither did the hoped-for expansion of demand. As a result profitability declined (see Tables 6.6 and 6.7).

AEI's problems did not end there. Until the merger with GEC, AEI's biggest fight was internal. It was in essence four separate companies, British Thomson-Houston, Metrovick, Ediswan-Hotpoint and AEI Overseas. However, the main antagonists were the old rivals Metrovick and BTH. The rivalry which existed before they merged continued afterwards. Engineers dominated both groups, and resources were wasted producing competing designs rather than uniting forces to beat external competitors. Many reorganisations took place within AEI but there was no real effort to root out the old companies and integrate them into the new AEI. In one thing the engineers of BTH and Metrovick were united – they were opposed to AEI moving into the lighter side of engineering, and encouraged all moves out (see Figure 6.2).

In his book, Latham (1969) points to the fact that there was no lack of analysis in AEI. He, for one, as Financial Director seemed to know what was going wrong,

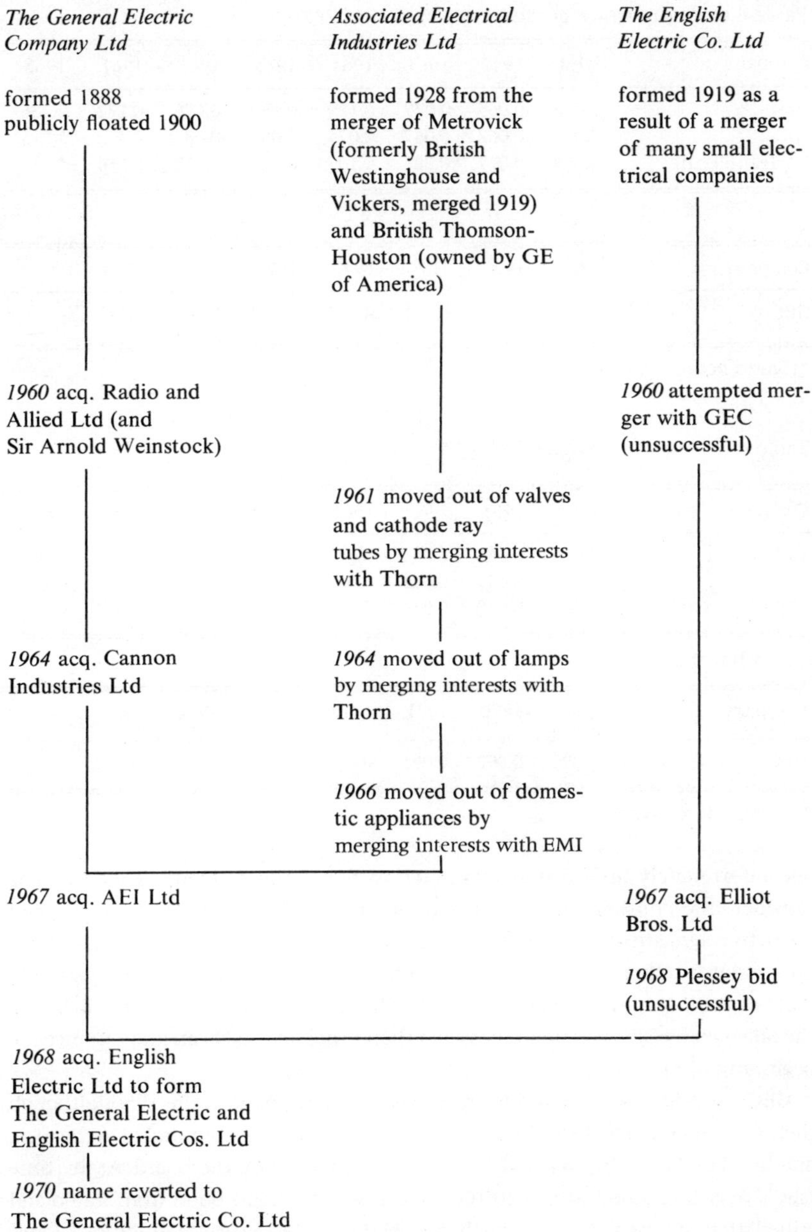

Figure 6.2 *Events leading to the merger of GEC, AEI and English Electric*

Table 6.6 *Rate of return of capital employed 1961–75*

Company	1961	1962	1963	1964	1965	1966	1967	1968
GEC	0.048	0.065	0.079	0.129	0.180	0.198	0.172	0.186
AEI	0.054	0.062	0.047	0.075	0.085	0.089	*	*
English Electric	0.068	0.077	0.088	0.107	0.126	0.129	0.136	*

Company	1969	1970	1971	1972	1973	1974	1975
GEC	0.146	0.132	0.144	0.160	0.237	0.266	0.273

*Figures not comparable.

Table 6.7 *Price–cost margins 1961–75*

Company	1961	1962	1963	1964	1965	1966	1967	1968
GEC	0.036	0.048	0.054	0.082	0.109	0.122	0.108	0.087
AEI	0.044	0.055	0.041	0.059	0.065	0.049	*	*
English Electric	0.041	0.050	0.056	0.064	0.078	0.075	0.069	*

Company	1969	1970	1971	1972	1973	1974	1975
GEC	0.091	0.092	0.091	0.095	0.131	0.145	0.132

*Figures not comparable.

but unfortunately little action was taken to rectify the problems. The factors he considered responsible for AEI's lack of profitability included (1) the abolition of restrictive agreements, (2) the slump in demand, (3) over-capacity, (4) the emphasis on standards rather than profits, and (5) the separate nature of the four constituent parts of AEI. It may have been that AEI did not have time to take action before the takeover by GEC was upon them, but their problems had been known since the beginning of the 1960s.

GEC itself had been suffering from weak management in the 1950s although their Chairman at the time, Lindley, was quick to see the potential of Weinstock, and by 1961 Mr Weinstock and his father-in-law were on the Board. At this time GEC's overdraft stood at £11,200,000 and it was Kenneth Bond from Radio and Allied that stopped it rising further. Although there were teething problems, GEC was committed to cutting costs, but it was not until Weinstock became Managing Director in 1963 that consistent financial control was introduced. In contrast to AEI, GEC strived to move out of the heavy side of electrical engineering and in 1965, GEC sold its turbo-generating interests to C. A. Parsons Ltd for £12 million.

Of all the firms in the industry English Electric was possibly the most stable at the time, but it was aware that the cut-back in demand for both power stations and telecommunications apparatus was going to hit the industry hard. In 1967, with the backing of the Industrial Reorganisation Corporation (IRC) it merged with Elliot Bros. Ltd (see Figure 6.2). However, the firms continued virtually as separate entities.

At this time, the IRC had a brief to seek out industries in which mergers could assist rationalisation and promote the introduction of new technology. The IRC was already familiar with the personalities involved as it had investigated the telecommunications industry in 1967 (no published report) and not long after, it was given the brief to promote the rationalisation of the heavy electrical engineering industry, as the CEGB's predictions of electricity demand implied overcapacity for industry.

The actual history of the take-over of AEI is well documented (Latham (1969), Jones and Marriott (1970)). It now seems obvious that AEI was bound to lose its fight against the merger, for the GEC bid had the backing of the IRC and the critical acclaim of the press. The merger was promoted to solve the problems of the heavy electrical engineering industry, but in no way can the merger between AEI and GEC be described as the answer, unless the answer is seen in terms of personalities (the most impressive being that of Mr (now Sir) Arnold Weinstock) and in terms of styles of management. GEC was no longer a major competitor in turbogenerators. If it took over AEI and reduced AEI's capacity autonomously this would leave the market to English Electric, C. A. Parsons Ltd, and A. Reyrolle & Co. Ltd (the latter two forming Reyrolle-Parsons). In fact, Weinstock later offered AEI's heavy electrical engineering capacity to English Electric. This action could be interpreted as either his willingness to let the heavy side go altogether, or as the catalyst for the later merger with English Electric. There is some suggestion in the events that the takeover of AEI was only the first step in gaining an even larger market share by taking over English Electric too (see below).

Certainly, the suggestion that personalities and management quality were the factors influencing the IRC's backing of the merger is supported by the following quote: 'All mergers large or small, succeed only when there is a strong and unified management at the top determined to exploit the opportunities for rationalisation which the merger provides. The quality of management is the key to success and the IRC has to be satisfied on this fundamental aspect before giving its support to any project' (IRC (1969)). GEC could only have wanted AEI in order to acquire size and prestige, for GEC was the smallest of the three firms and although growing, internal growth takes a long time. The acquisition of AEI also gave them a greater sphere of influence and a larger market share without the penalty of a period of cut-price competition to achieve it.

AEI's management did not consider the merger as the rational solution to the problems of electrical engineering (see Latham (1969)). Commenting on the marriage Latham says of GEC: 'Only ten per cent of the Company's total assets were used in engineering; in contrast over fifty per cent of AEI's assets were used in engineering or in cables, in which GEC were not involved.' He also points to the monopoly situation which arose as a result of the merger (in grid switchgear, telecommunications, lamps and lighting) which were 'overlooked' by the Board of Trade to enable the merger to go ahead. The joint company acquired a forty per cent share of the telecommunications business leaving Plessey with 40% and STC with 20%. Presumably telecommunications was not regarded as a cause for concern on the grounds that the main purchaser, the Post Office, was a monopsonist. The IRC opposed further reference to the Monopolies Commission on lamps alone. The role of the IRC was very important in all this. They backed the GEC bid. Weinstock not only sought their support but the support of others in the industry, including Lord Nelson of English Electric. In the height of the merger Grierson, one of the IRC instigators, resigned from his post at the IRC to become a director of GEC.

As will be seen from Figure 6.2 the incident which sparked off the merger of GEC and English Electric was Plessey's bid for English Electric in the following year (1968). Plessey, a rapidly growing firm, strong in telecommunications and automation, sought to extend its market by a merger with English Electric, but it had no experience in the heavy side of electrical engineering in which English Electric was mainly involved. To English Electric the merger had no logic and the bid was formally rejected. However, if it came to a take-over bid Plessey might just win as English Electric's shares were depressed by the publication of its half-yearly figures.

Talks concerning the future of the turbo-generating industry continued. As mentioned above, GEC had earlier offered English Electric AEI's turbo-generating interests but these included Larne in Northern Ireland, which had never made a profit, so Lord Nelson rejected the offer. However, here and at later meetings, it was suggested that a merger of the interests of both companies was the only solution for the industry, an idea not rejected outright by English Electric.

The possibility of the merger developed while English Electric remained threatened by Plessey. Although English Electric did not need GEC to fight off Plessey, it may have been difficult to see this at the time. It appears Lord Nelson soon became convinced of the rightness of the merger (after all English Electric had been after GEC in 1960) and it was he who approached the appropriate government departments, companies, and the IRC. The IRC were in favour of the merger, and as the Board of Trade would just have readily let the Plessey/English Electric merger go ahead, the merger was rushed through.

The announcement of the merger alarmed competitors. Plessey saw the dangers that might arise from the size of the shares which the new firm would have in important markets. Even Reyrolle Parsons[12] were worried by the prospect of its only competitor in heavy electrical engineering subsidising its product from other areas. However, the merger was not referred to the Monopolies Commission even though it created a monopoly (as legally defined) in domestic appliances (a 37% share of the market) and in heavy electrical plant (a 70% share in switchgear, 52% in turbo-generators) as well as reinforcing an existing monopoly in telecommunications). The reasons why the Board of Trade did not refer the merger appeared to be the IRC's backing and the statements made by Sir Arnold Weinstock and Lord Nelson that redundancy would be less if the merger took place. Promises of full compensation for those made redundant were also made.

The obligations placed on the new firm were that it must consult the Department of Employment as well as the unions about all redundancies and take into account regional policies. They also had to promise not to interfere with competition in any market and not to undertake any practices which would damage competition. In addition, they were obliged to appoint an IRC director. Such obligations were hardly binding and few checks were made to see they were being observed (IRC (1969)).

In the second report of the IRC (1969) it is stated that the role of the nominated director was to be associated with decisions affecting management structure and corporate strategy but not to intervene in the day-to-day management of firms. Commenting on events after the GEC mergers it is stated: 'In the case of GEC – English Electric, for example, which accounts for about forty per cent of the entire UK electrical/electronics industry, there remain many opportunities for further reorganisation. The Company has agreed to give full weight to the IRC's views on these matters and has not excluded the possibility of disposing of certain of its activities.' However, in the third IRC report (IRC (1970)) the list of firms which had appointed an IRC director does not include GEC despite the obligation to appoint a director undertaken two to three years earlier.

The main objective of the two mergers was to bring about rationalisation in the industry, and to do it less painfully than might be achieved otherwise. There is no doubt that GEC set about this task and, until the recent recession which started in 1974 hit the industry, it had done much to bring capacity into line with demand (see Chapter 8). The following section judges the success of the above mergers on commercial grounds and also considers whether or not

12 Reyrolle Parsons Ltd, also formed in 1968, was previously A. Reyrolle & Co. Ltd and C. A. Parsons Ltd. Later with IRC help it took over Bruce Peebles Industries. The merger of Reyrolle and Parsons was looked on favourably by the IRC and was made possible by GEC selling both GEC's and AEI's holdings in Parsons (36%) to Reyrolle which already had 18%. Thus GEC's main rivals in this sector owe them much. They also collaborate in a number of joint companies, e.g. the Bushing Company (see IRC (1969)).

GEC has kept the promises it made at its inception not to interfere with competition and not to engage in any practices which could damage competition.

6.3.2 The performance of GEC since the mergers

One of the ways of gauging the success of a merger is to look at it from the point of view of the shareholders and see what has happened to profitability. From the point of view of the economy as a whole, the success of the firm is better judged in terms of efficiency and whether or not the merger achieved its aim of bringing about rationalisation. Also the social judgement must be concerned with the economic and social consequences of creating a firm with substantial market power and any evidence of the abuse of this power must be weighed against any evidence of resource savings. Therefore, it is also necessary to look at GEC as an employer and to see whether or not the firm has acted in the public interest. Certainly for the shareholders of the newly formed companies there were immediate gains. The final bid value of AEI's shares was over 70/- (350p). Throughout 1968–69 GEC shares stood at a 50% premium above the market average of 193p, while the price/earnings multiple was 35 (*The Times*, 5 May 1973). Their position slipped slightly in 1971–72 (a premium of only 8% was recorded) as the market waited for evidence of the benefits from the merger to appear. Share prices improved again later. Recently GEC announced that shareholders would receive a cash handout totalling £178 million which the firm has amassed from the sale of assets resulting from the mergers with AEI and English Electric. (A matter that will be returned to later.)

Two measures of profitability can be calculated from the published figures, (i) a rate of return on capital employed and (ii) the price–cost margin. In practice both are rather gross measures but they give some indication of the profitability of firms. The problem with the rate of return on capital is, of course, the inevitable problem of valuation of capital – what is to be classified as a capital asset and how to assign a value to it – a particularly vexing problem in the presence of inflation. In addition, the assets of both AEI and English Electric were revalued after the merger on a different accounting basis which further complicates matters.

GEC's rate of return on capital (Table 6.6) improved dramatically from the beginning of the 1960s, this trend continued until the absorption of AEI and English Electric, when the rate of return dropped back a little to a still respectable level for a firm partly engaged in heavy electrical engineering (see Table 6.9). However, after 1971, the year GEC itself considered the rationalisation following the merger to have been completed, the rate of return on capital employed by GEC rose again. It has averaged 23.4% p.a. from 1972 to 1975, despite the economic climate of the 1970s.

A measure of profitability which does not rely on the subjective valuation of capital assets is the price–cost margin, the mark-up over marginal cost which would not be present in a perfectly competitive market equilibrium. If we assume

Table 6.8 *The values of k for selected product groups of GEC 1970–74*

Product groups	1970	1971	1972	1973	1974
Power engineering	100.0	106.9	103.0	95.8	87.6
Industrial	100.0	103.8	101.3	92.7	85.6
Electronic, tele-communications and automation	100.0	102.7	98.9	88.1	73.5
Cables and components	100.0	103.4	98.5	83.0	94.0
Consumer products	100.0	100.2	92.3	76.2	71.4

constant long-run marginal cost this would be identical to the ratio of profits to sales revenue. However, the profit figure used is the net profit before tax and interest and the resultant estimate of the price–cost margin, in fact, includes normal profit. In 1965 (see Table 6.7) all three firms had a price–cost margin of around 5%. Part of the recent increase may reflect a lessening of competitive pressure, but it could also reflect an increase in efficiency in a situation where entry is restricted.

The unit factor requirement efficiency measure of k is difficult to calculate for this merger because of the many and varied products of the firms concerned and the changing proportion in which their output has been produced over time (e.g. for a while GEC was not producing generators while the other two did). Since 1970, GEC has produced profit and turnover figures for its product groups individually, lessening the problem of identifying the composition of its output. Unfortunately, these product groups are not as homogeneous as their names suggest, but by making heroic assumptions (which would not be defended too strongly) it has been possible to assess the efficiency of certain sectors of GEC but only for the period since 1970. The following product groups have been identified as producing output which can be classified to a single MLH industry group.

Product Group	*Output Classification*
Power Engineering	MLH 361
Industrial	MLH 333
Electronic, Telecommunications and Automation	MLH 363
Cables and Components	MLH 362
Consumer Products	MLH 368

The calculated values of k are shown in Table 6.8. The index of wage cost used takes into account the differences in wages between male and female workers over the period and the profit figure used is net profit before tax.

Not very much can be deduced over this short period of time. However, Table 6.8 shows that in all cases k rises from 1970 to 1971 – implying a decrease in efficiency – and falls from 1971 –implying an increase in efficiency. (Only in the case of Cables and Components does k turn up again and that is in 1974.) GEC themselves regard the period up until 1971 as being the period of reorganisation after the mergers. From 1971 onwards, they regard the reorganisation as being completed, i.e. after 1971 GEC regards itself as a completely new firm, thus the increase in efficiency after 1971 would fit in well with their views of how things have worked. (It is also from 1971 that we see an improvement in profitability.)

Bearing in mind that the product groups are not homogeneous (see above), the fact that all the ks behave in the same way lends some support to the idea that the merger did lead to increasing efficiency although a direct pre- and post-merger comparison cannot be made.

A comparison with other electrical engineering firms over the same period is again difficult, as they mostly operate in more than one industry. However, it has been attempted and GEC's k factors are compared with firms specialising in particular products (see Table 6.9). Although the assumption that these firms are one product or one industry based is a strong one for Plessey, STC and Thorn, it is not so strong for Reyrolle Parsons, Hoover and BICC.

The first conclusion that can be drawn is that, except in the case of STC and Hoover (where the ks decline from 1970 and turn up in 1974), the pattern of the ks for all the other firms follows those of GEC. More strikingly, by 1974, the GEC's k factor is lower in every industry group and lower throughout the period, except in the Domestic Appliance industry. This leads to the conclusion that the merger has increased the efficiency of GEC relative to its main rivals, at least in these products.

What has been happening in terms of the size of operations? The size of capital employed in value terms has grown over the period since the merger. The capital commitment of GEC has risen from 104.5 million in 1966 to 681 million in 1975, at historic cost (Figures from *Extel*). However, immediately after the two mergers, it was not as much as the sum of the three companies, even though inflation occurred over the period. Apart from the new ventures that had already been undertaken by AEI, there have not been any major new factories constructed but many old ones have been closed down and sold off as part of the rationalisation process. Getting rid of the oldest plant and equipment should raise the average productivity of the capital employed without new investment. Obviously, as the reason for the merger was excess capacity, one would expect the closure of plants which, in fact, occurred. In addition there is evidence of actual reductions in output. The Labour Research Department (1974) contrasted the sales of GEC for the financial year ending March 1970 with those for the financial year ending March 1974. During that period, sales in current prices rose 28% while pre-tax profit rose 160%. Deflating sales by a general price index for manufactured goods,

Table 6.9 *A comparison of k factors with GEC's principal competitors*

Heavy Electrical Engineering MLH 361

	P_0/P_I	GEC division k	Reyrolle Parsons k
1970	100	100.0	100.54
1971	104	106.91	118.25
1972	103	103.00	111.75
1973	96	95.79	99.64
1974	92	87.58	93.16

Insulated Wires and Cables MLH 362

	P_0/P_I	GEC division k	BICC k
1970	100	100.00	103.40
1971	104	101.65	106.99
1972	98	96.79	100.73
1973	86	81.58	88.92
1974	96	92.38	99.58

Telecommunications MLH 363

	P_0/P_I	GEC division k	Plessey k	STC k
1970	100	100.00	94.69	103.56
1971	103	102.76	101.35	102.42
1972	101	98.96	100.43	95.77
1973	94	88.13	91.27	88.23
1974	92	75.53	89.33	89.23

Domestic Appliances MLH 368

	P_0/P_I	GEC division k	Hoover k	Thorn k
1970	100	100.00	93.44	95.71
1971	100	100.26	93.04	95.78
1972	96	92.30	84.42	90.93
1973	87	76.18	76.61	80.17
1974	80	71.41	82.12	75.77

N.B. Differences between firms in the same year merely reflect differences in the ratio of profits to sales, and this may be a result of factors other than differences in factor requirements.

which rose approximately 50% over the period, they conclude that, unless all the profit increase is due to increased efficiency and GEC's prices have risen less than elsewhere in the economy, output has been falling. In fact, the real value of sales from 1969–70 to 1975–76 fell, although it may have recovered to its 1969 level in 1976–77 (*Sunday Times*, 19 December 1976).

At the same time there has been an increase in the foreign import of many products also produced by GEC. The main competition is coming from overseas and is, therefore, facing higher barriers to entry than domestic producers, from whom there is no effective competition. Thus, even foreign competitors where they exist cannot reduce the high price–cost margin of GEC and for many products there is virtually no competition at all.

On the employment side there has been a marked reduction in the number of employees, although this has been associated with a rise in productivity. Data on employment is not available before 1968, but when AEI was taken over by GEC it had 74,800 employees and the joint company had approximately 128,000. The merger with English Electric created a workforce of 240,000 but by 1969 this was down to 228,000 a trend which continued until 1973, when employment levelled out at 170,000. The level at the end of 1976 was 166,000 (see *Sunday Times*, 19 December 1976) and is likely to fall further due to cutbacks in Government expenditure.

Thus there has been a cutback in capital equipment (new investment is only just picking up), a cutback in employment and a cutback in output, but profits have risen. Where are these increased profits coming from? It has been shown that efficiency has been increasing, but has it increased sufficiently to explain what has happened? In order to answer that one must say something about what is happening to costs and prices. Unfortunately, it is very difficult to say very much about GEC's costs and prices because its output is very varied and it is involved in many MLHs, both electrical and non-electrical. On the whole it can be assumed that GEC faces the same costs as other producers (though this might not be true of the cost of its labour input in various sectors). The differences in efficiency arise from their different utilisation of these resources.

Examining data on input prices for products in various MLHs, it is easy to see that costs have been soaring recently. Although these indices are confidential, it is possible to say that from the time of the merger in 1967 until 1974, GEC faced costs in telegraph and telecommunications which had risen steeply, but not as much as the rise that has taken place in the index of average output prices over the same period. The same is true of the price indices for electrical goods where the average price index of output rose much faster than the index of input prices. However, in the case of domestic appliances, the cost increases which the firm faced were not likely to have been compensated for by rapid increases in output prices.

Thus for MLHs 363 and 361, average prices were rising much faster than the costs of raw materials and fuels. However, this was not the case for domestic electrical appliances. The degree of protection each market faces is probably the explanation. In the telephone industry, the buying policy of the main purchasers, the Post Office, has been to buy British – this has only broken down recently. Previously, agreements between the Post Office and suppliers, of which there are only three, allocated work at agreed prices on a quota system. Recently, the Post Office has been buying abroad to encourage more competitive pricing. In electrical machinery the main purchaser is the Central Electricity Generating Board and there are only two suppliers (a situation which the CEGB favoured for a long time). There is virtually no foreign competition. However, for domestic electrical equipment, although GEC technically has a monopoly there is much more competition from overseas producers because of the very nature of the products. British industry has been less able to pass on cost increases in this section.

On the question of prices, there are problems as many products are made to order and not for mass production. Comparing British prices with those of the EEC for electrical engineering products, the NEDO industrial review to 1977 on the industry comments that, as the higher tariffs of the UK are reduced (as part of our commitment on entry to the EEC), then the UK products will have a small net disadvantage in price against the original members of the EEC. In other words, our prices are generally higher than those of the Continent (supporting our contention that British manufacturers were able to keep prices up because the only competition was from overseas).

To some extent price increases have been held back by the Government's pricing policy. It was reported in the *Guardian* (18 June 1974) that GEC was pressing for price increases over about twenty product ranges after its victory over the Price Commission in the High Court on the previous day. This case concerned the interpretation of the Pay Code in relation to profits. A high proportion of GEC's profit was coming from the income it derived from investing spare cash in the money market. This source of profit has been forming an increasing proportion of total profits, and stems originally from the sales of at least 48 major establishments at home and abroad during the rationalisation following the merger. The interest amounted to £8 million in the financial year ending 31 March 1973, £13 million April–December 1973 and was estimated to reach £50 million in the future (see *Guardian*, 18 June 1974), while GEC's cash balances now stand at £330 million and are rising, from an original overdraft of £55 million at the time of the merger (*Sunday Times*, 19 December 1976).

The Court ruled that this income was to be excluded from the area of the Stage Three profit controls. The Price Commission had opposed this as they wished to stop GEC from applying for and getting price increases. Once this element of profit was excluded GEC's margins were sufficiently low to enable them to press for price increases. By the end of the month (29 June 1974), the *Guardian* was reporting that GEC was planning to by-pass the normal procedures set up under the Price Commission and introduce a package of price increases 'which is probably the largest ever presented by a British firm'. To notify the Price Commission would only call for too much administrative time and effort. The product prices of GEC had been frozen since November 1972, although competitors had been allowed price increases because of higher costs, which GEC also faced. The suggested price rises were up to 33% on domestic appliances. GEC felt there was no need to notify the Price Commission (which was simply a delaying factor) as they had already notified them in May of the intended increases which had been rejected at the time. It would appear these large price increases went ahead without further delay.

We have already seen how GEC compares in efficiency with other firms. In terms of profitability its performance also holds up well. GEC's competitors tend to be different in different sectors of the market, its main competitors being Reyrolle Parsons in heavy electrical engineering, Plessey and the Standard Telephone Company in telephone and telegraph apparatus and in cables with BICC also. In automation, radio and radar apparatus and electrical appliances there are many competitors including Thorn, EMI, Hoover and Philips plus overseas companies which only import and do not manufacture here.

1973 is the latest year for which data on all the companies are available and at the time GEC's price–cost margin of 13.1% was only beaten by STC (a subsidiary of ITT), Thorne and Hoover, while its rate of return on capital was beaten only by Thorn and Hoover (Table 6.10). Certainly for a firm concentrated in the heavy side of electrical engineering GEC's performance looks impressive. Those firms concentrated in the heavy side are by no means as profitable as GEC and GEC ranks high among firms which are almost exclusively on the lighter side of engineering. However, it must be borne in mind that this high ratio is in part due not to manufacturing or trading, but to interest from investments made in the money market (see above). In terms of the size of capital employed, GEC is by far the biggest firm. This is also true of absolute profits and turnover.

One aspect of GEC's performance since the merger which cannot be overlooked is its competitive behaviour – has the company, with so much monopoly power, been acting in the public interest? The TAM agreement, mentioned earlier, finally broke up about 1970. However, the Post Office and its suppliers worked very closely together when it came to ordering equipment. Even so, a few rows occurred between the Post Office and its suppliers over the introduction of equipment and over competition. In 1974, a row occurred over the Post Office purchasing equipment from Pye (a subsidiary of Philips) to break up the ring (GEC, STC and Plessey) supposedly broken up earlier. GEC, Plessey and STC attempted to protect their position, pointing out that Britain would be the only country to open up its market in a time of contracting demand. Earlier the telecommunications firms dragged their feet over the introduction of electronic equipment (*Financial Times*, 11 January 1974). At the end of January 1974 the

Table 6.10 *GEC's performance compared with industry averages*[a]

	1963	1964	1965	1966	1967	1968	1969	1970	1971	1972	1973
Price–cost margins (%)											
GEC	5.4	8.2	10.9	12.2	10.7	8.7	9.1	9.2	9.1	9.5	13.1
Telecommunications[b]	14.9	14.4	15.1	10.1	10.4	10.5	11.0	10.4	10.0	10.7	12.6
Heavy electrical[c]	*n.a.*	*n.a.*	*n.a.*	*n.a.*	16.8	12.8	9.4	7.7	*-ve*	1.5	5.9
Cables	7.5	7.7	7.9	8.2	8.0	7.1	6.1	6.9	8.4	8.7	8.1
Domestic electrical appliances[d]	9.3	11.6	11.7	10.9	10.4	9.8	10.0	9.6	8.5	11.4	11.8
Rate of return on capital (%)											
GEC	7.9	13.0	18.0	19.8	17.2	18.6	14.6	13.2	14.4	16.0	23.7
Telecommunications	20.4	21.6	22.22	13.4	15.3	15.9	17.0	17.5	15.2	12.0	17.2
Heavy electrical[c]	10.2	17.4	17.5	16.9	16.1	24.7	12.5	8.7	*-ve*	1.6	8.6
Cables[c]	15.1	14.0	15.7	16.9	13.9	13.9	13.9	14.9	15.8	17.3	20.7
Domestic electrical applicances	20.1	24.4	24.4	20.1	18.5	23.0	29.2	23.4	20.2	24.2	29.4

[a]Not including GEC itself. The indsutry averages are weighted by turnover figures from EXTEL AEI and English Electric results not allowed for except in post-merger results.
[b]One firm only until 1968.
[c]One firm only.
[d]Three firms 1963–67, four firms 1968–73.
N.B. The calculation of all such measures is limited by the availability of the relevant data.

Post Office placed an order with Thorn-Ericsson for a £30 million contract for an international telephone exchange. The unions and the employers both condemned the action although STC kept fairly quiet (it is a subsidiary of an American company). Only Plessey was in a position to supply the equipment and the Post Office claimed that Plessey could not have supplied the right sort of equipment needed to meet the exceptional growth in international traffic. The British companies' arguments against the opening up of competition really rest on the fact that they do not wish to speed up the progress towards the latest technology until they have fully exploited the developments in which they have invested time and money. These disputes held up the development of the electronically stored programme controlled telephone apparatus for which GEC has the contract. Thus, although the ring had officially ceased to exist about 1969, it was still very much in evidence opposing any attempt by the Post Office to widen the basis of competition.

In July 1974 the Office of Fair Trading referred the cable makers to the Monopolies Commission because of the possibility of parallel pricing (*Guardian*, 17 July 1974). The *Financial Times* (8 April 1975) pointed out that the OFT was aware of an international cartel when it made its reference to the Monopolies Commission in the previous July. Such export agreements are registered and kept on a secret list. The Monopolies Commission could only look at the agreement from the point of view of UK public interest. The market for insulated cables was split in the UK between BICC, 40%; GEC/AEI, 20%; Pirelli, 20%; and Delta Enfield, 15%. Although the Monopolies Commission was due to report in July 1976, at the time of writing no report has appeared.

As a result of this investigation it came to light that the telephone cable makers had been operating a secret agreement in respect of sales to the Post Office. This agreement operated from 1965 to the end of 1974 and was not registered under the Restrictive Practices Act. The Post Office had the right to sue, believing it had lost money and in March 1975 threatened to do so. The four companies concerned, BICC, STC, Pirelli General Cable Works Ltd, and Telephone Cables Ltd (owned by GEC) claimed it kept prices down, 'by allowing an orderly pattern of business with the Post Office' (*Guardian*, 8 March 1975). Over the period of the Agreement the Post Office had contracted for £400 millions worth of business with the firms in the cartel.

The cable makers immediately instituted a new agreement and registered it with the Restrictive Practices Court but it was considered too restrictive. In the meantime, an argument between the Post Office and the cable makers over the right to see accounts caused the Post Office to impose a ban on tenders to the cable makers.

The dispute was not finally settled until the beginning of 1976 (although the decision on the agreement came earlier).[13] The cable makers agreed to the Post

13 The Restrictive Practices Court gave its judgement on 20 November 1975.

Office having access to their books, past and future, while the Post Office agreed to lift its ban on tenders, so long as the tenders were submitted competitively and the restrictive agreement was put 'on ice'. Therefore, the industry now faces fully competitive tendering, while the Post Office has dropped the idea of suing.[14]

Thus GEC has again been involved in situations where using its market power – in conjunction with others – has not been in the public interest. The companies concerned have not been prosecuted. This was part of an agreement between the Post Office and the firms to end a quarrel, which none of them wanted to see continuing indefinitely.

6.3.3 Future prospects and conclusions

In an article on the lifting of the ban on tenders by the Post Office, the *Financial Times* (8 January 1976) concluded: 'The Post Office's negotiated victory could hasten the process of concentration which is already under way in the telephone cable industry. Just before Christmas STC announced that one of its two cable plants would have to close. The possibility of one of the suppliers eventually quitting the race must also be increased.'

In addition the electrical engineering industry has seen a large cutback in demand for telephone equipment (mentioned above) and power station plant.

The telecommunicatious industry is aware that its future looks bleak, due to a natural contraction of demand compounded by the cuts in government expenditure and the Post Office's adoption of economic pricing. So far Plessey has been most badly hit; GEC declared redundancies in February (*Financial Times*, 23 February 1977) which were followed closely by Plessey's announcement of intention to close three factories at Kirby, Speke and Sunderland with a subsequent loss of 4,000 jobs (*The Times*, 3 March 1977). In the heavy electrical sector there is significant over-capacity, not only in Britain but in world markets. This was highlighted in the *Financial Times* (2 October 1976) where it was pointed out that the international industry was working at approximately half of capacity and that this was not a short- or medium-term phenomenon. Demand is unlikely to return to its pre-1974 levels for some time.

Once again the cutback in demand has led to pressure for rationalisation in the industry and in view of the needs of each manufacturer to be of at least some minimum size (see Epstein (1971)) this is taken to imply further mergers. (Sector Working Party papers on the engineering industry generally suggest that the government's industrial strategy may be the new vehicle for rationalisation.) The alternative might be for the Government to accept some responsibility for these periods, especially where it has actively encouraged expansion in the past. It already helps to keep research and development going in times of depressed demand.

14 The four major companies are repaying £9 million to the Post Office, it was revealed by the OFT in June 1978 (*Financial Times*, 13 June 1978.)

The CEGB now favours one supplier and the severity of the situation might result in a rash decision to create two multinationals, or one British firm or even two vertically integrated firms, which may be regretted when demand picks up again and the company or companies begin to use their increased market power.

In a final assessment of the 'success' of the mergers of 1967–68, the present cutback in demand creates difficulties. However, from the point of view of creating an integrated firm, the GEC mergers can be said to have succeeded. There is, for instance, none of the rivalry between the old component firms which in the case of AEI reduced efficiency. From the point of view of the shareholders and the stock market the merger has also produced benefits. GEC is one of the more successful electrical firms despite its involvement in heavy electrical engineering. What evidence there is would seem to suggest that GEC's efficiency improved once the rationalisation period was completed in 1971. This evidence can be supplemented by the general impression from meetings with an official of GEC that GEC is very cost conscious – there certainly appear to be very few of the normal 'perks' associated with top management on view at GEC headquarters in Stanhope Gate, even if it is off Park Lane. The main characteristic of Weinstock's management of GEC has been and remains tight financial control, each establishment having to stand on its own feet and produce a profit.

However, the performance of British electrical engineering exports has not been too impressive, particularly on the heavy side. The share of GEC's sales coming from exports rose from about 16% in 1965 to 21% by 1974. However, Britain's traditional markets are being taken away from her by the more competitive European and Japanese firms. The British producers do not seem to function well outside the scope of their restrictive agreements. This may force the situation to a head in the new crisis of over capacity, making a merger sound like the only solution to declining home demand, whereas the firms might support themselves as individual enterprises if they were more aggressive in overseas markets. (It must be added that the trade barriers imposed on importers to this country by the public purchasing bodies through their detailed specification, which exceed those required elsewhere, are very successful, but they also have the impact of making British firms less competitive overseas because designs are not standardised.)

All in all, the merger must be viewed as a success but at a high cost of increased market power, which GEC has used despite promises not to do so. There has also been a high social cost in terms of lost employment which has not necessarily been any less than if the mergers had not taken place (see Chapter 8). Pressures are again building up for a final merger of all turbo-generator interests and possibly further rationalisation in telecommunications. Before any decision is taken it should be kept in mind that a monopoly, in times of depressed demand might be fairly powerless, but once demand begins to improve again it will be in a position to put its market power into operation. The fact that the main buyers are technically monopsonists unfortunately does not provide consolation; GEC has managed to get the better of them in the past. Such buyers are monopolists in providing their services to the public so that cost increases can be easily passed on. The Post Office has been showing more vigilance on the prices its suppliers charge despite the large profits it has made recently (often a cause of not being cost conscious in a public body). Whatever the outcome of these recent moves, it is to be hoped that the public authorities keep a watchful eye on the behaviour of the electrical giants, in particular GEC, it being the largest and most powerful of them all. It is important to remember that just because the producers in some sectors of electrical engineering may have to be of a certain-size, it does not imply that all the sectors have to be controlled by the same firm. The Government must face the fact that it helped to create GEC and, therefore, it has some responsibility to it in times of depression. But, it also has a responsibility to the public at large and should be willing to take punitive action when necessary and not be continually backing down or ignoring situations blatantly against the public interest, as it has since the formation of GEC in 1967–68.

6.5 **Success versus failure**

From the evidence presented in the two cases studied, it is possible to highlight the factors which contributed to the failure of the British Leyland merger and the success of the GEC merger (at least judged from the point of view of efficiency).

We have seen that they were begot in similar circumstances. The industries in which both were located were going through difficulties due to increasing competition as a result of liberalising trade policies at home and abroad. Both industries were very susceptible to changes in Government policy, though in different ways – GEC directly through cuts in Government expenditure and BLMC indirectly through changes in taxation and credit controls.

Both mergers had the backing of the IRC and it was the IRC which appears to have been the major influence in preventing referral to the Monopolies Commission. The mergers were of note because of the personalities involved (the IRC being a great believer in personalities) and because of the size of the firms they created. Thus, at the same time as the Government was actively promoting competition it was also pursuing a policy which created firms through horizontal integration, thereby reducing competition and incidentally increasing aggregate concentration.

In both cases, the firms taken over were firms more concerned with engineering standards than with profits. BMC had got away with this in early years because of the existence of excess demand and the absence of real competition from overseas owing to a lack of capacity. AEI, on the other hand, had managed to sustain itself through its reputation and through numerous cartels and restrictive agreements. Once domestic and international competition increased neither was really strong enough to withstand the new pressures and profitability declined.

Finally another similarity springs out from the pages of the case studies. Neither of the mergers appeared to have any industrial logic to them: the firms were matched on the basis of the belief that the managerial skill of one group was superior to the other and that larger firms would be more successful overseas.

So, formed in similar circumstances and with similar potential, one succeeded while the other failed. A further examination of similarities and differences and how both firms handled the problems they faced may highlight the factors making for success and failure.

The first problem common to both BL and GEC was that the firms were the outcome of a series of mergers not all of which had previously been successful, i.e. those forming AEI and BMH. The case study of British Leyland shows that even today the firm does not consider itself one unit and not until the Government became directly involved was an integrated view of the company formed. Apart from minor changes, the separate divisions remained in production in much the same way as they had before the merger. This led to many inefficiencies in production. Internal rivalry does not seem to be as much of a problem as it was to AEI but lack of integration increases both production and information costs. GEC, on the other hand, has managed to overcome the problem of integrating the separate units into one company. Although it also keeps its brand names, internal rivalry between plants is minimised because the style of management does not allow engineers to be wasteful in the duplication of research effort. GEC placed able men into management jobs immaterial of the company for which they had worked previously. Therefore no one group felt frustrated.

The style of management leads into the second problem that faced both these firms, that of managing a large organisation. The text indicates that they chose different styles of management and produced different results. In the case of British Leyland the initiative was taken away from plant managements so that decisions were made by committee, and this meant that delays were inevitable and no-one felt responsible for any decision. Functions were duplicated and central staff grew in number. Thus administration costs rose without any benefits arising from faster decision making or tighter financial control.

Both firms suffered from a rapid turnover of middle management. However in GEC things eventually sorted themselves out. The differences were striking. One of the first actions of Weinstock was to reduce central staffing and to confer the power of decision making on his managers in the field. Each plant was made a profit centre and had to prove itself viable. Managers were given a free hand but were called to account, and although at first this caused many losses eventually things stabilised, enabling managers to have the kind of responsibility they needed to do their job, and giving the firm the kind of cost and profit consciousness it sought (see *Sunday Times*, 19 December 1976).

The IRC had sought the formation of both firms as the solution to the rationalisation needed in both industries. For GEC this was to involve a reduction of capacity, for BLMC this meant scrapping expensive model variants and re-equipping. How successful were the firms in achieving this aim? Certainly the newly formed GEC wasted no time in closing plants, in particular its oldest. It realised many of its assets, which has meant that at no time since the merger has GEC had a cash-flow problem. Between 1968 and 1973 it reduced employment from around 240,000 to about 170,000, while raising output per head. Although certain sections of the industry now face the problem of over-capacity, this has been due to circumstances beyond the control of the firm and not anticipated at the beginning of the 1970s. The evidence on the BLMC merger is that for whatever reason (and it may well have been due to the response to the GEC redundancies) British Leyland hung fire on over-manning and there is still room for further substantial rationalisation.

Neither company can be held up as a shining example of a firm investing in new plant and equipment, although GEC's investment plans have expanded recently (see *Sunday Times*, 19 December 1976). GEC had the money to do this but preferred to lend it to financial institutions. British Leyland was criticised by Ryder for paying out too much to its shareholders.

Both had problems in the field of labour relations. For British Leyland this was a continuation of a long history of bad industrial relations, while for GEC they mainly occurred as a result of the merger itself. GEC's methods of handling the problem may not be to everyone's taste (see Chapter 8) but after the initial problems, the presence of Sir Jack Scamp on the Board, the setting up of the NJCC, the willingness of top management to go to individual plants, the relatively small size of many of its manufacturing units and the fact that much of its labour is not unionised, all contributed to the absence of any major strikes crippling the whole enterprise. British Leyland's problem was deep rooted and although the new management spent much time attempting to improve labour relations, the results were not very encouraging. Without entering the debate about the optimum size of firm from the point of view of industrial relations, it does seem that managers in BLMC lacked the authority to make decisions and were not immediately responsible for their plants, and in consequence the workers may well have felt disaffected not knowing quite to whom to go with a grievance.

Both industries rely heavily on subcontracting for components. In the car industry it appears that most of the initiative for standardisation has come from the component manufacturers, whereas in electrical engineering GEC has been keen to standardise components as this cuts the cost and the production time of such things as generators. GEC has also followed a policy of securing component suppliers, if necessary taking them over, thus reducing their costs further (alternatively turning excess capacity over to the manufacture of components) (*Sunday Times*, 19 December 1976).

Finally we must remember that differences in efficiency are not everything. The case study of BLMC shows no evidence of the firm using its monopoly power to exploit the customer (although plenty of evidence of a misallocation of resources in an inefficient firm). Prices have not kept pace with cost increases mainly due to increased foreign competition. In the case of GEC we have seen this only applies to domestic appliances. In many areas GEC has been operating in heavily protected markets, and we have noted in the text instances where this has left a legacy of defensive attitudes to new competition (for instance in telephone apparatus) whereas British Leyland has been operating principally in a world wide market where it has many competitors. The fall in the output price relative to input prices, shown in Tables 6.4 and 6.5, can be attributed to an increase in competition. This, combined with the world recession, has contributed to the firm's poor financial performance in recent years. Table 6.9 shows the ratio of output prices to input prices facing GEC and its competitors. It would appear that in 1973 and 1974 the firms were having some difficulty in passing on cost increases although over the period from 1967 to 1974 costs had risen less than output prices for all products but domestic appliances. This difficulty in raising prices was due not to competition but to the influence of the Price Commission from November 1972 until the second half of 1974, after which GEC went ahead with substantial price increases.

In commercial terms the GEC merger was more successful and much of this success must be attributed not just to its greater effective market power but to the style of management which allows middle management its head while keeping tight financial control, and to a large extent this seems to be a matter of organisational structure. However, the inheritance by GEC of good industrial relations and by British Leyland of a history of hostile attitudes between management and labour must surely have also played an important part. Correcting this situation in such a large, complex firm as British Leyland would not have been easy anyway, but the attempted centralisation of authority was the wrong way to go about it.

References

British Leyland Motor Corporation, *Annual Report and Accounts*, various years 1968–75.

Counter Information Services (1973), *The General Electric Company Limited (Anti-report 2)*. CIS pamphlet.

CPRS (Central Policy Review Staff) (1957), *The Future of the British Car Industry* London: HMSO.

Dutton, P. A. (1978), *A Case Study of the G.E.C. – A.E.I. – English Electric Mergers*, Centre for Industrial Economic and Business Research Paper, No. 81, University of Warwick.

Electrical Industry Public Relations Committee (1956 approx.), *Agreed Prices in the Heavy Electrical Plant Industry* (pamphlet), Editorial Services Ltd, for the Committee.

Epstein, B. (1971), *Politics of Trade in Power Plant*, London: Trade Policy Research Centre.

Expenditure Committee of the House of Commons (1975), *Fourteenth Report*, London: HMSO.

Industrial Reorganisation Commission, *Reports to the Secretary of State for Industry*, London HMSO.
– (1968), First Report and Accounts, Dec. 1966–March 1968.
– (1969), Report and Accounts for the year ended 31 March 1969.
– (1970), Report and Accounts for the year ended 31 March 1970.
– (1971), Report and Accounts covering the period 1 April 1970 to 30 April 1971.
Jones, R. and O. Marriott (1970), *The Anatomy of a Merger*, London: Cape.
Labour Research Department (1974), *Labour Research*, **63**, No.9, LRD.
Latham, Sir Joseph (1969), *Take-over (The Facts and Myths of the G.E.C. – A.E.I. Battle)*, London, Iliffe.
Leech, D. and J. Cubbin (1978), 'Import Penetration in the UK Passenger Car Market: a cross-section Study, *Applied Economics*.
Monopolies Commission, London: HMSO (1956), *Report on the Supply of Electronic Valves and Cathode Ray Tubes.*
– (1957), *Report on the Supply and Export of Electrical and Allied Machinery and Plant.*
– (1958), *Report on Electric Lamps.*
Office of Fair Trading, London, HMSO (1975), *1st Report November 1973–December 1974.*
–(1976), *2nd Report 1975.*
Restrictive Trading Agreements, *Reports of the Registrar of Restrictive Trading Agreements* (R.L.Sich), London: HMSO, various reports 1959–72.
Rhys, D. G. (1972a), *The Motor Industry*, London: Butterworth.
–(1972b), 'Heavy Commercial Vehicles: The Survival of the Small Firm', *Journal of Industrial Economics*, **20** (July), 230–52.
Ryder, Sir Don et al. (1975), *British Leyland: The Next Decade*, London, HMSO.
Salmon, E. A. (1975), 'Inside British Leyland', *Management Today*, (November), 59–61, 114.
SMMT (Society of Motor Manufacturers & Traders), *The Motor Industry of Great Britain*, various years 1968–75.
Turner, G. (1971), *The Leyland Papers*, London: Eyre and Spottiswoode.

7

Mergers and the product mix: a case-study of the brewing industry

The sheer volume of merger activity in the brewing industry makes it an obvious candidate for our study. An equally compelling reason is that recent developments in the product mix offered by this industry have been surrounded by controversy. In 7.4 we will attempt to resolve some of this controversy and in particular will consider how far any changes in the product mix have been the result of mergers. Section 7.1 describes the change in the structure of the brewing industry, in 7.2 we provide some discussion of the tied house system, in 7.3 we assess how efficiency has changed during the period being considered, and in 7.5 we provide a summary and conclusions.

7.1 **Market structure**

By any of the criteria normally applied the brewing industry has experienced a dramatic change in concentration. In 1930 there were 1,418 breweries and 559 brewing companies. By 1960 the equivalent figures were 358 and 247, and by 1973, 162 and 88, respectively (Brewers' Society).

The decline in the number of brewing companies has been almost entirely due to mergers. Of the 146 companies that ceased to brew independently between 1960 and 1974 inclusive, only 22 did so because they were wound up (Osborne (1978)). The merger activity that led to the decline of independent brewers was until 1971 entirely horizontal. In that year Grand Metropolitan Hotels took over Truman, Hanbury and Buxton and in the following year, as well as this company taking over Watneys, there were three other takeovers by non-brewing companies. Insofar as Grand Metropolitan Hotels and Clydesdale Commonwealth Hotels, who took over Dudgeon & Co., were able to provide increased numbers of outlets for the beer their acquisitions produced, there was an element of vertical merging.

Table 7.1 shows the number of mergers undertaken by the major companies, or by their constituents before their takeover, and the number of brewers who were involved. The most important mergers since 1960 were those of:

Table 7.1 *Post-1960 mergers leading to the formation of the major brewing companies*

Companies	No. of mergers	No. of brewers involved
Allied	8	10
Watneys[a]	13	13
Bass Charrington	37	38
Whitbread	26	26
Courage[a]	13	13
Scottish and Newcastle	4	5

Source: Osborne (1978).
[a]Not included are the takeovers of Watneys by Grand Metropolitan Hotels or Courage by Imperial Tobacco.

(I) Tetley Walker, Ind Coope, and Ansells, in 1961, to form Allied Breweries;
(II) Bass, Mitchells and Butler, with Charrington, in 1967, to form Bass Charrington;
(III) Watney Mann with Grand Metropolitan, who already owned Truman, Hanbury and Buxton, in 1972;
(IV) Newcastle with Robert Younger and Scottish Breweries, in 1960, to form Scottish and Newcastle.

Neither Whitbread nor Courage carried out takeovers which had the repercussions of those above, though naturally some of their mergers were of particular importance to themselves.

An important feature of the mergers of the 1960s is that they transformed companies whose outlets were concentrated in particular regions into companies with outlets throughout the country. The most obvious example was the merger of Ind Coope, Ansells and Tetley Walker whose outlets were in the South, Midlands and North respectively, though all of the majors, with the exception of Guinness and Scottish and Newcastle, have undertaken similar geographic growth.

As would be expected from the amount of merger activity undertaken by the majors their importance within the market has significantly increased. *Censuses of Production* put the five-firm concentration ratio at 18% in 1954 and 62% in 1968 and it was estimated by *Market Research GB* (February 1975) to have risen to 71% by the mid 1970s. The latter estimated the percentage market shares to be:

Bass Charrington	20
Allied Breweries	16
Whitbread	12
Watneys	14
Scottish and Newcastle	9

Courage	9
Guinness	8
Others	12

An alternative measure of the relative importance of the major companies is the number of outlets they control. Osborne has estimated the total number of outlets, including hotels and off-licences, controlled by the majors in 1974 to be:

Bass Charrington	10,946
Allied	9,750
Whitbread	8,964
Watneys	8,100
Courage	6,900
Scottish and Newcastle	1,770
Guinness	1
	46,431

Ranking by the number of outlets controlled produces a similar (Whitbread and Watneys switch positions) order as when ranking by share of production but conceals that Scottish and Newcastle have significantly fewer outlets than Courage and indeed slightly fewer outlets than Greenall Whitley, who are comparatively minor producers, and that Guinness is an important producer but has not invested in British tied houses.

7.2 The tied house system

A considerable degree of vertical integration exists in the Brewing Industry. In 1967, (NBPI (1969)), 78% of outlets in the UK with full on-licences, mostly public houses, were owned by brewers. The actual degree of control is higher through the provision of loans by the brewing companies to the free sector, including registered clubs, in exchange for exclusive trading agreements. This does not exceed the degree of control over outlets exercised by producers in certain other industries, particularly wallpaper and petrol production, but the unique feature is that freedom of entry is strictly limited by licensing laws.

Tied public houses are staffed either by tenants (76.9% of tied houses in 1969, according to the Monopolies Commission (1969)) or managers (23.1%). Whilst in managed public houses the owning company takes full responsibility for the setting of prices, tenants are generally given freedom to determine their own prices in non-public bars. The consensus amongst writers on the industry is that the trend is towards the replacement of tenants by managers.

The tied system has been subject to vigorous debate, notably between the Monopolies Commission (1969) and the brewers (through the Economists' Advisory Group (1969)), the latter being supported by some academics, particularly Hawkins and Radcliffe (1971), but for the moment we have two comments:

(a) The tied system represents a barrier to both entry into brewing and to expansion by existing brewers. It would be possible but risky for other major brewers to follow Guinness's lead and promote nationally but not own outlets (though Scottish and Newcastle only control outlets in the North of England and in Scotland so to an extent they have done this). There would be no guarantee that brewers who did own outlets would buy their products or, if they did so, would not show preference to house brands when carrying out promotion. This fear is given foundation by the high proportion, 90%, which the Monopolies Commission (1969) found sellers' own beer formed of the total sold. Therefore if the potential for economies of scale in brewing exists its exploitation would be likely to be accompanied by the takeover of other brewers in order to secure their outlets.

(b) When determining the causes of merger activity in the UK brewing industry the picture is confused by the possibility of defensive mergers – the most often cited being the formation of Allied Breweries – in the face of threats from companies outside the industry tempted by the value of assets represented by tied property.[1]

7.3 Efficiency changes in the Brewing Industry

Before we examine changes in the total factor requirement we shall consider the results of earlier studies of efficiency in brewing. Of these the most pertinent to our work are those undertaken by Cockerill and Rainnie (1975) and by the Price Commission (1977). The former adopted the engineering approach to estimate the economies in brewing attributable to scale. They conclude that the great majority of economies may be derived at one million bulk barrels, that this represents the minimum efficient scale, MES, and that plants of twice this size will have costs lower by less than 5%.

This estimate of the MES for brewing assumes significance when compared to the actual size of plants in operation. Table 7.2 reveals that in 1974 the average plant size of only two companies exceeded the estimated MES and that none of the average plant sizes in any of the other majors came anywhere near it. Perhaps just as important, the number of breweries in operation by the majors in 1974 was as high as 47% of the total of breweries owned or taken over by the majors in the period beginning 1958; the building of new plants was obviously not accompanied by extensive rationalisation of those already in existence.

The strength of the conclusions that can be drawn from the above naturally depends on the reliability of the estimates. On *a priori* grounds one might expect an upward bias when using the engineering approach. For instance, where engineers within buying rather than supplying companies are interviewed, as

1 Naturally in a perfect market such under-valuation of a company would not be possible, nor would one expect a company to maintain property the opportunity cost of which would justify selling.

Table 7.2 *Breweries in operation in 1974 and their capacity*

	Breweries in operation 1974[a]	Average plant capacity 1974[a] ('000 bulk barrels)
Bass Charrington	13	575.4
Allied Breweries	8	747.5
Whitbread	17	264.1
Watneys	8	655.0
Scottish and Newcastle	3	1,233.0
Courage	8	421.3
Guinness	1	1,700.0

[a]As estimated by Osborne (1978).

was largely the case with Cockerill and Rainnie's work, their judgement might be clouded by optimism about gains from size, especially where merger activity has been undertaken ostensibly to achieve such economies. Neither would they necessarily be objective about diseconomies of scale, especially where these were found in management. Nevertheless, with the average plant capacity of the majors in 1974 at 551,000 bulk barrels the magnitude of the bias would have to be very large before it could be validly claimed that the merger-waves in brewing have resulted in the exploitation of the full potential for economies of scale.[2]

The Price Commission (1977) are highly critical of developments by the majors. They found that within the period 1974 to 1976 the average wholesale beer price charged by large brewers exhibited a bigger increase, and was higher in absolute terms in each of the years, than that charged by a sample of either regional or local brewers, and yet the majors enjoyed the lowest return on sales in any year of the three sizes of company. The Commission further argue that the majors had 'derived no apparent advantage from larger scale, [and] more concentrated operations'.

Two further studies are worth mentioning at this juncture. Elzinga (1973) adopted the survivor technique to estimate plant economies of scale in the US brewing industry. He shows that between 1959 and 1972 the number of plants in the range 538,000–717,000 bulk barrels was larger than in other ranges and remained fairly constant. The greatest increase was displayed by the number of

2 A large measure of support is, in any case, afforded to Cockerill and Rainnie's conclusions by the results of a similar study undertaken by Scherer (1975) which puts the MES at a considerably higher capacity, the two estimates apparently diverging because, whilst Cockerill and Rainnie defined the MES as that at which further cost reductions amount to less than 2% with a further doubling of output, Scherer considered any cost changes relevant whatever the magnitude.

plants in the highest range, beginning at 2,870,000 bulk barrels. No other trends were readily apparent. As is often the case when applying the survivor technique one is confronted with very real problems when it comes to interpreting the results, but US firms would seem to have exploited the available scale economies to a greater extent than UK firms.

Franks, Broyles and Hecht (1976) have considered the effects of mergers on the prices and dividend of shares in UK brewing and distilling and were primarily concerned with the distribution of gains between acquirers and acquirees. They find that gains to the acquirer relative to the acquiree are on average made prior to the merger, and that gains are on average made by the acquirer subsequent to the merger, though they concede that the credit for this cannot be entirely apportioned to the mergers. One cannot draw on the results of Franks, Broyles and Hecht's work for any indication of what has happened to efficiency in brewing and distilling for the reasons discussed in Chapter 4.

We turn now to the consideration of our own efficiency measure, *k*. The major problem when assessing how *k* for the brewing companies has changed is that published price data is poor. Data from which the wholesale price index is constructed is supplied to the Department of Industry by the Brewers' Society but there is a question about the relevance of wholesale prices, based on the free-trade published price-lists of a sample of brewers, given the degree of vertical integration in the industry. An accurate price-index would have to reflect a weighting for the transfer price between breweries and tied outlets. One cannot decide *a priori* what the relationship between the wholesale price to the free-sector, and that to the tied, might be.

An index of prices more representative of those actually received by brewers can be constructed by dividing total consumer expenditure on beer by quantity sold. Fielding, Newson and Smith, stockbrokers who have an undoubted expertise on brewing, have estimated that in 1970 50% of alcoholic drink was sold through tied outlets. It would appear, therefore, that, when calculating the total factor requirement for brewing, a more accurate estimate of prices will be derived from using consumer expenditure on beer divided by volume of beer sold, i.e. the average outlet price. Consumer expenditure in these calculations is net of duty, the overall incidence of duty as a percentage of consumers' expenditure on beer is given in the *Customs and Excise Report* (various years). This figure is also used as a proxy for total industry revenue when calculating *k* for the industry as a whole. The data in Table 7.3 indicate that wholesale prices inclusive of duty have risen at a lower rate than average outlet prices inclusive of duty and had we used the wholesale price series in our calculations of *k* our results would have been different. We are satisfied, however, that the average outlet price, net of duty, is the appropriate one to use.

In Table 7.3 the profit figures (measured before tax and post interest) refer to a sample of companies in the industry; this sample is of most firms covered by

Table 7.3 *k and its components for brewing 1955–72*

Year	P_0/P_I 1967 = 100	(a) Π/R	(b) Π/R	(a) k_1 (%)	(b) k_2 (%)	$\frac{WPI}{OPI}$
1955	73.2	0.181		59.9		1.10
1956	71.5	0.192		57.8		1.10
1957	78.4	0.192		63.3		1.10
1958	80.2	0.199	0.604	64.3	31.8	1.10
1959	83.5	0.202		66.6		1.04
1960	80.2	0.218		62.7		1.03
1961	76.7	0.213		60.3		1.04
1962	88.5	0.200		70.8		1.01
1963	89.5	0.212	0.564	70.5	39.0	1.00
1964	85.8	0.195		69.1		1.04
1965	90.9	0.204		72.3		1.02
1966	92.9	0.195		73.9		1.00
1967	100.0	0.189		81.1		1.00
1968	91.1	0.189	0.556	74.8	40.4	0.99
1969	99.6	0.177		81.9		0.97
1970	94.8	0.172		78.6		0.94
1971	102.3	0.175		84.4		0.90
1972	92.8	0.172	0.532	76.9	40.6	0.89

Sources: (*a*) EXTEL; (*b*) *Census of Production*.
P_0 = index of output prices
P_I = index of input prices
Π = profit before tax, after interest
R = total revenue
WPI = wholesale price index
OPI = outlet price index

EXTEL and comprises all of the majors and the majority of other companies covering almost 90% of total output in later years. As a further check we have used data from successive Censuses of Production to calculate gross profits (total revenue minus the cost of materials and labour) and used these estimates in the calculation of k_2.

It is clear from Table 7.3 that between 1955 and 1972 the total factor requirement rose steadily. When the arbitrarily chosen structural breaks 1963/64, 1966/67 and 1969/70 are introduced into the series the average k in the latter of each pair of periods is the higher and the difference highly significant; when other breaks are used the picture remains the same. Whatever the benefits that may have been reaped from the restructuring of the industry an increase in efficiency, at least until 1972, was not one.

k may also be estimated for individual companies. Price and cost data are not available for individual brewing companies and there was no obligation for companies to publish their turnover figures before 1968. Fortunately, Tetley Walker and Ind Coope had published their turnover for some years before they merged with Ansells to form Allied Breweries, and similarly Charrington United before its merger with Bass, to form Bass Charrington. Turnover for the subsidiaries of Whitbread has not been published but the parent has published such data throughout the period being considered. There is no suitable data on turnover for Watney Mann after 1972. The estimates of k in Table 7.4 are based on the assumption that the output and input price indices of the particular companies would be similar to national averages; k in any year will therefore only differ cross-sectionally because of differences in Π/R. It has proved possible to extend the period considered in Table 7.4 to 1974[3] with prices in 1973 and 1974 made exclusive of VAT as well as duty.

What is very striking from considering the trend in the total factor requirement of the majors is that the picture would appear very different when the ks for 1973 and 1974, and possibly 1972, are included from when they are omitted. Between 1962 and 1972 Allied Breweries had an average k higher than its constituent companies (Tetley Walker 11.6 lower, 1955–59, and Ind Coope 10.7 lower between 1957 and 1960). The average k of Charrington United Breweries between 1963 and 1967 was insignificantly different from that of Bass Charrington between 1968 and 1972; the merger would appear to have had no effect either way on efficiency. In the case of both Allied Breweries and Bass Charrington the efficiency of an important constituent company, Ansells and Bass respectively, has been ignored through lack of data on turnover for the period before the mergers. If the date of a structural break in the trend in Whitbread's estimated k is selected arbitrarily as 1966/67, the average total factor requirement in the period to 1972 was 13.9 higher than between 1955 and 1966. Whatever may have been the efficiency of the companies that Whitbread took over, that of the parent company fell between 1955 and 1972.

In the nine years before its takeover by Grand Metropolitan the efficiency of Watneys fluctuated wildly with the average total factor requirement between 1968 and 1972 3.4 higher than that between 1964 and 1967.

After 1972 it would appear that a startling increase in efficiency occurred. k falls because return on sales, Π/R, stayed virtually constant when apparently the price of variable inputs rose dramatically without any accompanying increase in output prices. It may well be, however, that our assumption that factor proportions stayed constant after the 1968 *Census of Production* would in this case be spurious. In 1967 the cost of labour formed approximately forty per cent of variable cost. Between 1967 and 1974 the cost of manual labour employed in brewing, according to the *Department of Employment Gazette*, more than trebled and that of non-manual workers generally almost doubled. It would be surprising

3 1973 P_0/P_I :78.06 1974 P_0/P_I :70.39.

Table 7.4 *Total factor requirements: major brewing companies*

	Allied Breweries			Bass Charrington		Whitbread[a]	Guinness	Scottish and Newcastle	Watneys
Year	Tetley Walker	Ind Coope	Ansells	Charrington United	Bass				
1955	66.41		*n.a.*			66.08			
1956	64.19		*n.a.*			64.00			
1957	87.92	71.40	*n.a.*			70.72			
1958	71.60	73.62	*n.a.*			72.30			
1959	74.40	77.06	*n.a.*			75.29			
1960	*n.a.*	73.04	*n.a.*			72.50			
1961	*n.a.*	*n.a.*	*n.a.*			68.60			
1962		79.55				80.56			
1963		80.08		81.80	*n.a.*	80.18			
1964		77.82		78.40	*n.a.*	*n.a.*			76.47
1965		82.42		83.40	*n.a.*	82.23			82.06
1966		84.35		85.20	*n.a.*	85.11	85.30		84.43
1967		90.74		92.20	*n.a.*	91.72	91.54		90.51
1968		82.33		83.55		85.11	82.85	81.84	82.32
1969		91.04		91.44		93.21	90.72	89.05	90.03
1970		86.41		86.17		88.92	85.77	84.91	85.96
1971		92.47		92.10		94.54	92.58	90.31	92.20
1972		82.57		82.58		85.10	84.10	81.69	83.39
1973		68.71		69.22		70.35	70.25	66.73	*n.a.*
1974		63.60		63.21		63.55	64.53	63.84	*n.a.*

[a]The accounting year changed for Whitbread in 1964, meaning that no data is available for that year.

if the brewing industry had not taken steps to reduce its labour intensity during a period of rising labour costs, though it must be conceded that if this did occur it was not reflected in a fall in the number of workers employed by the majors.

A second source of bias might arise from assuming the rate of change in the prices charged by the majors was similar to those charged by the industry as a whole. The Price Commission found that for the period after 1974 the prices of majors increased at a faster rate than smaller companies; if this were the case during the period we consider, the increase in efficiency experienced by the majors would appear exaggerated.

If indeed an increase in efficiency did occur in the 1970s it would not appear valid to assume that this was caused by the merger waves. If the fall in *k* for companies that carried out mergers is compared to the fall in that of Guinness that did not, it might be concluded that the mergers allowed the former to merely match Guinness's increase in efficiency. However, the total factor requirement of, for example, Higsons Brewery fell from 81.91 in 1972 to 61.63 in 1974, that of Boddingtons from 76.71 to 57.42 and that of Youngs from 85.04 to 63.66 (three firms not untypical of other small companies), yet all of these companies had a turnover in 1974 of less than ten million pounds. Thus whatever the source of the change in efficiency the industry appears to have enjoyed in the 1970s it would not seem to be the result of the increased size of the majors.

Our conclusions are broadly in agreement with those of the Price Commission. The restructuring of the brewing industry has not resulted in gains to efficiency. Further it would appear that until the early 1970s efficiency was actually falling and that any increase since then enjoyed by the majors has been matched by the smaller non-merging companies.

The decline in efficiency experienced by the industry before the 1970s is somewhat surprising, but the trend in the *k* resulting from using data from the *Census of Production* does not lead us to substantially change our view. Had we used a wholesale price index, suitably adjusted for changes in duty, the results might have been different for the period after 1970 but probably would not have been prior to this. When the constituents of *k* are considered it is found that *k* rises because, whilst the ratio of output prices to input prices increased, the return on sales did not increase accordingly. The obvious rejoinder is that the rise in output prices represents improvements in the quality of the product. Quality change we consider below although we can state here that we believe that as far as beer, at least, is concerned, we consider this a rather weak counter-argument; we draw no conclusions on changes in the quality of outlets.

7.4 The effects of mergers on the product mix offered by the brewing industry

The Brewing Industry has the dubious distinction of having developed its own 'Voice', a pressure-group of consumers who prefer to alter directly, largely through propaganda, producers' policies regarding their products rather than switching allegiances to other products as economic man is traditionally supposed to behave. The voice in question belongs to the Campaign for Real Ale. Its complaints are, amongst others, that the range of products has been reduced and, perhaps more interestingly, that the characteristics of these products have been changed. This section will assess the truth of some of these claims and discuss how far any changes have been the result of the change in concentration in brewing. It may fairly be said that economists have tended to concentrate on the effects of mergers on efficiency and/or market power and to have largely ignored their effects on product mixes. This is a modest attempt to redress the balance.

(a) *Range of choice*

If the number of brands offered by the brewing industry has fallen, other things being equal, a loss in welfare will have occurred. The Monopolies Commission (1969) believed that in 1967 there were three thousand brands of beer available. Both Mark (1974) and Gooding (*Financial Times*, 24 April 1974) claim that the number has been halved and this would seem a commonly held view though from where it is derived is not clear.

The number of brands offered throughout the country may have fallen but this does not mean that the range accessible to the individual consumer will necessarily have contracted if the history of the industry is that of 'local monopolies' being 'broken up' (Hawkins and Radcliffe (1971)) and replaced by national companies strongly competitive through advertising, and selling each other's products through reciprocal agreements.

This argument is highly dubious. The Monopolies Commission reported that in 1967 'ninety per cent of beer sold was brewers' own beer' and that at that time 'all brewers bought beer from and/or sold beer to other brewers'. Therefore it was neither true that the range of choice in individual public-houses had significantly increased – if local companies had reciprocal agreements it would actually have decreased – as a result of the merger-boom of the 1960s, nor that the availability of 'foreign' (the industry's term) brands was limited to public houses owned by the national companies.

It may have been true, though, that increased competition was introduced into the market. If a local monopoly was taken over by a national company then to a large extent one monopoly was merely replaced by another. The benefit of competition may be experienced, however, through the effects of more intense marketing. Given the increased mobility of the public all forms of marketing, and in particular advertising, will encourage people to travel to drink thus weakening the market-power of the local monopoly. If the reaction of the company which experiences falling sales is simply to retaliate with its own advertising it may be argued that the consumer has not benefited.[4] If a company chooses to react with alternative strategies: price cutting, improving the facilities in its outlets, increasing the range of products it sells, the consumer may well benefit, though the gain to the consumer would have been greater had the initial competitive act taken this latter form.

The fallacy of this thesis is that the evidence does not suggest that the UK was dominated by local monopolies before the restructuring of the 1960s. Using information supplied by Osborne (1978) it has been possible to locate the site of all brewing companies operating in 1960. Excluding home breweries, of which there were 13 in 1960, one can state with certainty that approximately 7,700,000 people lived in towns with at least two breweries and approximately 6,700,000 lived in towns with three. This does not reflect how well the rest of the population who lived outside these towns was served but with not particularly strong assumptions it is possible to make an estimate. The catchment areas of breweries in which their public houses would have been located would have varied in size with the maximum distance over which their draught beer could travel without its quality being affected. Brewery-fermented beer is not a good traveller but it can certainly travel easily over at least thirty miles; Davenports (Birmingham), for instance, supply draught beer to Liverpool and Bristol. If one assumes that public houses would be supplied to two thirds of this distance and circles are drawn of twenty miles radius, with their centres at the location of the breweries, there are practically no areas in which there are not two, and usually three, circles overlapping in England, with the West Country the major exception. Wales is less well-served and competition in Scotland is limited to the conurbations of the Central Lowlands.

The conclusion that can be drawn from this is that before the restructuring of the industry the majority of consumers were in the catchment area of at least two and usually three breweries. Indeed, considering that Caernarvonshire, Merionethshire and most of the Scottish Highlands would not otherwise have been supplied with any beer at all, the circles should have been drawn larger and the potential competition each brewery offered assumed to be at a correspondingly higher level. If brewers were profit-maximisers they would have attempted to populate their catchment areas to the full with their pubs, subject to two constraints. First the licensing laws would have provided some check to competition, and second, the number of pubs that would be established in any area would be limited by the level of demand there and it would have been possible for individual pubs to enjoy local monopolies in their areas. Nevertheless, though the degree of potential competition might be expected to exag-

4 This is adopting the no doubt extreme view that all advertising is persuasive rather than informative. Casual empiricism would suggest that advertising from the brewing industry is particularly barren of fact.

gerate the degree of actual competition, it would seem invalid to assert that before the 1960s the British beer market was dominated by local monopolies. The range of choice offered to consumers would appear unambiguously to have been reduced.

(b) The characteristics of beer

There is no doubt that over the last twenty years[5] a new type of beer has been gaining an increasing share of the market. The brewers have never denied this and until they became the object of press and pressure-group criticism had not been at all defensive about any changes in the products they sold.

The brewing process (Cockerill (1975)) consists of 'the production of a fermentable liquid (called wort) from the basic ingredients of water, sugar, malt and other cereals – the conversion of the sugars of the wort into alcohol and the clarification and stabilisation of the brew through fermentation and storage'.

The difference between the production process of traditional beer and that of the new product is that the latter is pasteurised to kill the yeast and prevent further fermentation, filtered to remove all solids and, because no natural carbon dioxide is produced after fermentation, this is injected before packaging to force the beer out of the barrel – 'the top pressure' method.[6] Criticism is usually concentrated on the first and last with such epithets as 'dead' and 'fizzy' appearing on the pages of 'What's Brewing', CAMRA's newspaper. The industry is also accused of adding chemicals to the brew, for instance to standardise ('burtonise') the water or to allow the head to be maintained longer.

The product in question is usually termed 'keg' by its critics, though the term was originally coined for promotion purposes by Flowers Brewers, now a subsidiary of Whitbreads, whilst traditional beer is called 'draught'. The brewing industry prefers to differentiate between brewery-fermentation and public-house fermentation. It is more convenient to use keg and draught but the usage should not be considered pejorative.

CAMRA claims that keg is inferior in quality to draught. Judging between products must be a matter of taste but it is possible to draw some conclusions about which might provide the better value for money in terms of whatever characteristics have been quantified.

In 1972 *Which* carried out a comparison of keg with draught beer and published the original gravity and percentage of alcohol by volume of the keg and draught brands of each of the major brewers. It referred to an index of bitterness and the measurements using this have been kindly provided by the Consumers' As-

5 It was first introduced on a very limited basis in the 1930s by Watneys.

6 Matters are complicated, leading to confusion in definition, by some beer which is not pasteurised or filtered being delivered under top-pressure, usually because it will then keep longer. It is assumed that statistics include this type as draught.

sociation. The original gravity, OG, refers to the ratio of the weight of unfermented liquid to an equal quantity of water. The stage at which fermentation is stopped will depend upon the brewer and he will be very unlikely to allow the yeast to convert all of the sugar. However, unless the OGs are very close they will serve as a reasonable guide to the relative strengths of different beers. Moreover, if *Which* scientists are correct, it 'determines flavour, body and condition'.

The use to which these data is put need not end at a simple comparison. *Which* reported the public bar prices that had been paid for the beer it tested and it is therefore possible to compare the prices of keg and draught brands after adjusting for differences in the amounts of some of their characteristics, i.e. to construct hedonic prices. *Which* is rather vague about the details of its survey and given the differences regionally between prices and even, occasionally, amounts of characteristics of the same brand the data should be treated with some caution. However it might still be expected to provide some indication of national averages. In order to remove the influence of tax, which in 1972 accounted for 30% of revenue from beer, all prices are exclusive of duty, the amount which has to be paid on a brand depending on its original gravity.

Regressions (1) and (3) in Table 7.5 show that if a keg dummy is omitted as an explanatory variable there is only a low correlation between the price of beer and the specified characteristics. When it is included however, the R^2 and F statistics assume high values. The results indicate that in 1972 producers of beer received 2.7p more from a pint of keg beer than would have been the case with a pint of draught beer with the same amount of the specified characteristics.

Separate regressions have been run using samples which included and excluded Guinness and Harp which, whilst keg, might be considered to have peculiar characteristics which might be expected to have intrinsic prices. In fact, whilst Harp's quality adjusted price (measured by its position in relation to the regression line), is 1.3p, which would support this contention, that of Guinness is only 0.04p so that whatever additional characteristics are embodied in the latter are provided relatively cheaply. When Harp and Guinness are excluded from the sample the keg dummy coefficient is slightly reduced.

What is surprising from the results is that the 't' statistics for OG, alcohol content and index of bitterness are usually of a low order (except in equation 6) and the signs of the coefficients are sometimes the opposite from those expected if one assumes that more of all characteristics is supplied in more expensive products. In case the explanation lay in multicollinearity separate regressions were run omitting each of the explanatory variables in turn, without any improvement in the results, and indeed when all these were omitted and only the keg dummy was retained as an independent variable, the resulting R^2 and 'F' statistics were hardly affected.

This does not necessarily mean that keg represents lower value for money. There may be some characteristic, present in the former but absent in the latter,

Table 7.5 *Hedonic prices of beer*

Eqn no.	Dependent variable (price exclusive of duty per pint)	Constant	Original gravity (degrees)	Alcohol content (%) by volume	Index of bitterness	Keg dummy	Advertising (£)	1972 Constant dummy	1972 OG slope dummy	1972 Index of bitterness slope	R^2	F (degrees of freedom)
(1)	Draught and keg in 1972 pooled (including (Guinness and Harp)	432.6 (1.1)	−0.4097 (−1.07)	0.6927 (0.25)	0.0799 (1.11)	—	—	—	—	—	0.24	1.03 (3,10)
(2)	Draught and keg in 1972 pooled (including Guinness and Harp)	257.5 (1.6)	−0.2404 (−1.5)	0.1879 (0.16)	0.0734 (2.5)	2.69 (6.95)	—	—	—	—	0.88	16.5 (4, 9)
(3)	Draught and keg in 1972 pooled (excluding Guinness and Harp)	−279.2 (−1.02)	0.2962 (1.1)	−2.376 (−1.37)	−0.3341 (−3.1)	—	—	—	—	—	0.57	3.6 (3, 8)

(4)	Draught and keg in 1972 pooled (excluding Guinness and Harp)	−51.2 (−0.41)	0.064 (0.52)	−0.9136 (−1.15)	−0.0533 (−0.8)	2.05 (5.9)	—	—	—	—	0.93	23.1 (4,7)
(5)	Draught and keg in 1972 pooled (including Guinness and Harp)	53.07 (0.19)	−0.0362 (−0.13)	−1.6895 (−0.82)	0.0647 (1.35)	—	0.5×10^{-5} (3.56)	—	—	—	0.68	4.8 (4, 9)
(6)	Draught and keg in 1972 pooled (excluding Guinness and Harp)	−370.18 (−2.14)	0.3816 (2.2)	−2.9714 (−2.7)	−0.1653 (−2.02)	—	0.3×10^{-5} (3.66)	—	—	—	0.85	10.2 (4, 7)
(7)	Draught in 1960 and 1972 (deflated) pooled	−49.3 (−1.8)	0.0507 (1.9)	—	0.0135 (0.69)	—	—	102.9 (1.18)	−0.0973 (−1.15)	−0.0175 (−0.24)	0.64	8.5 (5, 24)
(8)	Draught in 1960 and 1972 (deflated) pooled	−39.1 (−1.49)	0.0407 (1.6)	—	0.0165 (0.85)	—	—	—	0.0024 (1.4)	−0.0426 (−0.59)	0.62	(10.2) (4, 25)

Numbers in parentheses in cols. 3–11 refer to '*t*' values.

which earns it the higher price. It is claimed by critics of the brewing industry that advertising has played an important part in persuading the public to purchase keg. A discussion of this will be postponed to later in this chapter but here we make some estimate of the importance of advertising in raising the price of keg, either by persuading the public to value more highly the characteristics peculiar to keg (or informing it of keg's virtues) or by creating the illusion of characteristics. When the keg dummy is omitted, but the 1972 expenditure on advertising each of the brands in the sample is included as an explanatory variable, the results show the coefficient to be highly significant. When the keg dummy and amount spent on advertising are both used as explanatory variables (the results of this are not shown) the coefficient for the latter becomes insignificant. This reflects the heavy bias of beer advertising towards the promotion of keg. Given that keg and draught must be regarded as close substitutes it is hard to see how this could not be regarded as at least a partial explanation of the price differential between them.

Hedonic prices may also be used to compare prices in 1972 with those in 1960. The source is again *Which*; in 1960 it tested a wide range of beers including twenty-four that were draught. It would be surprising, given that keg is more expensive than draught, if the average price of the total sampled in 1972 were not higher than the average in 1960. What would be more interesting would be to compare the prices of draught beer in 1972 which has supposedly remained the same product during the intervening period and therefore would not contain any peculiar characteristics, with those in 1960, after taking account of the differences in the amounts of their characteristics. Prices in 1972 have been deflated by the index of the weighted average of prices of inputs as used in the construction of the *k* series described in 7.3. The dependent variables in regressions (7) and (8) are therefore draught beer prices excluding duty in 1960 and 1972, pooled.

Between 1960 and 1972 the average shadow price of omitted characteristics – which would be reflected in the size of the constant – and/or the shadow prices of included characteristics – could have changed. Therefore constant and interaction dummies have been included in (7). As there is no *a priori* reason why the real price of omitted characteristics must necessarily have changed the constant dummy has been omitted in (8). The change in the sign and significance of the OG coefficient suggests multi-collinearity. This does not matter if we are simply concerned to show that the real price of draught beer has risen; though there is perhaps no stronger *a priori* reason to suppose the prices of included characteristics would have changed rather than those that were omitted, the decision as to which is the correct specification is not crucial; if the amounts of characteristics in 1960 at 1960 prices is compared to the same amounts at 1972 prices, the average predicted real price exclusive of duty will rise from 3.8p to 5p regardless of whether a constant dummy, as well as a slope dummy, is utilised to take account of the change in price.

It is of relevance to this study that the real price of an important constituent of the product mix offered by brewing, draught beer, should have risen. But what has happened to the price–cost margin for draught beer? $\Delta\,(P_0/P_I$ where P_I is the weighted average of input prices, is a reasonable substitute for $\Delta\,[(P_0 - MC)/P_0]$ as long as efficiency has not declined within the industry with brewers using more variable factors of production to produce each pint. Cockerill and Rainnie (1975) have shown that at least the potential for scale economies exists in brewing so it would not be legitimate to employ the return on sales as a surrogate for the price–cost margin in order to check our results. If efficiency, defined as the ratio of output to inputs has remained constant, it is sufficient that P_0/P_I has risen to conclude that an increase has occurred in the price–cost margin: if the assumption of constant efficiency is relaxed, because firms approach their production frontier, or because of technical progress or because of scale economies, it is not necessary that P_0/P_I increase for an increase to have occurred in the price–cost margin. It would appear, therefore, that either the price-cost margin for draught beer increased between 1960 and 1972 or that efficiecny declined or both.[7] Given the upward trend in k between 1960 and 1972 reported in Table 7.3 it would seem rash to draw too strong conclusions about what happened to the price–cost margin.

To return to the differences between keg and draught it might be argued that the price of the former is higher because of peculiarly keg characteristics and that any judgement between the two must be purely subjective. This would have more force if the comparison were simply between two products which were both distributed either nationally or regionally. In fact the comparison is between largely nationally distributed keg with largely regionally distributed draught and certainly the average distribution area of keg brands is far higher than that of draught. It is a trivial assertion that in the absence of any consideration about price a consumer would prefer to be supplied with a product which has the amount of each of its characteristics specified by him. If regional differences in product reflect regional differences in taste, one would expect that each regional brand would approach nearer the ideal combination of characteristics for consumers in any region than would a national brand. In the trade-off between the price of a product and the closeness with which it approaches this ideal combination, it would be impossible *a priori* to state where consumers preferences might lie.

7 It would be natural for the Brewers to claim that the prices of the brands *Which* sampled in either of the periods were not representative of national averages. As an index of public-bar prices is not published it is not possible to verify this. However, as average outlet prices, (total expenditure on beer)/(volume of beer sold), rose by 112% between 1960 and 1972 whilst the average price of the draught beers sampled by *Which* was 102% higher than the average in 1960, there seems no reason to doubt the accuracy of *Which*'s surveys.

Table 7.6 *Beer sales by type (percentages)*

	1954	1968/9	1972[a]	1975
Draught bitter	24	28	27	25
Keg ale	1	14	19	20
Draught mild	40	24	18	12
Pale ale, stout (including draught stout) and brown ale	34	30	27	28
Lager (including draught)	1	4	9[b]	15
	100	100	100	100

Sources: NBPI (1969) for 1954 and 1968/69, Cockerill (1974) for 1972 and 1975 (predicted).
[a]Cockerill's estimate for 1972 agrees with that of MINTEL for keg's share and though other amounts differ the ranking remains the same.
[b]Cockerill describes this as almost certainly an understatement.

The results of the hedonic price analysis would suggest, however, that the question of whether consumers would prefer to return to regional variation at higher prices does not arise as for at least three important characteristics a higher price is apparently charged when they are supplied in national keg brands than in regional draught. It is conceivable that were keg to be supplied on a smaller scale the price differential would be even higher but it would be surprising if the inclusion of keg characteristics would give rise to economies of a much higher scale than other beer characteristics. If indeed no real trade-off between range of choice and price exists it can be stated quite categorically that the introduction of keg has resulted in a welfare loss because keg characteristics could have been included in brands distributed on a far lower scale than at present with variation in other characteristics being maintained. In short, whilst economists may not be able to arbitrate between the brewers and CAMRA about whether keg should have been introduced, they can at least express regret that keg brands are either distributed nationally or at least on the scale of a very large region.

The final, and perhaps most important, questions to be answered are why keg was introduced, and why it should have been distributed on a much larger scale than would appear justified by the costs associated with keg characteristics.

(c) Reasons for the introduction of keg

Not surprisingly, the brewing industry, by which we mean the Majors, claims that keg was introduced in response to public demand. The evidence it cites is that keg has dramatically increased its market share. Table 7.6 is testimony to this.

What is significant, claims the brewing industry, is not only that sales of keg are gaining in importance but that this coincides with a decline in bottled beer sales and an increase in the sales of lager. The former is important, it argues, because there was a strong demand for less flat beer which could only be satisfied by the addition of gaseous bottled beer to the flat draught. When an alternative was available, bottled beer sales were hit. Reinforcing this was the increasing affluence of young drinkers and the growth in the number of female drinkers, both sections allegedly preferring their beer gaseous and cold. The growth in lager sales, the argument continues, was not coincidental but reflected the same trend; the industry asks why so much objection is made to keg bitter but not to lager, the manufacture of which, at least in this country, has all the factors deplored in that of keg. This defence is not limited to the brewing industry's public relations organs but is supported by some academic observers, notably Hawkins and Radcliffe (1971).

As was suggested in (b) above, whatever the demand for 'keg type' characteristics might be, their introduction into beer need not have been accompanied by a reduction in regional brands. It is possible to deplore recent developments in brewing's product mix without making any judgement on the quality of keg.

It is however very difficult to discuss consumer preferences given the amount and trend of advertising expenditures and given the tied system. Virtually all of the expenditure on advertising non-canned or bottled beer is devoted to promoting the sales of keg beer. In 1972, according to MEAL, £2,536,800 was spent on press and TV advertising of the keg brands, excluding Guinness, that *Which* tested whilst £208,900 was spent on advertising draught, a ratio of 12 :1 ; if Guinness is included with keg the ratio rises to 15 :1. Either ratio would be lower than the corresponding ratios over the period 1968–71. Between 1960 and 1974 the amount spent on press and television advertising of all beer, including lager, after deflation by the retail price index, increased by an annual compound rate of five per cent. When the amount spent on lager is omitted the annual compound rate falls to four per cent.

One would ideally wish to distinguish between expenditure on advertising of keg and draught and on canned and bottled beer. Unfortunately it is not possible to do so before 1968. Since that date the approximate percentage of total advertising devoted to canned and bottled beer each year was as follows. 1968, 50; 1969, 41; 1970, 52; 1971, 43; 1972, 38; 1973, 37; 1974, 28. (Source: *Monthly Digest of Advertising Expenditure* (Media Expenditure Analysis Ltd, 1968–74).)

It would appear that the marked increase in real expenditure on beer advertising can be ascribed to an increase of that on keg. It is conceivable that the total effect of such advertising was to alter the relative shares of the market for keg enjoyed by different brands and to leave the market for draught beer unaffected. This would seem over-stretching the bounds of possibility. It is not easy for consumers to distinguish from the advertising whether the product in question is keg or draught; no attempt is made by the advertisements to differentiate the two. Therefore, it would not generally be possible for consumers to recognise the target audience as consumers of keg rather than draught; if such recognition were possible it might reduce the elasticity of demand for keg with respect to advertising. Even if the product being advertised could be recognised as keg, draught is to a large extent its substitute so that consumers might not only be expected to switch loyalty between keg brands but between beer brands in total. We have not made any attempt to estimate precisely the influence of advertising of keg on the demand for draught but it would seem significant.

Critics of the brewing industry have argued that the tied system provides brewers with the power to impose products upon consumers. This would be the case even in the absence of local monopolies. The argument which brewers have consistently maintained is that they offer a product mix of beer and pub and that the price of beer should not be taken in isolation from changes in pub-amenities. This would seem a reasonable contention but the corollary is that if in the total product mix the quality of beer is weighted less heavily than the amenities of the pub, whilst consumers may feel that quality has deteriorated, this need not be reflected in their transferring allegiance to a pub selling the beer they would prefer. The critics of the brewing industry have apparently not chosen to spell out the logic of the relationship between keg and the tied system if indeed the success of one is to be laid at the door of the other. Perhaps it is because whilst bruising to the brewers their critics do not escape unscathed. Not only does it suggest that consumers as a whole consider the quality of beer they drink relatively unimportant, so that CAMRA is not 'voicing' the preferences of the majority, but it does not easily allow criticism of the trends in the amenities offered by pubs. If major brewers are imposing music, fruit machines, etc., on a public that would prefer the traditional pub format this certainly would be reflected in a fall in their profits and a rise in those of smaller brewers who from preference or lack of capital have not 'modernised' to the same extent.

Differences between price elasticities would provide an obvious motive for brewers to use whatever market-power they possess to direct demand from draught to keg. Moreover, if the consumers of keg were more susceptible to advertising than those of draught, perhaps because they were younger, this would also explain the brewers' marketing policies with respect to draught and keg; in the latter case the result would be an increase in the total volume of sales as well as merely changing the market-shares held by keg and draught. There is probably some validity in both these explanations but regardless of any differences in the elasticities of demand with respect to prices and advertising between keg and draught a very powerful reason for brewers attempting to increase the sales of the former lies in the differences in the production methods of the two products. The maintenance of draught beer in retail outlets requires skill and attention. Keg requires little of either. Originally keg was sold to such outlets as sports and social clubs where the necessary skill would be less likely to occur and it might not receive attention for long periods. To a lesser extent the same danger to the brewer from leaving responsibility for the maintenance of his beer to the vendor exists when selling to public houses. *Ceteris paribus* brewers would prefer to sell keg instead of draught. More important even than this, the production method of keg allows it to be transported easily. Because with draught beer the fermentation process is still continuing it needs to be handled carefully when travelling. Though there are some notable exceptions, draught beer is not sold as national brands. If brewers wished to exploit economies of scale in production[8] the introduction of keg would be an obvious prerequisite; the alternative would be to produce nationally only bottled or canned beer, themselves brewery fermented.

It is important to note that this is a difference between the methods of production of keg and draught rather than their characteristics as perceived by consumers. Naturally the two are not totally independent and indeed CAMRA complains bitterly about the effects on taste of pasteurisation. To the extent that these effects were introduced in response to a change in consumer preferences and to the extent pasteurisation gives rise to economies of a national scale, it would not be possible to state categorically that keg should have been supplied on a smaller scale; the trade-off between regional variation and lower cost would then arise. If the significance of either of these factors is minimal, it is legitimate to distinguish between the minimum efficient scale for supplying keg characteristics and for supplying beer produced by the keg production method.

This now indicates the relevance of mergers to this section. The development of keg beer made economies of scale viable. If economies of scale could not have been achieved unless keg beer were introduced and if mergers in brewing were motivated by the desire to exploit these economies it would seem clear that the development of keg led to the mergers. Similarly, if indeed the attraction to brewers of keg was that it made possible production on a national scale, then had the mergers not taken place neither would the determined effort by brewers to shift demand from draught to keg. As there was, no doubt, some genuine demand for keg characteristics it would seem likely that these would have been supplied in modified versions of draught brands; if keg proper were sold this would not have been accompanied by the current massive amount of advertising.

It is likely that there were a number of reasons behind the mergers in brewing of which the desire to exploit scale economies might not even have been the most important; the obvious alternative explanations would be the potential a horizontal merger would offer to increase market-power and, if other arguments

8 It would not, however, be necessary to introduce keg in order to exploit economies of scale in marketing. It would be perfectly possible to promote nationally a product which differs in characteristics from region to region. Whitbread Trophy provides an example of this.

than profit-maximisation are allowed for in managers' utility functions, to increase a company's rate of growth. Whatever the reason, and in all probability there were a combination of reasons behind any one merger, once a merger had taken place it would still be in a company's interests to exploit whatever potential existed for scale economies and therefore to promote keg. In that sense the promotion of keg was more a result, than its development was a cause, of the mergers in brewing.

7.5 Concluding remarks

The conclusion that may be drawn from the evidence presented in this chapter is that the restructuring of the brewing industry has not been in the public interest. The efficiency of the industry actually declined during most of the period considered and when this was reversed and efficiency substantially increased, the improvement was shared by the small, as much as by the larger, brewers.

It is not surprising that the mergers in brewing led to a reduction in the range of choice open to consumers. What is to be deplored is that this reduction was accompanied by higher prices. We cannot make any judgement on whether keg beer is inferior to draught but we can regret that the introduction of keg characteristics has been associated with a reduction in choice without any obvious resulting benefits.

It is sufficient to describe an industry in which mergers have until recently been accompanied by a decline in efficiency and certainly have not resulted in gains from scale economies, and in which the product mix would appear to have unambiguously deteriorated, to demonstrate that a welfare loss has occurred. When one can add to this that the product mix has changed because it suited the brewers and that this change was made acceptable to consumers by a massive marketing exercise, the picture only becomes bleaker.

We do not prescribe a remedy for the problems confronting either the brewing industry or the consumers of beer though it would be tempting to call for the big brewers to be simply broken-up. We certainly, however, echo the Price Commission's recommendation that the Government review its attitude to the industry.

References

Brewers' Society, *Brewers' Almanac*. Reference has been made to several editions. Since 1972 it has been succeeded by the *Brewers' Statistical Handbook*.

Business Monitor Series (1975), *Brewing and Malting 231*, HMSO.

Cockerill, A.J. (1974), 'Mergers and Rationalisation in the Brewing Industry', *Brewer* (July).

– (1975) 'Market Structure, Economies of Scale and Technical Efficiency – International Perspectives for the Brewing Industry', *International Institute of Management, Seminar Proceedings, 2nd Conference on Economics of Industrial Structure*, Berlin.

Cockerill A.J. and Rainnie, G. (1975), 'Concentration and Economies of Scale in the Brewing Industry', unpublished paper, mimeographed.

Consumers' Association, *Which?* (November 1967, August 1970, April 1972).

Cowling, K. and McGuinness, A. (1975), 'Advertising and the Aggregate Demand for Cigarettes', *European Economic Review*, **6** (3) (July), 311–28.

Economists' Advisory Group (1969), *The Economics of Brewing*, a paper prepared for the Brewers' Society.

Elzinga, K. (1973), 'The Restructuring of the US Brewing Industry', *Industrial Reorganisation Review*, **1**, No.2, 101–14.

Euro-Monitor Publications Ltd (1975), *Market Research in Great Britain*, **15**, No.2 (February).

Fielding, Newson & Smith, Stockbrokers, *Report on the Brewing Industry*, various years.

Franks, J.R., Broyles, J.E. and Hecht, M.J. (1976), 'An Industry Study of the Profitability of Mergers in the United Kingdom', paper presented at the *Conference of the European Finance Association*:

Hawkins, K. and Radcliffe, R. (1971), 'Competition in the Brewing Industry', *Journal of Industrial Economies*, **20** (November), 20–41.

Hutt, C. (1973), *Death of the English Pub*, Arrow.

Legion Information Services Ltd, *Statistical Review of Press and TV Advertising*, all years 1960–67.

Mark, J. (1974), 'The British Brewing Industry', *Lloyds Bank Review* (April).

Media Expenditure Analysis Ltd, *Monthly Digest of Advertising Expenditure*, all years 1968–74.

Monkton, H. A. (1966), *A History of English Ale and Beer*, Bodley Head.

Monopolies Commission (1969), *Beer*, HMSO.

National Board for Prices and Incomes (1966), *Costs, Prices and Profits in the Brewing Industry*, Report No.13, HMSO.

–(1969), *Beer Prices Report No. 136*, HMSO.

Price Commission (1977), *Beer Prices and Margins*, HMSO.

Osborne, K. (1978), Raw material of a book, proposed title *The Rape of the British Brewing Industry* proposed date of publication 1978. Data can be obtained from the authors of this book.

Scherer, F. M. (1975), *The Economics of Multiplant Operation*, Cambridge, Mass.: Harvard University Press.

Stone, R. (1945), 'The Analysis of Demand', *Journal of the Royal Statistical Society*, **58**, 286–382.

Vaizey, J. (1960), *The Brewing Industry 1886–1951*, Pitman.

Wilson, R. (1974), *Who's Who in Brewing*, Northwood Publications Ltd.

8

The employment effects of mergers. A case study of GEC

8.1 **Introduction**

As seen in Chapter 6, GEC is a very large company with interests in most sub-sectors of electrical engineering. More recently it has diversified into non-engineering production (e.g. by the takeover of Schreiber). Over the period since the mergers with AEI and English Electric, GEC has reduced its workforce from around 240,000 at the time of the merger to 166,000 at the end of 1976. The main rationalisation occurred between 1967 and the end of 1971 when about 40,000 jobs were lost from the company. The incidence of the redundancies is recorded in Appendix A.8.1. GEC's prosperity and viability, of course, has a big impact on the electrical engineering industry's prospects. In particular, this must be true of those industries in which GEC gained or enhanced its monopoly[1] position through the merger. The Mergers Panel at the time had access to market shares data, but this information was not made public and one suspects the reason for this may have been that the market share acquired exceeded that laid down as a maximum in monopoly legislation.[2]

This chapter sets out to do two things. The first is to place the GEC merger within the context of other changes occurring within the engineering industries which also had an impact on employment. Throughout the period GEC was undertaking no significant new investment so that the increases in efficiency recorded in Chapter 6 were partly achieved by closing down labour intensive plant and reducing labour hoarding. These involved redundancies on a wide scale. The second part of the chapter, therefore, looks at how GEC handled the redundancies viewed from the company's position and the response of the unions. The interest here centres on the impact of redundancies on communities. Of particular interest is the problem of monopsony in the labour market.

1 Monopoly is used here as it was at the time the mergers took place, that is a 30% share of domestic sales.

2 The market share data for the AEI/GEC merger was considered too confidential to publish.

The labour market is singled out for special attention because, in actuality, the reallocation of resources which occurs in Williamson's trade-off model (Williamson (1968)) does not take place instantaneously nor costlessly. His calculations make no allowance for the imperfect functioning of the factor markets into which redundant resources are released. In particular, labour is of interest primarily because it is a human resource and because unlike other inputs labour cannot simply be stored while not in use. It must be maintained during periods of unemployment which not only introduces problems of the distribution of income, it also diverts money from other uses which may also have positive net discounted present values such as schools or hospitals or factories. Also during such periods labour may see a deterioration of skills through lack of use which may make an individual's time searching for a job longer and involves a loss for society too. In addition there are political and social implications arising from making people rather than plant unemployed. When a firm makes a decision about whether or not to make labour redundant, it will only take into account the costs which it bears directly such as the costs of firing; these include redundancy payments, which are spread over all employees like insurance cover, plus any settlement they agree with the unions over and above their legal obligations. They will not take into account the costs imposed on society or the individuals concerned.

The main reason that the IRC, the Government ministers and the press were in favour of the merger between GEC and AEI and English Electric was that it would increase the efficiency of the resources employed by all three firms. This would obviously involve a shedding of labour as at the time labour productivity was a problem for AEI and English Electric. At the same time the industry faced a sharp reduction in the anticipated level of demand and it was felt that the GEC management would be the most effective in achieving the rationalisation needed to bring the industry's employment levels into line. These are therefore the reasons which are put forward to explain the redundancies which followed. However, theoretically, there is an additional reason why the merged firm would require less labour than the three un-merged firms. Increases in product market power can result in a smaller demand for labour simply as a result of the firm using its market power to maximise its profits by reducing output and increasing its price–cost margin. This will occur even though the firm has no power in the labour market, i.e. it accepts the wage rate as given (see Figure 8.1 for the extreme example of the monopolist versus the competitive industry's demand for labour). If in addition the firm is gaining power in the factor market too, this can have implications for the wage rate as well as the level of employment (See Figure 8.2).

Of course these simple diagrams assume that labour supply is competitive. In reality the firm usually faces unionised labour with its aim to raise wages. Unions are often considered to be distorting the competitive wage. However,

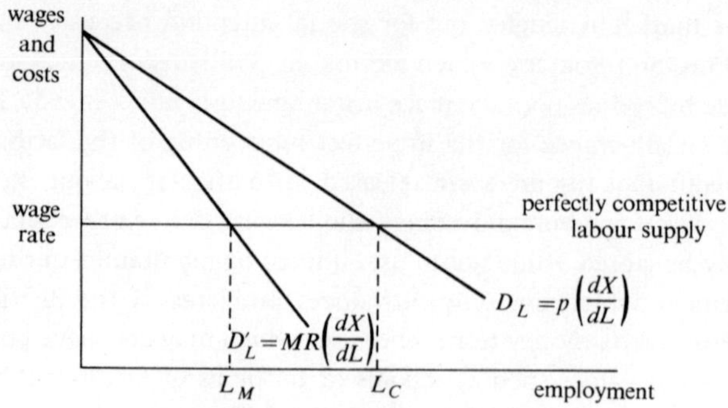

Figure 8.1 *The monopolist's demand for labour*

Key: D_L = Competitive demand for labour
L_C = Competitive employment
D'_L = Monopolist's demand for labour
L_M = Monopolist's employment

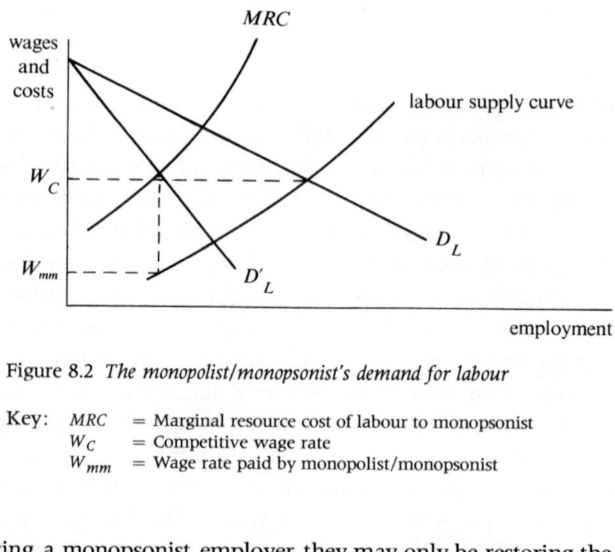

Figure 8.2 *The monopolist/monopsonist's demand for labour*

Key: MRC = Marginal resource cost of labour to monopsonist
W_C = Competitive wage rate
W_{mm} = Wage rate paid by monopolist/monopsonist

when facing a monopsonist employer they may only be restoring the wage rate towards its competitive level thus restoring relative prices. Even so, employment would still be below the competitive level.

The empirical question arises, to what extent is a firm such as GEC a monopsonist in the labour market? Obviously at a national level it is not so even for quite specialised skills. However, consider the example of a local labour market. Previous to the merger there were two or three competing firms, but after the merger there was only one employer. Engineers could be made redundant on two counts. One might be that it is a cost-saving merger and economies of scale decrease the need for engineers. The second might be that the increase in market power results in higher prices for engineering products which decreases the derived demand for engineering labour. If the market is such that there are no other employers of engineering labour, then the merged firm has monopsony power. Redundant men may find difficulty in finding alternative jobs and it will be extremely hard to find jobs which utilise their skills within their own labour market. Mobility is the usual answer to this problem but this raises social and even moral problems of uprooting people from their homes, still a sensitive topic in the UK.

Finally, before we examine the merger in the context of the industry as a whole and its effects on local labour markets, we must support the proposition, so far taken on board, that redundancy leads to unemployment. As mentioned above, this is not the case in the Williamson trade-off model, but in reality the labour market does not work instantaneously, nor is it always very good at working efficiently. One of the reasons why redundancy gives rise to unemployment must be that the release of a large number of people together on to the labour market takes some time to work its way through the system. Many other suggestions have also been made in the literature. Strong contesters for the main explanatory variable are the personal characteristics, age and skill status of those made redundant. Generally, youth suffers less unemployment on being made redundant than the older generation (see Daniel (1972), Kahn (1964) and Wedderburn (1965) and also the econometric results of MacKay and Reid (1972) and Herron (1975) although the latter two find age has more of a threshold effect on unemployment duration than a positive linear relationship). Skill is also generally considered an asset in finding a new job. In addition to these major characteristics the list could include mobility (see Wedderburn (1964)) and the kind of job search tactics employed by the searcher. Personal characteristics are not the only factors. The general state of demand will have a tendency to influence the average length of a spell of unemployment following redundancy, as will the timing of the redundancies, i.e. whether or not other redundancies are occurring at the same time.

Generalising from the results of surveys on unemployment following redundancy, it would be untrue to say everyone suffers some unemployment on being made redundant, but the average spell of duration has been about two months, differing from region to region. However, the distribution is highly skewed and some individuals are still unemployed over a year after the initial redundancy. These statistics are recalled here so that in reading the numbers which follow it will be possible to keep in mind the personal and social loss from the unemployment following the redundancies when seeing the benefits of increased efficiency for GEC (see Chapter 6) and the engineering industries.

8.2 Changes in engineering employment and the GEC mergers

The GEC mergers with AEI and English Electric were not the only forces for change occurring in the engineering industry in the second half of the 1960s. Besides other significant mergers, such as that between A. Reyrolle & Co. Ltd and C. A. Parsons Ltd, there also occurred a host of changes in the environment in which firms operated. The tightening up of government competition policy has already been mentioned in Chapter 6. Changes in government legislation affecting the employer and employee also occurred about the same time; these included the introduction of SET (repayable to manufacturing employers), the introduction of earnings related benefit and redundancy payments. The need for mergers was the conventional wisdom of the time and was considered the best way of bringing about rationalisation in an industry with excess capacity, which was facing a further reduction in demand. However, attempting to separate out the effect of the mergers on engineering employment is very difficult, because of all the other changes that were occurring at that time. First, it is necessary to establish what changes were observed in important economic relationships. Some occurred at the macro level, while others were more specific to engineering.

8.2.1 Changes in macro employment relationships

At the level of the whole economy, the Phillips relationship between the rate of change of money wages and unemployment appeared to become unstable about 1966. The relationship eventually reappeared with a noticeable outward shift, so that a given level of unemployment was associated with a higher rate of change of wage increases. Also there appeared to be a break in the usual relationship between the level of vacancies and the level of unemployment; while the Verdoorn law relating productivity to output was called into question by the fact that in some industries in which productivity was rising, both employment and output were falling.

Evidence that unemployment had become a poor proxy for demand in the Phillips curve relationship was provided by the NIESR (1970). But this was only true in aggregate not at a regional level. This they interpreted to mean that the unemployment variable was no longer reflecting the true position of excess demand. The change that had occurred in the national unemployment–vacancies (*U–V*) relationship could be caused in two ways. (1) The underlying *U–V* relationship may not have changed, but the dispersion of unemployment between the sub-markets may have changed, so that unless labour mobility increased, the national *U–V* relationship would be affected, producing a structural change. Alternatively, (2) the underlying *U–V* relationships may have shifted. Such behaviour might affect the national relationship or the sub-market effects might cancel each other out.

There was some evidence of a change in the dispersion of unemployment rates between the regions. They came closer together in the third quarter of 1966.

However, there is no real way of knowing how this would affect the Phillips' Curve; it might have lowered the rate of increase of earnings, while in actuality all the regional Phillips' curves shifted out. These shifts also occurred at industry sub-market level, and seemed to indicate the reason for the regional shift was the industrial basis.

Considering the *U–V* relationship again the NIESR (1972a) found a break between 1966–III and 1969–III which could not be ascribed solely to structural change in the relative rates of regional unemployment – it appeared the *U–V* relationships had shifted at the sub-market level.

The causes of such shifts in the *U–V* relationship and hence the Phillips curve was the centre of the debate between Gujarati and Taylor. Gujarati (1972) considered the shift to be due to a reduction in the labour supply of a voluntary nature, while Taylor (1972) stressed that all the extra unemployed were not all happy to be unemployed and that a shortfall in demand was the root cause.

Factors that Gujarati put forward that made employment less attractive were changes in government legislation, such as the Redundancy Payments Act (operative from December 1965, providing lump-sum payments on redundancy), the National Insurance Act (operative from 6 October 1966, which introduced earnings related benefit) and legislation which provided for increased Social Security payments. Employment would be reduced as some people would be better off not working. Without engaging in a political debate it is possible to counter that argument with the fact that it was only possible to get redundancy pay if one was made redundant, certainly not for simply leaving one's job. Once unemployed, those involved found it extremely difficult to find other jobs, which was not a symptom of labour shortage. Taylor's explanation was that other government legislation was increasing the fixed costs of employing, and this forced employers to reduce their labour hoarding. Such factors as SET redundancy payments and the levies of the ITBs accounted for the labour 'shake-out'. Output was increasing while employment fell. Employment could only be increased by a stimulus to demand. (See Taylor (1972).)

Certainly no-one would deny that deflation took place in 1966 and 1967, but the supply based arguments and the evidence of underlying structural change in unemployment relative to vacancies suggested that traditional demand-orientated policies might not work to cure this type of unemployment. What was strange about the situation was the maintained, fairly high level of vacancies. The NIESR (1972b) produced evidence to show that after a slight initial fall, productivity was rising during this time of increasing unemployment. Why then did vacancies not fall if unemployment was increasing? If it was really true that employers could not get all the employees they wanted, why did they let more of them go in 1970 and from 1973 onwards? It may have been that the high level of vacancies reflected increased selectivity on the part of employers but it must be borne in mind that this was the period in which the Department of

Employment was making a determined effort to get employers to register all vacancies. Thus the vacancy statistics began to be inflated by vacancies which would previously have gone unregistered. This discredits the arguments that vacancies had simply become a better measure of demand and since, used as a proxy, they showed the Phillips' Curve had not shifted, the level of unemployment should not be a cause for concern. Whatever the cause of unemployment, it implies resources are not being fully utilised. As a result there must be some loss of output. One of the more interesting questions perhaps was, why was productivity rising as employment fell, a phenomenon usually associated with rising output and employment? One reason may have been that the increased fixed costs of employment, mentioned above, and the existence of the redundancy payments scheme enabled firms to get rid of low productivity workers (presuming they could identify them). At this time there was also a growth in productivity bargaining which would help to raise average productivity. At the same time, many industries were going through a period of rationalisation, mainly through merger (coming about as a result of government policy). Productivity rose as the oldest plant and equipment was closed first. It could also have resulted from the achievement of economies of scale.

Certainly there was some change in employment behaviour during the period. This conclusion is backed by the findings of Briscoe and Roberts (1977). Looking for structural breaks in employment functions at sector and SIC order industry level, on purely statistical grounds, they found that most industries in fact experienced their strongest breaks around 1963. However, looking on economic criteria, they found the mid-1966 break point to be significant. The aggregate break is confirmed by Knight and Wilson (1974) who not only found a reduction in labour hoarding, but of those workers retained many were only working on short time.

Evidence would therefore point to a change in employment behaviour in the economy as a whole in the second half of the 1960s. The causes appear to be manifold, including changes in government legislation affecting both the costs of employment and the costs of being unemployed. Also, there was a deflation and a prices and incomes policy which bit most severely in 1966 and 1967. From July 1966, there was a complete standstill on wages, from January 1967, a zero norm but with increases in exceptional circumstances. The severity of the 'bite' however was possibly marginal for those who remained in employment (see Clegg (1971)). In addition, there was a general change in the structure of industry towards larger units, due to the merger activity of the early 1960s and the mergers of 1966 onwards (the latter group being actively encouraged by the Government). In view of all this it is not surprising to find the old relationships breaking down. Attributing the effects to each of these factors is more difficult.

8.2.2 Evidence of change in the electrical engineering industry

Engineering was an industry in which extensive change was occurring. The *U–V* relationship fell into the National Institute's high shift category; while Briscoe and Roberts (1977) found the strongest evidence of a structural break in the employment function of the engineering SIC in the first quarter of 1967.

Other evidence specific to electrical engineering, concerning the rate of growth of output, employment and productivity is to be found in Wabe (1974), Chapter two. There were significant differences in the rate of growth of output of the various sectors in electrical engineering from 1963 to 1971. The average growth in output was 20.8% while electronics grew 81.3% and wires and cables 52.9%. The growth in output has to be compared with what was happening to employment and productivity. In most cases employment grew, if only slightly, but in electrical machinery it fell 21% over the period. Looking at man hours, rather than 'heads', the fall in employment in other sectors is also noticeable. However, productivity increased noticeably over the period averaging a 21% increase per man for all engineering and 32.7% per man hour. Interestingly, the industry with the largest increase in productivity, electrical machinery, was the industry with the largest fall in employment. The Verdoorn relationship implies that high productivity industries will be those with the highest rate of growth of output. When this relationship is fitted, Wabe finds the electrical machinery observation a noticeable outlier (as is 'other vehicles'). Although output rose, it did not rise sufficiently to explain the large increase in productivity. Also, these increases are normally associated with rising employment, whereas employment fell dramatically from 1963 to 1971. However, such facts are quite in keeping with an industry going through a process of rationalisation, as was electrical machinery after the merger of GEC with AEI and English Electric.

Certainly the concentration figures would reveal a change in structure taking place (see Table 8.1). How was this change taking place? Working on data for an earlier period, Hart, Utton and Walshe (1973) attempted to assess the role of mergers in increasing concentration. Out of their sample of thirty industries, of those experiencing increasing concentration (21) ten were assessed to have done so through significant merger activity. Of these, line apparatus, electric cables and telegraph and telephone apparatus were amongst those also experiencing increasing output. Merger activity in the electrical engineering industry may have significantly increased concentration at this earlier date. Later, however, no discernible changes occurred because the industry was already highly concentrated.

It was admitted, at the time of GEC's merger with English Electric, that the new firm would gain a monopoly in at least two MLHs, 361, electrical machinery

Table 8.1 *Structural change in the engineering industry*

MLH SIC 1968	Industry	Five-firm concentration ratios 1963	1968	Percentage change
361	Turbogenerators	*n. a.*	86.8	—
	Switchgear	60.9	77.7	27.1
	Transformers	45.0	76.7	96.4
	Industrial Motors	56.4	64.6	14.5
362	Cables for telecommunication, other insulated wires	91.7	98.2	7.1
363	Line Apparatus	96.2	99.9	3.8
	Telecommunications	94.0	96.4	2.6
368	Cookers	60.0	85.9	43.2

and 368, (previously 365) domestic electrical appliances. Even so the merger was not referred to the Monopolies Commission by the merger's panel. The degree of control in sub-markets ranged from 30 to 90%. The data on the earlier merger is confidential, but as there were previously only four major firms in telecommunications, Plessey, AEI, GEC and STC, the merger between AEI and GEC would have had little impact on the five-firm concentration ratio for the industry. Over the period, the five-firm concentration ratio for telecommunications increased only 2.6% and for line apparatus 3.8%. As already seen in Chapter 6, the GEC mergers were backed by the Industrial Reorganisation Corporation and were intended to be both the vehicle of rationalisation and the proponent of the 'white-hot' technological revolution. Any benefits it did bring had to offset the increase in market power, which was not confined to the product market, but also occurred in some regional and specialised skill labour markets. Examples of the firm using its power in the product market can be found in Chapter 6. In the labour market, the process of rationalisation resulted not only in fewer jobs for engineering skills, but in many instances the labour force found itself facing fewer potential employers. There are many consequences of such developments, but an implication is the possibility of exploitation of the labour force and/or a growth in union militancy.

Another feature of the period was the increase in productivity in engineering. The increased efficiency of GEC has been demonstrated in Chapter 6. These changes took place against a background in which employment was falling while output increased. Work has been done at SIC order level by Briscoe and Roberts (1977) to see whether or not there was a change in the relationship between engineering output and employment. Adopting a Ball and St Cyr employment function (see Ball and St Cyr (1966)) they investigated the possibility of statistically significant structural breaks in the function, which they found for 1967 and 1971. However, when they use economic criteria and test for a break in 1966, they find that after the structural break, the speed with which employment adjusts to its desired level rises, implying that an increase in efficiency occurred in this industry. A more direct look at what was happening to labour hoarding in the industry was undertaken by Evans (1974). Constructing an index of labour hoarding, he finds differences between MLHs which correspond with individual business cycles, but there are two general boom years, 1964 and 1968. In both MLH 361 and 368, a change in behaviour is noticeable after 1968 when labour hoarding decreases rapidly. For MLH 363, there is a sharp drop in hoarding in 1968, although later there is a rise followed by a fall in 1971. The average amount of hoarding in these MLHs is less than their overall average from 1959 to 1971. For electrical goods the decrease in labour hoarding occurred against a background of rising output, although at the same time the industry was experiencing over-capacity, and falling employment. Output of domestic electrical appliances is slightly obscured by the SIC revision in 1969. Employment definitely fell in 1966 and 1968 but started to rise again in 1969, but this must be partly due to the reclassification. In the case of telegraph and telephone apparatus, employment rose steadily until the end of 1967, but fell until the beginning of 1970 when it started to level out. Output statistics are difficult to obtain but those available seem to indicate that throughout the period there was a steady rise, although a slight fall occurred from the end of 1968 to mid-1970.

Thus for the electrical engineering sector there is some evidence of changes taking place in the unemployment–vacancies relationship, in the employment–output relationship and in productivity and labour hoarding, much of which is dated later than the 1966 break observed in aggregate.

It may well have been the change in legislation, followed by the deflation of 1966 which sparked off a reappraisal of the employment situation but the vehicle for the required rationalisation was the merger wave of 1967 and 1968 which also changed the market structure in which the firms operated.

8.2.3 Employment and productivity in MLHs 361, 363 and 368

Finally we look at employment and productivity within the industries in which GEC acquired a monopoly (as defined by the monopoly legislation of the time).

Employment figures are available at MLH level[3] but there have been many discontinuities in the series. The most notable one, before the switch from the card count method to the Census of Employment, was the change in industrial classification. However, with the help of the Department of Employment, it was

3 Department of Employment Gazette (various).

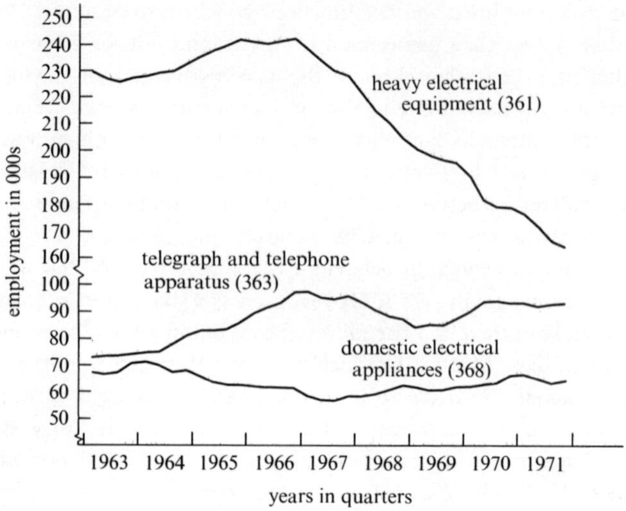

Figure 8.3 *Employment levels in MLHs 361, 363 and 368*

possible to construct a quarterly series from the monthly series on a continuous basis. In Figure 8.3 we plot the three employment series. This reveals that in both MLHs 361 and 368, employment was lower by 1970–71 than it had been in the early period before the merger, while for MLH 363, employment was in total greater but had levelled off since the merger.

Although the index of industrial production for these industries is confidential, it is possible to give some indication of what was happening in these industries in terms of productivity. The productivity indexes are derived from the output series (for which thanks is due to the Department of Industry) and an index of employment based on the series depicted in Figure 8.3.

The main problem with these (and any other output series more readily available) is that they tend to record deliveries of finished output rather than work in progress, so that employment is more likely to be related to the recorded output figures of some future date. In the case of MLH 368 (Domestic Electrical Appliances) this is not likely to be a real problem. Once a factory is tooled up there is little delay between the decision to produce, production and delivery. However, this is not true in the cases of MLH 361 (Heavy Electrical Equipment) and MLH 363 (Telegraph and Telephone Apparatus). Inquiries within the heavy electrical industry and statistical experimentation reveal a production lead of 8 quarters over employment in MLH 361 and 4 quarters in MLH 363. Allowing for this lead reveals statistically significant increases in productivity over the period. However, this is a normal finding; the question should rather be, has the rate of growth of productivity changed? (See Table 8.2: the series was split in 1967

Table 8.2 *Changes in the rate of growth of productivity 1963–71*

MLH (SIC 1968)	Annual rate of growth of productivity (%)[a]		
	1963–71	1963–67	1968–71
361	2.2	1.2	5.6
363	3.6	6.0	2.9
368	3.2	1.4	4.6

[a]Estimated by an exponential time trend

Source: Constructed from data provided by the Departments of Industry and Employment

not 1968 because of problems of degrees of freedom.) In both MLH 361 and 368, but not in MLH 363, there is evidence of a speeding up of the rate of growth of productivity in the late 1960s. This is possibly not so surprising for demand in MLH 363 remained quite buoyant relative to the fortunes of other engineering sectors (after an initial fall) and it was, at the time, still protected by the TAM agreements (see Chapter 6), all of which possibly reduced the need to improve productivity in this sector.

It is not, of course, possible to say categorically that this increase in the rate of growth of productivity for electrical machinery and domestic appliances was solely due to the two GEC mergers. But the GEC firm had a substantial share of all three markets and one of the main reasons put forward in favour of the mergers was that they would improve the efficiency of the industry. Certainly they must have contributed to this improvement in productivity.

8.3 **The redundancies**

Having noted the changes taking place at industry level, we turn now to examine how part of the fall in employment was achieved within the major firm in the three MLHs discussed above. This section deals with the actual redundancies, how they were handled by GEC and how the unions responded. From interviews with trade unions, we will discuss how the redundancies hit particular towns and communities, and will attempt to stress the reasons for the redundancies, whether or not they were justified and how the redundancies have affected industrial relations within GEC. We attempt to provide an impression of how GEC approached the redundancies and developed their policy towards them and how the unions reacted, their experience of particular redundancies and how they reacted to them. All the opinions are our own and although spokesmen for both GEC and the unions have kindly made suggestions on points of fact and opinion, the names of all such spokesmen are withheld to preserve their anonymity. Finally we will try to assess the evidence and look to the future. Can the loss of 74,000 jobs within one firm over a period of eight to nine years be left, in future, simply to the firm and unions to fight over? This is a substantial share of the total employment in the electrical engineering industry and should concern us all.

8.3.1 A view of GEC's approach

It has to be remembered that the GEC mergers with AEI and English Electric were backed by the Industrial Reorganisation Corporation (IRC) and had the support of the Central Electricity Generating Board (CEGB). We have seen from Chapter 6 that they can be considered successful both in the commercial sense and in the sense that they achieved one of the main objectives of the merger, the rationalisation of the electrical engineering industry. There is no doubt that GEC itself felt the mergers to be justified and that, in a sense, they felt the opposition they encountered to the following redundancies to be somewhat unfair, as the redundancies would have occurred one way or another, whether or not the merger went ahead. In fact, GEC has always claimed 'that the mergers would safeguard employment for those remaining'.

Obviously, mergers between firms producing competing products will result in the loss of some 'duplicated' jobs when product ranges are standardised. However, in a growing firm these need not cause unemployment if growth creates alternative jobs elsewhere. Unfortunately, the GEC mergers took place at a time of a considerable reduction in demand for engineering products. (In fact from the evidence of the Reports of the IRC it would seem that they were envisaged as the method by which rationalisation could be achieved.) On top of this it would not be unjustified to say that AEI at least, and possibly English Electric, were over-manned. (For example AEI's output per man in telecommunication was far below that of GEC's – GEC telecommunications with 15% more manpower than AEI produced nearly 100% more output (in terms of sales) than AEI – figures from GEC internal document.) Thus the introduction of GEC management techniques would undoubtedly produce a further fall in manpower requirements unless output were to increase, a possibility ruled out by the state of demand. In all this, the reduction in demand was the overwhelming factor giving rise to the redundancies.

The worst possible alternative to the merger might well have been the bankruptcy of one of the firms, most likely AEI, in which case shareholders and employees would have lost everything. As it was, the merger protected the interests of the shareholders and provided generous terms for those made redundant. It is relevant to note a suggestion made by the AEI Chairman to his Board in 1956 that they needed to reduce costs by 6% p.a. This was to be achieved by a 10% cut in total manpower and a 7½% cut in capital equipment. This would imply a cut of 7,500 in AEI's 1967 workforce of 74,800. Therefore it is quite clear that the redundancies were planned as a result of AEI's unprofitability and due to existing excess capacity, even before the really large drop in demand was known. GEC itself achieved a 5% cut in employment between acquiring English

Electric – giving GEC a combined labour force of 240,000 – and 1969 when employment stood at 228,000. (For the figures see Jones and Marriott (1970).) Redundancies then were inevitable and GEC had been, in a sense, created to deal with the problem. Thus not unnaturally it got a great deal of blame for 'causing' redundancies which it felt to be unfortunate but inevitable. Faced with its task GEC set about achieving it in the best way it could.

GEC's justification for the actual closure of Woolwich Telecommunications rests mainly on the excess capacity in the sector, the age of AEI's plant and on AEI's plan to close Woolwich. However, the criticism which was aimed at GEC, on the whole, was mainly over its handling of the incident. The closure came as a shock. At the time there was no formal mechanism through which the company and the unions could consult, although consultation occurred during the long notice period. After the initial 'bad press', GEC did much to ease the situation; they encouraged other firms to recruit, they assisted in placement along with the Department of Employment (then the DEP) special office, priority being given to disabled persons and foremen. In addition they made special provision for the 400 apprentices and trainees, allowed time off for interviews and let people leave within their notice period without allowing this to affect redundancy payments. This approach was adopted in the following redundancies. It is difficult to estimate the impact of the redundancies on employment in the area, but the DEP Survey of the Woolwich area[4] covering five closures found that half the workers were re-employed within a month and that on average they acquired jobs that were neither better nor worse than at AEI. In addition, the Woolwich redundancy scheme was considered, at the time, to be most generous and the actual closure of the plant occurred in April 1969, fifteen months after the announcements, although possibly this was not part of the original plan. After Woolwich, GEC adopted a policy of consultation which involved the setting up of a National Joint Consultative Council (NJCC). This occurred after the merger with English Electric, as part of GEC's promise to consult with the unions (and the Department of Employment) about planned redundancies. (Although informal discussion had taken place previously, from time to time.)

The Council is made up of a full-time official, representatives from the unions with substantial GEC membership, and senior members of GEC management, initially led by Sir Jack Scamp who acted as the Chairman. The Council is flexible enough to allow for the presence of either the Chairman or the Managing Director of GEC and Managing Directors of subsidiary companies when required. The Council can meet when either management or the unions wish it, but it should meet at least every three months. The general aim in setting up the NJCC was to improve communications between management and unions. GEC's explanation for the need for the NJCC is summed up as follows:

4 See Daniel (1972).

> The concept of the Council arose, on the Union side, out of the sense of employment insecurity which the mergers produced in some parts of the Company. Among management, the concept of the Council acknowledged that Trade Unions have an important and justified interest in the timing, location and character of major merger rationalisation; indeed, in any matters which could have a significant impact on employment.[5]

Although, initially, proposals involving redundancies were referred to within NJCC meetings, it was soon established that proposals should be announced locally and conveyed simultaneously to national officials of appropriate trade unions.

It appears to us that the existence of the NJCC kept GEC on its toes. Obviously the unions were going to oppose redundancy whatever the cause; they would challenge the basis of proposals. GEC businesses, however, never made a proposal involving redundancy without first trying to fully research the situation and consider all the possibilities. This is the reason why, in their opinion, even after consultation they rarely revised their proposals. Most of the discussions about proposals were held between local management and employee representatives, but meetings at the establishments affected also took place involving Head Office and local company representatives together with national, local and plant union representatives. At these meetings, management tried to explain the reasons for its proposals and the union representatives opposed them to the very best of their abilities. (The unions, of course, can never be expected to accept redundancy automatically. The most that can be expected is reluctant acquiescence, and only then if the proposals are found to be soundly constructed.) Then the task of negotiating redundancy terms would begin. This was always done at plant level (as are wage negotiations) where redundancies were occurring. There is significant evidence that employee representatives at plant level prefer to be involved directly in these negotiations (see next section).

How did GEC businesses make decisions concerning which plants to close when faced with over-capacity? The rationale appears to be that each plant was considered on its merits. It was and still is a question of which of the plants are viable. GEC has never presumed that a GEC plant (or GEC operating company management) would be better than AEI's or English Electric's. The demanding challenges of trade union representatives ensured that the company prepared its case properly. It is never pleasant to have to tell people that there is no longer a job for them; none of the decisions were taken lightly. In December 1975 employment levels in GEC were about 170,000 and had been since 1973. By December 1976 they were around 166,000.[6] This level does not take into account

5 Source: A GEC internal document.

6 See the *Sunday Times*, 19 December 1976.

the subsequently announced employment level reductions in the telecommunications business caused by Post Office cut-backs, nor what might occur as a result of over-capacity in the manufacturing sector of Britain's power generating industry. On the other hand, many of GEC's businesses are expanding and employment levels should be relatively stable. A proportion of the original reduction in numbers resulted from the selling of businesses and not redundancy or normal turnover.

Since the period of rationalisation following the merger, the role of the NJCC has been expanded to discuss pensions, business forecasts etc. This the unions were very keen to do. There has been an attempt to introduce plant level joint consultative councils (PJCCs). The NJCC, in fact, produced terms of reference but they were not mandatory. In fact, only about twelve units used these precise terms of reference because most plants already had satisfactory consultative arrangements. GEC believes consultation and involvement to be very important in achieving a smooth running organisation.

It is interesting to note that GEC's attitude to the recent Government cutbacks is one of acceptance. There appears to be no antagonism towards the Government, who have, in a sense, created GEC then left it to 'carry the can'. It is true that GEC donated funds to the Conservative and Liberal parties (see *Electrical Review*, 8 August 1975) for the first time recently, but that was mainly over plans to nationalise the aircraft and shipbuilding industries, which GEC opposes.

8.3.2 A view of the union position

A full list of the unions included in the NJCC covers most of the engineering unions, in both manual and staff employment areas. Most of the information here is compiled from interviews with officers of the Amalgamated Union of Engineering Workers (AUEW) and the Association of Professional and Executive, Clerical and Computer Staff (Apex). We are grateful to a number of union officials at national and local level for their co-operation and comments. However, no personal acknowledgements are given, and the opinions expressed, unless otherwise stated, are our own. We shall consider first the attitude and response of the unions to the redundancies following the GEC mergers.

The AUEW has at a national level the policy of full employment (which no doubt is an objective of most unions). Their policy has, therefore, always been that no man should be made redundant unless he had another job to go to, and then if and only if he was not taking that job away from another man. The initial reaction of the AUEW to the idea of the NJCC was to refuse to join. They feared it was the machinery for a 'national plan' for GEC redundancies, to which they were opposed (see above section). However, after meeting with top management a formula was agreed upon and it was on the basis of this formula that the NJCC approach was developed. The formula included the following:

(i) The maximum time for notification of proposed redundancies was to be given.
(ii) The union representatives were to be notified before the announcements were made public.
(iii) No compulsory redundancies.
(iv) No national policies on redundancy terms.
(v) The Unions retained the right to take normal action where and when they felt it necessary. Notification and consultation did not oblige them to acquiesce.

In achieving this formula, they felt that they did the best they could to lessen the impact of the redundancies. The NJCC unions believe that their pressure, through the NJCC, reduced the number of redundancies if not the number of jobs lost. It was pressure from them that got the company to agree to such things as time off for job search, extension of the closure periods and the use of alternative methods of reducing numbers. (It may well have saved much time and effort if these rights had not been fought for after every redundancy announcement. At this kind of level (outside the realm of compensation) a 'national plan' may have benefited all.) It is over the desirability of a national plan for redundancy that Apex appears to be in disagreement with the AUEW. In the interview with the officials of Apex the impression conveyed was that Apex felt it was easier for GEC to implement the redundancies because of the plant level agreements. (GEC would probably have found it cheaper than a national agreement which would have had to satisfy all, at the level of its larger, higher paid units). However, both unions were in agreement about the problem they faced in maintaining the level of employment. Many employees were quite willing to give up their jobs without having an alternative job to which to go. The main reason cited by the unions for this apparently irrational behaviour was the lump sum redundancy payments scheme, *ex gratia* and long service payments. Possibly many individuals did not realise the actual state of the labour market – it had always been fairly easy to get a job previously, so they took the opportunity offered them and volunteered for redundancy.

The unions themselves were surprised by this attitude to redundancy and the AUEW noticed a difference in attitude according to skill status. The unskilled worker and the semi-skilled were happy to volunteer for redundancy but the skilled who were tied to the industry were more militant. They could see that these redundancies did not simply mean a change of job, but a reduction of job opportunities. However, foremen and technicians did not seem to be interested in preserving jobs. It all points to the differences in the ability of the various parties to transfer their skills to another employer, particularly to one outside the industry. Officials sometimes felt themselves being more militant than the men they were representing.

During its existence the NJCC has earned for itself the nickname 'the burial party' and as a result it would appear the shop stewards have a mistrust of it. Union members also became suspicious of national involvement, thinking that their representatives were sanctioning the redundancies. In fact the unions only knew of the redundancies one to two days before the public announcement and then they fought the redundancies all the way. This mistrust has resulted in very slow progress in the implementation of the plant level JCC's. The opposition appears to come mainly from the shop floor. The AUEW, and possibly other unions, see the PJCC's as giving shop stewards an opening to develop greater accountability, but Apex feel that their image as minor sacking committees may be too strong to overcome. Apex feels that as a consultative committee the NJCC was not very successful. After all, they were presented with a *fait accompli*. However, the AUEW emphasised its importance in achieving common action policies among trade unions. They believe it enabled them to get better deals for the redundant men than if they all had negotiated separately. The impression one gets is that they feel it is GEC who is very keen to retain the NJCC, as GEC still follows a policy of notifying through the NJCC any redundancies that now occur solely from product demand factors.

What of the unions' attitude to the actual mergers? The unions were not consulted before the AEI merger took place. It was not a particularly popular merger. Although Sir Jack Scamp was held in high esteem by the unions (and he may have been the reason why some unions agreed to the NJCC scheme later), GEC generally did not seem to have such good industrial relations as either AEI or English Electric had before the merger.[7] Apex, for one did not see the rationale of the merger, for although GEC was a profitable concern it was the smallest of all three companies and it was not so experienced on the heavy side of the industry. (Possibly a better combination would have been AEI and Reyrolle Parsons.)

Over the Woolwich closure, the unions feel that although the closure went ahead despite their opposition, this was inevitable due to the changes in Post Office orders. However, had AEI been handling the redundancies, they have the impression that they would have come later and more humanely, or alternatively the Government would have been forced to step in. As it was, union pressure and the publicity the closure received enabled the redundant men to get much better terms than they would have otherwise achieved. It was this initial debacle which the unions feel caused the Government to insist on consultation for the redundancies arising from the merger with English Electric. In fact, during the period in which the NJCC was formed, Sir Jack Scamp gave assurances that no more redundancies would be announced until February 1969.

The unions are proud of their success in reducing the numbers actually made

7 That is from the unions' point of view, the terms of employment etc. were considered better in the other two firms. This comes over also in Latham (1969)

redundant as they forced the company to look for alternative methods of reducing manpower through natural wastage and transfers. They are adamant in their support of 'no compulsory redundancy' and, on the whole, have been successful (although presumably not in the case of the closures). Apex now realises that, in its effort to reduce the impact of redundancy, they were less thoughtful about future job prospects and that many of the jobs which GEC 'created' for redundant men were simply vacancies that had come about through natural wastage and had not been filled. These were not new jobs, simply existing jobs. Thus there was a net loss of jobs.

Certainly, the unions and the union membership have a mistrust of GEC which stems mainly from the redundancies and their handling of them. The AUEW believe that it may have been the shop floor opposition which was responsible for GEC's failure to take over Kent Bros. However, the unions cannot and will not deny that GEC is a successful firm. Part of this success they see as coming from its tendency to 'buy-in' firms in order to get hold of their management or organisation. The impression one gets of the unions' view of GEC is that it is a firm only concerned with obtaining a particular return on capital, and any concessions they do make, over the handling of redundancies, and the implementation of such things as equal pay and the pension scheme, have to be forced upon them.

With regard to the impact of the redundancies on the unions themselves, besides making them more wary of the total job situation within the industry, the AUEW does not believe it has affected their total membership, as many redundant men found jobs elsewhere in engineering. However, they do think it has had a possible impact on the skill structure. In some areas, where no alternative work of a similar nature was available, skilled men were forced to take unskilled or semi-skilled jobs, while no new skilled jobs were being generated. This point is borne out in the following remarks.

8.3.3 Evidence on actual redundancies

Not long after the formation of the NJCC, GEC produced a list of its major factories categorised according to three categories.

1. Factories whose future had been confirmed, although they would be subject to change as trade and commercial considerations dictated.
2. Factories whose future had been confirmed but in which there would be some product change which might involve some redundancy, although new products would be introduced.
3. Factories whose future had yet to be determined and were at the time the subject of a detailed survey by GEC.

At this time, over 100 establishments were classified in the first category, 5 in the second and 19 in the third.

It is important to remember that although GEC probably did this in good faith (after all it had been accused of springing the Woolwich redundancies on the unions) it did cause a great deal of worry for the workers who knew their factories were at risk but had not had actual notification of redundancies. With regard to the actual number of jobs at risk, there were about 17,365 in category 3 (approximately 9% of employment in larger establishments), but this excludes 20,000 employees in smaller establishments, the fate of whom was not revealed in the issued list. The purpose of this announcement is not perfectly clear because eighteen months after its release, 11 out of the 19 mentioned were still unaffected by major reorganisation. GEC itself admitted this had an unsettling effect on many employees, a point which comes out vividly below.

8.3.4 **Kidsgrove, Stoke-on-Trent**

The original site at Kidsgrove, Stoke-on-Trent, was owned by English Electric and had employed about 6,000 employees. After the merger with GEC, the computer side of the business was sold off to ICL but GEC retained Industrial Controls and Industrial Automation and Projects. (Projects had the task of finding orders for the Controls and Automation divisions.) According to the list of GEC factories, Kidsgrove's Automation division was categorised under category 3. (No mention of Industrial Controls at Kidsgrove was made in the original list.) It was later in 1969 that the redundancies were announced. At first 600 redundancies were announced and Industrial Automation was to be closed. The reason given was there was not enough work to support both Kidsgrove and another division at Leicester.

GEC's first action was to separate the sites which had been managed together by introducing separate management and separate negotiations. However all the unions and all the workforce joined together forming a joint committee and forced all negotiations to take place together. Joint industrial action was also threatened unilaterally and this initially delayed further action by management.

Eventually the redundancies became inevitable and the NJCC officials were brought in. One of the large plant level meetings was held at which the management heard all the unions' arguments against the closure and then adjourned. When the meeting was reconvened the announcement was made that despite the arguments the redundancies would go ahead. During the meeting news came through of planned industrial action and the meeting again adjourned. On reconvening, the management announced its intention of postponing the decision for the time being. At the start of the struggle the local site management was removed from the negotiating arena. It was felt by the workforce (and possibly by GEC) that they were not unsympathetic to the cause of preventing the division. Their place in negotiations was taken by Mr Neild (previously industrial relations manager for British Leyland) and Mr Sadler (from GEC Leicester, the rival town). The actual naming of redundant men had been delayed but eventually they were announced and once this happened, much of the will to fight disappeared. One of the reasons for the unions' resistance to the naming of individuals was that the company were constantly revising the numbers when put under pressure. The actual number of compulsory redundancies came down in the end to 130[8] (of which 30 to 40 were staff). The militancy was not without its effect. Work began to be transferred to Stoke-on-Trent from Rugby. This was mainly the assembly of televisions and domestic appliances (which presumably eventually placed Kidsgrove in Category 2). Hence, between 1959 and 1971, there was the unusual situation of GEC making people redundant on the one hand and recruiting on the other. Many people were actually re-employed by GEC in a different capacity and after losing the protection of their long service with the company, which affects such things as holiday, sickness and pension rights. Apparently GEC (at the time of these interviews in late 1975) employed as many people at the site as they ever had.

The impression comes over strongly that the workers at Kidsgrove became convinced that GEC had no concern at all about the local community or for the impact of their actions on that community. GEC showed no responsibility to the area and were possibly surprised by the solidarity and militancy of the Kidsgrove workers. It is important to remember that GEC was the only major employer of this type of skilled labour to be found at Kidsgrove and, up to then, had done all its own training. During the days of English Electric, a job at Kidsgrove brought security; it was quite well paid in comparison with most jobs in the area. (The other main occupations had been in the pottery, mining and steel industries.) A job with the firm had meant a good salary, status and security. Thus the news of the planned redundancies unnerved people. Bad cases of nerves in the area became known as the 'GEC disease'. The militancy had other effects. It made the fight to get the numbers reduced stronger. The remaining employees decided to go out for what they could get. Kidsgrove had always had a fairly placid workforce, but a by-product of the fight was a substantial rise in the rate of pay of those remaining, while trade union membership rose substantially. The past relationship between the workforce and their employer had broken down.

The other thing that the employees found most difficult to accept was the logic behind the redundancies. Kidsgrove appeared to be a fairly viable concern, efficient and in a traditionally low pay area. Also, up to this time, it had good industrial relations. There was a shortage of orders but, at the time of deciding to base activities in Leicester, GEC was having trouble finding workers. It was even offering a free pint to anyone who was willing to talk to the personnel officer about the possibility of going to work for GEC. (The suspicion that the

8 A further reduction of 230 occurred in 1971 according to Appendix A.8.1 acknowledged by GEC).

closure at Kidsgrove had been chosen on the grounds that less opposition would be experienced there than in Leicester might, of course, seem attractive to those involved, even if it were not the case.)[9] Certainly, GEC did not seem impressed by Kidsgrove's arguments that it was more cost conscious than Leicester. A cost-saving measure, involving the employment of clerks instead of draughtsmen to do routine work, would be lost in the transfer of work to Leicester, where GEC planned to employ draughtsmen to replace the clerks. Obviously, without the figures on the individual plants, it is impossible to make a judgement. GEC's policy had always been one of treating each plant on its merits, but where two plants are both viable but there is a shortage of orders, a decision must be made. It would appear GEC were surprised by the response to their proposal to close the Automation Division. The opposition which they encountered probably contributed to the supply of alternative work for the factory. Reactions to closures differed greatly from area to area as mentioned before, but close-knit communities such as the one at Kidsgrove probably put up the most resistance, as they had the most to lose.

8.3.5 The East Lancs. Road and Napier, Liverpool

These establishments comprised one site. Originally owned by English Electric, the East Lancs. Road made switchgear and domestic appliances and Napier made diesels. The whole site has contracted. The Napier section is not in use at all now as the diesel manufacture was transferred to Newton-le-Willows and Rugby.

As well as the redundancies in 1969 – a loss of 1,455 jobs at both plants and a further 1,600 elsewhere in Liverpool in that year alone (see Appendix A.8.1) – further redundancies have taken place recently, 300 in switchgear (announced 1970–71 and completed by April 1972) and a further 240 in domestic appliances in 1975. These redundancies are post-rationalisation, but simply add to the problems of the area. The unions feel this is all part of a ten year plan which has severely affected both the Manchester and Liverpool areas.

The people of Liverpool are not so much worried by the redundancies as by the permanent loss of jobs. No new jobs are coming to replace those lost. The closure and other reductions in the labour force have hit very hard those employees with specific skills, e.g. switchgear design engineers. Where was it possible for such men to get another job with the same status, pay and responsibility? Liverpool is a depressed area, with a high unemployment rate and there are people who have never had a job since they were made redundant from GEC. Those who did manage to get another job tended to find it was one with a lower skill requirement and, no longer protected by their long service to their

9 GEC argued that engineering expertise was available more readily in Leicester than in Kidsgrove.

employer, they took a cut in pay and lost out on such things as increments and pension rights.

The effect on the community has been extensive. Obviously GEC no longer needs to recruit at the same level as it did previously. This has meant a loss of training opportunities for young people. In the 1960s, GEC was taking 190 apprentices a year, by 1974 this was down to 4. On top of the loss of the skilled jobs, it has been roughly estimated that each skilled job lost involves the loss of 12 support jobs throughout Liverpool. The area of the East Lancs. Road has been particularly hard hit; the community has almost died with many shops disappearing. Those involved felt, at the time of the negotiations, that none of the arguments about community or unemployment rates had any effect on the GEC management's decisions on the closure and subsequent redundancies.[10] The closure on the East Lancs. Road must be seen in the context of what was happening elsewhere in Liverpool. Netherton, which had been English Electric Aviation, was closed in 1969 (1,400 redundancies) and the premises purchased by Lucas Aerospace (presumably some engineers were re-employed here). British Domestic Appliances at Huyton has suffered recent redundancies, while English Electric Computers at Huyton was closed down. Telecommunications at Clayton-le-Moors is suffering from the cuts in Post Office orders, while at Freckleton (near Blackpool) English Electric Aviation became GEC Plastics requiring different skills.

8.3.6 Stoke and Spon Street, Coventry

The Stoke works at Coventry comprised different divisions, exchange and manufacture, and telecommunications, the former buying floor space from the latter. One of the other GEC factories, Spon Street, originally electronics, had its work transferred to Leicester. As exchange and manufacture did not have enough room in Stoke they moved into Spon Street. The move meant the transfer of GEC-Elliott Process Automation Ltd Supervisory Systems from Spon Street to Leicester. This involved the transfer not only of jobs but of workers to Leicester. This the unions opposed, wishing to keep the jobs and the people in Coventry. When eventually the transfers were agreed to, it was on condition that they would be of a temporary nature and as soon as any vacancies occurred in Coventry they would be offered the chance of returning to Coventry. Jobs were not available in Coventry because the work had been transferred to Leicester.

There was much bad feeling in Coventry at the time over the transfer of work to Leicester. It meant a loss of job opportunities and about 150 redundancies were declared. However, the impact on Coventry was much less dramatic than either Kidsgrove or Liverpool. The reason must be that GEC is not the only

10 We have seen GEC's reason for this, but for those on the receiving end such attitudes are difficult to accept when not only men's jobs are at stake but the viability of the community.

employer of skilled engineering labour in the area and Coventry was at the time a more prosperous area. Even when, in 1968, they closed AEI Aircraft Instrument Works in Coventry and sold the premises to Rotax Ltd there was no big up-turn in the local unemployment level among engineers although 430 were made redundant. (In addition, others 'bought in' by Rotax were later made redundant too.) However, this transfer had a big effect on individuals who took jobs in Leicester in the hope that they would shortly be returning to Coventry.

8.3.7 GEC and the community

The evidence presented above gives support to the view that GEC is not over-concerned about the communities in which it operates, and in which it is often the major employer of skilled workers. The profitability of each manufacturing unit in the long run appears to be the most important factor. This was particularly hard for the employees of AEI and English Electric establishments to accept. They had been used to a different kind of treatment.[11] (Possibly it is one of the many reasons AEI and English Electric failed to be as profitable as GEC.)

Not only in the case of Woolwich was work transferred from one region to another to 'create' new jobs in, say, a development area where they are eligible for grants and Regional Employment Premiums (although the flow did not always go in this direction). There was bad feeling about this at Woolwich where some men actually trained the workers in Scotland and found they had lost their jobs in consequence. (See CIS (1973).) Obviously, the decision to close or reduce the capacity of a plant is based on all the factors – it is not simply based on the age of the machinery or the age of the premises; it would have to take into account the availability of supplies and their cost, its credit worthiness in the area, grants for retraining, the amount of empty floor space, the wage rates in the area etc. Sometimes the decision will, therefore, seem illogical and often callous to those involved and the local communities.

The impact on the people and the community at Kidsgrove and Liverpool are not isolated cases. Similar stories could be told about Manchester, Witton in Birmingham, Lincoln and the coilmakers of Hackbridge. The decline of the communities is not solely due to the action of GEC but, being a major employer in each area, its action has had a dramatic effect on the areas involved.

8.3.8 GEC and the unions

We have already seen how GEC's consultative machinery developed and how it is viewed by GEC and the unions. It is a non-negotiating body (partly at the request of the unions). In fact, little if anything in GEC is agreed on a firm-

11 The paternal attitude of both firms is documented in Jones and Marriott (1970) and Latham (1969).

wide basis, the new pension scheme being the only exception (and this because of government legislation). Hendricks (1975) suggests that a firm only undertakes plant level bargaining if it considers that firm level bargaining would involve paying higher wages. Certainly the bargaining power of the employer and the unions is not equal at plant level. GEC appears to prefer non-unionised labour but equally it does not strongly support Trade Associations. Recently, however, there has been a large increase in unionisation within GEC which dates from the time of the mergers. Even so there are no closed shops in GEC factories. GEC employs cut-off clauses, i.e. after certain skill or responsibility levels employees have the right to belong to other unions.

With regard to top management, the unions have few complaints over the way they are treated and general conversation gives the impression they have much respect for such men. Trouble has however occurred at middle management level. Although we are not especially at liberty, for good reasons, to reveal our sources, conversations did reveal cases of victimisation which were by no means isolated. Incidents involving the gradual reduction of working space, the removal of the telephones and finally desks and chairs were reported from different sources and occurring, in different GEC businesses, to shop-stewards and union officials who were militant in their opposition to redundancies. In such cases it is difficult to assess if sectional managers were acting individually or under instruction, particularly as GEC top management always maintained that union officials were free to do their work unhindered. In practice, this was not always the case when there was a dispute with the company taking place.

8.3.9 The attitude of Government

In many of these disputes local MPs became involved, most notably at Woolwich. Pressure was often forthcoming from local press and traders dependent on the general prosperity of the area for their trade. Deputations of workers approached the Secretary of State for Industry, but in no case did the Government intervene. On the other hand GEC has not been slow to take advantage of any Government grants that were available.

It is true to say GEC accepts the Government as a factor likely to cause a disturbance in its environment by policy changes but it is not a firm which is constantly blaming the Government. The Government, in its turn, has left GEC alone to get on with its 70,000 plus redundancies in the time since the merger, never stepping in with an argument in favour of a doomed community. Chapter 6 showed how its lenient attitude over the acquisition of market power has resulted in problems, while this section shows how its decision to stay neutral in this case has resulted in the undermining of communities and contributed to rates of unemployment (particularly in inner city areas) with which it now has the problem of dealing.

8.4 Costs and conclusions

This chapter has attempted to show how the merger between GEC and its former competitors AEI and English Electric affected national and local labour markets. It has also attempted to bring the numbers on redundancies to life by examples of how closures or reductions in employment affected certain communities.

The mergers occurred at a time of change within the Engineering industry. They were advocated because it was believed that the newly merged firm would be better able to deal with all the problems the industry faces. This chapter has highlighted evidence of that change and concentrated on its impact on local labour markets.

The second half of the chapter shows the dilemma which society faces when it attempts such *improvements* and when it creates organisations, which not only have the strength to implement these improvements, but have the additional power to add to unemployment if they utilize their market power.

It is only possible to make a rough estimate of the costs of the redundancies, as no survey of the duration of unemployment was made specifically for GEC men. (Some of those made redundant from the AEI Telephone Works at Woolwich were included in the survey conducted in the Woolwich area and reported in Daniel (1972).)

Given the assumptions of a perfectly competitive labour market, redundancy cannot be said to *cause* unemployment, for if the market is working smoothly all those made redundant should be re-employed instantaneously at the same wage.[12] Unfortunately labour markets do not work in this way. Simply placing a large number of workers on to the labour market at the same time can cause a 'hiccup' in the normal flows on to and off the unemployment register which may take some time to work through and increase unemployment, at least for a while. We have also seen that certain local labour markets cannot be described as perfectly competitive. In addition, part of the reason for the redundancies was a decline in demand and the general deflation made finding a job more difficult than if the redundancies had occurred in times of buoyant demand. Also, it is obvious that in reality, labour is not homogeneous and the personal characteristics of a worker, as well as the methods he uses to find a job, will influence the speed with which a job is found and the type of job taken. Finally, for most workers, the labour market is a very localised concept. Thus, unemployment may occur following a redundancy in one region, while vacancies exist elsewhere for those occupations.

The only information on the redundancies arising from the rationalisation following the mergers is contained in Appendix A.8.1. Apart from the qualified

12 However if all demanders of labour had product market power they would demand less labour than competitive industries, leading to the conclusion that 'full' employment would be reduced if not the wage rate.

estimates, the figures have been agreed to by GEC. The original sources for the information came from Counter Information Services (1973) and the unions. Unfortunately, we have no information on the experience of those actually made redundant (apart from those included in the Woolwich survey). Surveys do, however, tell us that the distribution of unemployment after redundancy is usually skewed with a long right-hand tail (e.g. Daniel (1972), Herron (1975), Kahn (1964) and MacKay and Reid (1972)). Unfortunately, there are so many factors which determine the length of this tail, it would be impractical, in dealing with so many redundancies, in so many different regions to take it into account in our estimation of the transaction costs following the redundancies.

What is used instead is the national average duration of unemployment (derived from the Department of Employment Gazette) which assumes that all unemployed in each duration group experience the median unemployment in that group, while those in the top unbounded group only experience 52 weeks unemployment. The assumption being made is that on average the unemployment suffered after a redundancy from GEC was equal to the average duration of employment at that period. In one way our measure will tend to overstate the total amount of unemployment resulting from the redundancies as it is known that a certain (varying) percentage experience no unemployment at all. However, assuming that no one experiences more than one year's unemployment will tend to bias down the estimate. The total unemployment for each half year is calculated from Appendix A.8.1 and average duration. However, the duration figures are, in fact, the actual duration being experienced at roughly the midpoint of the half year, not strictly the likely average duration of someone made unemployed at that point in time. In addition these spells of unemployment are not completed spells. However this measure is the only one directly available to us. How to evaluate the cost of this unemployment does raise a problem. The unemployment should be evaluated in terms of next best alternative occupations. Two estimates are, therefore, provided. One assumes that all could be re-employed as skilled men and the other assumes the next best alternative to be non-skilled employment (within engineering). This provides an upper and lower bound. The upper bound will undoubtedly overstate the cost as not all the men (or women) being made redundant were engineers. On the other hand, assuming all become labourers is, from the experience of the surveys (mentioned above), far too gloomy. (There was insufficient information in most cases to identify men or women, staff or manual redundancies.)

The value of lost wages was calculated by multiplying total numbers of weeks of unemployment by the gross weekly earnings (including overtime) for skilled men and labourers paid on the payment by results scheme (PBR), evaluated at June of each year. (PBR was considered to relate more directly to output than time rates.) The total value added to labour lost as the result ot redundancy is calculated in current values and presented in Table 8.3.

Table 8.3 *The total value-added lost from the redundancies*

Date	Redundancy total	Average duration of unemployment in weeks[a]	Total unemployment in weeks	Skilled rate in June (current rate)	Labourer's rate in June (current rate)	Estimates of wages lost: Upper £000's	Estimates of wages lost: Lower £000's
1968 I	10,911	19.8	216,037.8	£24.51	£18.10	5,295.086	3,910.284
1968 II	—	19.3	—			—	—
1969 I	4,262	20.4	86,944.8	£26.70	£18.56	2,321.426	1,613.695
1969 II	5,912	19.2	113,510.4			3,030.728	2,106.753
1970 I	457	20.1	9,185.7	£29.17	£21.22	267.947	194.921
1970 II	1,202	19.6	23,559.2			687.222	499.926
1971 I	4,694	19.5	91,533.0	£31.50	£23.03	2,883.289	2,108.005
1971 II	10,447	19.8	206,850.6			6,515.794	4,763.769
1972 I	1,922	22.2	42,668.4	£33.77	£26.05	1,440.912	1,111.512

Source: Department of Employment Gazette (various).
[a]For the first half of each year, the April estimate is used; for the second half, the October estimate.

An interesting alternative approach to calculating the macroeconomic costs of unemployment is presented by the Manpower Services Commission (1977). By assuming full employment corresponds to an unemployment register of 500,000 they allocated the remaining registered and unregistered unemployment to the industrial sectors. The additional output resulting from this extra employment was calculated from employment functions or the use of average output per head. From this, the resulting increase in GDP was calculated (less the allowance for special measures). Although this approach is to deal with the cost of aggregate unemployment, it points to the loss of output resulting from unemployment, only part of which is picked up in the measure used in Table 8.3.

The calculations result in quite substantial costs, but they are only the financial costs. If we were to add in the personal costs to the individuals particularly the loss of self respect, then truly the transaction costs would be high and their effects long lasting. To do this, however, would involve quantifying subjective loss, an exercise fraught with even more difficulties than the one attempted here.

Perhaps more important than such calculations is an awareness that it is the relationship which should exist between a large firm carrying out significant redundancies and the Government which is important. Can firms really be expected to take into account the personal problems they will be creating for their employees or even the problems of the town in which the redundancies occur? Here the Government's role is important and yet in no case did the Government step in with alternative suggestions or aid. (Although the Department of Employment did its best, in some cases a radical new policy was needed to deal with the problem – an initiative which could only come from Government.)

GEC's handling of the redundancies from the top cannot be criticised except that it was impersonal (it had to be with so many individuals to deal with) and the issuing of the list of categorised establishments possibly caused more uncertainty than calmed fears. However, from the point of view of individuals and communities, the redundancies often had quite serious effects. The actual carrying out of the redundancies was not always as smooth as it should have been and despite union efforts the contest for jobs was not always equal. In addition, the merger and the following redundancies put the relationship between the firm and the unions on a new footing. It formalised the relationship, and business done before on an informal, *ad hoc* basis now has a procedure. This has tended to correct the balance of power to some extent but not completely.

The GEC merger was undoubtedly successful in terms of efficiency, and in terms of rationalising the industry to meet the lower level of demand, but it was at a price. The price was paid by individuals who found themselves with no prospect of employment in the job they had always done and by the communities who found their nature changed.

Appendix A.8.1

GEC redundancies from 1968 to the end of the rationalisation period (Numbers confirmed by GEC)

Year	Name and/or location of establishment	Announcement date	Total number involved	Voluntary* redundancies
1968	AEI Telecommunications Ltd			
	Woolwich	February		
	Blackheath	February	5,230	1,095
	Sydenham	February		
	Harlow	February	451	365
	Witton (Birmingham)	May	1,650[a]	
	Wythenshawe	May	300	200
	Alridge (Staffordshire)	May	430	80
	AEI Aircraft Instrument Works, Coventry	May	1,650[a]?	
	Willesden	May	1,200[a]?	
1969	Chamberlain and Hookham, Birmingham	May	570	
	GEC-Elliott Automation Ltd, Stafford	May	300	
	Industrial Controls, Cross Heath	May	150	
	Industrial Systems, Industrial Controls and Process Automation, Kidsgrove, Stoke-on-Trent	May	135	
	Watson & Sons	May	100?	
	Main Line Locomotive Parts, Newton-le-Willows	June	1,200	
	Rugby	June	140	
	Witton	June	1,200	
	Liverpool	June	200	
	Moseley Road, Manchester	July	930	
	GEC East Lancs. Road, Liverpool	July	305	
	Napier (Liverpool)	July	1,150	
	Netherton (Liverpool)	July	1,400	
	Ashton-under-Lyme	August	140	
	Chesham	August	40	
	Whetstone	August	230	
	Walthamstow	August	810	
	Accrington	August	285	
	Stafford	August	305	[b]
	Bradford	August	50	[c]
1970	Loading Coils, Woolwich	February	70	
	Witton Moulded Plastics Ltd	April	60	
	GEC Power Engineering Ltd, Whetstone	May	60	

	GEC Semiconductors Ltd (Microelec.), Witham	July	80	
	Trafford Park Research Laboratory, Manchester	July	55	
	GEC Electrical Components Ltd, East Kilbride and Motherwell	October	(850)	transfers to Motherwell
	Marconi-Elliott Computer Systems Ltd, Borehamwood	October	50	
	GEC Transformer Co. Ltd, Wythenshawe	October	750	
	Accrington Bushings Unit	November	(41)	transfers
1971	GEC Semi-Conductors Division, Glenrothes	April-Nov.	125	redeployment
	GEC Marconi-Electronics Ltd, Gateshead	February	9	
	GEC Marconi-Electronics Ltd, Chelmsford	February	180	
	GEC Transformers Ltd, Thanet (Hackbridge & Hewittic Electrical Co. Ltd)	February	85	
	Dorman Diesels Ltd, Stafford	February	98	
	GEC Switchgear Ltd, Nelson	February	?	
	High Power Laboratory Stafford	February	30	
	GEC Semi-Conductors Ltd, Lincoln	March	50	
	Witton Moulded Plastics Ltd, Colne	March	175	
	Modern Wheel Drive, Slough	April	280	
	GEC Switchgear Ltd, Amersham	April	200	
	Marconi-Elliott Avionic Systems Ltd,	April	120	
	Elliott Flight Automation, Rochester (or GEC Marconi-Elec. Ltd)	April	400	
	AEI Scientific Apparatus Ltd, Harlow	April	260	
	GEC Switchgear Ltd, Liverpool	May	350	
	English Electric-Hewittic Rectifiers Ltd, Hersham	May	180	
	GEC Power Engineering Ltd, Stafford	May	178	
	NRC and Stafford Estates Labs.	May	60 ?	
	English Electric-Hackbridge Transformers Ltd, Hersham	May	180	
	Hirst Research Centre, Wembley	May	75 ?	

. . .

	MO Valve Co. Ltd, Hammersmith	May	65 ?	
	London Transformer Products Ltd, Willesden	May	80	
	Micanite and Insulators Ltd, Walthamstow	May	290	
	Walsall Tubes and Sections Ltd, Winsford	May	90	
	GEC Marconi Elec. Ltd,			
	Basildon	May	80	
	Bradford	May	70	
	Engineering Products Division, Trafford Park	June	311	
	GEC Transformers Ltd, Bridgend	June	270	
	Witton Moulded Plastics Ltd, Witton	June	80	
	GEC Semiconductors Ltd,			
	Glenrothes	July	150	
	Witham	August	300	
	Witton Moulded Plastics Ltd, Witton	August	70	
	Associated Automation Ltd, Willesden	September	130	
	GEC Elliott Automation Ltd, Kidsgrove	October	230	
	English Electric/AEI Turbine Generators Ltd, Willery Works, Rugby	October	200	
	Power Equipment, Trafford Park	December	9,100	5,571
1972	GEC Elliott Automation Ltd, Lewisham and Greenwich	January	100	
	GEC Marconi Eec. Ltd: Marconi Communications Ltd, Wembley Works	January	500	
	GEC Transformers (Hackbridge) Ltd, Hersham	January	450	
	GEC Marconi Electronics Ltd, Chelmsford	January	605	
	GEC Power Engineering Ltd, Stafford	January 1969– September 1973	2,674	1,840
End of rationalisation				

*Voluntary redundancies are included in total number involved.

[a]This cutback was decided before the merger.

[b]200 additional jobs 'created' at neighbouring GEC factory.

[c]200 additional jobs 'created' at Bradford.

? Numbers not known or not confirmed by GEC.

References

Ball, R. J. and E. B. A. St Cyr (1966), 'Short term employment functions in British manufacturing industry', *Review of Economic Studies*, **33**, 179–97.

Bowers, J. K., P. C. Cheshire, A. E. Webbe and R. Weedon (1972), 'Some Aspects of Unemployment and the Labour Market', *NIER*, **63**, 75–88, NIESR.

Briscoe, G. and C. J. Roberts (1977), 'Structural Breaks in Employment Functions', *The Manchester School* (March), 1–15.

Clegg, H. (1971), *How to run an Incomes Policy and why we made such a mess of the last one*, London: Heinemann.

Counter Information Services (1973), *The General Electric Company Limited: An Anti Report*, CIS.

Daniel, W. W. (1972), *Whatever happened to the Workers in Woolwich? A Survey of Redundancy in South-East London*, Political and Economic Planning Broadsheets, No. 537.

Durbin, J. (1970), 'Testing for Serial Correlation in Least Squares Regression when some of the Regressors are Lagged Dependent Variables', *Econometrica*, **38**, 410–21.

Evans, G. (1974), 'The Labour Market Mechanism and the Hoarding of Manpower' in J. S. Wabe, *The Problems in Manpower Forecasting*, Saxon House, Farnborough.

Gujarati, J. (1972), 'The Behaviour of Unemployment and Unfilled Vacancies: Great Britain 1958–71', *Economic Journal*, **82**, 195–202.

– (1972), 'A Reply to Mr Taylor', *Economic Journal*, **82**, 1365–8.

Hart, P. E., M. A. Utton and G. Walshe (1973), *Mergers and Concentration in British Industry*, NIESR, Cambridge University Press.

Hendricks, W. (1975), 'Labour Market Structure and Union Wage Levels'; *Economic Inquiry*, **13**, 401–16.

Herron, F. (1975), *Labour Market in Crisis*, London: Macmillan.

Jones, R. and O. Marriott (1970), *The Anatomy of a Merger*, London: Cape.

Kahn, H. (1964), *Repercussions of Redundancy: a local survey*, London: Allen and Unwin.

Killingsworth, M. R. (1970), 'A Critical Survey of Neoclassical Models of Labour', *Oxford Economic Bulletin*, **32**, 133–165.

Knight, K. G. and R. A. Wilson (1974), 'Labour Hoarding, Employment and Unemployment in British Manufacturing Industry', *Applied Economics*, **6**, No. 4, 303–10.

Latham, Sir Joseph (1969), *Take-over (The Facts and Myths of the GEC–AEI Battle)*, London; Iliffe.

MacKay, D. I. and G. L. Reid (1972), 'Redundancy, Unemployment and Manpower Policy', *Economic Journal*, **82**, 1256–72.

Manpower Services Commission (1977), *MSC Review and Plan 1977*, MSC, London: HMSO.

Nadiri, M. I. and S. Rosen (1969), 'Interrelated Factor Demand Functions', *American Economic Review*, **59**, 457–71.

NIESR (1970), 'The Change in the Relationship between Unemployment and Earnings Increases: A review of some possible explanations', *National Institute Economic Review* (November), No. 54, 44–63.

– (1972a), 'Unemployment', *National Institute Economic Review* (February), No. 59, 18–19.

– (1972b), see Bowers, J. K. et al.

Roberts, C. J. (1974), *A Survey of Employment Models*, Centre for Industrial Economic and Business Research Paper No. 30, University of Warwick.

Taylor, J. (1972), 'The Behaviour of Unemployment and Unfilled Vacancies: Great Britain 1958–1971: An Alternative View', *Economic Journal*, **82**, 1352–65.

Wabe, J. S. (1974), 'Practical Difficulties in a Manpower Forecasting Exercise', in J. S. Wabe, *Problems in Manpower Forecasting*, Saxon House, Farnborough.

Wedderburn, D. (1964), *White Collar Redundancy, A Case Study,* University of Cambridge, Department of Applied Economics, CUP.

– (1965), *Redundancy and the Railwaymen,* University of Cambridge, Department of Applied Economics, CUP.

Williamson, O. E. (1968), 'Economics as an Anti-Trust defense: the Welfare Trade-offs', *American Economic Review,* 18–36, Reprinted in Rowley, G. K., *Readings in Industrial Economics,* **2** (1972), London: Macmillan.

9

Mergers and technological progressiveness: the case of the British computer industry[1]

In 1968, with the blessing of the Industrial Reorganisation Corporation, English Electric Computers Ltd, Plessey (computer division), and International Computers and Tabulators joined together to form the only existing British computer company of any size, International Computers Ltd. There had also been considerable earlier merger activity in the industry, involving Elliott Automation, Leo Computers Ltd, Ferranti, and General Electric in just the post-1960 period.

In relation to this industry the IRC state in its first report, that this was a 'sector which is of great importance to the country's export effort, where the pace of technical change is rapid and where there is intense competition from powerful companies in the US, Europe and Japan'. It is reasonable to argue therefore that the main justification for the 1968 merger was on the grounds of technological progressiveness. It was felt that only as a merged industry could British computer manufacturing compete with its US rivals on a technological level. In fact it can be argued that as the rate of technological progress in the computer industry has been so fast it is only by keeping up technologically that a firm can stay in existence. The benefits from technological change cannot be matched by any other competitive mechanism. This is further reinforced by the existence of increasing returns to scale in computer manufacture which coupled with IBM's world market share of approximately 70% makes the chance of any small company using price cutting as a successful competitive weapon very remote. (For further documentation of these points the reader is referred to Stoneman (1976) Chapter 5.) One can further argue that if the British computer industry was to make inroads into the US position of supremacy then it must be on the basis of technological superiority.

We therefore have a merger where the effects on the rate of technological progressiveness are of paramount importance in its evaluation. Moreover by

1 We wish to thank Norman Ireland, other members of the University of Warwick Industrial Economics Workshop and an anonymous referee for comments on an earlier draft of this chapter.

investigating whether these benefits have been realised we can also gather some indication as to the validity of the views of Schumpeter (1942) on the relationship between progressiveness, firm size and market structure. Our task therefore in the present context is to analyse to what extent the formation of ICL has enabled the British computer industry to advance technologically at a rate faster than it would have done. Of course one expects gestation lags in the effects of mergers and this can be taken care of in the discussion of the results. One would expect however that if any benefits were forthcoming there would be some indication within seven years (i.e. the post-merger period covered by our data) of the merger taking place.[2]

For this industry we have not even attempted to estimate our static efficiency measure k. The reason is related precisely to the technological change with which we are so concerned. Our efficiency measure shows how input per unit of output changes over time. In this industry the nature of the inputs has changed so much the question has little relevance in isolation from the technological change question. For example between 1963 and 1968 the industry changed from a position of bought-in inputs being valued at 20% of sales to one of 43% of sales. Moreover in our time period the nature of the inputs has varied from transistors and capacitors, to integrated circuits to large-scale integration. Our problem is that we cannot isolate improvements in efficiency from improvements in inputs, or what is the same, efficiency changes from changes that lead to the use of and design of machines using the latest components. And this latter is precisely what we mean by technological change.

We may consider a computer to be a bundle of characteristics (following the work of Griliches (1971)). By valuing these characteristics we can generate the price of each machine but we can only observe the price of the machine and not the price of the characteristics. However, if we observe price changes over time this can be due to a change in either the price of the characteristics or the amount of characteristics in a given machine.

Technological change may take the form of either product innovation or process innovation. We would expect however that machines just being launched would exhibit both the state of the art as regards product technology and be constructed using the most advanced processes. Thus, although one could argue that machines already on the market will also be constructed on the latest processes, it is the new machines being launched that are most likely to exhibit the benefits of the latest technology. We expect these changes in technology to reduce the costs of supplying a given set of characteristics as embodied in these newly introduced machines.

We start therefore with a comparison of the relative prices of newly introduced

2 Thanks are due to Diane Ellwood and Warren Ho for their invaluable help in the preparation and manipulation of the data.

machines across manufacturers pre and post merger. If relative prices reflect technology differences then this will tell us how well ICL has performed relative to its US competitors. However in general one would not expect relative prices to reflect technology differences. If one manufacturer has lower costs as a result of technology changes he has the alternatives of maintaining his current price and increasing his profit per machine or reducing prices relative to other manufacturers and increasing his market share (although this course begs the question of retaliation). It is suggested therefore that technological progress may be reflected in either relative prices or the relative profitability of newly introduced machines across manufacturers. This comparison of profitability is our second task.

The price comparison we perform is one between the price of each manufacturer's machines in their year of introduction and what they would have cost given the characteristics prices apparent in the prices of IBM machines. Differences in the two 'prices' are then analysed for trends over time.

We can relate prices of a manufacturer's machines to characteristics levels embodied in those machines by the empirical relationship (i)

$$\log P_i = \sum_{j=1}^{m} \alpha_j \log C_{ij} \tag{i}$$

where P_i = observed price of machine i
C_{ij} = level of characteristic j embodied in machine i
α_j = valuation of characteristic j.

If we let a_j, $j = 1, \ldots, m$, be the valuation of characteristic j apparent in IBM machines, we may write that:

$$\log P_i - \log \hat{P}_i = \sum_{j=1}^{m} (\alpha_j - a_j) \log C_{ij} \tag{ii}$$

where $\hat{P}_i$ = price of machine i given the IBM valuation of characteristics.[3]

We may interpret (ii) as that differences in the price of a machine in relation to the IBM equivalent price depend on the level of and the difference in the apparent valuation of characteristics. By looking at the time pattern of movements of $\log P_i - \log \hat{P}_i$ we can observe changes in the relative prices of different manufacturers' machines. In fact to isolate the time pattern we perform regressions of the type (iii)

$$\log P_i - \log \hat{P}_i = f(t) + u_i \tag{iii}$$

where $f(t)$ is some function of the date of introduction of the machine. As can be seen $f(t)$ will reflect differences in characteristics valuations. Any observed trends in $f(t)$ over time can, then, in conjunction with the profit data, be related to merger activity.

3 The data sources used were CCL (1962–74), IDC (1961–74) Shirley (1969) and Smythe (1970, 1975). All logs are to base ten.

Before moving on to the results a short digression on what these characteristics equations represent seems in order. The equations are to be viewed as descriptive rather than deterministic. The question asked is, what are the apparent prices of characteristics embodied in IBM machines, and then given these prices how do the prices of other manufacturers' machines compare? We are not asking how are the prices of each manufacturer's machines determined. It is similar to the difference between measuring the price and explaining the price. Although price changes will be reflected in the time variables, all we expect to find out is whether measured prices have changed and not why. If it were a deterministic model then the interpretation of the estimated coefficients would be open to a number of identification problems. If one were able to get over these and state, for example, that the estimates of (i) and (ii) reflected cost curve coefficients, then the advantage would be that prices could directly reflect technology differences. However, we do not feel that we are able to do this and thus put such an interpretation on the coefficients. We consider the equations as descriptive and therefore, when discussing technological progressiveness, we also look at profitability as has been argued above is appropriate. The conclusions are drawn from relative movements in prices and profitability and no attempt is made to explain why prices have changed, this being considered an analysis with many pitfalls which would provide what for us is not an essential piece of information.

The first empirical task is to calculate the value of a_j, i.e. the apparent valuation of the characteristics of IBM machines. For this purpose we performed a regression on equation (iv). The sample is all IBM machines introduced between 1960 and 1974.[4]

$$\log P_i = \alpha + \beta_0 \log C_i + \beta_1 \log S_i + \sum_{n=1}^{16} \gamma_n D_{ni} + u_i \qquad \text{(iv)}$$

where P_i = price in £'000
C_i = cycle time in μ secs
S_i = maximum store in '000 bits
D_{ni} = dummy variables for the year of introduction

The initial results were as follows (t-statistics in brackets)

$$\begin{aligned}\log P = \; & \underset{(0.09)}{0.03} - \underset{(-4.10)}{0.56 \log C} + \underset{(10.20)}{0.73 \log S} \\ & + \underset{(3.39)}{1.04 D_{61}} + \underset{(4.45)}{0.81 D_{62}} + \underset{(2.73)}{0.84 D_{63}} + \underset{(3.98)}{0.81 D_{64}}\end{aligned}$$

4 This choice of characteristics was conditioned by some earlier work (Stoneman, (1976)) where a choice was made from approximately 50 relevant characteristics. A high degree of multicollinearity between characteristics indicates that these two are in fact representative of a number of relevant characteristics. The omission of any software characteristics is due primarily to data shortage, but it is felt that very little bias will be introduced as a result of this omission.

$$+ \underset{(0.74)}{0.13D_{66}} - \underset{(-0.27)}{0.08D_{67}} - \underset{(-3.18)}{0.85D_{68}} + \underset{(1.27)}{0.39D_{69}}$$

$$+ \underset{(1.07)}{0.25D_{70}} - \underset{(-0.82)}{0.20D_{71}} - \underset{(-0.96)}{0.21D_{72}} - \underset{(-0.41)}{0.09D_{73}}$$

$$\underset{(-0.91)}{0.28D_{74}}$$

$$R^2 = 0.89 \quad \hat{R}^2 = 0.83 \quad N = 45 \quad F = 16.96$$

As can be seen the time dummies are significant and positive prior to 1965 but generally negative and not significantly different from zero (except for 1968) for the later period. We have thus reduced the time dummies to a 'generation' dummy reflecting whether the machine was introduced in the 1960–64 period (when it is 1) or not (when it is zero). This yields the results shown in equation (v). The constant is excluded as its inclusion led to an estimate not significantly different from zero.[5]

$$\log P = \underset{(-3.37)}{-0.393 \log C} + \underset{(45.40)}{0.706 \log S} + \underset{(6.22)}{0.804G} \tag{v}$$

These estimates appear to indicate that the prices of characteristics embodied in IBM machines are constant over the period 1960–75, with a shift parameter lowering prices for the machines introduced post-1964. To test this result we have performed an F test to see if the coefficients have changed pre- and post-1964 and the hypothesis of no change is not rejected. We are reasonably satisfied therefore in these constant shadow prices. However, they are only constant in money terms. All prices are current, and thus the constancy hides the fall in the real price of these characteristics. Given these estimates we predict for each machine a value of $\log \hat{P}_i$ from the coefficients of (v) for use in equation (iii).

We have chosen the manufacturers for comparison on grounds of UK market share, thus excluding Univac and Control Data Corporation, and current status, for although RCA and Rank Xerox Data Systems operated during the study period both had ceased computer manufacture by 1975. This left Burroughs, IBM, Honeywell, and GE. The latter two merged in 1970, thus we can also investigate simultaneously the effects of this merger. (The methods used for com-

5 As equation (v) does not contain a constant, R^2 has no meaning. However to indicate its explanatory power, the R^2 of equation (v) including a non-significant constant was 0.81. Theil suggests in such cases that one uses

$$1 - R^2 = \frac{e'e/n}{y'y/n}$$

where $e'e$ is an estimate of the disturbance variance and $y'y$ the sample second moment of the dependent variable (Theil (1971) p. 178). For equation (v) the resultant estimate of R^2 is 0.988.

parison are such that no bias is introduced by the exclusion of now defunct companies.)

In Table 9.1 we show the results of estimating (iii) on data bases consisting of machines introduced by different manufacturers. We have represented time by a series of dummy variables for the year of introduction of the machine, with 1965 being included in the constant. We are thus estimating (vi).

$$\log P_i - \log \hat{P}_i = \bar{\alpha} + \sum_n \bar{\gamma}_n D_{ni} + u_i$$

$$n = 1 \ldots 4, 6 \ldots 16 \qquad \text{(vi)}$$

It may be noticed that initially we represent time by a dummy for each year but in calculating log $\hat{P}$ we used a 'generation' dummy. Given that in the estimates of (iv) the annual time dummies presented the pattern shown above, it is felt that we have less chance of introducing bias using the estimates shown in (v) than using estimates derived from (iv). We do, however present below also a number of estimates of (vi) in which time is represented by 'multi-period' dummies in the manner of our calculation of log $\hat{P}$.

Consider just the results on Honeywell/GE machines,[6] apart from 1967 and 1972, the time dummies are insignificant, the constant is insignificant, but the dummy introduced to represent machines marketed by GE prior to the Honeywell merger indicates that GE machines were more expensive. Perusal of the coefficients on the time dummies shows however a reversal in sign pre- and post-1967. This is recognised in the second set of estimates where the dummies are collapsed into a time dummy for the period 1960–67 and one for GE machines. This result, incorporating the insignificant constant, indicates that prior to 1967 machines introduced by Honeywell were cheaper than their IBM equivalents but post-1967 this was no longer the case – the prices were not significantly different. Machines introduced by GE were more expensive than both the IBM and Honeywell equivalents.

In equations 3 to 8 we cover British machines and Burroughs' machines. The first point to note here is that the constant is often significant, which in the absence of significant negative dummies implies that the machines covered are more expensive than their IBM equivalents. If we consider the results on Burroughs first (equation (3) Table 9.1) we see that although time dummies for 1964, 1969 and 1973 are significant and negative, and in all years post-1964 the coefficients approach significance, there is no particular time pattern to the estimated coefficients. Equation (4) was an attempt to find a pattern similar to Honeywell but the variables are insignificant and the explanatory power is very low. When we look at the results for the British machines (equations 5–8), where dummies

6 In the results presented in Tables 9.1, 9.2 and 9.3, a * on a t-statistic indicates significance at the 5% level, and a * for a coefficient indicates that no observations were included on that variable in the sample.

Table 9.1 $\log P - \log \hat{P} = \overline{\alpha} + \sum_n \overline{\gamma}_n D_n$

	Honeywell/GE coeff. 1	t	Honeywell/GE coeff. 2	t	Burroughs coeff. 3	t	Burroughs coeff. 4	t
Constant	−0.085	−0.733	0.007	1.24	0.871	2.847*	0.042	0.426
1960	*				*			
61	−0.466	−1.587			*			
62	−0.057	−0.192			−0.423	−0.978		
63	0.402	1.848			−0.519	−1.587		
64	−0.178	−1.137			−1.246	−2.880*		
65								
66	−0.237	−1.566			*			
67	−0.594	−2.621*			*			
68	0.101	0.684			−0.699	−1.863		
69	0.301	1.530			−0.985	−2.628*		
70	−0.273	−1.676			*			
71	0.292	1.482			−0.653	−1.743		
72	0.314	2.222*			−0.644	−1.924		
73	0.092	0.465			−1.237	−3.502*		
74	*				*			
75	*				*			
60–64								
60–67			−0.281	−2.975*			0.299	1.947
70–75								
ICT								
ICL								
Ferranti								
Leo								
EE								
Elliott								
GE	0.503	4.859*	0.485	4.733*				
R^2	0.623		0.311		0.604		0.147	
$\hat{R}^2$	0.510		0.285		0.392		0.108	
N	57		57		24		24	

are included for both time and manufacturer (ICT is included in the constant) the initial estimates in (5) show no significant coefficients, but (6), (7), (8) show a significant constant with isolated significant dummies. The estimates in equations (6) and (7) indicate that British machines were priced lower relative to their IBM equivalents pre-1965, but the Elliott machines were, even accounting for this, cheaper still. In Equation (7) the negative coefficient on ICL machines is significant, i.e. machines introduced by ICL were cheaper than those introduced by the manufacturers who individually existed prior to the formation of ICL, but as can be seen in equation (8), this result is very sensitive to the removal of non-significant variables. In all, these estimates do not support the existence of any

British coeff. 5	t	British coeff. 6	t	British coeff. 7	t	British coeff. 8	t
0.484	1.826	0.359	3.076*	0.359	3.087*	0.213	2.9111*
0.229	0.463						
*							
−0.205	−0.413						
−0.291	−1.032						
−0.465	−1.572						
−0.179	−0.638						
−0.162	−0.517						
−0.027	−0.082						
−0.201	−0.418						
−0.471	−0.860						
−0.036	−0.066						
−0.230	−0.362						
−0.185	−0.323						
−0.327	−0.598						
−0.701	−1.227						
		−0.260	−2.06*	−0.260	−2.064*		
		−0.121	−0.07				
−0.211	−0.450	−0.288	−1.727	−0.359	−2.572*	−0.212	−1.953
0.391	1.212	0.397	1.321	0.397	1.326		
0.162	0.593	0.215	0.884	0.215	0.887		
−0.278	−1.294	−0.236	−1.531	−0.236	−1.536		
−0.370	−1.913	−0.379	−2.454*	−0.379	−2.463*	−0.342	−2.522*
0.342		0.247		0.239		0.109	
0.641		0.155		0.161		0.080	
65		65		65		65	

trend in the prices of British machines relative to IBM machines that may be related to the merger.

The main problem with these results is that our estimates indicate that Burroughs and British machine prices are different from those of IBM, as shown by the significant constant. To explore this possibility we have estimated equations as in (vii).

$$\log P_i = \hat{\alpha} + \hat{\beta} \log \hat{P}_i + \sum_n \hat{\gamma}_n D_{ni} + U_i \qquad \text{(vii)}$$

Our estimation method to date has constrained the coefficient $\hat{\beta}$ to unity, it is now free to vary. In fact from equation (ii), we would expect that if the valuation of

Table 9.2 $\log P = \hat{\alpha} + \hat{\beta} \log \hat{P} + \sum_n \hat{\gamma}_n D_n$

	All manufacturers coeff. 1	t	Honeywell/GE coeff. 2	t	Honeywell/GE coeff. 3	t	Burroughs coeff. 4	t	British coeff. 5	t
Constant	0.849	4.790*	−0.167	−0.664	0.064	0.325	1.439	4.490*	1.453	5.865*
$\log \hat{P}$	0.665	11.496*	1.037	10.173*	1.060	10.94*	0.497	3.976*	0.462	5.187*
1960	−0.206	−0.594	*				*		−0.464	−1.253
61	−0.465	−1.357	−0.471	−1.585			*		*	
62	−0.015	−0.068	−0.075	−0.253			−0.180	−0.578	−0.272	−0.739
63	−0.002	−0.016	0.434	1.837			−0.275	−1.156	−0.150	−0.684
64	−0.329	−2.473*	−0.187	−1.168			−0.410	−1.111	−0.532	−2.475*
65										
66	−0.202	−1.551	−0.236	−1.545			*		−0.323	−1.548
67	−0.278	−1.695	−0.575	−2.456*			*		−0.177	−0.767
68	−0.117	−0.861	0.128	0.769			−0.345	−1.243	−0.137	−0.593
69	−0.015	−0.114	0.305	1.531			−0.174	−0.524	−0.081	−0.383
70	−0.256	−1.643	−0.273	−1.663			*		−0.047	−0.172
71	−0.121	−0.770	0.310	1.512			−0.092	−0.284	0.073	0.277
72	0.262	1.921	0.308	2.149*			−0.018	−0.062	0.127	0.338
73	−0.242	−1.525	0.108	0.530			−0.871	−2.387*	0.162	0.538
74	−0.291	−1.339	*				*		−0.359	−1.383
75	−0.199	−0.749	*				*		−0.017	−0.052

60–64										
60–66										
60–67					−0.282	−2.196*				
60–68										
70–75										
ICT										
ICL										
Ferranti										
Leo										
EE										
Elliott										
GE	0.278	2.341*	0.510	4.799*	0.487	4.519*				
British	0.101	1.182								
Honeywell	−0.151	−1.694								
R^2	0.677		0.835		0.697		0.887		0.664	
$\hat{R}^2$	0.629		0.780		0.681		0.813		0.561	
N	146		57		57		24		65	

characteristics is different the value of log P_i − log $\hat{P}_i$ will change with machine size, i.e. $\hat{P}_j$, and thus we are just allowing for this possibility.

The problem with estimating (vii) is that if log $\hat{P}_i$ is not independent of log P_i, i.e. if IBM prices are influenced by the prices of its competitors then ordinary least squares estimates of the coefficients in (vii) may be biased. For British manufacturers' machines it may be reasonable to consider that IBM prices are exogenous, in that IBM and ICL do not compete on equal terms in any market except the British. For Honeywell and Burroughs the exogeneity is less acceptable. However, if one is willing to consider price leadership as a reasonable description of IBM's market behaviour then estimating (vii) may not lead to too great an error. Acceptance of the price leadership principle leads one to also argue that the ceofficients in (iv) arise solely from IBM's pricing policy given its costs and are independent of the other firms' prices.

In Table 9.2 we present OLS estimates of (vii). The first point to note is that if we are to observe a manufacturer's price equal to the IBM equivalent price then the constant and the coefficients on the dummies must be insignificantly different from zero and the coefficient on the IBM price must be unity. In the first results, across all manufacturers, these conditions are not satisfied, but after disaggregation we can see that for Honeywell/GE machines the constant is insignificant and the coefficient on price is approximately unity, but the GE dummy and the 60–67 dummy are significant. This just confirms our earleir result. For Burroughs and British machines the coefficient on price is significantly different from unity and approximately equal to 0.5 and the constant is significantly different from zero with an estimate of approximately 1.5. These results for Burroughs and British machines imply that British and Burroughs machines are more expensive than their IBM equivalents when we consider small machines (as measured by log $\hat{P}$) but as machines get larger the IBM equivalents are dearer. This implies that the non-IBM machines have a higher fixed element in their price but a lower marginal cost for extra characteristics. If we consider an estimate of $\hat{\alpha}$ to be 1.5 and the estimate of $\hat{\beta}$ to be 0.5, these figures suggest that IBM machines are dearer for machines with an IBM price above £1m but cheaper for machines at less than £1m. This should be considered an approximation given the possible sources of bias.

It would seem given our results that a comparison of the performance of Burroughs and the British sector would be a reasonable one, the differing price structures of IBM and Honeywell making a comparison with these less valid. If we continue to look at the results for Burroughs (Table 9.2 equation 4) there does not seem to be any time trend in the dummies and this result is also apparent in equation (5) for the British machines. In Table 9.3 further investigation of the British sector is undertaken with combinations of time and manufacturer dummies. In equation (1) there seems not to be any significant time pattern although there is a possible change in sign for the dummies prior to 1967 (or prior to 1964 if we judge only by significant coefficients). This is reflected in equations (2) and (3) which indicate that prior to 1964 the prices of UK machines were lower relative to IBM prices (at all sizes) than they were post-1964. Elliott machines were cheaper and Ferranti machines dearer even taking into account other factors. However, when we come to look for a change in relative prices due to the formation of ICL, i.e. a significant ICL dummy or a significant 1970–75 dummy (allowing a lag for the merger to take effect) we cannot isolate it. Thus the results we have may be summarised as follows.

(a) The prices of Honeywell/GE machines match the prices of their IBM equivalents for all machine sizes, but machines introduced by GE appear to have been higher priced, and machines introduced prior to 1967 seem to have been lower priced than their IBM equivalents.

(b) The prices of Burroughs and British machines relative to their IBM equivalents fall as size increases. Apart however from differences in price due to a machine being introduced by Ferranti or Elliott, or introduced prior to 1964, the prices of British machines and the prices of Burroughs machines showed no marked change in their relationship relative to IBM, and thus each other, over time.

Thus in our view of prices we do not observe any changes that we can attribute to the merger, i.e. the pre-merger pattern is repeated post merger.

The next step is to look at the movements of profitability over time. If we assume, and it seems reasonable to do so, that input prices move similarly over time for each manufacturer, then with our results on prices we suggest that one can interpret movements in profitability over time in this industry as reflecting technological change. The variable we have isolated as the best indicator is the profitability of newly introduced machines. We cannot measure this. What we can measure is company profitability. Given that a newly introduced machine has a limited life and will contribute to profits with a lag on its introduction date, it seems reasonable to argue that company profits will reflect the technology of machines introduced in the previous one to three years rather than any other period. Thus changes in relative profitability (measured by the profit/sales ratio) are to reflect technological change. The first point one must make is that one expects the level of profits to reflect much more than the level of technology, e.g. scale economies, transfer prices, efficiency etc., but it is felt reasonably reliable to interpret changes in relative profitability as reflecting technological ability. Of course changes in, for example, the efficiency of production could lead to changes in profit but not for any significant period of time and in this industry in particular, the gains from changing technology are so great that it must swamp other factors. In the extreme a company not advancing technologically but maintaining price competitiveness as we have shown it has been maintained, would have to eventually price below cost and in the meantime its profitability would be falling.

Table 9.3 $\log P = \hat{\alpha} + \hat{\beta} \log \hat{P} + \sum_n \hat{\gamma}_n D_n$ *(British sector only)*

	coeff. 1	t	coeff. 2	t	coeff. 3	t	coeff. 4	t	coeff. 5	t
Constant	1.473	6.435*	1.247	8.516*	1.256	8.403*	1.193	7.931*	1.217	6.363*
log *P*	0.435	5.496*	0.509	7.693*	0.505	7.410*	0.499	7.267*	0.524	7.113*
1960	−0.195	−0.563								
61	*	*								
62	0.028	0.084								
63	−0.206	−1.062								
64	−4.20	−2.063*								
65										
66	−0.172	−0.887								
67	−0.094	−0.433								
68	0.035	0.156								
69	0.253	0.751								
70	0.317	0.808								
71	0.422	1.104								
72	0.489	1.088								
73	0.523	1.292								
74	−0.017	−0.045								
75	0.397	0.094								

60–64			−0.217	−2.389*	−0.217	−2.366*				
65–67					0.045	0.387				
70–75									−0.172	−1.966
ICT										
ICL	−0.304	−0.940	0.022	0.192	−0.003	−0.030	0.101	0.906		
Ferranti	0.688	3.052*	0.639	2.931*	0.642	2.919*	0.500	2.288*		
Leo	0.228	1.214	0.257	1.465	0.257	1.457	0.257	1.414		
EE	−0.135	−0.906	−0.081	−0.718	−0.079	−0.698	−0.078	−0.663		
Elliott	−0.257	1.914	−0.321	−2.882*	−0.320	−2.854*	−0.337	−2.923*		
R^2	0.685		0.714		0.714		0.685		0.561	
$\hat{R}^2$	0.652		0.678		0.673		0.652		0.547	
N	65		65		65		65		65	

Table 9.4 *Profit/turnover ratio*

Year	ICL	IBM (UK)[a]	IBM Corporation	Burroughs Corporation	Burroughs Machines Ltd[a]	
1965	—	—	0.269	0.074	0.155	—
1966	—	—	0.248	0.110	0.175	—
1967	—	—	0.243	0.116	0.117	—
1968	—	0.274	0.271	0.136	0.170	—
1969	0.048	0.280	0.275	0.145	0.244	—
1970	0.059	0.291	0.268	0.150	0.226	—
1971	0.067	0.212	0.248	0.142	0.177	(0.168)[b]
1972	0.022	0.195	0.259	0.144	0.053	(0.068)
1973	0.065	0.193	0.262	0.162	0.054	(0.068)
1974	0.067	0.175	0.264	0.152	0.027	(0.037)
1975	0.067	0.183	0.251	0.171	0.005	(0.038)
1976	0.080	0.176	0.269	0.166	−0.027	(0.052)

Source: EXTEL. All profits are pre-tax. Honeywell is excluded because its profits and turnover figures include a large non-computer element.
[a] Covering the British subsidiary of the US parent companies.
[b] In this column profits are not reduced for exchange losses due to changes in the value of the pound.

In Table 9.4 we have set out the data on the profit/turnover ratio (the level of profitability of IBM illustrates the dangers of comparing levels). Although Honeywell is excluded due to data problems, we have argued above that an ICL/Burroughs comparison is the one on the surest statistical footing as regards prices, thus this will be the most important one here. We can however make references to the IBM data. The first point is that the IBM Corporation profit rate is remarkably constant over time, although its UK subsidiary shows a falling ratio of profits to sales. Burroughs Corporation shows a slightly increasing ratio over time but the UK division shows a remarkable decline in profitability. Once one corrects for losses due to exchange rate changes then the post-1970 picture is one of fluctuating but falling profitability. Finally the ICL figures, which will not be so affected by exchange rate losses, show a steady rate of return (apart from 1972) with the rise in 1976 above all previous levels reflecting the introduction of its 2900 range of machines. With respect to Burroughs Machines Ltd the performances of ICL as shown by profitability would seem to be one of improvement over time, and with respect to IBM (UK) a similar conclusion seems appropriate. The comparison with the IBM Corporation and Burroughs Corporation, also shows ICL in a good light but the areas of operations of the two large companies relative to ICL are so different the comparison means little. The comparison to the UK subsidiaries is the relevant one and that shows, especially relative to Burroughs, an improvement over time or at least no deterioration over time. In fact given that in the time period under consideration RCA and Rank Xerox have left the industry, the improvement is notable. In fact in 1976 ICL itself purchased the operations of Singer Business Machines on their decision to leave the industry.

Thus we can conclude that the performance of ICL relative to at least Burroughs, which seems to be closest in price terms and probably the other firms too, has been one of improvement over time. This we consider to reflect technological capability.

Our next step is to consider our counter factual. If we are to consider this improvement over time as due to merger we must ask whether the industry would have fared any differently without merger. We are going to pose the question in two parts, as follows.

(a) Given the same R & D expenditures would the rate of advance have been the same in the non-merged industry?

(b) Would the R & D expenditures have been the same in a non-merged industry?

On the first question there seem to be three relevant points:

(i) Was it possible for the British industry to exhibit a faster rate of technological advance? As there are reasonable grounds for believing that IBM undertake protective R & D (Stoneman (1976)) there would appear to have been possibilities for faster advance. The existence of protective R & D can affect our earlier conclusions, in that if its extent has changed over time then our results should show a faster relative rate of advance for IBM than they do. Due to its nature, however, the chance of drawing any reliable conclusions, given the poor data, is small.

(ii) Would the competitive pressures have been any greater without the merger? Here one would answer no, for the main competition was and still is from the US companies.

(iii) Would the R & D process have been more efficient? Here we are asking whether, given the same competitive pressures, repetition of R & D in two companies would have been more efficient. The answer must surely be in the negative.

We can suggest therefore that without merger the rate of advance would have been slower with the same R & D expenditures. The second question concerns the level of R & D expenditures. Here the question revolves around the role of government. Between 1968 and 1975 ICL received £50.4m from the British Government to support R & D, plus the benefit of a Buy British Government procurement policy. Given the reduced effectiveness of R & D expenditure in a non-merged industry, it is unlikely that this support would have been available at any greater level to compensate, in fact one could reason that less help would have been forthcoming. There seems little supporting evidence either that funds would have been available from other sources.

The evidence thus suggests that the merger has been successful in terms of

Table 9.5 *Market shares (%)*

Manufacturer	1966	1967	1968	1969	1972	1973
ICL (ICT, EE, etc. pre-1968)	34.4	32.4	41.0	49.4	34.7	32.9
IBM	43.2	42.5	23.4	27.7	38.4	39.7
Burroughs	3.9	1.3	6.4	3.0	3.9	3.7
Honeywell	5.8	6.9	5.4	7.9	7.0	7.0
Others	12.7	16.8	23.8	12.0	16.0	16.7

Sources: Various reports of the Department of Trade and Industry to the Select Committee on Science and Technology 1969–74. The figures in Table 9.5 of course show year by year variation but no strong trends on which to base any conclusions.

comparative performance on prices and profits vis-à-vis US companies in that if anything the performance of ICL has relatively improved slightly in the post-merger period.[7] It is felt however that the relatively unspectacular nature of the improvement hides the fact that the counter factual is one in which the rate of technological advance would have been slower relative to the other companies.

Prior to drawing our final conclusions we can look to two other areas for further support:

(a) The analysis of patent data

(b) An analysis of market share data

A detailed investigation of patent applications is not really feasible for the 1960–76 period, and even if it were there must be some qualification to any results because it is not really clear whether patents are an input or an output of the research process and thus whether they represent a good indicator of success in research and development. However there is evidence that indicates that the British industry's performance with regard to patents has been the equal of IBM's (SCST (1970) para 874, p. 157).

The final indicator of performance that we can look at is market shares. One would expect that the company with technological superiority could increase its market share. In Table 9.5 some data on market shares is presented. The problems with drawing any conclusions on the basis of this data are that the UK government has a 'Buy British' policy (although one can get over this problem by data disaggregation) and that compatibility is of overriding importance in computer selection. This latter point at the simplest level means that if a firm has an IBM machine with IBM based software, its computing costs are much lower if that

7 It could be argued that a more dramatic improvement actually occurred but the rate of advance of the US companies was stimulated by the merger thus hiding it. This hardly seems likely given the worldwide nature of their operations.

software can be used on the next machine purchased, and thus it has an incentive to buy an IBM compatible machine.

Thus the overall conclusion that the main body of work and these peripheral comments imply is that the UK computer industry has at least been able to hold its own against the US companies. (It should however be noted that this does not take account of any changes in protective R & D taking place in the non-UK sector.) We have argued that this performance could not have been maintained if the British industry had not merged in 1968. However perhaps of as much significance is that this performance has been achieved in a situation where IBM spends more on R & D than ICL's total turnover.[8] The efficiency of their R & D process is therefore of commendable quality.

References

CCL (1962–74), *British Commercial Computer Digest*, Pergamon Press.

Griliches, Z. (1971), *Price Indexes and Quality Change*, Cambridge, Mass.; Harvard University Press.

International Data Corporation (1961–74), *Computers and Automation.*

Schumpeter, J. A. (1942), *Capitalism, Socialism and Democracy.* New York; Harper Row.

SCST (1970), Select Committee on Science and Technology, *U.K. Computer Industry*, Vol. II, HC 272 (Session 1969–70), London; HMSO.

Shirley, D. (1969), *Choosing a Computer*, London; Business Publications Ltd.

Smythe, C. (1970, 1975), *Choosing a Computer*, London: Business Publications Ltd.

Stoneman, P. (1976), *Technological Diffusion and the Computer Revolution*, DAE Monograph No. 25, Cambridge: Cambridge University Press.

Theil, H. (1971), *Principles of Econometrics*, Amsterdam: North Holland.

8 ICL's R & D expenditure between 1969 and 1971 was £45m, in 1969 IBM spent $288m, in 1970 $300m, its budget for 1972/73 was $500m.

10

Vertical integration via merger: Courtaulds and the textile industry

10.1 The history of acquisitions

Over the course of the 1960s and early 1970s Courtaulds carried through a continuous stream of mergers with firms operating in various segments of the textile industry. As a result of these mergers, plus investment in textile plant and equipment, Courtaulds emerged in a position of dominance in most sectors of the industry.[1] A rather narrowly based cellulosic monopoly was transformed into a vertically integrated fibre-textiles firm. A list of major acquisitions is reported in Table 10.1 where it can be seen that the process began with a bang in 1963 with seven substantial acquisitions concentrated largely in the Knitwear, Hosiery and Garment sectors. The eight acquisitions in the following year included two very large spinning companies, Fine Spinners and Doublers (with an acquisition price of more than £12 million) and the Lancashire Cotton Corporation (more than £16 million). There followed a lull in activity during 1965 and 1966, but this was followed by a further spate in 1967 and 1968, the twelve acquisitions in 1968 including some quite large ones (e.g. Northgate Group (£6 million plus) and Ashton's). The acquired companies covered the whole range of textile activities (Spinning, Hosiery, Knitwear, Foundation Garments, Wholesaling), but also included International Paints. One perhaps significant aspect of this period was that the Monopolies Commission report on Cellulosic Fibres, and therefore on Courtaulds, was being drafted and finally presented in 1968. The recommendations, as we see later, included what amounted to a call for a standstill on Courtaulds takeovers in the textile industry but the Government delayed acting on the report until the following year, 1969. From 1969 onwards acquisitions of textile companies continued but at a reduced rate. One major attempted acquisition, that of English Calico in 1969, was aborted after Government intervention.

1 Knight (1974) reports that over the period 1962 through 1969 out of a total of £175 million spent on acquisitions, £146 million was spent on acquisitions in the textile industry.

Table 10.1 *Courtaulds acquisitions 1963–74*

Date acquired	Company	Business
1963		
July	Foster Clay & Ward	Knitwear manufacturer
August	Bairns Wear Ltd	Knitwear, children's wear, rug wools, yarns and knitting
October	Morton Sundour Fabrics	Furnishing fabric manufacturer
October	Berne Silk Ltd Victor Marks Ltd Lester and Cann Ltd	Fabric manufacturer and merchant converters
November	Susan Small Holdings Ltd	Garment manufacturer
December	James Nelson Ltd	Acetate flake
December	Meridian Ltd	Underwear, knitted outerwear, hoisiery manufacturer
1964		
January	George Brettle & Co.	Hosiery manufacturer
January	Barracks Fabrics Printing Co.	Fabric printing
March	Fras. Hinde & Sour Ltd	
June	Premier Dyeing & Finishing (Holdings)	Dyeing and finishing
August	Fine Spinners & Doublers	Yarn spinning and doubling
September	Lancashire Cotton Corporation	Yarn spinning and doubling
September	J & J Hayes Ltd & Greenhalgh & Shaw Ltd	Carpet yarns, yarn spinning
December	Spray & Burgess	
1965		
January	Joseph Sunderland & Co. Ltd	Weaving
January	Samuel Heap & Son	Dyeing and finishing
October	Derby & Midland Mills (1935)	Garment manufacturer
1966		
January	Kayser Bondor Ltd	Hosiery manufacturer
June	Aristoc Ltd	Hosiery manufacturer
October	Ballito Hosiery Mills Ltd	Hosiery manufacturer
1967		
June	Wolsey Ltd	Knitted outerwear and underwear manufacturer
August	R. & W. H. Symington (Holdings) Ltd	Foundation garments
September	Bell Nicholson & Richard Lunt (Group) Ltd	Textile wholesaling
September	Bradbury Greatorex & Co. Ltd	Textile wholesaling

Table 10.1 *continued*

Date acquired	Company	Business
September	S. C. Larkins & Sons Ltd 60% interest in MaCanie (London) Ltd	Textile wholesaling
November	Samuel Farmer & Co. Ltd	Hosiery, underwear and knitwear
December	Sharp Perrin & Co. Ltd	Garment manufacturer and children's wear
1968		
January	I & R Morley Ltd	Knitted outerwear, hosiery, underwear
February	Prew Smith Knitwear Ltd	Knitwear manufacturer
February 1968	M. Duke & Son	Garment manufacturer
February	Henry Lister & Sons Ltd	Fabric manufacturer
February	Clutsom-Penn International Ltd	Elasticated fabric manufacturer
March	Northgate Group	Foundation wear, lingerie, outerwear
March	Sir Thomas & Arthur Wardle Ltd	Dyers and finishers, chemical manufacturer
March	Contour Hosiery Ltd	Hosiery manufacturer
July	Ashton Bros & Co. (Holdings) Ltd	Spinning, weaving, dyeing, finishing and converting
August	International Paints	Paint and varnish manufacturer
July	R. Rowley & Co. Ltd	Garment manufacturer
November	Moygashel Ltd	Spinning, weaving, dyeing, finishing and fabric manufacturer
1969		
February	Hunter Barr & Co. Ltd	Hosiery manufacturer
April	Lindsay Bros. (Belfast) Ltd & G. Rushbrook Ltd	Fabric manufacturer
	Celanese Building Components	Building materials
	Shorko Films	
	Percy Taylor	Hosiery
1970		
January	Charles Turner & Co. Ltd	
1971		
September	C. H. Fletcher & Berry & Fletcher Ltd	
	D. S. Howland Ltd	Garments
	Tubbs Lewis	
	BTB Paints	
	Hughes & Young	

Table 10.1 *continued*

Date acquired	Company	Business
	West-Riding Hosiery Ltd	Stockings and tights
	Crepe Weavers Ltd	Knitted fabric
	Morna Fabrics (1949)	Knitted fabric
1972		
	Harwood Cash & Co. Ltd	Cotton doubling
1973		
	H. Harrison and Co. Ltd	Dyers
	Lansil Ltd	Acetate and triacetate flake and yarn
1974		
	Swan Lane Spinning Ltd	Spinning and doubling
	John Ferguson	Jersey

Source: EXTEL Statistical Services.

It will be seen from the above list that weaving is mainly significant by its absence. Knight (1974) reports that the weaving industry was rather fragmented, or dominated by small private companies which proved difficult to acquire. Courtaulds therefore set up large new weaving plant on green-field sites, like Skelmersdale, away from the traditional weaving areas. As a result of this real investment, together with the large-scale acquisitions in the other sectors, Courtaulds helped to transform the industry. To establish some of the effect of this on market structure Herfindahl measures of concentration are reported in Table 10.2 for various segments of the textile industry. It can be seen that there is a remarkable correspondence between concentration increase and those industries into which Courtaulds was integrating. Other sectors of textiles revealed a largely unchanged or reduced level of concentration over this period.

This chapter will first examine theoretically the possible consequences of an extension of vertical control by a monopoly supplier of an intermediate good. The particular characteristics of Courtaulds and the textile industry will then be examined so that we will be in a position to develop our theoretical expectations of the consequences of this series of mergers. We will then confront these predictions with empirical evidence on the economic performance and behaviour of Courtaulds.

10.2 The impact of vertical control

It is obvious that vertical integration will tend to take place when costs are lowered by substituting planning for the price mechanism. It has been argued that market intermediation can involve significant transactions costs and that an extension of the firm can avoid many of these. Thus haggling, although privately

Table 10.2 *Herfindahl concentration measures for textiles*[a]

MLH	1963	1968
412 Spinning	0.0260	0.0414
413 Weaving	0.0091	0.0214
414 Woollen and worsted	0.0094	0.0110
415 Jute	0.0808	0.0795
416 Rope	0.0669	0.0761
417 Hosiery	0.0104	0.0191
418 Lace	0.0243	0.0207
419 Carpets	0.0376	0.0455
421 Narrow fabrics	0.0239	0.0253
422(1) Household textiles	0.0084	0.0121
422(2) Canvas	0.0107	0.0066
423 Textile finishing	0.0197	0.0336

[a]We are grateful to Michael Waterson for allowing us to use his estimates. They are based on Census of Production data. All the measures are biased down due to the method of estimation but comparisons of the estimates for 1963 and 1968 should serve to illustrate the process of structural change.

productive, is socially wasteful; the market for information poses many problems and imposes large screening costs; contracts, although not difficult to arrange in a static world, can become difficult to engineer in a changing world where devices introduced to allocate risk may themselves impose monitoring costs. Similarly it may be difficult for independent firms to adapt to stochastic shocks which affect the relationship between them. For these sorts of reasons it has been suggested that vertical integration can lead to significant gains both to the participants and to society in general (see Williamson (1971)). It must, however, be recognised that the extension and increasing complexity of organisations can lead to inefficiency. The underlying issue is not whether significant transactions costs exist when using market intermediation but whether transactions costs are significantly reduced by replacing market intermediation with a bureaucratic process, i.e. whether intra-firm transactions costs are lower than inter-firm. The managerial discretion literature clearly indicates that large, opaque organisations can be expected to generate considerable slack given that this will usually reflect the interests of managers. Under managerial control vertical integration may proceed in the absence of economies.

Up to this point we have proceeded as if there were no market power implications connected to the process of vertical integration. However in the case of monopoly at the level of an intermediate good, which accurately describes

Courtaulds' position in the market for cellulosic fibres, the general case is one where a vertical extension of control does imply the acquisition of market power where the market for the final product is initially competitive, even in the absence of dynamic effects, predatory pricing or price discrimination. As demonstrated by Machlup and Taber (1960), in the case of successive monopoly vertical integration will simultaneously result in price-reduction and increased profit. To the extent that monopolies are allowed to exist and their behaviour is unregulated vertical integration represents a third-best welfare optimum. This is not generally the case where the vertical extension is into a competitive industry. We will normally be faced with a welfare trade-off similar in character to the case of horizontal merger. We now turn to establishing this result and the determinants of the trade-off. The analysis at this point will rely heavily on Warren-Boulton (1974).

Texts in industrial economics have tended to expound the view that the vertical extension of monopoly has no market power implication. Thus it was observed that the monopoly supplier of an intermediate good could set a price for that good which would appropriate all the monopoly rents which were available for appropriation in the market for the final product. This can be true if one important assumption is met, that of fixed proportions in the production of the final product. If this assumption is replaced then it is immediately obvious that further profits can be appropriated by a vertical extension of control since such an extension would allow the firm to choose the cost-minimising input mix which the independent final product producer could not do because of the monopoly pricing of the intermediate good (see McKenzie (1951); Vernon and Graham (1971)). Thus, as in the successive monopolies case, it was suggested that vertical control would represent a third-best welfare optimum. Input distortions caused by monopoly could be eliminated and thereby both private profit and social welfare would be increased. But there is a further facet to the problem. In the process of establishing control over the input mix the vertically integrated monopoly is also establishing control over the final market for the other inputs which it did not previously control. Using Courtaulds as an example, the extension of Courtaulds' monopoly (of cellulosic fibres) into the textile industry would not only give it control over the use of cellulosic fibres in the production of textiles,[2] but would also give it control over the market for textiles which can be seen as a combination of cellulosic and other fibres. Thus Courtaulds establishes control over the other fibres which it has not previously controlled. The important question now resolves itself into whether or not the elimination of the input distortions fol-

2 This in itself would tend to result in the substitution of cellulosic fibres for natural fibres since the appropriate transfer price for cellulosic fibres would be their marginal cost whereas previously the independent textile company had to pay the monopoly price. Insofar as natural fibres are priced at marginal cost this adjustment following vertical integration would both raise profits and welfare.

lowing vertical integration will more than compensate for the extension of market power in the textile market, taking as given, Courtaulds' monopoly pricing of cellulosic fibres. The theoretical framework for resolving this question is due to Warren-Boulton (1974), following earlier work by Schmalensee (1973) and Burstein (1960).

For a trade-off to exist the price of the final product must rise as a consequence of vertical control, for if this were not the case then vertical control, by eliminating input distortions caused by monopoly in factor markets, would be unambiguously beneficial, at least in a second- or third-best sense. Making reasonable assumptions about cost and demand conditions allows Warren-Boulton (1974) to obtain the result that the price of the final product can be expected to increase following vertical control. To get the result he assumes a CES production function, constant costs in the production of each input and a constant elasticity of demand for the final product. In particular cases he can derive the result analytically but generally he relies on simulation. As Schmalensee (1973) discovered earlier this result is quite sensitive to assumptions about demand and cost conditions, but it is not unreasonable to accept the above characterisation of the fibre–textile industry. It is also necessary to point out that Schmalensee is assuming monopoly pricing for the final product after vertical control and obviously the outcome will also be dependent on the extent of vertical integration, i.e. how many firms are integrated and how many are left independent. The usual question of concentration in the final goods market thus arises but it is necessary to mention at this point that this is not generally independent of the question of vertical control and will be taken-up later.

If we accept the Warren-Boulton results as indicative of the expected outcome then we are faced with the usual sort of welfare trade-off discussed in Chapter 2. The rise in monopoly profits following vertical control consists of two components, one due to a change in efficiency and one due to a change in price. The magnitude of the change in profit will therefore be conditional on the importance of the monopolised input in the production of the final product (i.e. on δ, the share of cost due to the monopolised input) and on the elasticity of demand for the final product (η). As δ and η fall so the incentive for vertical control increasingly becomes the achievement of market power rather than the elimination of inefficiency. Warren-Boulton's results show that so long as $\sigma \geqq 1$ (where σ is the elasticity of substitution between rayon and other fibres) we may expect welfare to fall following vertical control, the fall being greater the lower are δ and η. The history of the textile industry would support the view that σ has increased and δ and η have declined. During the post-war period, as described in the discussion on the Courtaulds/British Celanese merger (Chapter 5), the advent of nylon, qualitative improvements in cotton cloth, and later the introduction of polyester fibres, implied a marked increase in competition for rayon, consistent with an increase in the elasticity of substitution between rayon and other fibres (σ) and a fall in the share of rayon (δ). Given that the price elasticity of demand for textiles may be historically declining (η), see e.g. Houthakker and Taylor (1970), then we have a picture of Courtaulds extending its control into textiles at a period in history when the market conditions would support the hypothesis that the incentive was market power rather than the elimination of inefficiency. An extension into textiles by Courtaulds at an earlier point in its history would have been more consistent with the elimination of inefficiency argument. There remains however, the possibility of the elimination of transactional inefficiencies as discussed earlier but before we look at the evidence it is necessary to discuss further implications of vertical control which will tend to reinforce the market power hypothesis.

A vertical extension of control as well as having a direct effect on market power also provides the preconditions for various indirect effects. By controlling the price of some inputs the vertically controlled enterprise can squeeze out independent private producers by an appropriate pricing policy. To be effective as an instrument for creating monopoly we have to assume that firms squeezed out cannot easily re-enter or enter the production of intermediate goods. Its effectiveness is thus predicated on the existence of barriers to entry to the intermediate goods industry. It is not difficult to think of many impediments to the entry of small textile firms into the production of rayon. The technology is certainly quite different and there are no small firms lying around to be taken over – this has been pre-empted by Courtaulds earlier activities. Given that they were also faced with another very dominant seller in the case of nylon (ICI) and with high tariffs on man-made fibre imports their position was clearly difficult. Indeed the 1970 textile recession led to claims by independent textile producers of predatory pricing by Courtaulds (see *Guardian*, 25 July 1970).

We can thus see that what might appear as a third-best welfare optimum can be expected to make the first-best infeasible as a dynamic consequence. Any trade-off analysis of the comparative-static type that we have discussed must recognise this. This would suggest that we err on the side of caution in accepting efficiency arguments.[3] One dynamic aspect of vertical control which may appear beneficial at first sight is the impact on the introduction of new products. The extension into textiles can be seen as providing a more secure base for the introduction of new fibres by Courtaulds in a situation where ICI (e.g. in the case of nylon and polyester) already had a dominant position. Thus vertical integration may allow the emergence of greater competition in the market for these newer fibres. The problem is that this could create the same problem of input distortion which we have already discussed. Courtaulds as an inefficient producer of these newer fibres could still find it profitable to introduce them because of ICI's monopoly pricing. This would be a further example of waste induced in the pursuit of monopoly profits. Only if the security provided by vertical integration

3 Other dynamic consequences related to the entry conditions for new firms would appear to work in the same direction, although they may be regarded as of less importance in this particular case.

induces truly new innovations will the preconditions for increased welfare be met. Such innovations could of course include new methods of producing existing fibres as well as new fibres.

We turn now to evidence on changes in Courtaulds' efficiency and market power over the period 1963 to 1974.

The empirical evidence

Courtaulds started the period in 1963 as essentially a man-made fibre producer and ended it as the dominant firm in the textile industry. At the end of this period Courtaulds was processing a large fraction of its own fibre production by spinning, weaving or knitting, together with some making-up of clothes, wholesaling and treatment of textiles. Most of the significant mergers had taken place by the end of 1968 and we therefore have a run of six years since that point with which to evaluate Courtaulds as an integrated textile producer. From 1963 to 1968 a rapid process of acquisition was in train. It can be viewed as a transitional period when more and more of Courtaulds' output was being consumed in its own subsidiaries.

Analysing Courtaulds' sales to third parties over the period 1969 through 1974, that is the period subsequent to the period of most active acquisition, we see that Textile Processing in total accounts for about 50%, Man-made Fibres about 35%, with a variety of activities including packaging and paint accounting for the remaining 15%.[4] Cotton Type Spinning and Weaving accounted for roughly 18%, Hosiery, Knitwear and Garments roughly 22%, and other Textiles and Textile Wholesaling about 9%. These figures relate to sales (both domestic and export) arising from UK production. Overseas production comprised almost a quarter of total output over this period.

Table 10.3 reports estimates of output and input price indexes for Courtaulds. It can be seen that in the case of the composite indexes the ratio of output price relative to input price has shown a persistent tendency to fall over the period, with perhaps a very slight rise in 1974. The average rate of decline has been of the order of 3% p.a. with the rate of decline since 1968 being rather *less* than the rate before that point. On the face of it this would seem to indicate either a steady improvement in efficiency and/or a fall in market power, a piece of evidence that may suggest some beneficial consequences arising from vertical integration. However, if we disaggregate then we find that whereas the Man-made Fibre price ratio shows a persistent and steady decline averaging over 4% p.a., the price ratio for Household Textiles shows a very modest decline averaging only 0.6% p.a.[5] The data for Household Textiles also indicate a tendency for the output

4 See F. Fishwick and R. B. Corm (1975) p. 192.

5 Other textile output price indexes span the Household Textiles index. Cotton Spinning and Weaving show a higher rate of growth whereas Hosiery and Knitwear show a lower rate.

Table 10.3 *Estimated k for Courtaulds 1963–74*

	(1) P_0^C	(2) P_1^C	(3) P_0^C/P_1^C	(4) P_0^M/P_I^M	(5) P_0^T/P_I^T	(6) Π/R	(7) k
1963	100.00	100.00	1.000	1.000	1.000	0.127	0.873
1964	100.07	102.59	0.975	0.955	0.986	0.146	0.833
1965	99.83	106.34	0.939	0.909	0.981	0.121	0.825
1966	97.70	109.64	0.891	0.854	0.968	0.109	0.794
1967	93.78	112.60	0.833	0.798	0.964	0.092	0.756
1968	97.25	120.82	0.805	0.763	0.928	0.091	0.732
1969	99.67	125.34	0.795	0.737	0.916	0.088	0.725
1970	102.66	136.88	0.750	0.690	0.910	0.083	0.688
1971	107.26	148.49	0.722	0.656	0.913	0.064	0.676
1972	111.74	159.60	0.700	0.625	0.915	0.067	0.653
1973	127.67	187.56	0.681	0.588	0.943	0.088	0.621
1974	168.18	244.85	0.687	0.559	0.939	0.122	0.603

Notes:

(1) P_0^C is a composite output price index for Courtaulds with weights derived from Fishwick and Corm (1975).

(2) P_I^C is a composite input price index; 0.6 (Man-made Fibre Input Price Index) + 0.255 (Textile Wage Index) + 0.145 (Cotton Price Index), intended to reflect price changes in those inputs entering the vertically integrated enterprise. The weights are based on Census of Production data.

(3) P_0^M, P_0^T are respectively the output price indexes for Man-made Fibres and Household Textiles, derived from Department of Industry sources (see Chapter 4 for details).

(4) P_I^M, P_I^T are respectively the input price indexes for Man-made Fibres and Household Textiles, derived from Department of Industry sources (see Chapter 4 for details).

(5) Π/R is the ratio of Courtaulds net profit before tax to Courtaulds sales revenue.

(6) k is the efficiency measure proposed in Chapter 4.

price to rise relative to the input price over the period since 1970. It is difficult to see how, on this evidence, the apparent gain in efficiency can be due to vertical integration.

Table 10.3 also reports estimates of the ratio of profit before tax to sales revenue (Π/R) for Courtaulds over the same period. If we argue that the primary impact of Courtaulds' restructuring of the textile industry would be felt within the UK then the profit and sales figures should refer to the UK.[6] However this breakdown is not available so our Π/R estimates relate to the worldwide operations of Courtaulds. In 1969 Courtaulds' total, worldwide sales to third parties

6 It could be argued that Courtaulds market power vis-à-vis foreign buyers has also increased as a result of the restructuring of the industry.

were £577 million, and their UK turnover was £452 million (domestic sales plus exports), but no profit figures are available for this split.

Column (6) of Table 10.3 reveals that the profit–revenue ratio was initially quite high (1963/65), then declined steadily to a minimum in 1971, subsequently climbing back to a similar position to that of the early 1960s.[7] This history could reflect general movements in the textile industry but is also consistent with adjustment problems posed by the rapid vertical extension into textiles through the 1960s and early 1970s.

The efficiency measure (k) reported in column (7) suggests a steady improvement in efficiency for Courtaulds over the 1963/74 period. The fall in profitability has not been as great as would have resulted from the fall in the ratio of output to input prices in the absence of any improvement in efficiency. It is important to note, however, that the fall in profitability for Courtaulds as a whole cannot be explained by any tendency for the price of textiles to fall relative to their input costs. The data tends to demonstrate that Courtaulds efficiency has grown because of productivity growth in the area of man-made fibres rather than in textiles and therefore has little connection with the vertical extensions of Courtaulds over this period.

Courtaulds, the textile industry and the state

The period of our analysis, 1963 through 1974, was one of intense interaction between Courtaulds and the state. The Monopolies Commission investigation of Courtaulds' dominant position in cellulosic fibres was initiated in 1965 and completed in 1968. The Commission concluded that continued acquisitions by Courtaulds in the textile industry could be against the public interest. It was recommended that no further acquisitions by Courtaulds should be allowed in any sector of the textile or clothing industries (including wholesaling and retailing) if Courtaulds share of capacity or sales in that sector exceeded 25%. In fact at that point in time (mid 1968) it was estimated that Courtaulds' market share for spinning was 30%, for filament weaving 22% and for warp knitting 35%.[8] In response to the recommendations the Board of Trade asked for a confidential statement from Courtaulds and the President of the Board of Trade (Douglas Jay) announced that there would be a review of tariffs and that he would have discussions with the company.[9] Courtaulds now sought to convince

7 As mentioned in Chapter 4, we would expect that the vertical extension of a firm will in itself tend to raise the profit–revenue ratio given that we are not accounting for the cost of capital. This in turn implies that k will be biased down as vertical integration proceeds. Our estimates will therefore *overstate* any efficiency improvement resulting from vertical merger.

8 See the *Financial Times*, 2 July 1969.

9 This process is fully documented in Knight (1974) pp. 130–40.

the Board of Trade that the Commission was wrong. Courtaulds had in fact, in previous discussions with the Board of Trade, argued for raising textile tariffs to the average level, whereas now it was set against reducing fibre tariffs to the same average.[10] Finally, on 22 July 1969, fifteen months after the Monopolies Commission report came out, the Government announced no change in tariffs and the acquisitions recommendation lapsed with the takeover of the issue by the Dell committee. Despite the recommendations of the Monopolies Commission a major acquisition (Ashton Bros.) went through in July 1968 and other smaller acquisitions followed in the same year and in the following year. However, in January 1969 Courtaulds made a bid for English Calico, the third largest British textile company, but the bid was withdrawn in February 1969 at the request of the Government. As can be seen in Table 10.1 other acquisitions continued to be made in each year up to 1974. Clearly the recommendations of the Monopolies Commission concerning the textile industry were not being acted on.

The interaction between Courtaulds and the state was not only via the Monopolies Commission and the Board of Trade. As already discussed, the Government decided against a tariff reduction in the case of cellulosic fibres but in the same year (1969) tariffs on Commonwealth imports of textiles were imposed following the recommendations contained in a Textile Council report. The sub-committee which drafted the report was in fact chaired by a Courtaulds director and also included A. M. Alfred, the company's chief economist, see Counter Information Services (1974). Courtaulds have been quite open about their attempts to secure a more restrictive import policy for textiles and have linked their acquisition of a dominant position in textiles to the achievement of this aim. Arthur Knight, their current chairman, explains that the acquisition of one third of the Lancashire textile industry was 'necessary to have any prospect of influencing government attitudes about imports' (Knight (1974) p. 49). The evidence would suggest that this assessment may have been close to the truth. Not only were tariffs introduced in 1969 but also, despite a promised lifting of quotas in 1972 following their imposition in 1966, the quotas were reimposed in 1971, see Counter Information Services (1974).

Knight also reveals another interesting facet of the interaction between the state and Courtaulds. At first sight one might conclude that the emergence of ICI in a position of power in both man-made fibres and textiles would be seen as a threat by Courtaulds. Knight, however, concludes that 'to have ICI as a strong vertical fibre–textile group would suit Courtaulds' interests taking the long view, because the interests of the two groups in dealing with Whitehall would coincide more than they would diverge, and it would thus strengthen any efforts to influence government policy'.

We conclude that the vertical extension of Courtaulds into the textile industry

10 Table 5.3 reveals the very high tariff rates on man-made fibres.

was not only intended to consolidate and possibly extend Courtaulds' product market power in a direct sense but was also seen as an instrument by which its dominant position could be secured by political influence. If another dominant firm like ICI followed suit then this would serve the same end. The links between economic power and political power will be raised again in the policy discussion in Chapter 14.

References

Counter Information Services (1974), *Courtaulds Inside-Out*

Burstein, M. L. (1960), 'A Theory of Full-Line Forcing', *Northwestern University Law Review*, **55** (February), 62–95.

Fishwick, F. & Corm, R. B. (1975), *A Study of the Evolution of Concentration in the UK Textile Industry*, Commission of the European Communities (October), 192.

Houthakker, H. & Taylor, L. D. (1970), *Consumer Demand in the US 1929–70*, Cambridge, Mass.: Harvard University Press.

Knight, A. (1974), *Private Enterprise and Public Intervention*, London: Allen & Unwin.

Machlup, F. & Taber, M. (1960), 'Bilateral Monopoly, Successive Monopoly and Vertical Integration', *Economica*, **27** (February), 101–19.

McKenzie, L. (1951), 'Ideal Output and the Interdependence of Firms', *Economic Journal*, **61** (December), 785–803.

Schmalensee, R. (1973), 'A Note on the Theory of Vertical Integration', *Journal of Political Economy*, **81** (March/April), 442–5.

Vernon, J. M. & Graham, D. A. (1971), 'Profitability of Monopolization by Vertical Integration', *Journal of Political Economy*, **79** (July/August), 924–5.

Warren-Boulton, F. (1974), 'Vertical Control with Variable Proportions', *Journal of Political Economy*, **82** (July/August), 783–802.

Williamson, O. E. (1971), 'The Vertical Integration of Production', *American Economic Review*, **61**, 112–23.

11

Diversification via merger: some empirical evidence

11.1 Introduction

The empirical evidence presented in this chapter relates to three aspects of diversifying mergers: risk pooling, capital transfer, and the related issue of merger as a search for investment opportunities. Thus the focus is on what were earlier described as 'strictly diversifying' aspects. As was argued in Chapter 2, the justification for selecting such a focus is stronger for a UK study than it would be in a US context, since the competition policies of the two countries result in UK firms being relatively less inhibited from seeking size economies and market power via non-diversifying growth.

Whether or not diversification (via merger or *de novo* expansion) *can* reduce risk is not a matter for empirical enquiry. In the absence of perfect positive correlation of two or more profit streams – a situation which can be safely disregarded – risk reduction follows from pooling individual sources by a mathematical necessity. The empirical question is, rather, *to what extent* risk pooling explains observed diversification patterns and diversifying mergers, and the magnitude of the risk-reducing effects of such mergers.

In the area of capital transfer, three empirical questions arise in connection with Williamson's affirmative case (Williamson (1970, 1975)) for conglomerates on grounds of efficiency in redeploying investible funds. First, the benefits of the hierarchical system which Williamson claims depend on firms being 'appropriately organised', i.e. being multidivisional (M-form). The incidence of M-form firms in the system as a whole is therefore an important question, as is the organisational form of the acquiring firms in diversifying mergers, if such mergers are to contribute to welfare via capital transfer effects. Secondly, some form of empirical support is needed for the basic contention that the hierarchical solution is in practice superior to the alternative, external capital market system. Thirdly, the efficiency of the hierarchical solution will depend among other things on the degree to which *all* industrial activities are embraced in the network of corporate linkages. In evaluating diversifying mergers in the present context, it is therefore

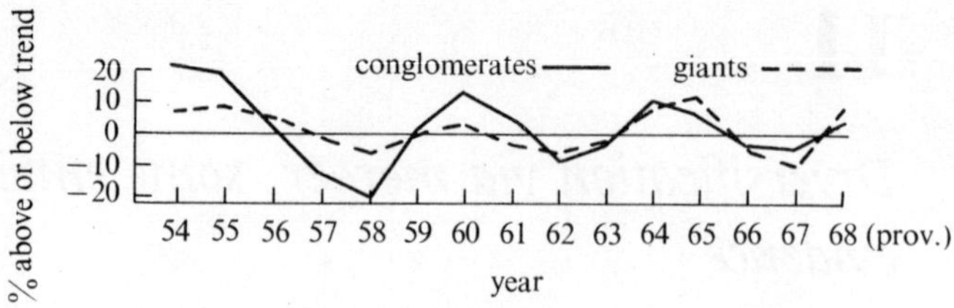

Figure 11.1 *Deviations from trend profits*

relevant to ask whether they occur in areas between which existing corporate links are strong or weak.

Empirical evidence relating to the merger-search hypothesis is relevant on account of the policy implications of this hypothesis in the context of capital transfer. The evidence set out in this chapter in connection with the hypothesis is mainly drawn from existing work, supplemented by some conclusions drawn from consideration of a sample of UK diversifying mergers that took place between 1965 and 1970.

11.2 **Risk pooling**

Studies of the role of risk pooling in diversification and merger have been numerous in the USA where they have generally produced negative results (Mueller (1977)). Only three studies have apparently been undertaken for the UK, by Utton (1969), Econtel Research (1969) and Kumps (1975).

All three compared the variability of profit between groups of 'conglomerate' or 'diversified' firms and a control group. Utton applied analysis of variance to a sample of eighteen diversified and a like number of firms specialising in the engineering industries, using profit-rate data for the period 1957–68. No statistically significant difference in the variance of profit between the groups was apparent. The Econtel study compared graphically the deviations from trend profits for a group of twenty UK conglomerates[1] with those for twenty-seven non-conglomerate 'giants' (Figure 11.1).[2] Here, after their 'full diversification' was effected by the early 1960s, 'the conglomerates experienced fluctuations which equalled (or even bettered) those of the giants, though these also were relatively stable'. Kumps calculated the coefficient of variation of profit rates for three groups among the 200 largest UK companies 1964–69: those which had grown principally by diversifying merger; those with no acquisitions; and those with principally horizontal and vertical acquisitions. The values obtained were 28%, 39% and 45% respectively.

1 See Econtel Research (1969).
2 See Econtel Research (1968).

Thus, the existing, relatively scanty UK evidence is somewhat conflicting, and two of the three studies focus on the effects of diversification in general rather than on diversifying merger itself. Against this background a simple test was undertaken for risk-pooling effects amongst two samples of diversifying mergers that took place in the UK between 1965 and 1970.

The approach adopted involved a simulation procedure using pre-merger data only. Thus the pre-merger profitability of firms which subsequently merged was compared with the profit series which would have been generated had the merger already occurred, i.e. the profit series obtained by simply combining the profit streams of the firms in question. This approach has the advantage of eliminating the need for the control group, since the merging firms are compared with their quasi-merged selves over the pre-merger period. It also minimises data requirements and problems arising over, e.g., other merger activity involving the firms under study. Moreover, the profits series for the simulated mergers are necessarily uncontaminated by transactions costs and synergistic effects.[3] Hence, risk-pooling effects, if present, are more readily observed.

The risk-pooling effects in two samples of UK mergers (one a subset of the other) were tested by this method. In all, 50 mergers were classified by the OFT in the diversifying category between 1965 and 1970. Data for the analysis were derived from a computer tape made available by Kuehn.[4] In all, data were available for 37 cases (the remainder being mainly mergers involving foreign or non-industrial firms). The larger sample consisted of all 37 cases. The subset comprised 15 'unambiguously diversifying' cases, where the merging firms shared no common (approximately 3 digit) industry prior to the merger. The average variability of profit (strictly, the mean of individual firms' variance of pre-tax return on assets) was calculated for three groups of firms in each sample: (a) the acquiring firms; (b) the firms with the higher pre-merger variability of profit, whether acquired or acquiring, and (c) the simulated merged firms. A *t*-test was applied to test the differences in mean variability of profit among the three groups.

Results of the exercise are reported in Table 11.1. From the viewpoint of the acquiring firms, the evidence of risk reduction is very weak. However, significant risk reduction is revealed in both samples for the participating firm with the higher pre-merger variability of profit. On the assumption that the forces determining the pre-merger variability of firms' profits continued to operate in the post-merger period, it may be inferred that the actual risk-reducing effects of the mergers were as shown in Table 11.1.

3 The simulation procedure would, of course, be inappropriate if the synergistic effects themselves were to be evaluated.

4 For further details see Kuehn (1975). We are extremely grateful to Doug Kuehn for placing his data tape at our disposal. Jonathan Palfrey rendered invaluable programming assistance in the empirical analysis reported in this chapter.

Table 11.1 *Risk-pooling via merger: statistical tests*

A. Simulated mergers vs. acquiring firms

Sample	Mean variability of profit %		*t*-statistic	Degrees of freedom
	Acquiring firms	Simulated mergers		
Smaller	0.124	0.036	0.567	28
Larger	0.249	0.093	1.351[a]	72

B. Simulated mergers vs. highest-variance firms

Sample	Mean variability of profit (%)		*t*-statistic	Degrees of freedom
	Highest variance firms	Simulated mergers		
Smaller	0.214	0.086	1.906[b]	28
Larger	0.476	0.093	1.974[b]	72

[a]Denotes significance at 10% or better.
[b]Denotes significance at 5% or better.

The very weak evidence from the point of view of the acquiring firms seems to suggest that risk reduction is unlikely to have been an important *motive* in these mergers, and consequently that any risk-reducing *effects* would have been incidental. The fact that risk was reduced for one party to the merger is most likely explained by the fact that, typically, relatively large acquirers took over firms considerably smaller but more profitable (and with higher variability of profit) than themselves. On average, the acquired firms were only 21.4% as large as their acquirers in the large sample and 8.1% in the small, and on average were more profitable by some 10.8%.

11.3 **Capital transfer**

On the evidence available at present the first structural condition for Williamson's case for conglomerates on capital transfer grounds – that the majority of large firms, responsible for the bulk of investment, have adopted a multi-divisional internal organisation – seems to be met. Two classifications of firms by type of organisational form have been made, by Channon (1973) and by Steer (1973). Both indicate that the 1960s was a period of marked internal re-organisation among the largest UK companies. There was a strong trend away from holding (H) companies and traditional, unitary (U-form) firms towards multidivisionals, and amongst these there was a reduction in the incidence of

Table 11.2 *Distribution of large companies by organisational form*

Organisational form	1970/72	(%)	1964/66	(%)
M (Multidivisional)	35	(29.2)	21	(17.5)
M′ (in transition to M-form)	40	(33.3)	12	(10.0)
$\overline{M}$ (Corrupted M-form)	7	(5.8)	17	(14.2)
H (Holding Co.)	14	(11.7)	37	(30.8)
U (Unitary)	9	(7.5)	14	(11.7)
X (Mixed)	4	(3.3)	6	(5.0)
Uncertain[a]	11	(9.2)	13	(10.8)

Source: Steer (1973)
[a]i.e. reliable classification available for one but not both periods.

Table 11.3 *Organisational form: merging firms*

Sample of 15		Others	Sample of 37	
M	6	10	16	(43.2%)
M′	6	9	15	(40.5%)
$\overline{M}$	0	1	1	(2.7%)
H	2	1	3	(8.1%)
U	1	0	1	(2.7%)
Unclass.	0	1	1	(2.7%)

Source: Steer (1973) with additional classifications.

the corrupted ($\overline{M}$)-form, in which central office is over-involved in operating affairs at divisional level. By the early 1970s the multidivisional organisation was easily the preponderant type, although as Table 11.2 shows only just under thirty per cent of the companies classified had achieved *pure* M-form. On the other hand the very low incidence of U-form firms is striking.

The incidence of M-form among firms involved in diversifying mergers is of particular interest, from the point of view of the possible significance of such mergers for the efficiency of capital transfer. Table 11.3 shows the breakdown for the diversifying merger samples, and records the organisational form of the acquiring firms in *1970/72*. In a number of cases, of course, M-form was adopted after (and in some cases perhaps because of) the merger. The incidence of M- and M′- form firms here is quite overwhelming.

The second piece of empirical evidence needed to substantiate Williamson's argument is that the claimed potential for more efficient reallocation of capital via the system of miniaturised, internal capital markets in appropriately organised firms is in fact realised. Up to the present such direct evidence has yet to be put forward, although there is some evidence showing a significant, positive impact of M-form organisational control on profitability amongst large UK companies (Steer and Cable (1978)).

The absence of more extensive evidence on this point would make it impossible to reach any firm conclusions on Williamson's arguments as a whole, were it not that evidence on the remaining necessary condition—that all industrial activities are satisfactorily linked by a network of corporate linkages – is both fairly clear cut and damaging to Williamson's case. Thus existing evidence on diversification (whether by M-form or by other firms) suggests that (a) it is confined mainly to large firms and (b) with few exceptions even these tend to have activities which are fairly narrowly concentrated in particular areas. In the most recent study for the UK, which looked at the largest 200 companies, Utton (1977) found that on average each firm operated in 9.4 three-digit industries, but with 80% of employment concentrated in only three industries, subsequent shares typically being 5% or less in a tail of 'quantitatively insignificant' activities. Moreover, the spread of activities appeared to be into industries with close technological or marketing links, most diversification being within rather than across two-digit industry boundaries. Thus indirectly the evidence does not seem to suggest a high degree of connectedness of all industries through corporate ownership links, as Utton says: 'The data for the UK . . . on the whole run counter to the popular view of a small number of very large conglomerates with tentacles stretching into every corner of industry.'

Direct evidence on the network of corporate ties among industries requires systematic information on the activities of individual firms which is not available from previous studies but is contained on the Kuehn data tape, where the principal industrial activities of all companies are listed. From this source it is possible to derive matrices showing, for all 67 industries in Kuehn's classification scheme, the number of firms active in industry j also active in industry i ($i \neq j = 1, 2, \ldots, 67$). No information is available about the scale of a firm's activity in any particular industry, although some size threshold must have been passed to have merited mention of the activity in Kuehn's data sources (EXTEL and the *Stock Exchange Yearbook*). However, from the capital transfer viewpoint it is the fact that a firm is engaged in an industry (above some minimum level) that is important, rather than the scale of operations, since this is enough for the internal information advantages to accrue.

Diversification matrices of the type described above were derived from the Kuehn tape for three groups of companies: pure M-form; M- and M′-form; and all firms. The industry codes listed on the original Kuehn tape related to 1965. We updated these codes adding in extra codes as companies broadened their activities through merger between 1965 and 1969, the final year covered by the data tape. Thus we obtained, for all three groups of companies, observations on the pattern of diversification in 1965 and 1969, although the latter excludes

Table 11.4 *Network of linked activities: M-form firms*

Composition of group	Diversification level			
	1965		1969	
1964/66	0	2,078	0	1,457
	1	126	1	596
	2	7	2	132
			3	20
			4	6
1970/72	0	2,000	0	1,369
	1	183	1	603
	2	22	2	175
	3	6	3	45
			4	6
			5	9
			6–8	4

diversification undertaken by internal expansion between the two years. As has been described earlier, the composition of the M-form and (M + M′)-form groups also changed over the period. For these two groups we therefore derived four matrices, as follows:

Composition of group	Diversification level	
	1965	1969
1964/66	A_{11}	A_{12}
1970/72	A_{21}	A_{22}

Thus comparison between A_{11} and A_{12} and between A_{21} and A_{22} shows the effects of the growth in the number of M-form firms alone, after eliminating the effect of diversification via merger (including the incidental diversification involved in any type of merger as well as diversifying merger *per se*), holding the group composition constant. Similarly the comparisons A_{21} with A_{11} and A_{22} with A_{12} show what the effects of the growing number of M-form firms would have been had there been no diversification via merger over the period. And the comparison A_{22} with A_{11} shows the combined effect of both developments. For the 'all firms' group we have, of course, only two matrices, based on the 1965 and 1969 diversification levels.

The matrices are too large to report in full and are in any case not readily digested by inspection. Tables 11.4 and 11.5 therefore summarise the ten relevant matrices for the three groups of firms, showing the number of elements in each

Table 11.5 *Network of linked activities: (M + M′)-form firms*

Composition of group	Diversification level			
	1965		1969	
1964/66	0	2,034	0	1,405
	1	159	1	609
	2	18	3	27
			4	9
			5	3
			6	1
	0	1,872	0	1,237
	1	243	1	612
	2	58	2	203
1970/72	3	15	3	72
	4	15	4	34
	5	4	5	25
	6–7	4	6–10	26
			11–15	2

matrix in which a pair of industries is linked by one firm, by two firms and so on. Since the matrices are symmetric, and since the leading diagonal shows just the total number of firms in each industry, the total number of relevant elements in each matrix is $\frac{1}{2}n\,(n-1)$ where $n = 67$: i.e. 2,211.

The evidence from Tables 11. 4 and 11.5 is very clear. Even when the multidivisional group includes M′-forms and the updated industry codes are used, over half the off-diagonal elements in the relevant diversification matrix are empty, and a further 30% of the links between pairs of industries depend on only one or two firms. Thus less than 10% of inter-industry links were joined by three or more M-form firms. Exclusion of the M′ firms and, more especially, using the original 1965 industry codes produces an even more extreme result. Of course, the original codes may have been incomplete and we know that *de novo* diversification after 1965 has not been taken into account. Furthermore, the list of known multidivisional firms must also be regarded as non-comprehensive. While these omissions mean that the industry coverage of M-form firms is systematically under-estimated it is unlikely that elimination of this bias would drastically alter the general result. Some confirmation of this is obtained when all firms are considered, the majority of which are, as previously stated, probably U-form. Thus, even when all firms are included, over 30% of the elements in the diversification matrix are zeros, and under 40% of pairs of industries are linked by 3 or more firms of any organisational type.

11.4 Empirics of the merger-as-search hypothesis

The hypothesis

The theoretical possibility that mergers, and especially diversifying mergers, may be undertaken as a form of search for new investment opportunities has been demonstrated elsewhere (Cable (1977)). The reasoning and the general circumstances in which such mergers are likely to occur are briefly as follows.

In the face of product and industrial life cycles, the need for companies to diversify and so disassociate their corporate life cycles from those of existing activities is obvious. Once it is recognised that knowledge of alternative production possibilities among existing firms is incomplete, 'search' – acquiring the information capital required to undertake 'new' activities – is evidently an essential feature of the diversification process. The fact that diversification occurs sometimes, but not always, by merger, may therefore be explained by the costs and attractiveness of merger as a search mode, relative to other modes.

Merger ranks as a mode of search since, among other things, it involves the acquisition of information embodied in the acquired firm. It differs from other modes in that (a) the 'information set' describing the new activity is acquired as a complete entity rather than in piecemeal fashion and (b) there is a substantial fixed cost element in merger search, due to the transactions costs of merger. Because of this it can be shown that merger search is likely to dominate alternatives on efficiency grounds beyond some critical level of disparateness of the new and existing activities and/or size of the acquired information set.

Thus the typical situation for merger search is where the acquiring firm faces declining investment opportunities and its search carries it relatively far from existing activities, where the quantity of information to be acquired is large. However, for merger search to be viable, it is also necessary that the information transferred via the merger is worth more to the acquiring than to the acquired firm; otherwise the acquisition price must exceed the buyer's benefit. Such differential valuations of the same information (on investment opportunities) are, it is argued, possible if there are opportunities known to the (relatively favourably placed) acquired firm which do not enter its optimal investment programme, or, if, because of differences in existing knowledge and opportunities, further (i.e. post-merger) search *based on the acquired firm's existing knowledge* would not shift its own efficient investment frontier, but would have this effect for the acquiring firm.

Some empirical evidence

Since firms resorting to merger in their search for investment opportunities will be experiencing difficulties in finding satisfactory projects, and since the better projects are most probably to be found where existing profitability is high, we should observe less profitable firms acquiring relatively higher profit firms. For this to be possible the acquiring firm will generally need to be relatively large. However, since the firm's internal information system can be overwhelmed by size and diversity beyond some point, *very* small acquisitions may not be worth while because the opportunity costs of management time are too great to warrant application to very small, albeit promising activities. Hence we might expect that acquisitions have to reach some threshold size, which is presumably larger for large firms.

Existing evidence offers some support for these propositions. In particular, Weston and Mansinghka (1971) found that companies heavily involved in the conglomerate merger wave of the 1960s earned lower returns on capital than a random sample of industrials prior to the merger wave, and roughly the same returns after it. Analysing the characteristics of some 700 acquired firms over the period 1948–68, Boyle (1970) found that the acquired firms in conglomerate mergers had higher levels and growths of profits than in horizontal and vertical cases, and characterised the conglomerate merger process as the acquisition of strong and financially viable firms by larger corporations. Unfortunately for the present purpose, the relative profitability of the acquirers was not reported. On the other hand, Conn (1976) has recently reported no significant difference in the mean profitability of acquired and acquiring firms involved in 36 pure conglomerate mergers in the period 1960–69.

Data for the sample of 37 diversifying mergers described earlier, shows that in 14 cases (37.8%) the acquired firms earned significantly higher profit rates in the five years preceding the merger than the firms which acquired them, and that overall the acquired firms were on average 10.8% more profitable. In the subset of 15 unambiguously diversifying cases where the parties had no industry in common, 53.3% of the acquired firms were earning more than their acquirers.

The UK data also show a strong tendency for the acquired firms to be smaller, with only 7 exceptions overall of which 2 were in the sub-sample. In this sub-sample the acquired firms were on average only 8.1% as large (in terms of assets) as the acquirers. To test for a possible threshold size for acquisition the 37 cases were divided into six classes according to the size of the acquiring firm, containing roughly equal numbers. The minimum acquisition size was then found for each. As a percentage of the class mean, the smallest acquisition fell very sharply, from nearly 50% in the smallest size class, but at an exponentially decreasing rate, apparently approaching an asymptote of between 1 and 2%. While it is clearly hazardous to draw firm conclusions, this asymptote value might be regarded as a reasonable minimum for the marginal division of a conglomerate bearing in mind prospects for its future growth, and that the average division size could be much larger.

The merger-as-search hypothesis is also consistent with a number of other observed or discoverable aspects of diversification and mergers. First, since the motive is the acquisition of information which is embodied in the acquired firm's personnel and other resources, it is to be expected that the existing management of the acquired firm will be retained, and the tendency for acquired firms to be left to operate as autonomous divisions, often under the existing management, has been widely noted (e.g. Mueller (1969)). Secondly, the theory links the firm's search process closely to its investment planning, so that the frequency of mergers prompted by search should vary directly with the level of pressure to invest in the economy. Again, the correlation between merger intensity and the level of business activity seems firmly established (e.g. Nelson (1959), Kuehn (1975)). Thirdly, the merger search hypothesis implies that diversification will be purposeful rather than random, i.e. will display some underlying logic in terms of production technology, marketing, R & D and so on. And this has been noted in the observed pattern of diversification and diversifying merger (Reid (1968), Narver (1969), Gorecki (1975)). Fourthly, the search cost function on which the hypothesis hinges is such that the first investment opportunities to be considered will be those closed to existing activities. By definition, both horizontal and vertical mergers involve the firm more deeply in its existing activities or in a technically related area, i.e. in 'close' activities involving total or substantial overlap of the relevant information sets. Thus we should not find diversifying mergers being initiated by firms operating in unconcentrated markets, or where there are few forward and backward linkages, *cet par.* Similarly, reinvestment in existing activities is by definition the closest possible opportunity available, so that firms initiating the sort of merger under consideration should tend not to be operating in rapidly growing industries. These expectations are wholly consistent with the evidence of Gort (1962, 1969).

Two further, more specific predictions can be spelled out from the search hypothesis. One is that, since merger search dominates other search modes, if at all, only beyond some critical level of disparateness, diversification by merger rather than *de novo* expansion should increase with some (proxy) measure of disparateness. A direct test was attempted using data on product acquisitions and additions among pairs of industries and the product structure of manufacturing firms by industry as reproduced in Wood (1971). The dependent variable (Y) was simply the ratio of product acquisitions to total product additions for any given pair of industries, i.e. the proportion of diversification activity from industry i to industry j in which merger was involved. The independent variable (X) was defined as $(1 - p)$ where p is an estimate of the proportion of firms active in industry i who were also active in j.[5] X was interpreted as a proxy for the disparateness of

5 The derivation was as follows. The original matrix gave the number of firms in each industry (n), and the number of products in the basic industry (p_0) and in each other industry (p_i, $i = 1, 2, \ldots, n$). Given that the number of firms active in the basic industry was by definition n, the probable number of *firms* active in each other industry was estimated as $n(p_i/p_0)$.

the industries, on the grounds that, insofar as firms' product structures evolve in a rational, cost-minimising way, the disparateness of the activities involved will be revealed in a diversification matrix which shows the proportion of firms that have actually bridged the distance from a given industry to some other. A semi-logarithmic equation yielded a highly significant relationship of expected sign:

$$\log Y = -0.49 + 0.66\,X \quad R^2 = 0.27$$
$$(t = 3.71) \quad F = 13.79$$

However, this result should be regarded as preliminary, in view of data limitations.

The second prediction is that M-form firms should be the first to initiate diversifying mergers *cet par.* Whereas the multidivisional can readily absorb a newly acquired unit, the U-form must either reorganise along M-form lines or accomplish the more difficult task of integrating the new firm into the existing, functionally arranged hierarchy. The consequently lower transactions cost for the multidivisional implies a downward shift in the merger search-cost function and dominance of merger search over other modes at a lower level of disparateness and/or size of the acquired information set. The organisational form data for merging firms in Table 11.3 is therefore of relevance to the merger search hypothesis. Since it is the ability of the firm to add extra quasi-autonomous units which is presently at issue, a case may be made employing a broad definition of M-form, including M′ and $\overline{\text{M}}$. Also, purely from an ease of expansion standpoint, the H-firm may share the M-form's advantages to some degree. On this basis the predominance of the appropriate organisational form in the sample is overwhelming. In any event, the fact that there was only one U-form firm is striking.

The bulk of the existing evidence not so far considered consists of studies of conglomerate merger performance, many utilising the capital-asset-pricing model. These have mostly produced neutral or negative findings (Mueller (1977)). Of itself this neither contradicts nor supports the merger search hypothesis. A successful search-motivated merger will by definition improve the profitability of the acquiring firm, but if initiated against a background of internally perceived, diminishing profit expectations, due to lack of investment openings, the improvement can be consistent either with a rise or decline in externally observed earnings, or with unchanged financial results. At the same time, the merger results in the realisation of a hidden asset in the acquired firm: information on existing and potential investment opportunities which does not improve its own prospects but is of value to the acquiring firm. As a number of merger studies have shown, for the acquiring firm the cumulative average residual (between *ex post* security returns and the estimated equilibrium returns predicted from the capital-asset-pricing model) is not greatly affected by merger, whereas for the acquired firm the residual rises sharply 9–12 months before the merger, when the news leaks out (Halpern (1973), Mandelker (1974), Ellert (1976)). While there are many possible explanations, this could reflect realisation of a unique, informational resource held by the acquired firm at the time of the merger.

11.5 Summary and conclusions

This chapter has considered certain aspects of diversifying merger, focussing on questions which are either relatively new or under-researched in the UK. This approach enables at least tentative conclusions to be reached as to whether the existing range of considerations in diversifying mergers (e.g. as enumerated by Gribben (1976)) should be extended or curtailed.

So far as risk pooling is concerned, existing studies for the UK were found to be few and somewhat inconclusive. A simulation analysis of 37 diversifying mergers which took place between 1965 and 1970, suggested very little reduction in risk from the viewpoint of the acquiring firms. On the whole it seems unlikely that risk pooling is either a major motivation or effect of diversifying merger.

In connection with the hierarchy vs. market issue in the transfer of capital context, it was found that the majority of the largest UK companies, responsible for the bulk of corporate investment, and the overwhelming majority of acquiring firms in diversifying merger cases have adopted the appropriate (multidivisional) form of internal organisation required by Williamson's arguments. However, systematic evidence confirming the realisation of the alleged advantages of such firms in the capital allocation process has yet to be put forward, and the network of inter-industry linkages provided by M-form firms as a group was found to be highly incomplete. In this situation, it could be argued that diversifying mergers which extend the existing network of linkages are urgently needed. However, further empirical evidence on the superiority of the hierarchical capital transfer over the external capital market is required before a defence of diversifying mergers on this ground is warranted.

While more detailed empirical evidence is necessary before firm conclusions can be drawn, it is possible that at least some of the diversifying mergers that occurred in the UK in the late 1960s may be interpreted as corporate search for more profitable investment opportunities. If so, two positive welfare effects may be anticipated, connected with the transfer of capital that is involved in such mergers. Thus, while the same reallocations could eventually come about via the external markets, merger can foreshorten the transfer process. According to the merger search hypothesis, search leading to merger follows recognition of declining investment opportunities in the initiating firm. Because of the asymmetric information held by firms and by the market, correction via the external market would take place only after the dwindling investment opportunities had fed through into reported profits. In view of the typical life-span of investment projects, and the relatively small impact of a deteriorating future on any one year's returns, this lag could be long. Hence, by removing the lag, search motivated mergers can contribute to the dynamic flexibility of the system. Secondly, in connection with the Williamson hypothesis, such mergers would mitigate the tendency towards only locally optimal reallocations of capital within the existing boundaries of conglomerate firms, rather than optimal transfers across the whole economy. Moreover, to the extent that conglomerates are formed by mergers of this type, their boundaries will not be irrationally drawn from a capital transfer point of view.

On the other hand, the typical circumstances envisaged for mergers motivated by search involve the demise of viable firms as separate, independent entities. The merger search hypothesis shows that information gain alone can be a sufficient motive for merger. Thus it cannot be relied upon that choice of external growth as a means of diversification is confined to circumstances in which there also exist potential size economies or other synergistic gains, or the acquired firm is failing (and hence its assets are undervalued by the market), or its growth is blocked by a discontinuity in the supply of finance etc. In the absence of such circumstances all that happens is that the life cycle of one firm – typically already large and well established – is extended at the expense of another – typically younger and smaller. The short-run effect is an increase in overall concentration, with attendant, incremental growth in the problem of maintaining the balance of economic and political power in society, against which must be set only the possible gain in the efficiency of capital transfer previously discussed. Moreover, in the longer term the balance of social gain and loss is more adverse in that, as Boyle (1970) has noted, it is the relatively young, profitable, small but growing concerns being acquired that might have risen to challenge the positions of large entrenched corporations which acquire them. Thus, insofar as it shows that the acquired firms in diversifying merger cases can be successful concerns, under no threat to their continued life and growth other than from takeover, the merger search theory lends support to the view that conglomerate mergers can impair the long-run corporate competitive process.

References

Boyle, S. E. (1970), 'Pre-Merger Growth and Profit Characteristics of Large Conglomerate Mergers in the United States 1948–68', *St John's Law Review*, Special Edition **44**, 152–70.

Cable, J. R. (1977), 'A Search Theory of Diversifying Mergers', *Recherches Economique de Louvain*, **43**(3) (Sept.), 225–42.

Channon, D. F. (1973), *The Strategy and Structure of British Enterprise*, Harvard University Press.

Conn, R. L. (1976), 'The Failing Firm/Industry Doctrines in Conglomerate Mergers', *Journal of Industrial Economics*, **24**, 181–7.

Dewey, D. (1961), 'Mergers and Cartels: Some Reservations about Policy', *The American Economic Review*, **61**, 255–62.

Econtel Research (1968), *Giants in British Industry,* Factual Series No. 4, London.
– (1969), *Conglomerates,* British Industry Series, London, 1969.
Ellert, J. F. (1976), 'Mergers, Antitrust Law Enforcement and Stockholder Returns', *Journal of Finance,* **31**, 2.
Gorecki, P. K. (1975), 'An Inter-Industry Analysis of Diversification in the UK Manufacturing Sector', *Journal of Industrial Economics,* **24**, 131–46.
Gort, M. (1962), *Diversification and Integration in American Industry,* Princeton.
– (1969), 'An Economic Disturbance Theory of Mergers', *Quarterly Journal of Economics.* 624–42.
Gribbin, J. D. (1976), 'The Conglomerate Merger', *Applied Economics,* **8**, 19–35.
Halpern, P. J. (1973), 'Empirical Estimates of the Amount and Distribution of Gains to Companies in Mergers', *Journal of Business,* 554–75.
Hannah, L. (1974), 'Mergers in British Manufacturing Industry 1880–1918', *Oxford Economic Papers,* **26**.
Kuehn, D. A. (1975), *Takeovers and the Theory of the Firm,* Macmillan.
Kumps, A. M. (1975), 'Conglomerate Mergers: The Case of Great Britain', Document de Travail CRIDE No. 751.
Mandelker, F. (1974), 'Risk and Return: The Case of Merging Firms', *Journal of Financial Economics,* **1**, 303–35.
Manne, H. F. (1965), 'Mergers and the Market for Corporate Control', *Journal of Political Economy,* **73**, (1), 110–20.
Mueller, D. C. (1969), 'A Theory of Conglomerate Merger', *Quarterly Journal of Economics,* 643–59.
– (1977), 'The Effects of Conglomerate Mergers: A Survey of the Empirical Evidence', IIM Berlin (mimeo).
Narver, J. C. (1969), *Conglomerate Mergers and Market Competition,* University of California Press.
Nelson, R. L. (1959), *Merger Movements in American Industry, 1865–1956,* Princeton.
Reid, S. R. (1968), *Mergers, Managers and the Economy,* New York, McGraw-Hill.
Steer, P. S. (1973), 'An Investigation into the Managerial Organisation of Firms' (mimeo).
Steer, P. S., and Cable, J. R. (1978), 'Internal Organisation and Profit: An Empirical Analysis of Large UK Companies', *Journal of Industrial Economics.*
Utton, M. A. (1969), 'Diversification, Mergers and Profit Stability', *Business Ratios,* 24–8.
– (1977), 'Large Firm Diversification in British Manufacturing Industry', *Economic Journal,* **87**, 96–113.
Weston, J. F. and Mansinghka (1971), 'Tests of the Efficiency Performance of Conglomerate Firms', *Journal of Finance,* **26**, 919–36.
Williamson, O. E. (1970), *Corporate Control and Business Behaviour,* Prentice Hall, N. J.
– (1975), *Markets and Hierarchies, Analysis and Antitrust Implications,* The Free Press, N.Y.
Wood, A. (1971), 'Diversification, Merger and Research Expenditures: A Review of Empirical Studies' in R. Marris and A. Wood (eds.), *The Corporate Economy,* Harvard University Press.

12

Economic performance and market structure

12.1 **Introduction**

This chapter both surveys and adds to empirical evidence on the link between market structure and economic performance and thus provides supplementary evidence on the impact of merger given that merger has been an important instrument in the modification of market structure in the UK (see Chapter 1). The second section is concerned with surveying and evaluating previous estimates of the relationship between concentration, advertising and price–cost margins (emphasising those for the United Kingdom). The third section summarises previous empirical work on the relationship between market structure and technical progress and briefly reports on new estimates using UK data. The fourth section reviews existing work on the impact of diversification on profitability and concentration and provides new estimates of these relationships.

12.2 **Concentration, advertising and price–cost margins**

The impact of mergers on economic performance can be established indirectly by estimating the relationship between market structure and economic performance given that merger activity has contributed importantly to the evolution of market structure within the United Kingdom (see Chapter 1). The most obvious element of industry structure which is determined by merger is the distribution of market shares, but other elements of structure follow from changes in market behaviour induced by merger. By creating market power merger can provide the necessary preconditions for advertising and, as we have seen in Chapter 2, this can have direct welfare implications. We will therefore be interested in knowing the impact of advertising on the degree of monopoly (the mark-up on marginal cost) via its effect on consumer behaviour. Advertising may also form part of 'excess capacity' which serves to maintain the degree of monopoly in the long-term. Our review of previous results will, in the case of price–cost margins, focus mainly on estimates for the UK. The voluminous literature dealing with the US has been adequately summarised in recent surveys by Weiss (1971, 1974).

Survey of empirical results

Empirical results on the concentration/economic performance nexus go back to Bain's 1951 article. There he related the rate of return on capital to the level of concentration in US manufacturing industry. The method of analysis was a simple cross-classification of the data where high concentration appeared to be associated with high profit rates. There followed much work in this area but the next major landmark was again provided by Bain in his introduction of a composite measure of the height of entry barriers into the analysis (Bain (1956)). Cross-classification of the data revealed high barriers to be associated with high profit rates. Again this stimulated much related work which is summarised in Weiss (1971). The next major innovation was by Comanor and Wilson who split up the composite barrier variable into its separate parts and estimated a continuous relationship between the rate of return on capital and the various components of market structure (Comanor and Wilson (1967)). Their results purported to demonstrate the importance of advertising and question the role of concentration. Subsequent research in the US tended to emphasise inter-firm analysis, partly because of the problem of defining meaningful industry level variables. We will not pursue the details of these studies except to say that Weiss in his two surveys of the literature in 1971 and 1974 has concluded that there are grounds for believing that a significant, but not very strong, positive relationship exists between profitability and concentration. The US evidence also suggests a significant relationship between advertising and profitability. The problems of interpreting these results are discussed below, but first we turn to the recent and rather scanty evidence for the UK.

Phillips (1972), Shepherd (1972), Holterman (1973), Khalilzadeh-Shiraz (1974), Caves (1975) and Hart and Morgan (1977) all follow, more or less, the standard Comanor and Wilson formulation of the inter-industry relationship with varied results. Only Phillips and Shepherd find concentration to have a significant effect in the presence of an array of barrier variables.[1] In contrast the advertising variable appears to be generally significant but it should be pointed out that the definition of the dependent variable in all cases includes advertising within it so that this result should be treated with some caution.[2] The same point applies to almost all the variables in the different studies which appeared to be significant. They are typically components of the dependent variable because of the way that variable has had to be defined when using Census of Production Data. Dutton (1976) follows the same general approach but adds a variety of interesting new variables in an attempt to capture the impact of government policy and international competition. She finds that the joint impact of concentration and advertising is positive and significant but concentration entered separately is insignificant.

1 However Hart and Morgan do find that the number of enterprises variable does retain its significance in the more general formulation.

2 The dependent variable in all cases has value added minus the wage bill as numerator.

Obviously the UK studies reported above do not offer strong support for a link between concentration and economic performance. However, they do raise fundamental questions concerning the specification of the relationships and the appropriateness of inter-industry, cross-section analysis of this type (Cowling (1976)). These issues will be briefly analysed below but a few recent studies have attempted to meet some of the theoretical points raised. Cowling et al. (1975) estimated a relationship of the Comanor and Wilson type but restricted the analysis to the UK food industry using firm-level observations. Both concentration and advertising appeared as significant variables. Nickell and Metcalf (1975) restricted their sample of observations in a somewhat similar fashion by taking a variety of products sold by supermarkets and approximated the price–cost mark-up by the difference between the price of nationally advertised brands and the price of the own-label brand. Again both concentration and advertising appeared significant. Cowling and Waterson (1976) focussed on the impact of changes in concentration over time and found a significant and positive effect in a broad industry cross-section. Hart and Morgan (1977) using a sample of 'comparable industries' failed to reproduce these significant results using the same specification, but it is necessary to point out that their sample included two industries, Bread and Brewing, where the growth in concentration was much higher than that of any other industry, and which therefore dominated the relationship, but where concentration change, as measured at national level, has a very limited meaning. This must put a serious question-mark against their results.

Specification problems in existing empirical work

Errors of omission[3] Probably the most serious and basic deficiency in much of the existing work is the omission of the price elasticity of demand from inter-industry studies. Theoretical analysis suggests no systematic relation between measures of concentration and performance where elasticities vary widely so that it is not surprising that we find some results with non-significant or only marginally significant relationships, or poor explanatory power (see the survey by Weiss (1971) and recent comments by Brozen (1973) and Phillips (1972)). Other parameters of consumer behaviour, such as the determinants of responsiveness to advertising messages, have also generally been omitted. The problem of these omitted variables, which are generally not easily measurable, may be to some extent circumvented by switching the focus to changes in industry performance. The recent work by Cowling and Waterson (1976) and Waterson (1976) has followed this course and reports significant, positive relationships between changes in concentration and changes in price–cost margins.

Buyer concentration is another variable, theoretically required but generally

3 This section does not attempt to cover the many social and technical factors which may help to explain the degree of collusion within a particular industry.

omitted, which it is possible to measure at reasonable cost. Its omission is likely to bias down the coefficient on seller concentration.

Errors of commission In this category it is possible to identify three areas where errors have arisen: (1) in the specification of the dependent variable, (2) in the specification of seller concentration, and (3) in the specification of the advertising variable. In the case of the dependent variable analysts generally have followed what Bain practised rather than what he preached (Bain (1951)): they have tended to use rate of return on assets or equity (Π/K) rather than the ratio of profits to sales (Π/R). In the constant cost case the ratio of profits to sales is equivalent to $(p - mc)/p$, the performance variable which oligopoly theory suggests is systematically related to market structure. The use of some measure of Π/K would require us to introduce variables explaining imperfections of the capital market, which need not be directly related with product market power, and would also justify the use of a capital–output ratio variable on the right-hand side of the equation. Insofar as Π/K is closely related to Π/R, which often appears to be the case, then such a misspecification need not be an important source of error. Whether Π/R is a good approximation to $(p - mc)/p$ is of course a real problem.[4] If we assume that the deviation of average cost from marginal cost is related to capacity utilisation, then including variables intended to capture this would appear relevant.

Seller concentration has usually been measured as the ratio of the output of the top n firms to industry output. Oligopoly theories suggest the relevance of the Herfindahl measure but this has been little used (see Weiss (1971)). Where it has been used it has appeared to perform rather better than the concentration ratio (see Stigler (1964), Cowling and Waterson (1976)), but of course the data required to compute the Herfindahl is not readily available. However, its computation by government statistical agencies would not only provide analysts with a theoretically more acceptable measure of concentration, but would also reduce problems of disclosure at the same time.

The advertising variable (A/R) used in previous studies would appear inappropriate (see Cowling et al. (1975)). Nevertheless, this variable has been a popular specification and seems to have helped in the explanation of profit rates or price–cost margins. How can this be explained? Firstly, it may be due to a fortunate sampling of industries or firms. Comanor and Wilson's significant coefficient in weighted regression is conditional on the exclusion of the automobile industry,[5] and Vernon and Nourse (1973) restrict their sample to firms in the top

4 The measure used by Nickell and Metcalf (1978) can be seen as one possible answer to this problem.

5 An industry which happened to have a high profit-rate and the lowest advertising–sales ratio – and apparently the high profit rate was not explicable in terms of the other variables included in the model

hundred by size which also have high advertising–sales ratios. Alternatively these results could be picking up an appropriations relationship rather than a barriers relationship.[6] When the advertising variable is correctly specified and the analysis is restricted to a fairly homogeneous sector, advertising appears as both a significant barrier to entry and a significant component of the market power of a specific firm (Cowling et al. (1975)).

Policy implications

There has recently been much doubt expressed about both the significance of the relationship between concentration and profitability and also, if the relationship is significant, about its meaning. On the first point the pendulum seems to have swung in favour of the importance of advertising and against the importance of concentration, see for example Comanor and Wilson (1967) and Khalilzadeh-Shiraz (1974). However, since the specification problems raised by these studies are serious the bases for this reassessment seem inadequate.[7] With a more satisfactory specification concentration appears significant (Cowling and Waterson (1976) and Waterson (1976)). We should also note that the general omission of buyer concentration will tend to bias down the measured effect of seller concentration.

If we accept that a relationship exists then the other arguments turn on the survival of the fittest (Demsetz (1973)) or the luckiest (Mancke (1974)). Firms get to positions of power because they are most efficient or by chance, and not by the deliberate acquisition of monopoly power. Whilst accepting that these are possible explanations they are not exclusive so we must turn to the evidence. We would expect efficiency to be more closely related to size than to concentration, whereas the reverse would be true of market power. However, the accumulated evidence for Europe suggests at least that biggest is not best (Samuels and Smyth (1968), Jacquemin and Phlips (1974)). For the US the position is a little more cloudy (Hall and Weiss (1967), Soloman (1974), Shepherd (1972) Gale (1972)). Hall and Weiss observe a positive and significant firm size effect, but it may be picking up market power effects; Shepherd finds a negative relationship, while Soloman and Gale both observe a significant and positive effect of market share.

In the case of Europe the implications of current structure–performance research seem umambiguous. Since size does not appear to contribute to efficiency, and concentration can be shown to have a significant impact on price–cost margins, static efficiency will fall with increased concentration. These results would seem in line with our case studies reported earlier.

6 There are clear theoretical underpinnings for such a finding, see Cowling et al. (1975).

7 This is not to imply that advertising is unimportant, see Cowling et al. (1975).

12.3 Concentration and technical progress

One of the more persistent propositions in economics is that relating technical progressiveness to market structure, its origins generally being attributed to Schumpeter (1942). As a proposition it is also one that has been subjected to extensive empirical investigation. Fortunately in the last few years this mass of literature has been itself studied and surveyed a number of times. Thus we have, for example, papers by Kennedy & Thirlwall (1972), and Kamien and Schwartz (1975) amongst others. The existence of these surveys enables us to avoid performing anything approaching an extensive survey of the field. In fact we will mainly refer back to these surveys. It seems beneficial to keep within the invention–innovation–diffusion framework of Schumpeter given our present purposes, although clarification must then be our first task. In what follows we will consider the typical technological advance to be one in which a new product is launched by one industry for sale to another industry or to the consumer. Given the subset of potential users of the new product we consider innovation to concern the question of what characteristics of the product determine an early taking up of the product by the first user and what characteristics of the first user distinguish him from other potential users. The diffusion problem concerns what characteristics of the product and the users determine the speed with which the innovation is spread across all its potential users. Although this gives a full picture of the users' technological change process we are left with the question of determination of the rate of new product launches. This is essentially the invention aspect of technical change. We interpret invention widely, as the generation of new ideas, and expenditure on R & D in so doing, as well as spending R & D funds on developing the idea to a marketable product.

In the present case we will start with the innovation aspect of technological change, i.e. the analysis of first users. The classic reference here is the work of Mansfield (1968) on the extent to which the four largest firms in the US iron and steel, petroleum, refining and bituminous coal industries account for a larger proportion of innovations carried out than their share of the market. On this crude test, coal and petroleum support the Schumpeterian view but steel does not. Although there are some results as a by-product of diffusion studies e.g. Griliches (1957) relating innovation date to profitability, our knowledge of this aspect of technological change has advanced little beyond Mansfield's study. For a detailed coverage one may look at Johnson (1975).

Although innovation is a necessary prerequisite it is the diffusion process that will really determine the effect of new technologies on the economy. Here the results are much thicker on the ground, although as Kennedy and Thirlwall point out (p. 60) British studies are not as common as US studies. The major result in all such studies is the existence of an S-shaped diffusion curve relating the % of firms using the new technology to time. Again Mansfield's work sits at the centre of the empirical evidence, relating diffusion to expected return and liquidity (positively) and the size of investment required (negatively). He also finds faster acceptance by large firms (with a positive second derivative). This latter conclusion is much disputed, as is any positive relation to the level of concentration. Recent work on diffusion in the UK, Ray (1969), Nabseth and Ray (1974), is concerned more with international comparisons and gives weak support for a negative relationship between early innovation and the speed of diffusion. Using the data arising from these two NIESR studies supplemented from other sources, Davies (1979) has made some advance on the questions of the effects of firm size and market structure. He views Mansfield's approach based on the logistic diffusion curve as essentially in error. His reasoning is that the logistic curve arises from the interaction of a falling number of potential adopters and an increasing probability of adoption by these non-adopters as the number of adopters increases, but the probability of adoption should be independent of firm size and not change in response to profitability changes over time. Davies argues that these two conditions cannot be met, and proceeds to build a model generating a log-normal diffusion curve. His model has three parts:

(a) The firm will adopt an innovation if its rate of return $r \geqq \bar{r}$ some target rate of return.
(b) Firm size is log-normally distributed.
(c) Either r will rise or $\bar{r}$ will fall with firm size and time.

Thus as time proceeds r rises (or $\bar{r}$ falls) and more firms will adopt the innovation, the pattern of adoption being log-normal because of the distribution of firm size. Similarly as r is larger (or $\bar{r}$ smaller) with larger firms, large firms will adopt early and small firms late. Davies' model fits the diffusion pattern of what he labels type A innovations – new processes which are capital intensive, exhibit scale economies and show a falling price over time. The diffusion of type B innovations which are simple, cheap, and fixed price is best represented by the logistic model. Given Davies' objection to the logistic, this is as it should be. He fails to isolate any clear cut relationship with market structure, finding that a greater variance of the log of firm size stimulated diffusion but so does a smaller number of firms. In essence therefore his model relates adoption to profitability, which is a major point in the diffusion literature, and then profitability to firm size and time. It should be noted however that his theory of technique choice arises from behavioural and not maximising or neoclassical postulates in common with some of the other recent literature in this field, Stoneman (1976), Nelson and Winter (1974).

Finally we turn to the invention and R & D stage. It is generally accepted that most R & D is spent on development rather than basic research which probably explains the result of studies on the sources of invention (e.g. Jewkes, Sawers and Stillerman (1959). This literature essentially places invention as external to large firms (either in the hands of individuals or universities) but the development of inventions within firms. Freeman (1976) stresses the invention role of large firms more strongly than some others, but eventually the literature reduces to a discussion of the relationship between R & D, firm size, and market structure. Again there is a dearth of research on the UK, but with reference mainly to the US, Kamien and Schwartz summarise the empirical results as:

(a) R & D activity increases more than proportionately with firm size only up to a point and then levels off or declines.

(b) There seems little support for a linear relationship between R & D and market structure, but a nonlinear one with maximum rivalry in oligopolistic market structures yielding high R & D (i.e. an inverted U relationship between R & D intensity and market structure) may be sustainable.

(c) Diversification and R & D are not strongly linked.

As a field of research this area is still very active and attention has recently been concentrated more on the theoretical as opposed to empirical relationships. The first area of concentration is attributed to Fisher and Temin (1973) where they emphasise that high R & D inputs do not mean (necessarily) faster technological progressiveness, they may mean less efficient research. Holding this in mind however the other results centre around the theoretical proposition of Arrow (1962) that the return to the inventor is greatest when the invention is used in a competitive market, and thus the stimulus to R & D is greatest under competition. The result concerns the return to the invention of a process innovation. Needham (1975) looks at the theory behind the R & D/market structure relationship with product innovation and suggests the opposite result. Needham's results are derived from Dorfman and Steiner (1954) type relationships and relate to the activities of the firm. We have attempted to supplement the empirical evidence for the UK by looking at R & D and market structure across industries building and testing a model on these lines. Details of the model and estimation procedure are reported in Leech and Stoneman (1976). The results provide little evidence of a relationship between R & D and market concentration, as measured by the Herfindahl index. This latest result for the UK is in line with much of the previous work which gives little support for a systematic link between market structure and technical progress.

12.4 The effects of diversification on market structure and monopoly power*

This section will be concerned with the effects of diversification on competition as measured by profitability (12.4.1) and changes in concentration (12.4.2). The studies analysed and the empirical results reported are based on the traditional structure performance method in which measures of performance are 'explained' by a set of structural variables through ordinary least squares

*This section has been written by Michael Kelly.

regression analysis. The literature dealing with the impact of diversification on financial variables, such as stock market valuations is not discussed.

Since all of the diversification data considered in this section include growth by internal expansion as well as by merger, a brief analysis of the relative importance of these two methods of diversifying is necessary. The theory that diversification will tend to take place through internal growth is based on considerations of efficiency. A firm will often find itself with excess capacity in one of its main functions (technological, managerial, productive, marketing) (Narver 1967). Consequently, it will diversify through internal growth in order to use its resources more efficiently. In addition, it will diversify into areas which complement its present activities. Therefore, complementary diversification is likely to take place through internal growth. On the other hand, conglomerate diversification is more likely to take place through merger. Efficiency considerations do not arise and acquisition enables the firm to acquire quickly the skills and experience needed in the new industry. An alternative theory emphasises monopoly power considerations as the major determinant of the method of diversification. Internal growth will increase the number of firms in the new industry and generally increase the level of competition, whereas a merger will have no direct effect on competition. *Ceteris paribus*, the firm will prefer to diversify by merger.

Evidence on this matter is rather limited. Hart et al. (1973) find that although mergers are becoming a more common method of growth, they are as yet confined mainly to horizontal mergers. This suggests that diversified growth takes place mainly through internal expansion. However, the OFT sample[8] of consummated, conglomerate mergers presents a different situation. Of 37 conglomerate mergers in manufacturing, 22 represent product extension or complementary diversification and 15 conglomerate diversification. If efficiency considerations were the primary motive for diversifying, we would expect to find that most diversified mergers were of the conglomerate type.

12.4.1 The effects of diversification on profitability

The theory most commonly used to support a positive relation between diversification and profitability is the cross-subsidisation argument, which appears to have been first applied systematically to diversified firms by Edwards (1955). Because diversified firms can readily transfer resources across the markets in which they operate, they can carry out practices such as predatory pricing, i.e. pricing below cost in order to drive out competitors. The division carrying out this policy does not jeopardise its own survival, because it can rely on funds from the other divisions of the company. After driving out the competing firms, the predator will be in a position to set monopoly prices which will more than cover the costs of the operation. In addition, similar practices can be used

8 Discussed in Chapter 11.

in non-price competition, such as R & D, advertising, and model changes, where, it is argued, the advantages goes to the firm with the greatest financial resources, not the greatest degree of efficiency (Edwards (1955), Scherer (1970)).

This theory has been used in several empirical studies, Imel and Helmberger (1971), Kelly (1969), Miller (1969), Rhoades (1973) as the basis of their attempt to establish a significant, positive relation between diversification and profitability. It is usually supplemented by the argument that diversified firms may be able to use some of their resources more efficiently than specialised firms and therefore be more profitable (Kelly (1969)). For example, they may be able to maintain a higher level of capacity utilisation if the demand for their products is subject to seasonable fluctuations. With the exception of Rhoades, diversification has been a minor feature of these studies; consequently, the cross-subsidisation theory has received little critical development. A selection of the results is presented in Table 12.1.[9] In all cases, the diversification index used is $Dv(1) = R_s/(R_p + R_s)$, where R_p is sales of primary products of the firm (or industry) and R_s is sales of secondary products. For convenience, the signs of the diversification variables are summarised in Table 12.2.

The results appear to conflict, positive results being obtained at the industry level and negative ones at the firm level. There are some theories which may explain this difference; these will be considered later. But it is necessary first of all to analyse the weaknesses of the theory used and the resulting specification of the empirical model.

The negative results have been interpreted to indicate that very profitable firms lack the incentive to diversify. They prefer to re-invest their retained earnings in the primary industry rather than branch out (Kelly (1969)) This complements the 'defensive diversification' argument of Weston and Mansinghka (1973). Their study of the performance of firms involved in conglomerate mergers indicates that conglomerates do not have higher profits than firms in general and in fact may have lower profits. They argue that these firms are diversifying because of falling profit rates in their current markets and therefore will not have higher profits than non-diversifying firms.

One recent consequence of this failure to find clear cut evidence that diversification does increase monopoly power, as indicated by increased profits, has been a trend towards complacency about diversification, particularly diversified mergers. Since they do not appear to increase monopoly power, it is suggested that strong policies against such firms are not needed. At the same time, greater emphasis is put on the potential benefits of diversified firms. Their cross-subsidisation ability enables them to avoid the capital market imperfections which can be a significant entry barrier for smaller firms. Therefore, they are in a

9 Imel and Helmberger do not report any equations which include a diversification variable, but state that negative and significant results were obtained with their 4-digit industry sample.

Table 12.1 *Results of previous studies: profitability and diversification*

Miller (1969) – sample: 106 'minor' industries (1958)

	Dep. var.	Intercept	*Sp*	4-*C*	*MC*-8	*A/R*	$\bar{R}^2$
1	Π/K	5.34	0.00589 (0.539)	0.0411 (3.51)	−0.117 (−2.72)		0.113
2	Π/K	6.68	−0.0241 (−2.76)	0.0336 (3.68)	−0.160 (−4.76)	0.557 (8.29)	0.467
Partial sample: Consumer goods inds. (35 observations)							
3	Π/K	5.86	−0.0189 (−1.25)	0.0482 (3.98)	−0.202 (−4.39)	0.597 (7.91)	0.708
Partial sample: Producer goods inds. (71 observations)							
4	Π/K	6.45	−0.0240 (−2.16)	0.0187 (1.40)	−0.104 (−2.14)	0.756 (3.27)	0.223

Rhoades (1972) – sample: 241 4-digit inds. (1963)

	Dep. var.	Intercept	*Sp*	4-*C*	$\dot{R}$	*K/R*	Producer good dummy	Geog. mkt	$\bar{R}^2$
5	Π/R	15.64	−0.081 (−3.346)	0.108 (3.316)	0.055 (3.023)	0.109 (4.860)	7.082 (6.115)	−0.082 (−2.590)	0.32
6	Π/R	6.02	0.029 (1.575)	0.148 (4.757)	0.059 (3.199)	0.124 (5.522)	6.730 (5.644)	−0.103 (−3.248)	0.29

Kelly (1969) – sample: 97 Food-Processing Firms (1950) (Weight $\sqrt{\boldsymbol{K}}$)

	Dep. var.	Intercept	Dv	$4\text{-}C$	$(4\text{-}C)^2$	$\frac{S}{4\text{-}C}$	$\frac{S^2}{4\text{-}C}$	$\frac{S^3}{4\text{-}C}$	A/R	$\dot{R}$	$\frac{1}{\log K}$	$\bar{R}^2$
7	Π/E		3-Digit									
		−15.8	−0.040	0.513	−0.004	0.505	−0.017	0.0002	1.21	0.007	3.85	0.586
			(−1.48)	−(2.84)	(−2.42)	(2.10)	(−1.91)	(1.99)	(2.78)	0.552	(1.13)	
8	Π/E		4-Digit									
		−12.8	−0.037	0.467	−0.003	0.448	−0.015	0.0002	1.17	0.010	2.95	0.590
			(−1.75)	−(2.64)	(−2.27)	(1.86)	(−1.65)	(1.73)	(2.74)	(0.756)	(0.841)	
9	Π/E		5-Digit									
		−10.0	−0.057	−0.465	−0.004	0.457	−0.015	0.0002	1.22	0.016	0.530	0.614
			(−2.94)	−2.71	(−2.43)	(1.97)	(−1.79)	(1.85)	(2.92)	(1.19)	(0.150)	

t-values in brackets

The variables:

- Π = profit level
- K = asset level
- R = sales revenue
- E = equity
- Sp = index of specialisation (= 1− index of diversification)
- $4\text{-}C$ = 4-firms concentration ratio
- $MC\text{-}8$ = marginal 8-firm concentration ratio
- A/R = advertising–sales ratio
- $\dot{R}$ = rate of industry growth
- S = firm market share

Table 12.2

Dep. var.	Ind. level	Firm level
Π/K	+	−
	(Miller (1969))	(Kelly (1969))
Π/R	+	−
	(Rhoades (1973))	(Imel & Helmberger (1971))

Key: (Π = profit level, R = total sales, K = assets)

position to compete with established large firms in industries with high entry barriers. In other words, diversification may increase competition in the Schumpeterian sense of only large firms being able to compete with other large firms.

However, such conclusions cannot be supported either by the underdeveloped state of the current theory or the inappropriate specifications of the models used in the empirical studies. A curious feature of the theoretical analysis is its failure to follow through its implications. This may be partly the result of the lack of effective criticism of the cross-subsidisation theory. The only positive point made seems to be that cross-subsidisation is not a sufficient condition for successful predatory pricing (Wetson (1973)); other conditions are needed, particularly entry barriers, or else the predator will not be able to enjoy the long-run monopoly profits which are needed to recover the losses suffered during the operation. It is also argued that there is little evidence that such practices are carried out.

Though the number of identifiable cases is quite small (e.g. the Safeways case, 1953, Mueller (1970)) this may simply reflect the difficulties of identifying anti-competitive conduct, particularly when production costs must be identified. Moreover, there is strong evidence of cross-subsidisation policies being used effectively to establish and preserve monopoly power in industries where firms are not necessarily diversified but overheads are high and need not be directly related to an individual product line (e.g. computers (Shepherd (1970)) and shoemaking machinery (Blair (1972)).

There are other gaps in the theory which appear to have been overlooked. For example, these practices will be effective only against specialised firms; they could not be used successfully in an economy characterised by diversified firms. Even against specialised firms, the effectiveness of the policies will vary inversely with the monopoly power of the established firm. Furthermore, the diversified firm must have established monopoly positions itself which will provide the funds needed for cross-subsidisation.

A central weakness of this line of reasoning appears to be the attempt to treat diversification as an additional characteristic of the firm independent of all others, which can be added to a set of traditional explanatory variables for regression analysis. This approach is reflected in Edwards' statement: '(The diversified firm) may possess power in a particular market not only by virtue of its place in the organisation of that market but also by virtue of the scope and character of its activities elsewhere' (Edwards (1955)). Without going to the opposite extreme adopted by Adelman, 'Absolute size is absolutely irrelevant' (Adelman (1961)) we should recognise that diversification is closely related to firm size. Therefore, the effects of diversification can be analysed initially within the framework of traditional analysis in which relative size is a major determinant of a firm's monopoly power. Again, this is implicit in the cross-subsidisation analysis but not fully recognised. The purpose of the cross-subsidisation activities is to give the firm a relatively large share of the new market; the benefits of monopoly power will accrue only after such a position has been achieved.

Consequently, a firm with a high degree of diversification will tend to have a smaller market share in each industry than less diversified or specialised firms of the same absolute size. One effect of diversification will therefore be to reduce the market power of the firm, *ceteris paribus,* i.e. assuming identical market conditions. In other words, we are ignoring relative industry growth rates or marginal profitability (Kelly (1974)) as motives for diversification. Our static theory predicts a negative relation between diversification and profitability because of this dilution of market shares and therefore market power. Moreover, the appropriate specification for a testable model is the multivariate, additive one used by the previously mentioned empirical studies. It must be emphasised that we are not arguing that the effects of diversification on profitability are entirely negative, but simply that one effect is negative and that this is the effect that will be picked up in additive, multivariate regression analysis. Moreover, this negative effect plays an important role in determining the pattern of diversification, as will be discussed in Section 12.4.2.

This theory has been tested with two samples: an intra-industry (the food-processing industry) and an inter-industry sample. Attempts have been made to solve several specification problems. In the first place, the sample for the inter-industry study must be selected so that the diversification index does not pick up the effects of vertical integration. For example, in Miller's (1969) partial samples, the specialisation index, *Sp,* performs successfully only with the producer goods sample and not with the consumer goods sample (Table 12.1, eqns 3 & 4). This may reflect the fact that diversification indices for producer goods industries are more likely to include an element of vertical integration than a similar index for consumer goods industries where final goods are likely to predominate over intermediate goods. Consequently, the inter-industry sample has been restricted to consumer goods industries to minimise the effects of vertical integration.

A second problem is the need to distinguish between complementary (or product extension) and conglomerate diversification. If a firm diversifies into an industry which is complementary in some way to its primary activity (e.g. in

R & D, production or marketing), diversification may have a positive effect on profitability because it allows the firm to use its resources more efficiently. Such an effect is likely to be present in our food-processing industry sample where brand loyalty, marketing skills, etc., can readily be transferred to new markets. An attempt has been made to separate the effects of complementary and conglomerate diversification by estimating a quadratic relation. Initially, diversification will have a positive effect on profitability because of the complementary factor but eventually the overall effect will be negative as the negative force of market share dilution becomes stronger and as opportunities for further complementary diversification decline.

The effects of complementary diversification can also be minimised by using a reasonably high level of aggregation. That is, with highly disaggregated industries there is a greater chance that diversification will be complementary than conglomerate. Note how the significance of the diversification index in the FTC study (Kelly (1969)) improves as the industries become more disaggregated (Table 12.1, eqns 7–9). Therefore the use of MLH industries in our two samples will reduce the effects of complementary diversification.

A further problem is that of omitted variables. Unless the model is specified completely, positive results may be obtained because the diversification variable is picking up the effects of an omitted variable such as firm size. For example, in Miller's (1969) full sample, the specialisation index is significant only in the presence of an entry barrier variable, the advertising–sales ratio (Table 12.1, eqns 1–2). Thus, the model specification needs to include a comprehensive set of determinants of monopoly power, such as concentration (C), entry barriers, (B), and firm size (K). Viz:

$$\frac{\Pi}{R} = f\,(\mathrm{Dv}, K, C, B)$$

When expressed in additive form, the model will allow us to examine the effects of diversification, holding other firms characteristics and industry conditions constant.

Finally, the index of diversification most commonly used $Dv(1) = 1-(R_p/R)$ (where R is total sales) is unlikely to be the most suitable for our purposes. In order to examine the market share dilution effect, we need to know the number of secondary industries as well as the gross sales in secondary industries. Consequently, we also use Berry's (1974) index:

$$Dv(2) = 1 - \sum\left(\frac{R_i}{R}\right)^2$$

where R_i is sales in the ith industry and R is total firm (or industry) sales.

Like the Herfindahl index $Dv(2)$ is determined by both the number of industries and the distribution of sales across industries. The more industries in which the firm operates or the more equal the distribution of sales across industries, the higher the value of $Dv(2)$. For specialised firms, $Dv(2) = 0$. A simple count of the number of industries in which the firm operates, $Dv(3)$ is also used.

The results are reported in Table 12.3. As expected, $Dv(2)$ performs best. Moreover, the quadratic form gives the only significant results (eqns 2, 3); $Dv(3)$ gives negative results in equation 1 but is significant only at the 10% level. For both samples, the optimum level of diversification suggested by the coefficients in equations 2 and 3 is quite low: 32% for the food-processing industry and 27% for the consumer-goods industries.

The results do give some support to the hypothesis that one effect of diversification is to dilute market power. Their limited success may reflect the fact that the model does not take into account the relative size of the industries entered; $Dv(2)$ measures the absolute rather than the relative level of sales in each industry. Moreover, a positive element of diversification is still present in the model: the effects of a reduction in risk and the variability of profits. Particularly in inter-industry studies, diversification may be associated with increased profitability because it reduces the incidence of business failure.

The above analysis is not intended to discredit completely the cross-subsidisation theory or to deny that diversification will have any positive effects on monopoly power. But it does suggest that the use of regression analysis with additive equations is inappropriate and will give misleading results, because it picks up the negative effects of spreading one's resources across several industries. A similar situation arises with regard to risk. On the one hand diversification may be a way of reducing the risk associated with fluctuating demand. On the other hand the firm will face new risks from entering a new industry. Just as the firm can reduce the latter type of risk, for example by entering industries with similar characteristics to the primary industry or by entering through external acquisition rather than by internal expansion, so it can offset the negative effects of reduced market shares. How this can be achieved will be discussed in the next section.

12.4.2 The effects of diversification on concentration

The theory that diversification will increase Schumpeterian competition can be evaluated by considering the effects of diversification on the number and size distribution of firms in the entered industry. Diversification through internal expansion will of course have an immediate effect on concentration by increasing the number of firms. However, diversification through acquisition will have no direct effect on concentration, unlike a horizontal merger; but the indirect effects, achieved through cross-subsidisation, may be of considerable importance. The effects on competition will depend largely on the scale and method of entry. If the diversifying firm acquires one of the large firms in the industry, concentration is unlikely to be affected and there will be no competitive benefits from the entry. However, it is argued that diversifying firms are more

Table 12.3 *Diversification and profitability: new estimates*

a. Food-processing industry

	Intercept	Dv_i (3)	Dv_i^2	K_i	A_i	A_i^2	$\sum C_j$	$\sum C_j^2$	$\sum A_j/R_j$	$\bar{R}^2$ [F]
(1)	−0.43717	−0.3778		0.005965	0.003149	-5.755×10^{-7}	0.2355	−0.002945	0.007363	0.323
	(−0.41349)	(−1.7128)		(0.6829)	(2.8568)	(−2.1775)	(3.6976)	(−3.2691)	(2.2547)	(7.1293)
					√√√	√	√√√	√√√	√	√√√
		(2)	(2)							
(2)	−1.2697	0.06289	−0.001033	−0.004376	0.002544	-5.3864×10^{-7}	0.2363	−0.002901	0.007860	0.326
	(−1.2031)	(1.8118)	(−2.0444)	(−0.5411)	(2.4707)	(−2.0280)	(3.5041)	(−3.0909)	(2.3884)	(6.4348)
			√		√√	√	√√√	√√√	√√	√√√

(1) Dependent variable: Π_i/R_i (ith firm, jth industry)
(2) 88 observations; weight: $K^{\frac{1}{4}}$; t-values in parentheses
(3) Explanatory variables: (Data averaged over 1965–69)

5% = √
2% = √
1% = √√√

(i) K_i = firm size (assets, £m)
(ii) A_i = firm advertising expenditure (£'000)
(iii) $\sum C_j$ = weighted industry concentration (weighted by the firm's sales) (%)
(iv) $\sum A_j/R_j$ = weighted industry advertising–sales ratio (%)

b. Consumer goods industries

	Intercept	Dv	Dv^2	K	A/R	C	C^2	C^3	$\dot{R}$	MEF	$\bar{R}^2$ [F]
		(2)	(2)								
(3)	1.5516	0.8960	−0.01742	−0.000206	−0.1201	0.9133	−0.02812	0.000189	0.1090	0.6771	0.308
	(0.1693)	(2.2656)	(−2.4874)	(−1.7186)	(−0.4537)	(1.5169)	(−2.0888)	(2.1790)	(1.9440)	(2.1089)	(3.6792)
		√	√√				√	√		√	√

(1) Dependent variable: Π/R

(2) 52 observations

(3) Explanatory variables (1969 data)

- (i) K = Average firm size (sales, £m)
- (ii) A/R = advertising-sales ratio (%)
- (iii) A = advertising expenditure (£'000)
- (iv) C = 4-firm concentration (%)
- (v) $\dot{R}$ = rate of growth (%)
- (vi) MEF = Minimum efficient firm size (%)

likely to acquire small firms with good growth potential than large firms with established monopoly positions. When the latter type is acquired the purchase price tends to approach the full market price (Scherer (1970)), whereas small firms, whose growth is hindered by capital market imperfections, can be acquired for less than their market value and funds from other divisions of the company can be used to promote their growth. (This implies that diversifying firms are better evaluators of the potentials of small firms than the capital markets.) Diversification by internal expansion is likely to have the same effects on concentration as this type of acquisition, because new entry will probably take place on a relatively small scale.

If diversification does take place in this way, the effects on the size distribution of firms will depend on how the expanding division of the diversifier acquires its extra sales. These may be gained at the expense of other small firms or of the large firms. The competitive effects are clearly different in each case. If growth is achieved at the expense of other small firms, the competitive benefits may occur only when the firm has become large enough to challenge the top firms (i.e. the marginal-concentration theory (Miller (1969)). Moreover, this competitive period may be temporary; having achieved a certain size, medium or large, the diversified firm may decide that further attempts to expand will be unprofitable and invest its funds elsewhere (Kelly (1974)). Thus, Schumpeterian competition will come to an end. However, if the firm's expansion is achieved mainly at the expense of the top firms, then diversification may lead to a permanent reduction in concentration levels.

Empirical studies on these topics have reached conflicting conclusions. Goldberg's studies (1973, 1974), have looked specifically at conglomerate mergers, and their effects on four- or eight-firm concentration. His conclusions are that such mergers have had no effect on concentration or the growth rate of the acquired firm. The latter is determined primarily by the pre-acquisition performance of the company. Since these mergers have no proven disadvantages (i.e. they do not increase concentration), Goldberg argues that strong policies against conglomerates are unnecessary. The fact that they seem to have no proven advantages seems to be irrelevant. However, one of Goldberg's samples consists largely of mergers in which the acquired firms had very small market shares, usually less than four per cent. The fact that such a firm's growth had no effect on the top firms is not unexpected.

Berry (1974, 1975) comes to opposite conclusions, though his studies are concerned with diversification in general. He distinguishes entry by large and small firms and takes into account the initial concentration level of the entered industry. His results indicate that entry into a low concentration industry will lead to a decline in four- or eight-firm concentration whether the new entrant is large or small. But if concentration is high, only entry by a large firm will reduce concentration. Moreover, in the latter case, 70% of the new entrants sales are obtained at the expense of the largest firms. Therefore, Berry concludes, diversification increases competition.

An alternative view is taken by Shepherd (1970). He considers how many industries have firms among their top four or eight which are branches of the largest firms in the economy as a whole. In 1950, 264 out of 926 product classes had at least one of the largest 100 firms among their top four. In 1958, 550 out of 1,014 product classes had one or more of the largest 100 firms among their top four. A similar situation existed in 1963. Shepherd argues that diversification tends to reinforce market power rather than increase competition, because the diversifiers become the largest firms in the entered industries. Utton (1974a) reaches a similar conclusion from a more limited sample. This type of data has its limitations. It does not tell us whether diversification takes place by internal expansion or by acquisition or whether the diversifier becomes one of the largest firms immediately or after a certain period of growth during which there may be a temporary increase in competition.

One way in which this result could be achieved would be for the diversifying firm to enter relatively small industries, where it could easily achieve a dominant position, and, equally important, where there would be less likelihood of coming into contact with other large diversified firms. A less frequently used criticism of diversification is that it will lead to a reduction in the overall level of competition. Firm *A* may be unwilling to compete with firm *B* in industry *X* where it has the advantage, because the retaliation from *B* will probably take place in industry *Y*, where *A* is more vulnerable. Entering relatively small industries would be one way of avoiding this conflict and may also increase the effectiveness of cross-subsidisation policies against established firms. Moreover, it would be a method for offsetting the negative effect of diversification, that of diluting market shares.

Such a strategy would help to explain the average value of the diversification indices listed in Table 12.4. The values for $Dv(1)$ tend to be quite low. The primary industry continues to play a dominant role in the development of the firm. There is little evidence that firms spread their assets equally across several industries. In the case of $Dv(2)$, the number of industries actually entered is significantly greater than the number predicted by the 'numbers equivalent' property of the index.

It is apparent that an examination of the case for Schumpeterian competition must consider the entire complex of firms, not just the top four or eight, and that a distinction must be made between the short-run and long-run effects of diversified entry. Some preliminary work on the first point has been carried out using Census data for 1963 and 1968. The Herfindahl index would be one way of capturing comprehensively the change in the number and size distribution of firms but would not reveal whether large, medium or small firms were being affected by entry. Therefore, the market shares of the top 100 companies

Table 12.4 *Mean values of diversification indices*

Food processing industries sample		
Dv(1)	=	21.8686
Dv(2)	=	21.8889
Dv(3)	=	2.0796
Consumer goods industries sample		
Dv(1)	=	8.2500
Dv(2)	=	26.4546
Dv(3)	=	4.8462
Average number of industries v. numbers equivalent		
1. Berry 1960:	9.9	v. 2.7 (Sample: 460
1965:	13.9	v. 2.9 large firms)
2. Food Industry:	2.0796 v. 1.2802	
3. Consumer Goods Industries:	4.8462 v. 1.3597	

have been divided into the following groups: firms 1–4, 5–8, 9–25, 26–50, and 51–100. The change in the market share of each group between 1963 and 1968 has been regressed against industry growth (*R*), the net change in the number of enterprises (*N*), and the change in the sales of the primary products of the industry accounted for by establishments classified to other industries (*Rps*). No variable measures entry by diversified merger, but *N* is likely to have effects similar to those of an acquisition of a small firm. *N* may underestimate the level of new entry, because it is net of firms which left the industry between 1963 and 1968. The present sample is taken from the 52 consumer goods industries discussed in Section 12.4.1. Of these, 37 contain at least 100 firms; the results presented in Table 12.5 are limited to these firms.

From these results it is possible to draw some tentative conclusions. First, the large firms (1–4) appear to be unaffected by any of the explanatory variables. Their market shares remain fairly stable regardless of the growth rate of the industry or the rate of new entry. The competitive struggles take place lower down the hierarchy. The medium sized firms (5–25) grow proportionately more than the industry growth rate, possibly because they are largely responsible for this growth. But in contrast to Berry's (1974) results, their market shares appear to be most vulnerable to new entry. Small firms (26–100) benefit from new entry probably because new entry takes place within this group and expansion takes place afterwards, through cross-subsidisation for example. Though the sample is incomplete and regression analysis cannot provide the complete answer,[10]

10 For example, we also need to know which forms are responsible for entry and whether they enter highly concentrated industries. Moreover, it would be useful to know to what extent, if any, the concentration measures, particularly the 4-firm concentration ratio, are subject to firm turnover.

Table 12.5 *Change in market shares and diversification*

Dependent variable: $\frac{\textit{market sales 1968}}{\textit{market sales 1963}}$

Group	Intercept	$\dot{R}$	$\frac{N'68}{N'63}$	$\frac{Rps'68}{Rps'63}$	$\bar{R}^2$ [F]
(1) (1–4)	1.4271	0.3325	−0.08260	−0.06985	0.028
	(4.9747)	(1.1238)	(−0.2318)	(−0.4615)	[1.3580]
(2) (5–8)	0.8434	1.2347	−1.2112	0.09495	0.106
	(1.8874)	(2.6789) √√	(−2.1826) √	(0.4027)	[2.4672]
(3) (9–25)	0.6959	0.7162	−0.4818	0.007522	0.365
	(4.0811)	(4.0722) √√√	(−2.2754) √	(0.08361)	[8.0890] √√√
(4) (26–50)	−0.5018	0.3210	1.4616	0.1239	0.889
	(−2.8025)	(1.7380)	(6.5721) √√√	(1.3109)	[99.349] √√√
(5) (51–100)	−9.0726	−0.6748	12.6695	0.4597	0.962
	(−13.1990)	(−0.9811)	(15.3022) √√√	(1.2784)	[307.837] √√√
(6) (Dept. var.: Herfindahl)					
	2.3329	−0.5063	0.009141	−0.06145	0.101
	(6.0689)	(−1.2769)	(0.01915)	(−0.3030)	[2.3867]

37 observations
t-values in parentheses; levels of significance 5% = √
2% = √√
1% = √√√

there are indications that diversification does not contribute to Schumpeterian competition; the largest firms in the economy appear to be insulated from the competitive process.

References to section 12.2

Bain, J. (1951), 'The relation of profit rate to industry concentration: American manufacturing 1936–40', *Quarterly Journal of Economics*, LXV (Aug.).

Bain, J. (1956), *Barriers to new competition*, Cambridge, Mass.: Harvard University Press.

Brozen, Y. (1973), 'Concentration and profits: Does concentration matter?' in: J. Weston and S. Ornstein, eds., *The Impact of large firms on the U.S. economy*, Lexington, Mass.: Lexington Books.

Caves, R. et al. (1975), 'Scale Economies in Statistical Analyses of Market Power', *Review of Economics and Statistics*, **57**, 133–40.

Comanor, W. S. & Wilson, T. A. (1967), 'Advertising, Market Structure and Performance', *Review of Economics and Statistics*, **49**, 423–40.

Cowling, K. (1976), 'On the Theoretical Specification of Industry Structure–Performance Relationships', *European Economic Review* (July).

Cowling, K. & Waterson, M. (1976), 'Price–cost margins and market structure', *Economica,* (Aug.).

Cowling, K., Cable, J., Kelly, M. & McGuiness, A. (1975), *Advertising and economic behaviour,* London: Macmillan.

Demsetz, H. (1973), *The Market Concentration Doctrine,* Washington, DC: American Enterprise Institute.

Dutton, P. A. (1976), 'The Impact of Government Competition Policy, Imports and Tariffs on Price–Cost Margins for British Manufacturing Industries', *Centre for Industrial Economic and Business Research,* University of Warwick, Discussion Paper, 65.

Gale, B. T. (1972), 'Market share and rate of return', *Review of Economics and Statistics* (Nov.), 412–23.

Hall, M. & Weiss, L. (1967), 'Firm size and profitability', *Review of Economics and Statistics* (Aug.), 319–31.

Hart, P. E. & Morgan, E. (1977), 'Market structure and Economic Performance in the UK', *Journal of Industrial Economics,* XXV (3).

Holterman, S. (1973), 'Market Structure and Economic Performance in UK Manufacturing Industry', *Journal of Industrial Economics,* XXII(2).

Jacquemin, A. P. & Phlips, L. (1974), 'Concentration, size and performance of European firms', Working Paper No. 7409, Institute des Sciences Economiques, Louvain.

Khalilzadeh-Shiraz, J. (1974), 'Market structure and price–cost margins in UK manufacturing industries', *Review of Economics and Statistics,* LVI (Feb.).

Mancke, R. B. (1974), 'Interfirm profitability differences', *Quarterly Journal of Economics* (May), 181–93.

Nickell, S. & Metcalf, D. (1978), 'Monopolistic Industries and Monopoly Profits', Economic Journal (June), 254–68.

Phillips, A. (1972), 'An Econometric Study of Price-Fixing, Market Structure and Performance in British Industry in the Early 1950's' in *Market Structure and Corporate Behaviour,* Cowling, K., ed. Gray-Mills, 1972.

Phlips, L. (1971), *Effects of industrial concentration: A cross-section analysis for the Common Market,* Amsterdam: North-Holland.

Samuels, J. & Smyth, D. (1968), 'Profits, variability of profits and firm size', *Economica* (May), 127–39.

Shepherd, W. G. (1972), 'Structure and Behaviour in British Industries with U.S. Comparisons', *Journal of Industrial Economics,* XXI (1).

Soloman, E. G. (1974), 'Market structure and performance of large firms', *Atlantic Economic Journal* (April), 34–44.

Vernon, J. M. & Nourse, R. M. (1973), 'Profit rates and market structure of advertising intensive firms', *Journal of Industrial Economics* (Sept.)

Weiss, L. (1971), 'Quantitative studies of industrial organization, in M. Intriligator, *Frontiers of quantitative economics,* Amsterdam: North-Holland, 363–403.

Weiss, L. (1974), 'The Concentration–Profits relationships and Anti-trust', in *Industrial Concentration: The New Learning,* H. Goldschmid, H. Mann, and J. Weston (eds.) Boston, Little, Brown.

Waterson, M. (1976), *Price–Cost Margins and Market Structure,* PhD Thesis, University of Warwick.

References to section 12.3

Arrow, K. J. (1962), 'Economic, Welfare and the Allocation of Resources for Invention', in NBER, *The Rate and Direction of Inventive Activity,* Princeton University Press.

Davies, S. (1979), *The Diffusion of Process Innovations,* Cambridge University Press.

Dorfman, R. & Steiner, P. O. (1954), 'Optimal Advertising and Optimal Quality', *Am. Ec. Review*, 826–36.

Fisher, F. M. & Temin, P (1973), 'Returns to Scale in Research and Development', *Journal of Political Economy*, **81**(1), 56–70.

Freeman, C. (1976), *The Economics of Industrial Innovation*, Penguin.

Griliches, Z. (1957), 'Hybrid Corn, An Exploration in the Economics of Technological Change', *Econometrica* (October).

Jewkes, J. Sawers, D. & Stillerman, R. (1959), *The Sources of Invention*, New York: St Martins Press.

Johnson, P. S. (1975), *The Economics of Invention and Innovation*, London: Martin Robertson.

Kamien, M. I. & Schwartz, N. L. (1975), 'Market Structure and Innovation: A Survey', *Journal of Ec. Literature* (March), 1–37.

Kennedy, C. & Thirlwall, A. P. (1972), 'Technical Progress: A Survey', *Economic Journal*, (March), 11–73.

Leech, D., & Stoneman, P. (1976), 'An Application of Random Coefficient Regression: The Case of R & D Expenditures and Market Structure', *Warwick Economic Research Papers*, No. 91, University of Warwick, Coventry.

Mansfield, E. (1968), *Industrial Research and Technological Innovation* New York: W. Norton.

Nabseth, L. & Ray, G. T. (1974), *The Diffusion of New Industrial Processes*, Cambridge: Cambridge University Press.

Needham, D. (1975), 'Market Structure and Firms R & D Behaviour', *Journal of Industrial Economics*, 241–55.

Nelson, R. & Winter, S. J. (1974), 'Neoclassical vs. Evolutionary Theories of Economic Growth', *Economic Journal* (December).

Ray, G. F. (1969), 'The Diffusion of New Technology: A study of ten processes in nine industries', *National Institute Economic Review* (May).

Schumpeter, J. A. (1942), *Theory of Economic Development*, New York: Harper.

Stoneman, P. (1976), *Technological Diffusion and the Computer Revolution*, DAE Monograph No. XXV, Cambridge University Press.

References to section 12.4

Adelman, M. A. (1961), 'The Anti-Merger Act', *American Economic Review*, **51**, No. 2, 236–244.

Berry, C. H. (1974), 'Corporate Diversification and Market Structure', *Bell Journal of Economics and Management Science*, **5**, No. 1, 196–204.

– (1975), *Corporate Growth and Diversification*, Princeton University Press.

Blair, J. M. (1972), *Economic Concentration*, New York: Harcourt Brace Jovanovich, Inc.

Edwards, C. D. (1955), 'Conglomerate Bigness as a Source of Power', in National Bureau of Economic Research, *Business Concentration and Price Policy*, Princeton University Press.

Goldberg, L. G. (1973), 'The Effects of Conglomerate Mergers on Competition', *Journal of Law and Economics*, **16**, Pt. 1, 137–58.

– (1974), 'Conglomerate Mergers and Concentration Ratios', *Review of Economics and Statistics*, vol. LVI, August, pp. 303–309.

Hart, P., Utton M. and Walshe G. (1973), *Mergers and Concentration in British Industry*, Cambridge University Press.

Imel, B. and Helmberger P. (1971), 'Estimation of Structure-Profit Relationships with Application to the Food-Processing Sector', *American Economic Review*, **61** (September), 614–27.

Kelly, M. (1974), *The Determinants of Diversification: A Simple Profit-Maximization Model,* Centre for Industrial Economic and Business Research, Discussion Paper No. 49, University of Warwick.

Kelly, W. (1969), *The Influence of Market Structure on the Profit Performance of Food-Manufacturing Companies,* Federal Trade Commission, Washington DC.

Miller, R . A. (1969), 'Market Structure and Industry Performance: Relation of Profit Rates to Concentration, Advertising Intensity, and Diversity', *Journal of Industrial Economics,* **17**, No. 2, 104–18.

Mueller, W. (1972), *A Primer on Monopoly and Competition,* New York: Random House.

Narver, J. C. (1967), *Conglomerate Mergers and Market Competition,* University of California Press.

Rhoades, S. A. (1973), 'The Effects of Diversification on Industry Profit Performance in 241 Manufacturing Industries, 1963', *Review of Economics and Statistics,* **55**, (May), 146–55.

Scherer, F. M. (1970), *Industrial Market Structure and Economic Performance,* Chicago: Rand McNally & Co.

Shepherd, W. G. (1970), *Market Power and Economic Welfare,* New York: Random House.

Utton, M. (1969), 'Diversification, Mergers and Profit Stability', *Business Ratios,* **3**, No. 1, 24–8.

– (1971), 'The Effects of Mergers on Concentration. U.K. Manufacturing Industry, 1954–65', *Journal of Industrial Economics,* **20**, No. 1, 42–58.

– (1974a), 'On Measuring the Effects of Industrial Mergers', *Scottish Journal of Political Economy,* **21**, No. 1, 13–27.

– (1974b), 'Aggregate versus Market Concentration', *Economic Journal,* **84** (March), 150–3.

Weston, J. F. (1973), 'The Nature and Significance of Conglomerate Firms', *St. John's Law Review* (1970), in B. Yamey (ed.), *Economics of Industrial Structure,* Harmondsworth: Penguin Books Ltd.

Weston, J. F. and Mansingkha (1973), 'Tests of the Efficiency Performance of Conglomerate Firms' in J. F. Weston & Ornstein (eds.), *The Impact of Large Firms on the U.S. Economy, Lexington: D.C. Heath.*

13

Mergers, market structure and the rate of price adjustment

13.1 Introduction

There is generally a wide measure of agreement among economists concerning the relationship between monopoly power and price levels. Much of the preceding analysis was specifically concerned with this question and its associated welfare implications. However, the relationship between industrial structure and price flexibility over time remains the subject of heated controversy. At the root of this debate lies the celebrated 'administered prices' hypothesis of which the most recent restatement is that of Means (1972). In this chapter we shall investigate both theoretically and empirically the influence of market structure on the rate of price adjustment in response to cost and demand changes. Any policy implications to emerge from our findings, particularly in the context of inflation, will be relevant to policies towards mergers since they are a crucial determinant of industrial structure.

It is generally accepted that organised markets display the greatest degree of price flexibility since, in these markets, all sellers are price takers not confronted with the problems of price adjustments. Arrow (1959) was the first to draw attention to the analytical problem created by the absence of market clearing mechanisms in the modern industrial economy. Thus the essential difference between competitive markets in the neoclassical tradition and quasi-competitive industrial markets is that, in the latter, price adjustments are carried out by each firm individually but not in isolation from its rivals. In practice, therefore, it is crucial to make the distinction between competitive markets with an institutional framework which ensures perfect price flexibility, and those which are conventionally termed competitive merely on account of their low level of industrial concentration.

In Section 13.2 we shall analyse, by means of a partial price adjustment model, the link between industrial structure and the optimal rate of adjustment. In Section 13.3 we shall outline the methodology of the empirical analysis. This will consist of time-series and cross-section regressions through which the relationship between price adjustment and market structure will be tested, and an analysis of co-variance which will be used to examine the stability of the adjustment process in a number of industries which experienced significant merger activity. The data used in this analysis together with their sources will be discussed in Section 13.4. The results of the tests concerning market structure and the rate of adjustment will be reported and evaluated in Section 13.5, and those relating to structural breaks in the adjustment process will be reported in Section 13.6. Finally, in Section 13.7 we shall put forward some of the policy implications which emerge from our findings together with a few concluding remarks.

13.2 The cost of price adjustment

In this analysis we shall not be directly concerned with price formation, although we shall assign to marginal cost and demand their traditional role in the determination of equilibrium price. Instead we shall focus attention on the firm's decision concerning the optimal *rate* of adjustment. Consequently, our analytical framework could be characterised by a 'dual-decision' approach, whereby it is assumed that the firm first determines the required magnitude of the price change which will restore equilibrium, and then decides what is the optimal rate of change over time. It achieves this by making a decision as to how much of the desired price change it should pass on in the current period. At the end of this section we shall have more to say about the implications of this methodology.

The basic approach adopted here owes its origin to Griliches (1967). It consists of a partial price adjustment model in which the costs of adjustment are a crucial determinant of the adjustment coefficient, λ – the latter representing the proportion of the desired price change which should be passed on in the current period. Our point of departure is to identify the variables which influence the adjustment process. The first is the degree of disequilibrium which is measured by the difference between the actual and the equilibrium price in the current period, $P_t - P_t^*$. The desired rate of adjustment is determined by the extent of disequilibrium, and while it persists, the firm's objective function will not be maximised and some profits will be sacrificed. The other relevant decision variable is the actual rate of price change, measured by the difference between the price in the current and the previous period, $P_t - P_{t-1}$ or ΔP_t. As will be argued below, the greater is this rate of price change, the higher will be the associated costs of adjustment.

In what follows we shall assume that these profit losses and adjustment costs are quadratic functions of the deviation of P_t^* from P_t and the absolute rate of change ΔP_t respectively. This assumption ensures that the profit losses and adjustment costs are positive and symmetric about the relevant variables and that they rise at an increasing rate. We would therefore suggest that as an approximation to the actual costs of adjustment, this assumption is not unduly contentious. The functional specification to which we refer is as follows:

$$C = f(P_t - P_t^*)^2 + g(\Delta P_t)^2 \quad f' > 0, \quad g' > 0 \tag{1}$$

The first part of equation (1) represents the profits forgone by adjusting price at anything less than the full amount required to restore equilibrium. These losses exert pressure on the firm to pass on the entire price change in the current period, i.e. to adjust prices instantaneously. It is not clear whether the pressure for an instantaneous adjustment is greater in monopolistic or competitive industries, and we must therefore conclude that very little can be said *a priori* concerning the relationship between profits forgone due to delayed adjustment and market structure.

Turning to the costs of adjustment *per se*, as defined by the second term of equation (1), it seems that traditionally these costs were purported to arise from the need to disseminate information about forthcoming price changes. This essentially involves sending out new price lists, and the very nature of these costs suggests that they are fixed: they do not vary with the degree of adjustment. However, our basic premise is that the costs of adjustment will be an increasing function of ΔP_t, with market structure playing a central role. The underlying rationale is based on the existence of two types of adjustment costs. The first stems from the required information concerning the adjustment behaviour of rivals. For when the desired rate of price adjustment is established and the new equilibrium price known, the firm faces the problem of co-ordinating its price changes with those of its competitors. This is a problem of dynamic oligopoly and its importance is related to the fact that there are risks in disregarding the average industry rate of adjustment. Suppose one firm's partial adjustment coefficient is consistently higher than the industry norm; consumers will eventually learn that in times of rising costs the firm's price will be higher than the average for the industry, with a resulting loss of demand. It is therefore crucial for firms to obtain information on the past and current adjustment rates of their competitors. But the costs of gathering this information will increase as the sampling population, in this case the number of firms in the industry, rises.[1] But since the latter is inversely related to industrial concentration, *ceteris paribus*, we may infer that the costs of search will be a decreasing function of industrial concentration. Thus we are hypothesising that due to the need for search, the costs of co-ordinating price changes with those of other firms in the industry fall as the level of concentration rises.

1 Stigler (1961) suggested that, in the context of consumers looking for low price sellers, the costs of search will be approximately proportional to the number of units searched, i.e. the number of firms approached. Scherer (1970) looked specifically at oligopoly and showed that the number of potential communication channels in the industry rises more than proportionately to the number of firms. This again suggests that search costs will rise with the number of firms in the industry.

Market structure will also affect the costs of adjustment through its impact on the losses associated with deviations from the average industry rate of change. We would hypothesise these losses to be inversely related to concentration assuming that product differentiation tends to increase with industrial concentration. For in this case, we would expect the cross price elasticities of demand to be lower in concentrated industries, and the demand shifts arising from differential adjustment rates to be correspondingly smaller. As regards the relationship between market structure and product differentiation, Cowling et al. (1975) found strong evidence that advertising levels are positively related to concentration, and this suggests a similar relationship for product differentiation.

In replacing equation (1) by a more explicit functional form we substitute $\Delta P_t - (\Delta P_t)^*$ for $P_t - P_t^*$ where $(\Delta P_t)^*$ represents the desired rate of adjustment, given that these two expressions are equivalent.[2]

$$C = a(\Delta P_t - (\Delta P_t)^*)^2 + (b/CR)(\Delta P_t)^2 \tag{2}$$

Thus a is the coefficient proportional to the profits lost through delayed adjustment and b/CR represents the costs of adjustment which are inversely related to industrial concentration (denoted by CR).

Assuming that the firm minimises adjustment costs in each period, we differentiate equation (2) with respect to ΔP_t and set it equal to zero:

$$\frac{dC}{d(\Delta P_t)} = 2a(\Delta P_t - (\Delta P_t)^*) + 2(b/CR)(\Delta P_t) = 0$$

This can be rearranged to give:

$$\Delta P_t = \lambda(\Delta P_t)^* \quad \text{where } \lambda = \frac{a}{a + b/CR}$$

or

$$\Delta P_t = \lambda(P_t^* - P_{t-1}) \tag{3}$$

Thus the optimal rate of adjustment is some fraction of the desired rate ($P_t^* - P_{t-1}$) in the current period. The partial adjustment coefficient, λ, which defines this fraction has an upper bound of unity and a lower bound of zero, and its actual size will depend on the relative magnitude of the parameters in the model. For example, in the case of a monopolist the costs of adjustment and hence the b coefficient would be reduced to zero and this would effectively raise the partial adjustment coefficient to unity ($\lambda = a/a$).[3] However, with more than

2 $(\Delta P_t)^*$ is defined as $P_t^* - P_{t-1}^*$ if the firm was previously in equilibrium and $P_t^* - P_{t-1}$ otherwise. Therefore in both cases $(\Delta P_t)^* = P_t^* - P_{t-1}$ and hence $\Delta P_t - (\Delta P_t)^* = P_t - P_{t-1} - P_t^* + P_{t-1} = P_t - P_t^*$.

3 In this situation the only costs are those associated with the deviation from the desired rate of adjustment and therefore the optimal rate will be an instantaneous one.

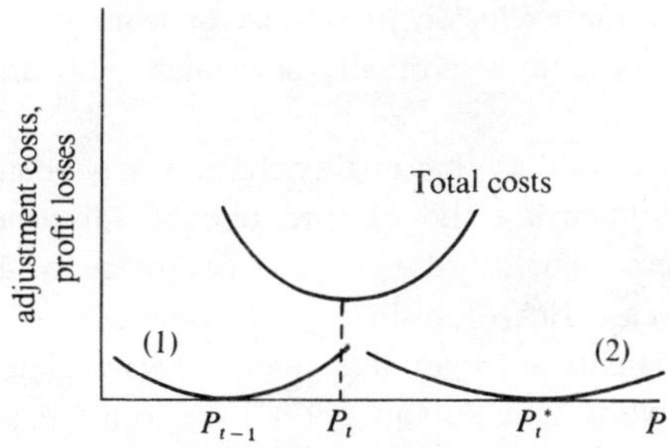

Figure 13.1 *The optimal rate of adjustment*
Notes: (1) Adjustment cost function, $f(\Delta P_t)^2$
(2) Profit loss function

one firm in the industry there will be non-zero adjustment costs, and consequently the adjustment coefficient will be less than its upper bound.

Thus far the analysis has been conducted at the level of the representative firm; but since the degree of concentration (CR) is common to all firms within an industry, equation (3) effectively defines the optimal rate of adjustment at the industry level. The relationships implied by the model can be best illustrated with the aid of a diagram.

In Figure 13.1 adjustment costs and profit losses are measured along the vertical axis and price along the horizontal axis. Three separate curves are depicted in the figure. The one which is at a minimum when $P_t = P_t^*$ represents the profit forgone through being in disequilibrium. The curve defined by the function $f(\Delta P_t)^2$ represents the costs of adjustment *per se*. Thus if prices do not change from one period to another there will be no adjustment costs. The total costs curve is the vertical summation of the other two just described.

The optimisation process implied in Figure 13.1 can now be elucidated. In the situation depicted the current price is to be raised since P_t^* is greater than P_{t-1}. An instantaneous adjustment would reduce the profits forgone to zero, but would raise the costs of adjustment to such a level that total costs will not be at a minimum. On the other hand, if this period's price is kept at the same level as in the previous period, adjustment costs would now be zero but total costs, once again, will not be minimised by this strategy. Thus, the optimal rate of adjustment and hence the current period price is given by the minimum point on the total adjustment costs schedule.

We recognise that another factor which could affect the adjustment process is inflationary expectations. Although this has come to be considered as a potentially important influence on pricing behaviour, there is no evidence which suggests that it is systematically related to industrial concentration. Consequently we do not expect the exclusion of this factor from the empirical analysis to lead to the bias which is normally associated with an omitted variable.

We must also consider the possibility that quality changes may be substituted for price changes thereby influencing the *observed* rate of adjustment. This would not constitute a problem if quality-adjusted price data were available, but unfortunately this is not the case. However, since what evidence is available on this subject suggests that quality changes may be a characteristic of concentrated industries (see Cowling and Cubbin (1971)) we would expect these industries to be more likely to reduce the *observed* rate of adjustment through quality change. Therefore, should we find a positive relationship between concentration and the speed of adjustment, it would not be the result of a favourable bias induced by measurement errors.

We conclude this section with the following qualification. Setting up the adjustment problem in terms of discrete price changes in each period emphasises the 'how much' question to the detriment of the 'how often' question which, it could be argued, is equally important but was not considered in this analysis. However, in the context of the period under investigation, i.e. 1963–74, we would suggest that the rate of inflation during this time was sufficiently high for the losses resulting from delayed adjustment to be large relative to the purely administrative costs of adjustment.[4] If this is accepted then it is not unreasonable to concentrate attention on the 'how much' decision, which is what has been done here.

13.3 The methodology of the empirical analysis

The empirical analysis involved estimating a set of price equations, one for each industry in the sample, from which the rate of price adjustment could be derived. The estimating equations were obtained from the partial adjustment model in the following manner: given that we had

$$\Delta P_t = \lambda(P_t^* - P_{t-1}) \tag{3}$$

this equation can be rewritten as:

$$P_t = \lambda P_t^* + (1 - \lambda)P_{t-1} \tag{4}$$

Replacing the equilibrium price P_t^* by a linear combination of cost and demand variables, equation (4) becomes:

$$P_t = \lambda\beta_1 C_t + \lambda\beta_2 D_t + (1 - \lambda)P_{t-1} \tag{5}$$

Where C_t and D_t represent current period industry marginal costs and demand respectively. However, since these variables are strongly trended, multicollinearity in the regressions is likely to result in imprecise estimates of the

4 The record of inflation in the United Kingdom during this period is outlined in Flemming (1976), Chapter 1.

coefficients and in order to overcome this problem we took the first difference of equation (5). Thus the functional specification which was used for estimation was linear in first differences, as defined by equation (6) below:

$$\Delta P_t = \lambda\beta_1\Delta C_t + \lambda\beta_2\Delta D_t + (1 - \lambda)\Delta P_{t-1} \tag{6}$$

Equation (6) was estimated for each industry using data on wholesale output prices, input prices, labour costs and a proxy index for demand which was constructed along the lines suggested by Lustgarten (1975). With this method, instead of using direct observations on the output of the industry whose price movements we try to explain – a procedure which would inevitably introduce simultaneity bias in ordinary least squares regressions –we use the weighted sum of output indicators of those industries which utilise the output of the industry in question for their own production activities. As the industry's output price is not related to the demand for other industries' output the simultaneity problem is effectively removed.

However, the equation estimates using this index did not provide any evidence to indicate that price adjustments are influenced by short-run changes in demand. The estimated coefficients were mostly insignificantly different from zero, and when significant they had the wrong, i.e. negative, sign. Furthermore, the inclusion of this variable made little contribution to the explanatory power of the regressions over and above that which was provided by the other variables. Consequently, the equations which included the demand index will not be reported here. It should be noted that this finding is supported by the recent empirical study of Godley and Nordhaus (1972).

The functional specification used to estimate the regressions which are reported in this paper was as follows:

$$\Delta WPI_{it} = \alpha_i + \lambda_1\beta_{1i}\Delta PIMF_{it} + \lambda_i\beta_{2i}\Delta ULC_{it} + (1 - \lambda_i)\Delta\, WPI_{it-1} + u_{it} \tag{7}$$

$$\beta_{1i} > 0, \quad \beta_{2i} > 0, \quad 0 < \lambda_i \leqq 1$$

where *WPI* denotes the wholesale price index, *PIMF* denotes the price index of materials and fuel and *ULC* denotes unit labour costs. The partial adjustment coefficient is λ_i, and α_i is the constant term included for estimation purposes only, since the theory does not suggest that it will be significantly different from zero.

The estimates of the partial adjustment coefficient were linked to concentration using multivariate regression analysis. In these regressions we did not attempt to derive an explicit functional form linking λ to *CR* on the basis of the analysis in the preceding section. To specify such a functional relation directly from the model would render our hypothesis unduly restrictive. Thus, whilst concentration remains the key explanatory variable in the regressions, the preferred functional form was determined empirically. Furthermore, although the lower bound of λ is zero, we expect it to be positive irrespective of the level of concentration. Consequently, a constant term was included in the equations.

In addition we expect the adjustment coefficients of the engineering and non-engineering industries to differ significantly because of differences in the length of the gestation period between input purchases and final output deliveries. To capture these differences we included a dummy variable in the regressions, taking the value of 1 for an engineering industry, and 0 otherwise.[5]

It should also be remembered that our estimates of λ relate to the 1963–74 period whilst the concentration measures relate to specific years within that time. Thus each estimate of λ represents an average for the period, but the concentration measures do not. Yet changes in concentration could influence λ since the latter may vary within each industry over time. Consequently, where the data permitted, we included changes in concentration as an additional explanatory variable. Hence, this variable was included on empirical rather than theoretical grounds.

The basic regression equation was as follows:

$$\lambda_i = A + b_1 CR_{it} + b_2 (CR_{it+\theta} - CR_{it}) + b_3 ED_i + u_i \tag{8}$$

where CR_{it} is the index of concentration of industry i in period t and ED_i is the engineering industry dummy.

Equation (8) was also transformed into a semi-log, log-linear, and quadratic functional form before estimation in order to test for different non-linear relationships between the speed of adjustment and concentration.

In this analysis we also need to consider the potential effect of Government price-controlling agencies. We refer in particular to the National Board for Prices and Incomes set up in 1965 and the Price Commission set up in 1973. It is commonly believed that the impact of these institutions is much greater in concentrated industries because the monitoring process is facilitated when relatively few firms account for a large part of the industry's output.

Thus within each industry the rate of adjustment can be partially controlled by these institutions. It is difficult to capture their effect directly in our regression analysis, but if the above hypothesis is correct, then, should the empirical results indicate a positive association between λ and concentration, the validity of the results would be enhanced. In this event the results would suggest that the activity of price controlling institutions is not as effective in imposing price restraint on oligopolists as market fragmentation is in restraining competitive firms.

13.4 The data

The dependent variable in the regression equations was the Wholesale Price Index (WPI) available monthly since 1963 and published in *Trade and*

5 We would ideally measure this effect using a continuous variable such as the stock/output ratio. Unfortunately this data is not available by MLH industry groups.

Industry. The indices are compiled free of value added tax (or purchase tax before its abolition) and represent price quotations by manufacturers.

On the explanatory variables side, the price index of materials and fuel (PIMF) was previously only available at SIC order level of aggregation. The necessary PIMFs were therefore calculated for industries defined at MLH level using information on input purchases which is published in the report on the Census of Production for 1968.

The unit labour cost (ULC) was based on the monthly index of average earnings by broad industry groups published by the Department of Employment. The index goes back to 1963 and comprises gross remuneration including overtime payments, bonuses and commissions.

To obtain the unit labour cost index we divided the average earnings series by a long-term (1963–74) productivity trend in each sector. We are therefore implicitly assuming that output prices are not adjusted in response to short-run changes in productivity.

To identify industrial structure we followed convention and used the five-firm concentration ratios. Three sets of concentration ratios were available to us; the 1963 and 1968 figures from the quinquennial census published in the summary tables of the 1968 report, and the more recent figures for 1971 published in the annual census report. It should be noted that the 1971 concentration ratios are not comparable with the figures for 1963 and 1968 because they are constructed on a different basis. Therefore in the regression equations we shall have to restrict our measure of concentration change to 1963–68.

As an alternative explanatory variable in equation (8) we used the Herfindahl index of concentration. This index is not available from official sources and was constructed by M. Waterson for 1963 and 1968 using employment data published in the 1968 census report.

13.5 The results

Our sample comprised a total of twenty-one industries identified at MLH level or below, and selected from seven different SIC orders. We attempted to cover the entire spectrum of industrial structure but our sample was ultimately restricted by the availability of data.

The equations were estimated initially by ordinary least squares. The estimation period extended from 1963 to 1974 giving 48 quarterly observations in total. The industry sample was divided into two groups, one comprising the engineering and the other the non-engineering industries. The basis for this division will be discussed later.

Since it is not uncommon for firms to carry large stocks of materials and to have fixed-price supply contracts as well as medium-term wage agreements, the equations were also estimated using lagged values of PIMF and ULC in order to allow for a delayed impact of input price changes. In four out of the twenty-one regressions a lagged variable provided an improved overall estimate.

The ordinary least squares results revealed significant negative serial-correlation in most regressions as measured by Durbin's '*h*' statistic. Since serial correlation coupled with a lagged dependent variable on the right-hand side of the equation leads to estimation bias, the ordinary least squares regressions were considered unsatisfactory and will not be reported here.[6]

The alternative estimation technique which was used involved a two-stage generalised least squares procedure. The data was first transformed by means of an estimated value of ρ – the serial correlation parameter – and ordinary least squares were then applied to the transformed data. The serial-correlation was thus removed so that ordinary least squares could be used without danger of bias. The method utilised to estimate the appropriate value of ρ in each equation was the Cochrane–Orcutt iterative technique (see Johnston (1972) p. 262).

The generalised least squares results for the engineering and non-engineering industries are reported in Tables 13.1 and 13.2 respectively. It is immediately apparent that the negative serial correlation was effectively removed, as testified by the 'h' statistics. The industry sample was divided into engineering and non-engineering groups on account of our *a priori* expectation that the respective adjustment coefficients come from two different populations. For we would expect the engineering sectors to have a longer lag than other industries because of differences in the complexity and duration of the manufacturing process. In effect the results supported this view. The mean coefficient of the engineering industries group was 0.3490 whilst that of the non-engineering group was 0.6515. The statistical significance of this difference in the means was confirmed by a *t*-test ($t = 2.2876$).

From Table 13.1 it can be seen that the constant term was in no case significantly different from zero, a result which is consistent with our specification. The price index of materials and fuel had a statistically significant impact on output price adjustments in all nine equations. The unit labour cost variable did not perform so well being statistically significant in six equations only. Its relatively poorer performance may have resulted from errors in measurement caused by using SIC order data for MLH industry estimates. The coefficients on the lagged dependent variable, which represent the regression estimate of $(1 - \lambda_i)$ were statistically significant and showed a widely diverging partial adjustment structure.

Table 13.2 presents a very similar picture. With only one exception the constant term in the equations was not significantly different from zero. The single exception was the Man-made Fibres industry equation in which the constant

6 Serial correlation was also present in the regressions incorporating the demand proxy, and consequently this suggests that it was not the result of omitting this variable.

Table 13.1 *Price adjustment equations: engineering industries. Dependent variable ΔWPI_t. Generalised least squares estimates*

MLH	Industry description	Constant	$\Delta PIMF_t$	ΔULC_t	ΔWPI_{t-1}	R^2	$F(3, 41)$	h	ρ
332	Metal working M-T	−0.3165	0.4508	0.0829	0.7137	0.8979	120.23	−0.2274	−0.3052
		(−1.2349)	(7.4005)	(0.7129)	(7.4814)				
333	Pumps, valves and compressors	−0.0757	0.1977	0.2749	0.6622	0.8683	90.07	−0.1437	−0.4019
		(−0.3579)	(5.8769)	(3.5830)	(7.6123)				
339/1	Mining machinery	0.0131	0.1281	0.1358[a]	0.7074	0.8131	59.46	−0.0796	−0.3663
		(0.0802)	(4.0446)	(2.5614)	(8.3059)				
361	Electrical machinery	−0.2649	0.1079	0.2328	0.8249	0.8640	86.82	−0.3433	−0.3819
		(−1.2490)	(3.7952)	(2.6495)	(8.2066)				
362	Insulated wires and cables	−0.3685	0.3551	0.0668	0.6942	0.8302	66.83	−0.3851	−0.4619
		(−0.6337)	(12.9345)	(0.4153)	(11.5047)				
363	Telegraph and telephone apparatus	−0.2067	0.1601	0.4496[a]	0.5286	0.4475	11.07	−0.0204	−0.2960
		(−0.3988)	(1.6704)	(3.1273)	(3.9969)				
365/2	Broadcast receiving equipment	−0.9320	0.1113	0.0482	0.3946	0.4586	11.58	[c]	−0.2154
		(−0.6269)	(2.4327)	(1.0448)	(2.0595)				
368	Domestic electrical appliances	−0.1715	0.1405[b]	0.1090	0.6398	0.8319	67.65	−0.2441	−0.1750
		(−1.2547)	(4.1957)	(2.1190)	(6.8627)				
369	Other electrical goods	−0.2717	0.1261	0.2348	0.6932	0.7442	39.75	−1.0606	−0.4025
		(−1.1548)	(3.9299)	(2.7536)	(6.1086)				

[a] ΔULC_{t-1}; [b] $\Delta PIMF_{t-1}$
[c] h statistic not calculable
t-ratios are given in parentheses

WPI = Wholesale Price Index
PIMF = Price Index of Materials and Fuel
ULC = Unit labour costs
h = Durbin's statistic adjusted for lagged dependent variable
ρ = Estimated serial correlation parameter

Table 13.2 *Price adjustment equations: non-engineering industries. Dependent variable ΔWPI_t. Generalised least squares estimates*

MLH	Industry description	Constant	$\Delta PIMF_t$	ΔULC_t	ΔWPI_{t-1}	R^2	$F(3, 41)$	h	ρ
272/1	Pharmaceutical chemicals	−0.1096	0.1375	0.3378	0.6123	0.6345	23.73	−0.1485	−0.2937
		(−0.3473)	(1.8500)	(4.2513)	(4.2376)				
272/2	Pharmaceutical preparations	−0.0857	0.1097	0.0659	0.7811	0.8637	86.60	[b]	−0.2539
		(−0.8878)	(4.9669)	(2.2282)	(7.8281)				
274	Paint	−0.0557	0.3023	0.1898[a]	0.6067	0.8551	80.64	−0.2055	−0.8772
		(−0.3352)	(8.6588)	(2.7492)	(10.0357)				
411	Man-made fibres	−1.0059	0.4179	0.5767	−0.0093	0.8912	111.93	−0.0860	−0.1509
		(−5.1227)	(10.5900)	(8.7805)	(−0.1436)				
414	Woollen and worsted	0.3595	0.3752	0.2016	0.3752	0.8513	78.27	−0.0737	−0.7249
		(1.4408)	(10.4533)	(2.2324)	(5.5757)				
419	Carpets and rugs	0.1609	0.3598	0.2322	0.4382	0.6443	27.76	0.1364	−0.2881
		(0.5761)	(4.9855)	(2.4764)	(4.1072)				
422/1	Household textiles	0.1588	1.0843	−0.0654	−0.1286	0.8996	122.44	0.1526	−0.2770
		(0.6135)	(11.4343)	(−0.8456)	(−1.3223)				
461	Bricks and refractory goods	0.0418	0.4205	0.0289	0.4986	0.8912	111.99	−0.4312	−0.4971
		(0.2283)	(11.9723)	(0.3606)	(6.4394)				
462	Pottery	0.1714	0.3871	0.2645	0.3767	0.7907	51.62	−0.0297	−0.0698
		(0.5863)	(5.5005)	(3.3928)	(3.5381)				
469/1	Abrasives	0.2372	0.8477	0.5215	−0.3956	0.6646	27.08	0.3756	0.0871
		(0.3573)	(5.4791)	(3.4699)	(−3.5748)				
473	Bedding	0.0771	0.4339	−0.0352	0.5998	0.8422	72.97	−0.2726	−0.5417
		(0.3517)	(7.5098)	(−0.5947)	(7.6105)				
483	Manufactured stationery	−0.2792	0.3331	0.2472	0.6494	0.9263	171.72	−0.3170	−0.3802
		(−1.2399)	(5.6304)	(3.1054)	(7.5511)				

[a] ΔULC_{t-1}
[b] h statistic not calculable
t-ratios are given in parentheses

WPI = Wholesale Price Index
PIMF = Price Index of Materials and Fuel
ULC = Unit labour costs
h = Durbin's statistic adjusted for lagged dependent variable
ρ = Estimated serial correlation parameter

term was negative and statistically significant. We would explain this result in terms of the influence of technical progress on output prices. It is well known that this industry has experienced considerable technical innovation during our estimation period, both in product specification and production methods. This technological trend is therefore reflected in a downward trend of output prices, although in the remaining industries it was adequately captured through the allowance made in labour costs for the growth of productivity.

As in Table 13.1, the price index of materials and fuel had a statistically significant impact on output price changes in all twelve equations and unit labour costs in nine equations only. The partial adjustment coefficients of this sample displayed considerable variability, and in two cases they were insignificantly different from zero implying an instantaneous price adjustment i.e. $\lambda = 1$. One interesting result was that the estimated coefficient for the Abrasives industry was negative and statistically significant thus implying that λ was significantly greater than one – its theoretical upper bound. The industry is highly concentrated and therefore this result may be explained in terms of rapid price adjustments which reflect full or over compensation for cost increases based on inflationary expectations.

Before going on to examine the relationship between the speed of adjustment and concentration, it should be noted that the estimates are based on a period of rising inflation and therefore are related essentially to upward movement in prices.

The equations linking concentration and adjustment coefficients were estimated by ordinary least squares. The linear regression results are reported in Table 13.3. Five alternative equations were estimated using different measures of concentration. In equations (1) and (4) the concentration change between 1963 and 1968 was included as an additional explanatory variable.

Taking equation (1) first, we note that the 1963 concentration ratio had a positive and statistically significant effect on the rate of price adjustment (λ). The estimated coefficient implies that for every percentage point increase in concentration the partial adjustment coefficient will increase by 0.0075. This is a plausible order of magnitude. The change in concentration from 1963 to 1968 had a positive coefficient which was not, however, statistically significant. We would attribute this result primarily to the problems of measurement associated with this variable. Our suspicion was confirmed by the fact that, using unpublished estimates of employment concentration ratios made available to us by the Office of Fair Trading, the coefficient on the concentration change variable turned out to be statistically significant at the 5% level. The estimation results were as follows:

$$\underset{}{\lambda} = \underset{(2.1844)}{0.3050} + \underset{(2.3067)}{0.0059}\, CR_{63} + \underset{(1.9819)}{0.0228}\, [CR_{68} - CR_{63}] - \underset{(-3.3265)}{0.4112}\, ED$$

$R^2 = 0.5173$; $F = 5.00$

Table 13.3 *Partial adjustment and industrial structure.*[a] *Dependent variable: partial adjustment coefficient (λ). Linear specification. Twenty-one industries sample*

Explanatory variables	(1)	(2)	(3)	(4)[b]	(5)[b]
Constant	0.1782	0.1852	0.3141	0.5191	0.5180
	(1.0662)	(1.1614)	(2.3464)	(5.9815)	(6.2056)
CR_{63}	0.0075				
	(2.9143)				
$[CR_{68} - CR_{63}]$	0.0091				
	(1.1433)				
CR_{68}		0.0076			
		(3.0069)			
CR_{71}			0.0066		
			(2.6734)		
H_{63}				2.1453	
				(2.3395)	
$[H_{68} - H_{63}]$				2.3986	
				(1.1611)	
H_{68}					2.1913
					(2.7774)
Engineering	−0.3821	−0.3775	−0.3549	−0.3649	−0.3630
dummy	(−3.4144)	(−3.5339)	(−3.2526)	(−3.2346)	(−3.3638)
R^2	0.4770	0.4756	0.4361	0.5175	0.5171
F statistic	5.17	8.16	6.96	5.36	8.57

[a] *t*-ratios are given in parentheses.

[b] In regressions (4) and (5) two sample observations were omitted (MLH 365/2 and 483) because the Herfindahl index was unavailable for these industries.

CR_{63} 1963 industry concentration ratio, being a weighted mean (weighted by sales) of component concentration ratios published in the Report on the 1968 Census of Production, HMSO, 1974.

CR_{68} 1968 industry concentration ratio derived in the same manner as CR_{63} using the same data sources.

CR_{71} 1971 industry concentration ratio by MLH groups published in the Summary tables of the 1971 Census of Production, HMSO, 1976.

H_{63} Estimate of the 1963 Herfindahl index calculated by M. Waterson from employment data published in the 1968 Census Report, HMSO 1974.

H_{68} Estimate of the 1968 Herfindahl index compiled in the same way as H_{63}.

Going back to equation (1) in the table it can be seen that the coefficient on the engineering industry dummy was negative and statistically significant thus confirming our earlier prediction. This coefficient shows that, on average, the adjustment rate in engineering sectors is considerably lower than in non-engineering sectors. Equation (2) presented a very similar picture. The coefficient on the 1968 concentration ratio was 0.0076 – almost identical in size to the coefficient on the 1963 concentration ratio – and it was also statistically significant at the 5% level.

In equation (3) the key explanatory variable was the 1971 concentration ratio which, as was indicated earlier, is not directly comparable with the 1963 and 1968 measures. It is therefore interesting to note that the coefficient on this variable was not only positive and statistically significant, but at 0.0066 it was not much smaller than the corresponding coefficients obtained in equations (1) and (2). This result would suggest that the relationship between concentration and the rate of adjustment is independent of minor differences in the measurement of concentration.

As a further test of the hypothesis we regressed the adjustment coefficients on M. Waterson's estimates of the Herfindahl index of concentration for 1963 and 1968. The results are reported in columns (4) and (5) of the table. The coefficient on H_{63} was positive and statistically significant. However at 2.1453 it was much larger than the coefficients obtained when using the concentration ratios. This can be explained by reference to the fact that the Herfindahl index is measured on a scale between zero and one, whilst the concentration ratio may range from just above zero to one hundred. As in equation (1), the coefficient on the change in the Herfindahl index ($H_{68} - H_{63}$) was positive but not statistically significant. Looking at equation (5) we note that the coefficient on H_{68} was almost of equal size to the one on H_{63}, and was statistically significant.

Generally, the results obtained for the engineering industry dummy coefficients were remarkably consistent in all five equations. They were negative and statistically significant in every case, and were restricted to between −0.3549 and −0.3821. The F ratios confirmed the statistical significance of the regressions.

The semi-log regressions reported in Table 13.4 gave as good a statistical fit as that of the linear specification.[7] The coefficients on all the concentration ratios were statistically significant at the 5% level, and those in equations (1) and (2) indicated that every percentage point increase in the concentration ratio raises the partial adjustment coefficient by $1\frac{1}{4}$%. As before, the coefficient on the concentration change turned out to be positive but not statistically significant, although it did gain significance when the data provided by the Office of Fair Trading was used for estimation. The result was as follows:

$$\log \lambda = \underset{(-4.7514)}{-1.0962} + \underset{(1.9679)}{0.0083}\ CR_{63} + \underset{(2.1955)}{0.0417}\ \left[CR_{68} - CR_{63}\right]\ \underset{(-3.6228)}{-0.7399}\ ED$$

$$R^2 = 0.5398; \quad F = 5.47$$

7 The alternative semi-log specification, i.e. $\lambda = A + \beta \log CR$ was also tried but the overall significance of the regressions was considerably lower than those reported in Table 13.4. Consequently these results will not be presented here.

Table 13.4 *Partial adjustment and industrial structure.*[a] *Dependent variable: partial adjustment coefficient (log λ). Semi-log specification. Twenty-one industries sample*

Explanatory variables	(1)	(2)	(3)	(4)[b]	(5)[b]
Constant	−1.3272	−1.3253	−1.0745	−0.7517	−0.7535
	(−4.7193)	(−4.9463)	(−4.6557)	(−5.1328)	(−5.3498)
CR_{63}	0.0125				
	(2.8732)				
$[CR_{68} - CR_{63}]$	0.0129				
	(0.9594)				
CR_{68}		0.0125			
		(2.9606)			
CR_{71}			0.0102		
			(2.3762)		
H_{63}				3.1849	
				(2.0585)	
$[H_{68} - H_{63}]$				3.5983	
				(1.0323)	
H_{68}					3.2599
					(2.4490)
Engineering	−0.6771	−0.6759	−0.6285	−0.6716	−0.6684
dummy	(−3.5961)	(−3.7653)	(−3.3405)	(−3.5275)	(−3.6707)
R^2	0.4933	0.4933	0.4265	0.5250	0.5247
F statistic	5.52	8.76	6.69	5.53	8.83

[a] *t*-ratios are given in parentheses.
[b] In regressions (4) and (5) two sample observations were omitted (MLH 365/2 and 483) because the Herfindahl index was unavailable.

CR_{63} 1963 industry concentration ratio, being a weighted mean (weighted by sales) of component concentration ratios published in the Report on the 1968 Census of Production, HMSO, 1974.

CR_{68} 1968 industry concentration ratio derived in the same manner as CR_{63} using the same data sources.

CR_{71} 1971 industry concentration ratio by MLH groups published in the Summary tables of the 1971 Census of Production, HMSO, 1976.

H_{63} Estimate of the 1963 Herfindahl index calculated by M. Waterson from employment data published in the 1968 Census Report, HMSO, 1974.

H_{68} Estimate of the 1968 Herfindahl index compiled in the same way as H_{63}.

Turning to the log-linear results reported in Table 13.5, it would appear that although broadly similar, these regressions did not provide as high a degree of explanatory power as either the linear or the semi-log equations. In particular, the Herfindahl measures of concentration no longer had a statistically significant impact on the rate of adjustment and, furthermore, in equations (3), (4) and (5) the significance of the regressions, as measured by the F statistic, was much reduced.

Finally, the quadratic functional form did not yield statistically significant

Table 13.5 *Partial adjustment and industrial structure.*[a] *Dependent variable: partial adjustment coefficient (log λ). Log-linear specification. Twenty-one industries sample*

Explanatory variables	(1)	(2)	(3)	(4)[b]	(5)[b]
Constant	−3.5729	−3.5630	−2.2841	−0.2017	−0.1253
	(−3.2126)	(−3.3495)	(−2.6046)	(−0.5095)	(−0.3473)
Log CR_{63}	0.7414				
	(2.7075)				
Log $[CR_{68}/CR_{63}]$	0.7771				
	(0.9842)				
Log CR_{68}		0.7399			
		(2.7981)			
Log CR_{71}			0.4473		
			(1.9357)		
Log H_{63}				0.1249	
				(1.1746)	
Log $[H_{68}/H_{63}]$				0.3443	
				(0.5439)	
Log H_{68}					0.1337
					(1.3022)
Engineering dummy	−0.6709	−0.6693	−0.6049	−0.6264	−0.6396
	(−3.5155)	(−3.6628)	(−3.0935)	(−3.0037)	(−3.1599)
R^2	0.4750	0.4750	0.3764	0.4202	0.4091
F statistic	5.13	8.14	5.43	3.62	5.54

[a] *t*-ratios are given in parentheses.

[b] In regressions (4) and (5) two sample observations were omitted (MLH 365/2 and 483) because the Herfindahl index was unavailable.

CR_{63} 1963 industry concentration ratio, being a weighted mean (weighted by sales) of component concentration ratios published in the Report on the 1968 Census of Production, HMSO, 1974.

CR_{68} 1968 industry concentration ratio derived in the same manner as CR_{63} using the same data sources.

CR_{71} 1971 industry concentration ratio by MLH groups published in the Summary tables of the 1971 Census of Production, HMSO, 1976.

H_{63} Estimate of the 1963 Herfindahl index calculated by M. Waterson from employment data published in the 1968 Census Report, HMSO, 1974

H_{68} Estimate of the 1968 Herfindahl index compiled in the same way as H_{63}.

estimates of the relationship between concentration and the rate of adjustment. Since this specification is clearly inappropriate, the results will not be reported.

To sum up, our results indicate that a consistently positive and significant relationship exists between industrial concentration and the rate of price adjustment. The results are given added support by the fact that the relationship is invariant with respect to the type of concentration index which was used and the year in which it was measured. Regarding the coefficient on the concentration change variable, which was not so well determined although it consistently had the expected sign, this result may be attributed to the influence of two factors. First, the lack of comprehensive data meant that the variable used in the regressions did not fully capture the concentration change which had taken place during the estimation period. Second, any lags between changes in market structure and changes in behaviour would obscure the relationship even further. Consequently, in Section 13.6 below we shall attempt to identify discrete rather than continuous changes in the price adjustment process of industries which experienced significant merger activity.

13.6 Structural breaks in the price adjustment process

An essential prerequisite for this analysis was a measure of changes in industrial concentration, over selected time periods, which would permit the identification of mergers with a significant impact on the industry.[8] In effect, the major problem with this analysis lay in the inadequacy of the data. The problem arose because of the non-comparability of the two sets of concentration ratios at our disposal. The ones available were for the years 1963, 1968, 1970, and 1972, and so would appear to provide considerable scope for measuring changes in concentration. However, the 1963 and 1968 concentration ratios are not comparable with those for 1970 and 1972 because the two sets are based on different levels of industry aggregation. Thus we can evaluate changes in concentration between 1963 and 1968 or 1970 and 1972, but cannot do so between 1968 and 1970 or 1972.

The non-comparability of these concentration ratios restricted our ability to measure changes in industrial structure which could be used to identify significant mergers. As most of the important mergers which affected the industries in our sample occurred in the late 1960s and early 1970s, if we were to use the 1963–68 concentration changes as the basis for identifying significant mergers we would run the risk of omitting important ones which took place after 1968.

To safeguard against such omissions we selected our sample of industries on the basis of two criteria: the incidence of important mergers in terms of the asset size of the taken-over firm, and the change in concentration from 1963 to 1968 and 1970 to 1972.

The sample which was selected for our analysis comprised six industries, four of which had experienced important mergers, with an increase in concentration of at least 20% during the estimation period. The remaining two industries did not belong to this category but were included for purposes of comparison, that is, in order to ascertain whether any structural breaks are confined to industries with significant mergers or are due to more general factors such as changes in the overall rate of inflation.

8 For a discussion of the link between mergers and concentration see Chapter 1.

To test for the significance of structural breaks in the equations we used the familiar 'Chow Test'. The data set was divided in two parts so as to obtain two separate estimates of the price adjustment equations in the two sub-periods. If the first period comprised *m* observations and the latter period *n* observations, then the *F* statistic which was used to test for structural breaks was defined as:

$$F(p, m+n-2p) = \frac{[\sum e^2_{m+n} - \sum e^2_m - \sum e^2_n]/P}{[\sum e^2_m + \sum e^2_n]/[m+n-2p]}$$

where $\sum e^2_{m+n}$, $\sum e^2_m$, and $\sum e^2_n$ are the residual sum of squares of the regressions using $m + n$, m, and n observations respectively. The number of estimated parameters in the equations is given by p. Since F has an 'F' distribution with p and $m + n - 2p$ degrees of freedom, if it exceeded the critical value for a predetermined level of confidence we rejected the null hypothesis of no structural break in favour of the alternative hypothesis. This result would indicate that the adjustment process in the post-merger period was significantly different from that of the early period. The industries selected for the analysis, with their respective concentration changes are reported in Table 13.6 below:

Table 13.6 *Changes in concentration*

MLH	Industry description	1963–68 % concentration change[a]	1970–72 % concentration change[b]
422/1	Household textiles	20	83
339/1	Mining machinery	40	10
368	Domestic electrical appliances	8	20
411	Man-made fibres	0	−3
419	Carpets and rugs	21	14
469/1	Abrasives	6	−3

[a]Based on the weighted concentration ratios used in the regression analysis.
[b]From the Census of Production Reports 1970 and 1972, Summary Tables.

The Household Textiles industry, traditionally fragmented, was subject to a large number of takeovers during the 1960s, a particularly significant one being that of Ashton Brothers Ltd by Courtaulds in the second quarter of 1968. The value of the assets taken over was £11.2 million. In the Mining Machinery industry the important merger was between the Dowty Engineering group and Anderson-Morris Ltd in the second quarter of 1970, with the assets acquired valued at £19 million. However, by far the largest merger in our sample was that between GEC and English Electric in the Domestic Electrical Appliance industry. The value of the assets taken over was £417 million and the merger took place in the second quarter of 1968.[9]

The Man-made Fibres and Abrasives industries, although highly concentrated, did not experience any significant takeovers or changes in concentration during the relevant period. In the Carpets industry an important merger took place in the second quarter of 1969 between the Guthrie Corporation and James Templeton Ltd. with the assets of the acquired company valued at £14.1 million.

Before reporting our results it should be stressed that our analysis did not aim at identifying the quarter when the structural change took place, but only at determining whether one had occurred in the post-merger period.

Our methodology was therefore to allow a period of six months after the merger had taken place as the basis for splitting up the sample period. Thus, in the case of the Mining Machinery industry with an important merger in the second quarter of 1970, the early estimation period was from 1963-I to 1970-IV and the post-merger estimation period was from 1971-I to 1974-IV. For those industries which had not experienced any significant mergers the estimation period was divided as follows: 1963-I to 1968-IV and 1969-I to 1974-IV.

In Tables 13.7 and 13.8 both ordinary and generalised least squares estimates are reported on account of the potential bias associated with serial correlation in the regressions. However, only the estimated coefficients on the lagged dependent variable are reported since the remainder are of no relevance to this analysis. As these coefficients represent the estimates of $(1 - \lambda_i)$ the implied values of λ_i are also reported in the tables.

From Table 13.7 it can be seen that the adjustment coefficient of the Household Textiles industry increased from 0.4873 in the early period to 1.279 – a value which is greater than its theoretical upper bound of unity. This suggests that during the post-merger period the price adjustment process in this industry involved an element of over-compensation for cost increases based, perhaps, on inflationary expectations. What is curious, however, is that the adjustment coefficient of the Mining Machinery, Domestic Electrical Appliances and the Carpets industries actually decreased in the later estimation period. This drop was from 0.3375 to 0.2724 in the case of the Mining Machinery industry, and from unity to 0.3387 and 0.6803 in the case of the Domestic Electrical Appliances and the Carpets industries respectively. Furthermore, the F ratio was statistically significant at the 5% level in two out of the three cases.[10]

9 For a detailed discussion of the changes in competition which occurred in the Electrical Engineering and Textiles sectors before and as a result of the mergers see Chapters 6 and 10 respectively.

10 The F test concerns the break in the overall relationship and is not specific to individual parameter changes. However, since a productivity trend was incorporated in the equations, we would not expect structural breaks to be associated with changes in the cost coefficients.

Table 13.7 *Split period estimates of the price adjustment coefficients: variable periods*[a]

Industry description	Estimation period	ΔWPI_{t-1} (*OLSQ*)	ΔWPI_{t-1} (*GLSQ*)	Implied λ	$F(4, 36)$
Household	1963 I–1968 IV	0.4571	0.5127	0.4873	
textiles		(2.9697)	(4.0822)		4.77[b]
(422/1)	1969 I–1974 IV	−0.2889	−0.2791	1.2791	
		(−1.9749)	(−2.4387)		
Mining	1963 I–1970 IV	0.5889	0.6625	0.3375	
machinery		(3.8189)	(4.5731)		2.97[b]
(339/1)	1971 I–1974 IV	0.5886	0.7276	0.2724	
		(3.1189)	(6.6859)		
Domestic	1963 I–1968 IV	0.0028	0.0880	1.000	
electrical		(0.0139)	(0.4284)		0.32
appliances	1969 I–1974 IV	0.6496	0.6613	0.3387	
(368)		(4.2928)	(4.4191)		
Man-made	1963 I–1968 IV	−0.1022	0.3549	0.6451	
fibres		(−0.4672)	(1.8089)		4.64[b]
(411)	1969 I–1974 IV	−0.0349	−0.0365	1.000	
		(−0.5022)	(−0.5230)		
Carpets and	1963 I–1969 IV	−0.0649	−0.0616	1.000	
rugs (419)		(−0.2941)	(−0.2732)		2.85[b]
	1970 I–1974 IV	0.2963	0.3197	0.6803	
		(1.9224)	(2.3105)		
Abrasives	1963 I–1968 IV	−0.0196	0.2654	0.7346	
(469/1)		(−0.0934)	(1.4514)		0.79
	1969 I–1974 IV	−0.3969	−0.4367	1.4367	
		(−2.4533)	(−2.7532)		

[a] *t*-ratios in parentheses
[b] denotes a significant *F* statistic at the 5% level.
WPI = Wholesale Price Index
OLSQ = Ordinary least squares estimates
GLSQ = Generalised least squares estimates

These results are puzzling and contrary to our *a priori* expectations, but they are open to an alternative interpretation. Consider, for example, the change in the Wholesale Price Index of Domestic Electrical Appliances during the 1963 to 1974 period. Between 1963 and 1966 this index rose by only 2.6% and, similarly, by only 2.1% in the next three years. By contrast, between 1969 and 1971 the index rose by 17.6%, and from 1972 to 1974 by 24.2%. It is clear from these figures that the rate of price increase from 1963 to 1968 was extremely small compared to the rate prevailing in the 1969 to 1974 period. Hence the period stretching from 1969 onwards represents a very different history of price movements than the six years which preceded it. The marked divergence of the rate of price increase between the two periods was also evident in the Mining Machinery industry, and to a lesser extent in the Carpets industry.

Therefore, these results may be explained by suggesting that, regarding these three industries, the absolute magnitude of the desired rate of adjustment in the 1963–68 period was so small that the costs of instantaneous adjustment were negligible and that therefore firms in these industries found it expedient to pass on the entire increase in price during the current quarter. Although this type of behaviour was not specifically discussed in the theoretical analysis it is intuitively plausible that for extremely small changes in the rate of price adjustment the costs of adjustment are effectively ignored. Thus in these situations a distributed lag structure of price adjustments would not be observed since changes would be effected instantaneously. It is clear that the type of behaviour described above is consistent with the estimated coefficients which were obtained.

Turning to the Man-made Fibres industry it can be seen from Table 13.7 that the estimated adjustment coefficient rose from 0.6451 to 1.000 and that the F ratio was statistically significant thus indicating a structural break in the equation. The coefficient of the Abrasives industry rose from 0.7346 in the early period to 1.436 in the later period but the F ratio was not statistically significant at the 5% level.

What may be concluded from the results presented so far? The results do not reveal a consistent set of reactions to merger activity and changes in the rate of inflation. Furthermore, in view of the fact that three industries in our sample showed a reduction of the adjustment coefficient in the later period it is evident that the sample observations used to obtain the pre- and post-merger adjustment coefficients are not strictly comparable. This is so because the early estimation period was characterised by relatively moderate price increases whilst in the later period all the industries in the sample had moved into the double figure inflation phase. The marked difference in economic conditions in the two periods may influence the adjustment behaviour of firms and consequently render our comparisons somewhat unreliable. More specifically in periods of rapid inflation firms may increase their partial adjustment coefficient so as to shorten the lag between cost and price increases. They would do so because, in times of inflation, lagging behind cost increases could lead to severe short-run liquidity problems. Therefore it may be that the observed increases in the adjustment coefficients in Table 13.7 are influenced to a greater extent by the overall rate of inflation in the 1969–74 period than by the incidence of mergers.[11]

It is particularly interesting that the two industries which exhibited an increase in the adjustment coefficient and had a statistically significant F ratio were characterised by either a high *increase* in concentration (Household Textiles) or an existing high *level* of concentration (Man-made Fibres). This evidence sug-

11 It is generally believed that key relationships such as the Phillips curve underwent a structural change in the latter half of the 1960s, at the same time as the rate of price and wage increase began to accelerate. For a discussion see Henry, Sawyer, and Smith (1976).

gests that in conjunction with inflation both a high level as well as a large increase in concentration have a similar effect in reducing the lag of adjustment.

In order to improve the comparability of our adjustment coefficients we re-estimated the equations by splitting up the period from 1968 to 1974 into one extending from 1968-I to 1971-II and the other from 1971-III to 1974-IV. This sample breakdown was used for all six industries because the small number of observations did not permit changing the estimation period to take into account the date of a merger. Nevertheless, since the earliest relevant merger was that of GEC and English Electric in the second quarter of 1968 we can be confident that the adjustment coefficients estimated from 1968-I to 1971-II would not have been influenced by the merger. More important, since both estimation periods lie within the higher inflation phase the comparison of adjustment coefficients will not be subject to those problems of interpretation discussed above.

From Table 13.8, in which the results based on these alternative estimation periods are reported, it can be seen that the adjustment coefficient of the Household Textiles industry rose from unity to 1.402 – i.e. to a value greater than its theoretical upper bound. In addition the *F* ratio indicated a statistically significant structural break in the equation. Moreover, since the estimate based on the 1968-I to 1971-II period was unity this indicates that the process of increasing the rate of price adjustment was already well under way by the early 1970s. The increase in the coefficient to a value greater than unity may be explained in terms of inflationary expectations and an attempt by the industry to increase price–cost margins over time, so that when met with cost increases prices were raised by a greater amount than that required to restore former price–cost margins.

In contrast to the results based on the 1963–68 and 1969–74 estimation periods, the adjustment coefficient of both the Mining Machinery and the Domestic Electrical Appliances industries did rise somewhat as can be observed in Table 13.8, although the *F* ratios did not indicate a structural break in the equations. Since the mergers took place in 1970-I and 1968-II respectively, these results would suggest that the mergers did not lead to a significant change in the price adjustment process. Furthermore they suggest that these industries did not respond to an accelerating rate of inflation with a substantial increase of their adjustment coefficients. They also support our hypothesis regarding the observed drop in the coefficients reported in Table 13.7 which was discussed above.

The coefficient of the Man-made Fibres industry increased from 0.5561 to unity and that of the Abrasives industry from 1.000 to 1.5798. By contrast, the coefficient of the Carpets industry fell from 1.000 to 0.6495 in the later period. In all three cases the *F* ratio was not statistically significant at the 5% level. It is interesting to note that both the Man-made Fibres and the Abrasives industry are highly concentrated while the Carpets industry is not. Thus the two increases in the adjustment coefficient were observed in concentrated industries whilst the only case of a decrease in the coefficient was in an industry of moderate concentration.

Table 13.8 *Split period estimates of the price adjustment coefficients 1968 I–1971 II, 1971 III–1974 IV*[a]

Industry description	Estimation period	ΔWPI_{t-1} (*OLSQ*)	ΔWPI_{t-1} (*GLSQ*)	Implied λ	$F(4, 18)$
Household	1968 I–1971 II	−0.4799	0.1846	1.000	
textiles		(−0.1550)	(0.7528)		3.35[b]
(422/1)	1971 III–1974 IV	−0.3699	−0.4023	1.4023	
		(−2.0358)	(−5.6413)		
Mining	1968 I–1971 II	0.6931	0.7585	0.2415	
machinery		(3.0769)	(4.5066)		2.43
(339/1)	1971 III–1974 IV	0.5658	0.7358	0.2642	
		(3.0819)	(5.5480)		
Domestic	1968 I–1971 II	0.5618	0.8991	0.1009	
electrical		(2.1683)	(6.2733)		2.34
appliances	1971 III–1974 IV	0.6769	0.7366	0.2634	
(368)		(3.7975)	(4.1605)		
Man-made	1968 I–1971 II	−0.0476	0.4439	0.5561	
fibres		(−0.2305)	(2.2265)		2.25
(411)	1971 III–1974 IV	−0.0441	−0.0445	1.000	
		(−0.5313)	(−0.5110)		
Carpets and	1968 I–1971 II	−0.2972	−0.2699	1.000	
rugs (419)		(−0.9787)	(−0.9879)		1.48
	1971 III–1974 IV	0.3547	0.3505	0.6495	
		(1.6501)	(1.9294)		
Abrasives	1968 I–1971 II	−0.1838	0.0370	1.000	
(469/1)		(−0.5789)	(0.1349)		1.63
	1971 III–1974 IV	−0.5337	−0.5198	1.5198	
		(−2.7816)	(−2.4737)		

[a] *t*-ratios in parentheses
[b] denotes a significant *F* statistic at the 5% level
WPI = Wholesale Price Index
OLSQ = Ordinary least squares estimates
GLSQ = Generalised least squares estimates

In conclusion, the following tentative inferences may be drawn. On the one hand it would appear that concentrated industries are more successful at raising their rate of price adjustment in times of inflation, as suggested by the results in Table 13.8. Also, the adjustment coefficients of the Household Textile industry in Table 13.7 would suggest that rapid increases in concentration through merger activity may have the same effect on the adjustment process. On the other hand the results in Table 13.7 would also indicate that when faced with very small increases in prices, firms may abandon the partial adjustment process in favour of full price increases in the current period. The rationale for such behaviour is that since in such circumstances the costs of price adjustment are negligible, they may therefore be ignored by firms which are contemplating an adjustment of price.

More interesting, perhaps, are the inferences which may be suggested regarding the impact of price-controlling institutions. In relation to the Conservative Government's anti-inflation programme, which also included the creation of the Price Commission in 1973, the results reported in Table 13.8 suggest that concentrated industries are equally if not more successful at withstanding the impact of the Price Commission than those of lower concentration. This is particularly significant because it is widely believed that the Price Commission can control more effectively the price increases of highly concentrated oligopolies than those of firms in less concentrated sectors of the economy. This hypothesis is based on the notion that it is easier to monitor an industry where a few large sellers account for a large proportion of the industry's output. However, the evidence presented here, whilst by no means definitive, casts some doubt on this view.

13.7 **Conclusions**

The findings which were reported in this chapter and which are based on United Kingdom data do not lend support to the proposition that oligopolists are sluggish in their adjustment of prices. The empirical evidence indicated that there exists a consistently positive and significant relationship between the rate of price adjustment, as given by the partial adjustment coefficient λ, and the level of industrial concentration. This conclusion appears to be in conflict with the 'administered prices' hypothesis, but the paradox can be resolved when it is remembered that Means refers to the inflexibility of industrial prices relative to those associated with 'perfect' markets in the neoclassical sense, whereas our analysis was confined specifically to industrial markets and the influence of their structure on the adjustment process.

On the question of changes in concentration the results were less clear cut primarily because of measurement problems. Yet the structural breaks analysis of the preceding section revealed that in the case of the Household Textiles industry which experienced a substantial increase in concentration through mergers, the rate of price adjustment was significantly higher in the post-merger period. Another related finding was that the increase in the overall rate of inflation was associated with a rise of the partial adjustment coefficients and, moreover, that this rise tended to be more pronounced in concentrated industries.

We conclude with the following policy implications. Since the relationship between the rate of adjustment and concentration was clearly established by the regression results, the effect of mergers must ultimately be to raise the speed of price adjustment. Thus in times of rising costs the short-run rate of inflation will be greater the higher is the level of concentration in the economy. In view of the generally well established influence of price level increases on wage increases and the recursive nature of this relationship, it would seem that, whether brought about by merger or internal growth, industrial concentration will render more intractable the attainment of the price stability objective.

References

Arrow, K. J. (1959), 'Toward a Theory of Price Adjustment' in *The Allocation of Economic Resources* (M. Abramovitz et al.) 41–51, Stanford: Stanford University Press.

Cowling, K. et al. (1975), *Advertising and Economic Behaviour*, London: Macmillan.

Cowling, K., and Cubbin, J. (1971), 'Price, Quality, and Advertising Competition: An Econometric Investigation of the United Kingdom Car Market', *Economica*, **38**, 378–94.

Flemming, J. S. (1976), *Inflation*, London: Oxford University Press.

Godley, W. A. H. and Nordhaus, W. D. (1972), 'Pricing in the Trade Cycle', *Economic Journal*, **82**, 853–82.

Griliches, Z. (1967), 'Distributed Lags: A Survey', *Econometrica*, **35**, 16–49.

Henry, S. G. B., Sawyer, M. C., and Smith, P. (1976), 'Models of Inflation in the United Kingdom: An Evaluation', *National Institute Economic Review*, No. 77, 60–71.

Johnston, J. (1972), *Econometric Methods*, New York: McGraw-Hill.

Lustgarten, S. (1975), 'Administered Inflation: A Reappraisal', *Economic Inquiry*, **13**, 191–206.

Means, G. (1972), 'The Administered-Price Thesis Reconfirmed', *American Economic Review*, **62**, 292–306.

Scherer, F. M. (1970), *Industrial Market Structure and Economic Performance*, Chicago: Rand McNally.

Stigler, G. J. (1961), 'The Economics of Information', *Journal of Political Economy*, **69**, 213–25.

14

Conclusions and public policy implications

There are various possible approaches to the problem of the control of economic power. Preventative measures, such as structural policies, may be available to control its emergence. If such structural policies are not ruthlessly pursued then we are left with the possibility of modifying the behaviour of the organisation possessing economic power by imposing and enforcing rules. Profit rate control, price control, advertising control would be cases in point. If such rules proved unsatisfactory then a reversion to a more structural approach (e.g. divestiture or mitosis) would be a possibility. Alternatively, a behavioural change may be sought via public takeover, either of the industry or of a firm or firms within an oligopoly group.

Given that the regulation of firm behaviour poses severe problems (some of which were discussed in Chapter 2) and given that public takeover is no obvious solution to the monopoly problem, even if politically feasible, then it follows that structural policy has a potentially significant role to play in controlling the emergence and impact of monopoly power in the economy. If we put the question of divestiture on one side for the moment then we are left with a requirement for an active anti-merger policy if we are to begin to control the extension of monopoly power. However, while in the case of large economies, like the United States, there may be little to lose from such policies in terms of static or dynamic efficiency, in the case of smaller economies attempts to maintain relatively deconcentrated structures may be faced with substantial social costs. To put the issue another way, merger activity leads with certainty to the acquisition of economic power but this may be balanced by the possibility of real resource savings. This requires us to know more of the cost savings which appear to have resulted from merger and provides a justification for the empirical work in which we have been engaged. However, it could be argued that all gains implicit in merger will be exhausted by the competitive process for the acquisition of these gains and therefore there is no trade-off (see Chapter 2). Since this position is not a generally accepted one and depends on rather special assumptions, we have accepted the case for examining gains in technical efficiency and this has provided a primary focus for our enquiry.

What has our enquiry revealed? Taking a broad sweep of the results the picture is one in which it is difficult to sustain the view that merger is in fact a necessary or sufficient conditon for efficiency gain. In many cases efficiency has not improved, in some cases it has declined, in other cases it has improved but no faster than one would have expected in the absence of merger (for a broad cross-section of cases, see the summary and conclusions section in Chapter 5 and also the conclusions of Chapters 6 to 10). There are one or two cases where we have seen an efficiency gain which has followed from the merger, these cases being where superior management has gained control over more resources. This aspect was probably the dominant view in the thinking of the IRC, but the evidence also forces us to recognise that it is just as likely that a merger based on such reasoning will fail as that it will succeed. We have drawn a comparison between the experience of British Leyland and GEC (Chapter 6), both mergers backed by the IRC. It is also undoubtedly true that ruthless measures to achieve efficiency gains do not take account of the full social costs (see the case of GEC, Chapter 8) and further that the calculus of such thinking should also recognise the inevitable economic power consequences. This is not strictly power within any particular market – it can have much wider implications and we have demonstrated some of these. Broad industrial policy becomes more and more entwined with the interests and objectives of individual corporations – witness Lancashire textiles and more recently the question of electric power stations.

Most important mergers in the UK have been horizontal and have therefore resulted in an increase in the degree of monopoly (Chapter 1). Evidence suggests that the welfare loss from the existence of monopoly positions in the UK can be substantial (Chapter 3). Cross-section evidence on the link between concentration and price–cost margins indicates that higher levels of concentration (to which merger has provided a considerable impetus, see Chapter 1) contribute to welfare loss, whereas the link between concentration and technical progress is by no means proven. Vertical mergers also, of which there have been a number of significant cases, have resulted in an extension of monopoly (see Chapter 10, and the case of British Leyland in Chapter 6).

As well as the various case studies which have been aimed primarily at measuring efficiency change following a merger or series of mergers, we have also developed detailed studies highlighting other aspects of the impact of horizontal merger. Our results suggest that such mergers have also led to (a) less product variety (see Chapter 7 for the case of brewing), (b) labour displacement in areas without immediate employment possibilities (see Chapter 8 for the case of GEC), (c) no observable increase in the rate of technological progressiveness (although perhaps some improvement over the counter factual) (see Chapter 9 for the case of ICL) and (d) market structures with more rapid rates of adjustment of prices to cost increases (see Chapter 13). More generally we have various pieces of evidence from our investigations that merger has led to no apparent improvement in international competitiveness or export performance (see e.g. the case of machine tools, TV sets and ball-bearings in Chapter 5).

The above discussion has related specifically to the question of horizontal and vertical merger with clear market power implications. Truly conglomerate mergers, with no direct product market power effects, although increasing in importance recently, have been the exception historically within the UK (see Chapter 1). However this is unlikely to be true of the future as and when opportunities for horizontal and vertical acquisitions are reduced. Evidence on the impact of such mergers is conflicting, but we feel it would be unwise to adopt the attitude that if diversified mergers tend to be 'neutral' in terms of efficiency and market power, then active policies toward such mergers are unnecessary. Broader implications relating to the acquisition of economic power would again have to be faced. In addition optimistic arguments that diversified firms may be a source of competition because of their ability to avoid capital market imperfections (Chapters 11 and 12) should be viewed with some scepticism. There is a tendency to compare the imperfections of *real* capital markets with the operation of ideal diversified firms. Moreover, as is pointed out in Chapter 12, there is no conclusive evidence that this resource allocation ability will be used to compete with other large firms.

Given the low level of efficiency gains realised relative to what could have been expected anyway, the potential social costs generated by increased market power, and the apparent lack of any other benefits, the evidence of the mergers of the 1960s would appear to argue against allowing mergers, especially those generating very large firms, to proceed without more control than has been exercised in the past. If increased social welfare is equated not only with greater output but also with a more egalitarian distribution of income, wealth and power then this view would be strengthened since merger involving the acquisition of monopoly power will result in a redistribution of income in favour of the recipients of profits, whether they be stockholders or managers (see Chapter 2), and economic power more generally will result from the pooling of assets irrespective of its impact on the degree of monopoly. If one considered a total ban on merger this would have have the effect of shutting-off an obvious avenue for circumventing restrictive practices legislation and would therefore contribute to the efficiency of existing legislation. To many observers such a policy may appear unreasonable – why not let the Mergers Panel or the Monopolies Commission assess each case on its merits? Surely it is irrational simply to apply a blanket refusal? Our first response would be that the evidence really does not support this view. The evidence suggests that bad decisions have been made in the past –mergers have been allowed which in some cases have been disastrous and in other cases have simply allowed the emergence of a substantial monopoly without any significant benefits. More fundamentally the whole approach has been biased in favour of acceptance since the parties involved have not been required to demonstrate that social benefits will result. Even if they were there is no institutional mechanism available for reversing the process should the outcome be found to be against the public interest. Our analysis and results therefore suggest that the array of policy options should be confined to a range, with an onus of proof on the merging firms to demonstrate social benefit at one end defining the mildest policy, and an outright ban at the other end defining the toughest policy. Within this range a variety of types of ban could be defined which might reasonably relate to the size of firms involved and their joint market share. Our observations of the problem over the past four years would lead us to favour strong measures and we would therefore lean toward a fairly strictly interpreted ban.

However even if strict controls were established over future mergers such that only a minority were allowed, this would still leave a highly concentrated industry structure, the legacy of the rather permissive merger policy of the past. A hard-line merger policy although important would still have to be seen as peripheral to the central issue of monopoly power in the economy. Our evidence suggests that there is little to be gained by increases in size but potentially much to be lost. Given this the question of divestiture should be raised. As well as asking firms proposing merger to justify it, we should also ask firms in dominant, powerful positions to justify themselves.

INDEX